SOCIAL LEARNING AND SOCIAL STRUCTURE

Northeastern University 1898–1998

Advisor in Criminal Justice to Northeastern University Press   **Gilbert Geis**

SOCIAL LEARNING AND SOCIAL STRUCTURE: A GENERAL THEORY OF CRIME AND DEVIANCE

Ronald L. Akers

Northeastern University Press   Boston

Northeastern University Press

Copyright 1998 by Ronald L. Akers

Library of Congress Cataloging-in-Publication Data

Akers, Ronald L.
   Social learning and social structure : a general theory of crime and deviance / Ronald L. Akers.
      p. cm.
   Includes bibliographical references and index.
   ISBN 1–55553–310–8 (cloth : alk. paper)
   1. Deviant behavior.   2. Criminal behavior.   3. Social learning.   4. Social structure.   I. Title.
   HM291.A4214   1998
   302.5'42—dc21   97–10291

Designed by David Ford

This book was composed in Adobe Trump Medieval by Graphic Composition in Athens, Georgia. It was printed and bound by Thomson-Shore, Inc., in Dexter, Michigan. The paper is Glatfelter Supple Opaque Recycled, an acid-free sheet.

Manufactured in the United States of America

02 01 00 99 98   5 4 3 2 1

This book
is dedicated
with love
and appreciation
to Caroline

My wife,
life companion,
and best friend

Contents

Tables

Figures

SOCIAL
LEARNING
AND SOCIAL
STRUCTURE

1

A Personal History of the Development of Social Learning Theory

In carrying out the purposes stated in the Introduction, I show the origin, development, and current status of the social learning theory of crime and deviance. This portrayal revolves around intellectual, theoretical, conceptual, and empirical issues. Such an approach risks giving the erroneous impression that the progress of the theory has been a straight line, guided only by scientific considerations and the next logical step needed for theoretical elaboration/specification or empirical testing. For a true picture, however, one must also paint in scenes of how the progress and problems of the theory have been affected by the vagaries of an academic career, opportunities, personal happenstance, and just being in the right (or wrong) place at the right time. Therefore, I begin with a brief history of my own involvement with the theory to provide some supplemental information to the reader who is interested in this dimension of its development and to flesh out its presentation.

I am unpersuaded by the extreme sociology-of-knowledge argument that all ideals, ideology, theory, and knowledge are simply reflections of the locations of their authors and promoters in a particular sociocultural context. I do believe, however, that personal history, being in a particular place at a particular time, does have some impact on a scholar's work. Certainly one's own ideas are strongly influenced by interaction with colleagues and students. This is one of the main reasons why books on theory in the social sciences often include biographical material on the authors. One's personal history, values, beliefs, and interests may influence one to pay attention to one problem and not another, to be intrigued

3

or persuaded by one line of argumentation and not another. They may introduce some element of "bias," and to know "where someone is coming from" aids in assessing her or his theoretical and value judgements. The old adage that "where one stands depends on where he sits" has some truth to it. Nevertheless, the validity of our ideas cannot be judged on that basis; the truth lies in the content of what is said, not in who says it. But in recounting the intellectual heritage of the theory it is informative to relate something of what Williams and McShane (1988) refer to as its "social heritage" as well.

Background

I can trace my introduction to Sutherland's differential association theory back to my undergraduate days (1956–60) at Indiana State University (known originally as Indiana State Normal School, as Indiana State Teacher's College when I enrolled, and simply as Indiana State College by the time I was graduated). At that time the primary majors available were secondary and elementary education, and most ISU students began careers in public school teaching immediately following graduation. I entered Indiana State with this as my goal, and until two months before graduation my intention was to teach in high school. Indeed, in the final quarter of my senior year I had a contract offer from the Vigo County school superintendent to teach social studies and English and to coach the cross-country team in a Terre Haute high school. At the last minute, I turned it down and decided to enter graduate studies in sociology.

Social studies was one of the "subject matter" specializations allowed within my secondary-education major, which included history, psychology, anthropology, sociology, and economics. There was no course in sociological theory or methods at the time, but several worthwhile sociology courses were offered as electives. I was very much attracted to sociology and anthropology (there was much less distinction between the two in those days than there is now) and took almost all of my electives in them. The courses included introductory sociology, social problems, sociology of education, juvenile delinquency, family, stratification, public opinion, and cultural anthropology.

It was in one of these elective courses (juvenile delinquency) that I was introduced to Sutherland's differential association theory. There was, as I recall, little theoretical content to the course, but the text covered, and the instructor devoted time to, "causes" of delinquency. Some attention was paid to biological, psychological, and sociological causes. Sutherland's theory, which the instructor interpreted to mean "differences in associations" with bad companions, was covered in this context. This introduction did not really convey the significance of the theory in the history of criminological thought; there was, instead, more emphasis on the concentration of delinquency in the lower class, on Merton's theory and Cohen's then relatively new book on gang delinquency, and on family factors in delinquency. For a term paper on social class and delinquency I read F. Ivan Nye's *Family Relationships and Delinquent Behavior* (1958).

In retrospect, I must admit that the theoretical differences and similarities between the control theory Nye presented in his book, the anomie theories of Merton and Cohen, and Sutherland's differential association theory pretty much escaped me. I thought the key sociological issue was lower-class status as a cause of delinquency. I spent the first few years of my life in a lower-class mixed-race neighborhood, and until completing high school I frequently returned to run around with my cousins and friends there. Although my upbringing included little in the way of "class consciousness," it made sense to me to hear that social class is important in understanding a whole range of social interactions, attitudes, and problems. It seemed pretty much settled that crime and delinquency was concentrated in lower-class neighborhoods. Thus, I was surprised and intrigued by the finding of little class difference in self-reported delinquency (measured by a technique developed by James Short in collaboration with Nye), as opposed to strong class differences in official delinquency.

That interest stayed with me into graduate school. After I took a seminar in criminology, it motivated me to do master's thesis research in 1961 replicating the part of the Short and Nye study dealing with social class and delinquency; my first published article was based on that thesis (Akers, 1964). By then, three other self-report studies had been published (Dentler and Monroe, 1961; Reiss and Rhodes, 1961; Clark and Wenninger, 1962). In the next decade, the self-report technique mushroomed to become the standard, most frequently used methodology in all studies of delinquency. For most of that time, virtually every published self-reported delinquency study noted my article in the string of citations to Short, Nye, Clark and Wenninger, and others. By 1972 it had become one of the most cited pieces in the criminological literature published since

1945 (Wolfgang et al., 1978).[1] In the thesis and article, I had no theoretical framework other than the hypothesis that delinquent behavior is related to social class. The only theoretical implications I drew were that the findings raised questions about theories that focused on the concentration of delinquency in the lower class.

However, I became thoroughly familiar with differential association theory and grew to understand its significance as the leading general criminological theory. My knowledge and interpretation of the theory was strongly influenced in graduate study (1960–61) with the late Oscar Ritchie at Kent State University, who directed the thesis, and in doctoral studies (1962–65) with Richard Quinney at the University of Kentucky, who directed the dissertation. At that time, there was great excitement among faculty and graduate students in the sociology of crime and deviance about the newly developing theories of the late 1950s and early 1960s. Although differential association theory received its due, most of the excitement was generated by Albert Cohen's and Richard Cloward and Lloyd Ohlin's theories of delinquent subculture, Vold's conflict theory, the conflict approach that Quinney was developing, and labeling theory (earlier introduced by Edwin Lemert and made highly visible when I was in graduate school by the publications of Howard Becker). I found all of these to be highly attractive intellectually, but I became more and more persuaded that Sutherland's theory made more sense as an explanation of criminal behavior than any of the others. However, I did nothing special with the theory in graduate school.

My major doctoral specialty within sociology was criminology and sociology of law (with an out-of-department minor in social anthropology). My dissertation was a study of political power and enactment of professional and licensure laws. I had come to this problem through studies in criminology and an interest in criminal and deviant behavior. What began as a study of white-collar crime among health professionals turned into a study in the sociology of law. The theoretical orientation of the dissertation was taken from Quinney's conflict theory of law. It included nothing on criminal behavior or differential association.

Development of the Theory

Robert Burgess and I arrived at the University of Washington in Seattle in 1965. We were untenured, acting assistant professors with unfinished dissertations who were assigned adjoining offices in the Department of Sociology. Burgess was one of the first behavioral sociologists specifically trained in psychological operant conditioning theory and research under Robert Hamblin at Washington University in St. Louis. Later, another behaviorally oriented sociologist from that program, David Schmitt, joined the UW faculty. Burgess's graduate training included intensive study of behavioral learning theory. At Washington University, he had access to the theories and programs of two of the top applied behavioral psychologists of the day, Nathan Azrin and Theodore Ayllon, who were developing behavior modification programs (in fact, token economies) at a nearby state mental institution in southern Illinois.

Burgess's specialty was social psychology, and his dissertation was an experimental test of an operant model of organizational communication patterns. He had also worked on a delinquency prevention project as a graduate student and had acquired some knowledge of differential association theory. I was quite familiar with the theory, but had acquired only a little knowledge of psychological behaviorism, mainly by reading George Homans while in graduate school. I was not overly impressed with Homans and did not see that his approach had much to offer for understanding crime and deviance. Burgess was already persuaded that all of sociology would benefit from the infusion of psychological behaviorism.

Because of our spatial, intellectual, organizational, and career proximity, it did not take long for the two of us to become friends and begin carrying on lengthy conversations about a wide range of mutual concerns. The most intensive of our talks had to do with the relevance of psychological behaviorism to sociology and criminology, especially the connections between Sutherland's learning theory formulated in the 1940s and operant psychology, which had begun at about that time but did not come into prominence until the 1950s. Were it not for this fortuitous juxtaposition, I believe, neither of us would have become involved in a behavioristic reformulation of Sutherland's theory. Moreover (as will become apparent below), there was a unique combination of faculty and graduate students at the University of Washington who also played a role in my early focus on theoretical issues in criminology.

Although I was drawn to Sutherland, during the early years at the University of Washington I was involved in the same kind of spirited discourse over the new theories of the late 1950s and early 1960s that I had encountered in graduate school. I became steeped in the subcultural and gang theories and studies of Cohen, Cloward and Ohlin, Short, and their colleagues; I knew the control theories of Nye, Reckless, and others. My mentor, Quinney, had work on differential association theory under way with Melvin DeFleur, an effort that they had begun while I was in graduate school. There were other exciting theoretical developments brewing at the time. I knew directly of Quinney's and Turk's style of conflict theory and incorporated it into my dissertation (which I completed during my first year on the UW faculty). I had studied Becker's widely heralded work on labeling theory. William Chambliss and I became good friends through team-teaching the social problems course and through our mutual interest in criminology. Chambliss was developing his conflict approach and doing some extremely interesting research, à la Sutherland, with Harry King, a professional thief, whom I came to know and with whom I continued to work after Chambliss left UW. Conflict theory was challenging functionalism in sociology. The whole intellectual atmosphere of the time was to question or revise existing theoretical perspectives and to develop new approaches. The political conflicts over the Vietnam War were still nascent, but there was already a distinct anti-establishment, underdog orientation in sociology.

One major contention, promoted by both conflict and labeling theorists but also widely endorsed by others, involved a shift in emphasis. They argued that the field should move from a focus on explaining the behavior of "ordinary" criminals and the lower class toward a focus on the establishment. Such a change would involve not only accounting for social control, law, and the criminal justice system but also studying white-collar and corporate crime (taking up a theme developed earlier by Sutherland). Chambliss persuasively advocated (and still advocates) this position. This was my inclination as well, and that was reflected in the dissertation project, in my articles on the political power of professions, and in teaching courses in criminology and sociology of law.

I had no intention of developing etiological theory or working specifically on differential association theory; my goals were to complete the dissertation, teach classes, and get enough published from the dissertation and other research to pass muster at tenure and promotion time. It was not until the interaction with Robert Burgess that I began to think seriously about refocusing on the question of criminal etiology and a general theory of criminal behavior. Burgess was very interested in promoting the behavioral perspective in sociology, and we had common career concerns—a desire to make an impact in sociology and to make tenure. Richard Emerson, who also was on the UW sociology faculty at the time, had made a major contribution to the field with his power-dependence theory (Emerson, 1962) and was later active in the group of social psychologists developing social exchange theory in sociology (Emerson, 1972a; 1972b). Burgess and I spent a good deal of time in discussion with him about behavioral sociology and how operant theory fits with sociological theory.

My friend had no previous inclination to develop his behaviorist interest with differential association theory and had little interest in criminology as a field of study. I was not inclined toward studying operant psychology. Once we perceived our common interests, however, we began collaborating. Burgess guided my reading and study of operant psychology and behavior modification, and I helped him with differential association theory and criminology. Although he was interested in social interaction and was a well-trained sociologist, Burgess tended to take a fairly strict Skinnerian approach and to agree with Homans that there is virtually no sociological principle or generalization that cannot be reduced to the basic behavioral principles of operant conditioning theory. I agreed that the operant principles were a very powerful explanation of behavior that, by attributing primary causes to the environment, fit sociological theory better than explanations of behavior that gave primacy to the internal emotional or biological states of the individual. But I leaned toward retaining cognitive concepts from the symbolic interactionist tradition and Sutherland's emphasis on interaction in primary groups. It seemed to me that the concept of "environment" in operant conditioning theory was fairly artificial, modeled on Skinner's apparatus for experiments with pigeons and other animals. It would mesh with sociology only if it were conceptualized so as to fit the naturally occurring social environments (studied with observational and survey techniques) with which sociologists were mainly concerned. In addition, I thought the "successive approximation" process in Skinnerian theory—involving gradual, incremental "shaping" in which all "behavior is constructed by a continual process of differential reinforcement from undifferentiated behavior" (Skinner, 1953:92) without assuming any cognitive processes— was too cumbersome and undirected to apply to most social behavior.

This leaning toward relying on cognitive processes pointed me in the same theoretical direction in which Bandura and other behavioral psychologists were moving.

Burgess and I agreed that Sutherland's theory was the most fruitful place to explore the ramifications of behavioral psychology for sociology beyond what Homans had done with regard to small groups. Both Sutherland's view and operant conditioning were self-consciously "learning" theories, involving behavioral acquisition, maintenance, performance, and change. We were fully aware that the disciplinary, theoretical, and methodological traditions of the two differed dramatically. We knew from our discussions (sometimes heated) with colleagues in the department that there was enormous skepticism among sociologists about the value and relevance of behaviorism to sociology.

Behavioral psychology was (and to a great extent still is) viewed in sociology as a mechanistic theory that treats humans as "hollow" automatons whose actions are the result of passive and mindless conditioning by environmental stimuli in exactly the way animals are conditioned. This was in contrast to symbolic interactionism theory, which stresses the thinking and reflexive individual interacting in society. Many of our colleagues were of the opinion that the two approaches were so incompatible that no integration of any kind was possible; indeed, it was fruitless to try. Burgess and I so violated the conventional wisdom that our efforts to blend Sutherland and behaviorism were later branded as "theoretically illiterate" (Taylor et al., 1973). Behaviorism was also viewed as hopelessly tautological. Moreover, some of our colleagues and students saw it as somehow bent to serving the establishment and maintained that greater knowledge of the behavioral principles would only lead to more effective, coldly efficient techniques of behavior and mind control by the power elite.

Burgess and I disagreed with this. We argued that knowledge of behavior can be put to use as readily in the cause of dissent and change as in the cause of maintaining the status quo. We pointed to Skinner's arguments in *Walden Two* that behavioral principles could be used to model a more humane and free society. It seemed unequivocal to us that operant principles contained the precise mechanisms of learning that Cressey had said were needed for differential association theory. While these principles emphasized the functional relationship between behavior and ob-

servable environmental consequences, they allowed for human awareness and placed the person at the center as acting upon the environment.
It was not simply a theory of reflex conditioning. We argued that, despite
being directed toward individuals and small groups rather than institutions or whole societies, it had the same formal characteristics as func-
tionalist theory in sociology. That is, both explained the form of the thing
to be explained (behavior in the case of operant theory, institutional
structure in the case of functionalism) by its consequences.

We also argued that Sutherland's fundamental idea of learning through
association or interaction with others in a social environment was entirely compatible with the basic notion in operant theory that the individual's behavior is shaped by interaction with the environment, whether
social or nonsocial. Sutherland's conceptions of differential association
and the balance of definitions favorable and unfavorable to crime is analogous to the Skinnerian concept of differential reinforcement as the balance of reward and punishment. Therefore, we began to explore the extent to which the symbolic interactionist concepts in the sociological
approach to learning and socialization incorporated into Sutherland's
theory could be compatible with the radical behaviorism of operant conditioning theory. In the beginning we leaned more heavily toward the
strict behavioral conditioning components of orthodox operant theory
and downplayed the symbolic interactionist components from Sutherland's theory. As I have mentioned, the more I developed the theory, the
greater the role I gave to direct cognitive processes more in line with
symbolic interactionism in sociology and the social behaviorism of Bandura and others in psychology.

As Burgess and I were working on this task during the fall of 1965, C.
Ray Jeffery's (1965) article "Criminal Behavior and Learning Theory" was
published in the *Journal of Criminal Law, Criminology, and Police Science.* I brought it to my friend's attention as an example of an effort by a
criminologist who was moving in the same direction we were. The more
closely we examined the piece, however, the more it became apparent
that Jeffery did not have the same goal that we did. He made no attempt
truly to revise or reformulate differential association theory. We believed
that his efforts fell short of what was needed, not only because of this
failure to integrate behaviorism and differential association but also because he relied on extrapolations from operant experiments with ani-

mals. He left out the already sizable body of operant research with human subjects that had much more direct relevance to differential association theory. We concluded that while Jeffery had made a good start his effort was incomplete. Moreover, although both he and Burgess and I wanted to introduce elements of behavioral psychology into criminological thought, his primary aim seemingly was to supplant differential association theory, while ours was to improve it. We believed such a revision could be done in a way that would integrate behavioral principles with the explanatory variables of differential association, and all of the previous modifications made to it by others, into a more general theory.

We completed the paper devoted to this purpose by examining each one of the nine statements in Sutherland's theory and revising it with behavioral concepts. To emphasize that the result was an integration of differential association and operant theory, in which the central process is differential reinforcement, we labeled the revision "differential association–reinforcement" theory. We presented the paper at the spring 1966 meetings of the Pacific Sociological Association (a revised version was published in *Social Problems* in the fall of 1966). The late Donald R. Cressey was present at the session. We were well aware that he was one of Sutherland's students, that he was one of the top criminologists, that he had revised all of the post-1947 editions of Sutherland's book, and that he was the main proponent of differential association theory. We had also been forewarned by others of his ability to devastate the authors of papers with his critical remarks. Therefore, it was with considerable trepidation that Burgess and I awaited Cressey's reaction. But he was very encouraging and expressed the opinion that Sutherland would have approved of our efforts. Indeed, he felt that Sutherland would have moved the theory in the same direction had he lived to see the work of the operant conditioners in the 1950s. (Later, Karl Schuessler, 1973:xvii, another Sutherland student, made the same point.) We were also encouraged by DeFleur and Quinney, who by this time had completed their work on stating differential association using the formal logic of set theory. They felt that incorporating reinforcement principles was important as a way of filling in some of the gaps in Sutherland's theory.

I began almost immediately to work elements of the theory into my lectures in the social problems course at the University of Washington. This was in the days before there were separate courses on deviance in sociology departments, and I taught social problems basically as an introduction to the sociology of deviance. Otto Larsen, a colleague and later chairman of the department, encouraged Burgess and me to write a general text in the sociology of deviance organized around the theory we had produced. He was very supportive of our work, both because he had a special interest in serving as a mentor to young faculty members and because he felt that we had come up with something different that would make good classroom material. Nevertheless, we thought his suggestion was premature and that our time would be better spent in writing journal articles, at least until gaining tenure and some scholarly credibility.

However, I determined to organize my lectures on various forms of deviant behavior as carefully as possible around social learning theory, in anticipation of the time when Larsen's advice could be followed and a social learning text on deviant behavior might be done. One of the first areas that I concentrated on was drug use and abuse. Alfred Lindesmith's theory of opiate addiction especially seemed to be compatible with the theory, and with the collaboration of Burgess and Weldon Johnson (at the time a doctoral student in sociology at the University of Washington) I published an article on this topic based on my lecture notes for the social problems course (Akers et al., 1968).

By 1968, I had gained tenure and promotion to associate professor. Not having to publish something every year gave me some breathing room, so it became more feasible to write a book. I began to work on the deviance text from a social learning perspective while on a visiting summer appointment at San Diego State University. By this time Burgess had moved on to apply behavioral theory to other issues in sociology, principally in family studies, and had begun to lose interest in working further with the theory or in the area of criminology. I continued writing the book, trying out ideas in my lectures and putting them into manuscript form over the next three years.

At about this time, Travis Hirschi joined the University of Washington faculty and introduced me to his control theory (which I came to call "social bonding"). Widely hailed as one of the most exciting theoretical innovations of the time, it almost immediately began to have a major impact on criminological theory and research. It soon became (and remains today) the most studied and researched of all criminological theories. The response to it and to his later work has placed Hirschi in the well-deserved position of being the most recognized and the most frequently cited criminological author (Cohn and Farrington, 1996a; 1996b).

Hirschi had brilliantly and creatively woven together all of the strands of existing control theory and of elements outside that tradition into a new theory of delinquency. I was most impressed with how he had not only laid out the assumptions, concepts, and propositions of the theory in a logical and coherent way but had also tied the concepts to clearly articulated empirical measures and tested the theory with his own primary data. Since the data had been collected as part of the larger Richmond Youth Study, on which Hirschi had worked as a graduate student, he did have them in hand before finalizing the theory. Nonetheless, he had come closer than virtually anyone else to the classic model of formulating a theory, deriving hypotheses, putting the concepts into operation, and then testing the hypotheses with data collected primarily for that purpose. His endeavor was close to being unique in criminological theory at the time and remains a model for others to emulate to this day. I became and remain immensely affected not only by Hirschi's intellect and theoretical insights but also by his example of how to be a good and supportive friend and colleague.

I was less enamored with his understanding of differential association theory. I felt (and still contend) that he misclassified Sutherland's original position (as well as the later Burgess-Akers reformulation) as the major example of "cultural deviance" theory (see Chapter 4 and Akers, 1996). Although there were parts of social bonding theory that I found wanting, it seemed to me to be a highly persuasive and empirically sound explanation of delinquency. I almost immediately saw great similarities and compatibility between social bonding and social learning theory. Social bonding, with its focus on social control and integration, had more of a structural element, but it also was a social psychological theory of individual delinquency that used explanatory concepts similar (though with different labels) to those of social learning theory. Hirschi disagreed, arguing that the two were not only different but incompatible approaches, with contradictory assumptions and propositions. He saw social learning theory (and virtually all other criminological theories) as concerned only with explaining why people commit crimes and become delinquent, while his theory concentrated on explaining why they did not. Our basic disagreement on this point continues to this day.

Partly because of these theoretical differences, Hirschi and I did no collaborative research. However, he became a good friend and very influential colleague. Immensely helpful and generous with his time, Hirschi laid aside his reservations about social learning theory and strongly encouraged me to continue with the book on deviant behavior from the social learning perspective. By this time, Rodney Stark had also joined the UW faculty. He and Hirschi had already developed a relationship with Wadsworth Publishing, and they were very instrumental in persuading Steve Rutter, then the Wadsworth sociology editor, to sponsor *Deviant Behavior: A Social Learning Approach.* The acknowledgment given Hirschi in the preface was an accurate reflection of the impact he had on me and the book: "I owe a special thanks to Travis Hirschi, who read and thoroughly reacted to every version and revision of the manuscript from the first to the last. Whatever integrity of content and facility of style the book possesses are much the result of his tireless attention to what I wrote and how I wrote it" (Akers, 1973:ix).

This does not mean that he agreed with me then or agrees with me now. In fact, he is probably the chief critic of social learning theory, and I in turn have been a critical thorn in his side. Anyone who reads the rest of this book will find many places where I take strenuous exception to some of Hirschi's views on social learning theory and disagree with some of his theoretical arguments. Let no reader mistake any of this as qualifying, in the least, our collegial and personal relationship.

By the time I left the University of Washington for a position in the School of Criminology at Florida State University, fall of 1972, *Deviant Behavior* was complete except for final editing. It came out that fall, with a 1973 publication date. Although it was intended for classroom use, I viewed its publication as the opportunity to promulgate social learning theory and gain it wider visibility in sociology and criminology. The model I had in mind was how Sutherland (and later Cressey) had presented and applied his theory in a textbook, *Principles of Criminology.* *Deviant Behavior* presented the theory with a fuller discussion of concepts and propositions than had been possible in the Burgess-Akers article. It showed how social learning theory relates to other theories of crime and deviance and gave a social learning explanation of drug and alcohol behavior, sexual deviance, white-collar crime, professional crime, organized crime, violent crime, suicide, and mental illness. It retained

Sutherland's and Cressey's concern with social structure and included preliminary ideas on how social learning process could relate to variations in the group rates of crime and deviance. The first deviance text to take such a strong and consistent theoretical approach, it was revised in a second (1977) and a third edition (1985).

Efforts to Test the Theory

While reworking the theory and beginning to write the textbook, I became convinced that the presentation of the theory and the value of the book would be greatly enhanced if I could report a direct empirical test of the new theory, as Hirschi had done for social bonding theory. Further, I felt that such a test should be done with survey data collected from the general population similar to the self-reported delinquency studies that had been pioneered by Short and Nye; I had used such studies in my master's research, Hirschi had used them, and by that time they were becoming more common. I proposed, therefore, to conduct a self-report study of alcohol and drug use among junior high and high school students in the Seattle area. There had been only a few surveys of drug use done in various communities and campuses around the country at the time. No such survey had yet been done that covered an entire school district and surrounding areas in a city the size of Seattle, and none had been done to test a specific causal theory. The study thus would both provide the first scientific data on how much drug and alcohol use there was in the adolescent population in the area and would allow me to test the propositions of social learning theory directly. I had just completed a study of alcohol prevention programs in school, and in that connection I had been meeting with a citizens' advisory group on which the superintendent of the Seattle school district served. He was very interested in the project and gave his approval to conduct the study in the junior and senior high schools of the city. I was still very much interested in the issue of the class distribution of delinquency, and I gained the approval of two suburban school districts to do research in their communities as well so that I could include both inner-city and middle-class schools. I served as a consultant to a suburban teen "drop-in" program and observed the growth of drug use outside the lower-class areas of the city.

The sale of liquor in Washington was solely in the hands of a public agency, and a fraction of the revenues from the board of liquor control was appropriated to the state agency on human services to fund research on and treatment and prevention of alcohol and drug problems. My proposal to the state to underwrite the study with some of this money was approved; work was to begin in 1969. However, for political reasons, Seattle's school superintendent withdrew his support. The approval of the suburban districts remained, but I felt that without the large number of respondents from the Seattle district the project would not have much value. I returned the research funds and canceled the study. The first opportunity to test the theory had been lost.

This disappointment did not convince me to give up on the idea of testing the theory directly with a large-scale survey, but it did result in putting the project on the back burner while completing the book. Also, through interaction with Clarence Schrag and Norman Hayner at the University of Washington, I had become increasingly interested in prisons and the sociology of corrections. Hayner and I collaborated (along with Werner Gruninger, my doctoral student at the time) on a National Institute of Mental Health (NIMH) grant to do cross-cultural study of prisonization. This project absorbed all of my research attention during my remaining time at the University of Washington, and most of my writing efforts when I joined the faculty at Florida State University in 1972.

After only two years at FSU, I moved on to the faculty at the University of Iowa. I had no desire to leave, and I was very satisfied with my colleagues and students there. But the offer from Iowa was hard to refuse, and in retrospect it afforded me an opportunity to test social learning theory that I might not have had remaining in Tallahassee. It was another example of being in the right place at the right time.

The next year, the director of the newly established Boys Town Center for the Study of Youth Development in Nebraska learned of my presence in the Midwest and invited me to join the center as a visiting fellow. I was asked to propose one or two research projects to be carried out during my tenure there that would be funded by the Boys Town Center. This offer presented a good opportunity to move forward with plans to test the theory in a natural setting. My proposal to do a survey of adolescent alcohol and drug behavior in the general population and among the residents of Boys Town (along with another proposal to conduct a study of knowledge and opinion of the law) was accepted by the center. I took a year's leave from the Iowa faculty and went to Omaha to do the research. Marvin Krohn (on whose doctoral committee I had served, with Charles Wellford as the chairman, at the FSU School of Criminology) had joined the University of Iowa sociology faculty the year after I had arrived. The theoretical and methodological abilities that have since made him one of the leading criminologists in the country were quite evident even then, and I asked him to come with me to do the projects as a post-doctoral fellow. Also, Lonn Lanza-Kaduce and Marcia Radosevich, who were graduate students at Iowa, went with me as pre-doctoral associates. It was this funded Boys Town project, eight years after my first efforts, that enabled the completion of a large-scale study to test the theory with data collected specifically for that purpose (see Chapter 7).

The timing of these events—formulating the theory in the 1960s and testing it in the 1970s—permitted its development and empirical verification in classic scientific form: (1) propose a general theory with defined concepts and propositions, (2) derive testable hypotheses and predictions from the theory, (3) construct reliable and valid operationalizations of the concepts, (4) collect data measuring the theoretical variables and the dependent variables, and (5) test the theoretical predictions against the empirical findings. I wish I could truthfully claim that all of this had been cleverly planned and rationally accomplished. It should be clear by now that I cannot.

The findings from the Boys Town Study strongly supported the theory. This was very encouraging, and I began almost immediately upon my return to Iowa to write up the findings and to search for other avenues for testing the theory. Through one of my doctoral students, Sherilyn Spear, I came to know Ronald Lauer, a pediatric cardiologist at the university, who had been conducting a longitudinal study of heart disease risk factors in an Iowa community. By that time, he had become particularly interested in smoking among teenagers as a significant risk factor, and we teamed up to propose a longitudinal research and prevention project on teenage smoking. Our proposal was approved and funded by the National Institute of Child Health and Human Development (NICHHD) and allowed a longitudinal test of social learning theory, this time specifically on teenage smoking behavior. Although I left Iowa for the University of Florida in 1980, before that project was completed (and Krohn became co–principal investigator with Lauer), I retained a role until the work was completed. The findings from that study once again strongly supported the theory and encouraged seeking other ways of testing it.

As before, the move to Florida was for personal and family reasons that had nothing to do with plans to continue testing the theory. In fact, it looked at first as if the move would disrupt the work that was under way in the smoking study. After arriving in Florida, I tried unsuccessfully to get funding for a large-scale study of adolescent substance use that included a longitudinal follow-up of the respondents in the Boys Town Study. At about the same time, Anthony La Greca and Gordon Streib approached me about collaborating on a research proposal to the National Institute of Alcoholism and Alcohol Abuse (NIAAA) for a longitudinal study of alcohol behavior among the elderly. I was not particularly interested in gerontology or in alcohol consumption in the older age group, but the opportunity to test the theory with such a population intrigued me. My previous research had only dealt with deviant substance use among adolescents. How much of the social learning explanation of substance use by the young would apply to the old? I was able to find out because our proposal to test a social learning model of drinking among the elderly was approved and funded by NIAAA. The findings showed that the theory applied to the drinking behavior of both groups.

Others were also testing the theory, measuring some or all of the major concepts, and the findings from those studies were very supportive. By the late 1980s, it seemed that the accumulation of empirical support for differential association, imitation, differential reinforcement, and definitions (as well as other parts of the theory) had become very impressive. But I felt that the theory needed to be tested more thoroughly with non-adolescent populations on behavior other than alcohol and drug use. Some of these efforts did not succeed because of lack of funding. For instance, although Scot Boeringer, one of my doctoral students, tested the theory on rape behavior among college men, a proposal submitted by the two of us and my colleague Constance Shehan to test it with arrested, convicted, and incarcerated rapists got no financing. But, through funded and unfunded research, social learning models of fear of crime in the adult population, cheating among college students, and acquaintance rape by college men were all tested.

In subsequent chapters, the nature and outcome of these investigations will be laid out in detail. I want to show how they fit together into an overall research agenda of theory testing and development extending over many years. This integrated theoretical/empirical enterprise, the basis for the continued development of the theory, culminates in the statement of the theory in Chapter 3 and in the proposal of the sssL model of social learning and social structure in Chapter 12.

Note

1. This is another example of how being in the right place at the right time with an idea can make a major difference in how much attention is paid to it and how it affects one's visibility in the field. I had no notion in 1960 that the research for my master's thesis would become one of a handful of early studies on which future developments in the self-report technique in surveys of delinquency in general adolescent populations would be based. I saw it as simply a re-test of one part of the large study by Short and Nye. I knew that beyond some early surveys among college students there were no other accounts in the literature of such self-report studies. I also knew that Short and Nye had produced a new technique and spent a considerable amount of time justifying self-reported behavior as a valid alternative to official measures of delinquency. My master's thesis supervisor, the late Oscar Ritchie, was able to convey to me that I was going into relatively uncharted waters. But the importance of the self-report technique and the role that my master's study could play in its development did not really sink in until after I had begun doctoral studies at the University of Kentucky. Richard Quinney, my major advisor and dissertation director, focused on how little self-reported delinquency research had then been done and urged me to publish the findings from the master's research.

2
Development and Revisions of
Differential Association Theory

The late Edwin H. Sutherland (1883–1950) is widely recognized as the most important criminologist of the twentieth century. He pioneered sociological studies of professional theft (1937) and white-collar crime (1940; 1949). Sutherland is best known, however, for his "differential association" theory of criminal behavior (Cohen et al., 1956; Schuessler, 1973; Gaylord and Galliher, 1988). He was the author of America's leading criminology textbook, and it was here that Sutherland presented his theory. The textbook had an intellectual and scholarly impact unmatched by any other work written primarily for undergraduate students. Translated into many languages, it affected criminological thought around the world.

Sutherland's Differential Association Theory

Criminology (1924) was Sutherland's first publication of any kind in this specialty (although he had been teaching the course for several years), and it served as the foundation for all his future work on the sociology of crime and delinquency (Schuessler, 1973:xiii). In this first edition, Sutherland made no mention of the theory of differential association, and indeed he was apparently somewhat proud of his eclectic, broad-minded, and unfocused "multiple factor" approach to crime (Schuessler, 1973; Cohen et al., 1956; Gaylord and Galliher, 1988). Although the second edition, published in 1934 and retitled *Principles of Criminology*, contained some preliminary, unsystematic theoretical notions, Suther-

land thought that his textbook did not promote any "abstract generalization." Therefore he was surprised when Henry McKay later mentioned
Sutherland's "theory" of criminal behavior (Schuessler, 1973). McKay referred to three sentences in the 1934 edition of *Principles of Criminology,*
which stated the "hypotheses of this book" as Sutherland's theory of
crime:

> First, any person can be trained to adopt and follow any pattern of behavior
> which he is able to execute. Second, failure to follow a prescribed pattern of
> behavior is due to the inconsistencies and lack of harmony in the influences
> which direct the individual. Third, the conflict of cultures is therefore the
> fundamental principle in the explanation of crime. (Sutherland, 1934:51–52)

This is an embryonic theory at best. The first two sentences merely
state general assumptions about human behavior; only the third one refers to crime. But it was a beginning, and in response to the urging, ques-
tioning, and criticisms of colleagues and students Sutherland continued
to work on the theory, with the central idea that "it seemed to me that
learning, interaction, and communication were the processes around
which a theory of criminal behavior should be developed. The theory of
differential association was an attempt to explain criminal behaviors in
that manner" (Schuessler, 1973:19).

This development resulted in the first published statement of differential association theory, in the third edition of *Principles of Criminology*
(1939:4–8). This 1939 version of the theory proposed that "the specific
causal process in the development of systematic criminal behavior" is
"differential association" with those who commit crime or with those
who are law-abiding. Sutherland presented differential association primarily as a processual theory of how individuals come to commit crimes.
His theory also had a structural dimension, which included statements
proposing that conflict and social disorganization are the underlying
causes of crime because they determine the patterns of differential association. This full version was initially given in seven succinct statements, or propositions (Sutherland, 1939:4–8). The first five of these referred to differential association, while the last two statements referred
to conflict and disorganization.

The final version of the theory was included in the 1947 edition of
Sutherland's criminology textbook; here, he dropped the concepts of con-

flict and disorganization. Sutherland retained them separately in comments about "differential social organization," the term that he suggested should be used in place of "social disorganization." It was not that Sutherland rejected a structural explanation. Instead, he came to see such explanations as culture conflict and social disorganization as levels of theory separate from differential association that would have to be evaluated on different grounds. Nevertheless, they must be consistent and indeed linked through the idea that differential organization explains why the person is exposed to the pattern of associations he has. Therefore, Sutherland perceived differential social organization as the cause of differences in group or societal crime rates, which is consistent with differential association as the explanation of differences in individual behavior. Today we would interpret differential social organization as a macro-level, or structural, theory and differential association as a compatible micro-level, or processual, theory. In spite of this recognized connection and frequent references to differential social organization throughout the book, Sutherland did not develop it as a general concept or provide a systematic statement of differential social organization as a theory of crime rates. Rather, he concentrated his efforts on fully explicating differential association as a processual theory of criminal behavior.

Sutherland also distinguished between "mechanistic" and "genetic" theories. The first focuses on the situation (or the personal pathologies of individuals), and the latter focuses on the processes existing before the situation (not the biological meaning of genetic). The differential association theory was in this sense more a genetic than a mechanistic theory of factors at work in the immediate circumstances. However, differential association operates at the nexus of the "person-situation complex" because the situation is defined "by the person in terms of the inclinations and abilities which the person has acquired up to that date" (Sutherland, 1947:5) The final version of differential association theory (Sutherland, 1947:6–7) was presented in a nine-statement format, with accompanying commentary:[1]

1. *Criminal behavior is learned.* Negatively, this means that criminal behavior is not inherited, as such; also, the person who is not already trained in crime does not invent criminal behavior, just as a person does not make mechanical inventions unless he has had training in mechanics.

2. *Criminal behavior is learned in interaction with other persons in a process of communication.* This communication is verbal in many respects but includes also "the communication of gestures."

3. *The principal part of the learning of criminal behavior occurs within intimate personal groups.* Negatively, this means that the impersonal agencies of communication, such as movies and newspapers, play a relatively unimportant part in the genesis of criminal behavior.

4. *When criminal behavior is learned, the learning includes (a) techniques of committing the crime, which are sometimes very complicated, sometimes very simple, and (b) the specific direction of motives, drives, rationalizations, and attitudes.*

5. *The specific direction of motives and drives is learned from definitions of the legal codes as favorable or unfavorable.* In some societies an individual is surrounded by persons who invariably define the legal codes as rules to be observed, while in others he is surrounded by persons whose definitions are favorable to the violation of the legal codes. In our American society these definitions are almost always mixed, with the consequence that we have culture conflict in relation to the legal codes.

6. *A person becomes delinquent because of an excess of definitions favorable to violation of law over definitions unfavorable to violation of law.* This is the principle of differential association. It refers to both criminal and anti-criminal associations and has to do with counteracting forces. When persons become criminal, they do so because of contacts with criminal patterns and also because of isolation from anti-criminal patterns. Any person inevitably assimilates the surrounding culture unless other patterns are in conflict; a Southerner does not pronounce "r" because other Southerners do not pronounce "r." Negatively, this proposition of differential association means that associations which are neutral so far as crime is concerned have little or no effect on the genesis of criminal behavior. Much of the experience of a person is neutral in this sense, e.g., learning to brush one's teeth. This behavior has no negative or positive effect on criminal behavior except as it may be related to associations which are concerned with the legal codes. This neutral behavior is important especially as an occupier of the time of a child so that he is not in contact with criminal behavior during the time he is so engaged in the neutral behavior.

7. *Differential associations may vary in frequency, duration, priority, and intensity.* This means that associations with criminal behavior vary in these respects. "Frequency" and "duration" as modalities of association are obvious and need no explanation. "Priority" is assumed to be important in the sense that lawful behavior developed in early childhood may persist throughout life, and also that delinquent behavior developed in early childhood may persist throughout life. This tendency, however, has not been adequately demonstrated and priority seems to be important principally through its selective influence. "Intensity" is not precisely defined but it

has to do with such things as the prestige source of a criminal or anti-criminal pattern and with emotional reactions related to the associations. In a precise description of the criminal behavior of a person these modalities would be stated in a quantitative form and a mathematical ratio be reached. A formula in this sense has not been developed and the development of such a formula would be extremely difficult.

8. *The process of learning criminal behavior by association with criminal and anti-criminal patterns involves all of the mechanisms that are involved in any other learning.* Negatively, this means that the learning of criminal behavior is not restricted to the process of imitation. A person who is seduced, for instance, learns criminal behavior by association, but this process would not ordinarily be described as imitation.

9. *Although criminal behavior is an expression of general needs and values, it is not explained by those general needs and values, because noncriminal behavior is an expression of the same needs and values.* Thieves generally steal in order to secure money, but likewise honest laborers work in order to secure money. The attempts by many scholars to explain criminal behavior by general drives and values, such as the happiness principle, striving for social status, the money motive, or frustration, have been and must continue to be futile since they explain lawful behavior as completely as they explain criminal behavior. They are similar to respiration, which is necessary for any behavior, but which does not differentiate criminal from non-criminal behavior.

In addition to now constituting a purely processual theory with neither culture conflict nor social disorganization included, this classic formulation unequivocally identifies the causal "processes which result in systematic criminal behavior" as *learning* processes. This is stated in a simple declarative sentence in the first proposition of the theory, and the terms "learned" and "learning" are repeated in five other statements (in the second through the fifth and in the eighth sentences). The second and third propositions make it clear that Sutherland identified this learning process primarily with verbal and nonverbal interaction in intimate groups.

The fourth statement introduces the idea that the content of what is learned includes both the behavioral techniques involved in crime ("sometimes very complicated, sometimes very simple") and the inclination (through motive, drive, rationalization) to break the law. In other words, simply knowing how to carry out a crime in the sense of going through the behavioral sequence is not sufficient to account for law-breaking, except in the negative sense that if the act requires a complicated set of tasks or skills that the person does not possess then he or she cannot commit the crime. Rather, the direction of previously learned motives, drives, rationalizations, and attitudes must orient the person toward being willing to violate the law.

Next, the fifth and sixth statements follow this up with explicit propositions that whether people become criminally inclined is based on "definitions" favorable or unfavorable to the law. These two statements lead, in the sixth proposition, to what Sutherland identifies as the "principle of differential association," the nucleus of the theory around which all the other elements revolve. It proposes that people commit crimes because they have learned "definitions" favorable to violating law in "excess" of the definitions unfavorable to violating it.

This is not a simple matter of association with "bad companions," nor does it involve associating only with particular "kinds" of people. The theory, rather, is directed at learning criminal behavior in communication with criminal and noncriminal "patterns" and "definitions." Although the 1934 version referred to associations with other persons who commit crimes, the final version of 1947 stressed the notion of contact with definitions favorable and unfavorable to criminal behavior. Therefore, Sutherland explains lawbreaking primarily by the differential exposure (created by this interaction) to others' definitions that are favorable to criminal behavior, balanced against contact with conforming definitions. Although it is to be expected that law-violating definitions are typically communicated by those who have violated the law, it is also possible to learn law-abiding definitions from them, just as one can be exposed to deviant definitions from law-abiding people (Cressey, 1960:49).

The seventh principle of the theory makes it clear that the process is not a simple matter of any exposure to either criminal or noncriminal association, but that the effects of associations vary according to the "modalities" of association—frequency, duration, priority, and intensity. Sutherland had earlier referred to "frequency and consistency," but he came to believe that "consistency" was just another term for "differential" (Schuessler, 1973), dropped it as a variable, and added the other modalities. He probably did not mean these to be exhaustive of all possible ways in which associations vary, but no one has yet suggested additional modalities, nor have I yet been able to come up with additions. The greater the extent to which individuals are exposed first (priority), more frequently, for a longer time (duration), and with greater intensity (importance, prestige, intimacy, or closeness) to law-violating definitions than to law-abiding definitions, the more likely they are to learn definitions favorable to deviating from the law and to break it.

To summarize, the differential association theory, as Sutherland presented it in 1947, proposes that one learns criminal behavior in a process of symbolic interaction with others, mainly those in primary groups, who present the person with both criminal and anti-criminal patterns, techniques, motivations, and definitional stances toward the legal norms. The balance of learned criminal and anti-criminal definitions determines whether one will be conforming or deviant with respect to a given legal code. If the balance of definitions is favorable to abiding by the law, the outcome is conformity; if violative definitions are in excess, criminal behavior is the result. This balance is based on the frequency, duration, priority, and intensity with which one is exposed to lawful or criminal definitions. If one is exposed to law-violating definitions and at the same time is relatively isolated from law-abiding definitions, or if he is exposed to the former first, more frequently, for a longer time, and with greater intensity than the latter, he will learn the techniques and definitions favorable to crime and will commit crime.

Although the theory was stated fully only in the textbook, Sutherland engaged in continuing dialogue with students and colleagues and often responded to criticism and issues raised about the theory in published and unpublished commentaries before devising the final version (see Cohen et al., 1956; Schuessler, 1973; Gaylord and Galliher, 1988). One of the most remarkable of these private commentaries was entitled "The Swan Song of Differential Association." Here Sutherland (somewhat tongue-in-cheek) took the stance of his strongest critics and tried to show that differential association is not an adequate theory of crime because, while it is a "necessary" cause of criminal behavior (crime does not occur in the absence of associations), it is not a "sufficient" cause (crime always occurs in the presence of associations). Certain other "extraneous" factors must be brought in to account for when crime does or does not occur in the presence of differential association.

The first of these is "opportunity." Since the objective conditions producing opportunities to commit specific crimes (e.g., the presence of victims against whom one may commit a violent crime, burglary, or robbery, being in a job that affords a chance for embezzlement, or other particular situations allowing the commission of a crime or deviant act) must be present for the crime to occur, differential association alone is insufficient as a cause of all crime. The second factor is intensity of need, but Sutherland dealt with it in a manner that also answered the question raised by the opportunity factor. He simply asserted that the level of need (as in the case of objective conditions) provides an opportunity for crime, but persons will not commit the crime unless they have learned to define the given need or opportunity situation as one in which a crime is appropriate. Another factor is the availability of "alternative behaviors," or noncriminal ways of satisfying the same needs or wants. This sounds very much like differential opportunity theory, as espoused earlier by Merton and later by Cloward and Ohlin. The answer, again, is that what are perceived as appropriate alternatives or means to satisfying the same needs is also a matter of definition of the situation.

At one time this concept of cause as a "necessary" and "sufficient" condition was the ideal toward which social science theory strove. Sutherland adhered to this standard of cause, and it fit into the methodology he adopted from Alfred Lindesmith of "analytic induction" (one also used by Donald R. Cressey, 1953), in which one keeps examining cases of what is to be explained, one at a time, until an exception to the explanation is discovered. At that point, the investigator either rejects the explanation or modifies it to include the differences found, and then moves on to the next case. At some point the theory fits all cases and provides both the necessary and sufficient conditions for crime to occur. But no theory of behavior, whether inductively constructed or not, has ever fully met these conditions of strict determinism. Therefore, to conclude that differential association is not both a necessary and sufficient condition for crime to occur is not meaningful, because it is exactly the same conclusion that would be reached about any alternative explanation. A more appropriate conception of cause is a probabilistic one in which the theory simply asserts that criminal behavior is more likely in the presence of a set of variables or processes, less likely in their absence, and different values of the variable produce different probabilities of criminal behavior occurring.

Sutherland also addressed the issue of the "ratio" of definitions favorable to definitions unfavorable (Schuessler, 1973). Although he believed that an exact quantifiable ratio was needed, he felt that while it was possible to produce such a ratio it would be extremely difficult. This seems to be based on his belief, growing out of his adherence to the technique of analytic induction, that the calculation of this ratio would mean adding up in some cumulative fashion, on a case-by-case basis, all definitions favorable and definitions unfavorable to which the person had been exposed over time. Beyond this, however, Sutherland provided a conceptual basis for interpreting the ratio and making predictions from it. If definitions favorable to crime are exactly counterbalanced by definitions unfavorable, the ratio is 1:1, or "unity." It is possible that there are patterns of association at one extreme in which essentially the only definitions to which individuals are exposed are favorable to crime. Sutherland gave "the criminal tribes of India" as an example of differential association at this far end of the continuum (Cohen et al., 1956:40). In such situations, the ratio is "far above unity" and criminal behavior is almost certain. On the other hand, one could be exposed only to highly conforming, conventional definitions; here, the ratio would be far below unity, with almost no chance of criminal behavior. The most common pattern in modern society is exposure to both criminal and anti-criminal influences, with individuals lying somewhere along the scale from far below to far above unity. As the ratio comes closer to unity for an individual, it "becomes increasingly uncertain" what the behavior will be (see Orcutt, 1987).

After Sutherland's death, Donald R. Cressey revised *Principles of Criminology* from the fifth through the tenth editions. He became the major proponent of differential association, clarifying it and applying it to various areas in criminology (see Akers and Matsueda, 1989). However, in all of the revisions of the text, Cressey purposely left the original nine statements of differential association theory unchanged from the way Sutherland had them in 1947. After Cressey's death, David F. Luckenbill revised the text for its eleventh edition (Sutherland, Cressey, and Luckenbill, 1992), and he too has changed nothing from the 1947 presentation. Both of Sutherland's successors were well aware of and discussed others' criticisms and suggested modifications of the theory. Cressey thought it best, however, to preserve the original form, even though "it seems highly probable that it [the theory] will have to undergo revision," because "[i]t would be inappropriate to modify the theory in such a way that research work now in progress would be undermined" (Sutherland and Cressey, 1960:vi).

Cressey's Analysis of Critiques of Differential Association Theory

Donald R. Cressey (1960) conducted an exhaustive review of the criticisms of Sutherland's theory that had accumulated up to the end of the 1950s. It is important to examine them because, even though one seldom encounters exactly these same criticisms, errors in interpreting differential association continue to this day. Cressey argued persuasively that many of these were simply misunderstandings or "literary errors" on the part of the critics. First, the theory was widely criticized on the grounds that not everyone who has had contact with criminals becomes criminal, and that even in environments that lean toward criminality (such as a neighborhood with high crime rates) most people most of the time are law-abiding. This criticism is invalid because it overlooks the fact that the theory specifically refers to the ratio of criminal to noncriminal contacts by individuals. Differential association does not propose that any environment in American society will be entirely criminal or that everyone in the same neighborhood will have acquired exactly the same ratio of definitions favorable and unfavorable to crime. Simply having some kind of contact with criminal patterns or being in an environment suffused with such patterns will not necessarily result in learning criminal behavior, because for some or most individuals the pro-criminal contacts are offset by anti-criminal contacts. This criticism is simply a misreading of the theory.

Second, Cressey noted that some critics misread the theory as referring only to association with criminals as a category of *persons*. In truth, as shown above, the theory hypothesizes that the effect on one's behavior comes from contact with *patterns* of definitions, regardless of "the person presenting them" (Cressey, 1960:49). Thus, one may be exposed to law-abiding patterns while associating with thieves and to law-violating patterns while associating with policemen. The terms of the theory do not require the person to interact directly with others who are committing violations. It is necessary only that one be exposed, directly or indirectly, to patterns of definitions favorable to the violation and be in a position to learn how to do the crime if more than commonly learned techniques are involved. Many offenses require little skill, and the crimes can be perpetrated simply by applying knowledge already acquired in a conventional context. Moreover, it is not simply exposure to criminal and anti-criminal patterns, but the relative frequency, duration, priority, and intensity of such exposure, that is crucial.

Third, some critics continued to refer to the limited scope of the 1939 version that mentioned only "systematic" criminal behavior, even years after the publication of Sutherland's final version, which dropped this adjective altogether. Fourth, differential association theory was criticized for not explaining why someone comes to have the differences in associations that produce the behavior. Again, such critics have simply not read the theory closely and have ignored Sutherland's explicit exclusion of this problem from its purview.

This type of misreading characterized some of the early research efforts to test differential association theory in the 1950s. For instance, Clinard (1952:285–329) found that black-market violators during World War II did not associate very much with other lawbreakers; he concluded that differential association did not account for such crime. This conclusion is based on a misunderstanding of differential association as referring only to interaction with other persons who are themselves active criminals. In fact, the violators in Clinard's study were aware of other violations and applied definitions of the situation that made these appear justified. Their techniques simply involved applying lawfully learned business and bookkeeping techniques unlawfully.

Similarly, Lemert determined from his studies of check forgery that, although differential association explained the behavior of professional check forgers, it did not account for either naïve or "systematic" (but nonprofessional) check forgers (Lemert, 1953; 1958). This conclusion was based on his finding that both the latter types were "isolates," who tended to forge checks on their own without working in gangs, tended to have no (or no serious) previous criminal record, had no intimate interaction with other kinds of criminals, and had picked up the techniques of forgery in the general process of learning to write checks rather than in learning to violate the law.

Again, this conclusion not supporting the theory mistakenly assumes that differential association hypothesizes that one learns techniques and definitions of crime only by interaction with others who are engaging in the same type of criminal behavior or that one can only learn definitions and techniques from criminals. Moreover, much of what Lemert reported in his study of forgers fits well with the differential association process. For instance, he found that they tended to justify their actions as not really a crime, or at best as a "relatively benign form of crime" (Lemert, 1953:298), and that they refrained from violent offenses, which they defined as wrong. This fits exactly into Sutherland's concept of definitions favorable or unfavorable to committing the crime. Lemert noted that these sentiments about check forgery were also held by the public at large and that knowledge of its techniques is acquired simply in the process of learning how to write and cash a check lawfully—even Lemert's college students knew how to do it. Both the techniques and definitions were learned from exposure to definitions found in the prevailing culture. Since there is no requirement in differential association theory for exposure to a specifically criminal value system or subculture in order to learn law violation, these findings support the theory. Lemert's conclusion that they did not was based on a misapplication of the theory.

Cressey (1960) pointed out that some critiques were not errors of reading or interpretation. For instance, he believed empirical "exceptions" to the theory could be found and that this was a problem for differential association. Cressey was operating from the same "analytic induction" approach that, as noted above, Sutherland had adopted; any exception to a theory must be considered fully and the theory must be rejected or modified immediately to take the exception into account (Schuessler, 1973). However, the probabilistic approach to testing more common today does not expect all cases to fit a valid theory. Exceptions can be found for the assertions of any theory, and no criminological theory fits all cases. The question is which theory does the best job of fitting the facts, has the fewest exceptions, is most supported by the empirical evidence, and does the best job of predicting criminal behavior.

Another common criticism of the day was that the theory of differential association does not adequately take into account "personality" or "psychological" variables. Cressey also viewed this as an acceptable critique, provided the critic could show precisely what personality variables were relevant. But this approach did not show which personality variables in particular must be taken into account or how doing so adds to or undermines differential association. Cressey pointed out that most often references to individual or personality differences turn out to be simply additional labels that are attached to the observed behavior without explaining the behavior. It is true that differential association theory does not explicitly account for differential receptivity or individual differences in responses to essentially the same set of proffered criminal and noncriminal associations. Rather, it does so implicitly by referring to the differential impact of individuals' histories of prior associations and learned definitions on current associations and definitions. How one responds when confronted with or seeking out new associations or definitions favorable or unfavorable depends on previously learned definitions and associations. This may not be a full answer, but it does as well or better than the usual response given by critics, which makes only vague references to some unspecified self-selective mechanism or personality trait (Cressey, 1960:51–54). Moreover, it had not been shown then (and still has not been shown) that such variables have a stronger relationship to criminal and delinquent behavior than do associations. It is not a sound critique of differential association to point out that it does not include psychological or personality variables when those variables themselves are not strongly related either to crime or to patterns of associations.

Cressey recognized two weaknesses in Sutherland's theory that could not be dismissed as erroneous or as readily nullified in the theory's own terms. The first was the difficulty of defining some terms of the theory in a way that permits empirical testing. Cressey was especially concerned that the crucial concept of definitions was itself not precisely defined and that the ratio of the "excess of definitions" could not be operationalized. He (along with the Gluecks) believed the concept of "excess" implied the almost impossible task of having to reconstruct exactly or make ongoing observations of all of the individual's prior criminal and anti-criminal contacts (differentiated by the modalities of association), add them up, and determine what the ratio was. Second, the theory left the learning process unspecified, giving no clue as to what in particular would be included in "all the mechanisms that are involved in any other learning." These two issues of clarification and operationalization of the concept of definitions and specification of the learning process became the focus of subsequent efforts to reformulate or revise Sutherland's theory, as discussed below.

Cressey's review covered the critiques of differential association in the 1940s and 1950s. Even though some of the same criticisms he reviewed are still being voiced, for the most part they are no longer relevant because of later developments in research and modifications of the theory. They are seldom repeated in contemporary criminological literature. It is more common now to find the theory criticized as a "cultural deviance" theory, a stance that began to be taken in the 1960s (Kornhauser, 1978; Hirschi, 1969; Gottfredson and Hirschi, 1990). The cultural deviance criticism attempts to show that differential association (as well as the social learning revision of the theory) is irredeemably flawed because it rests on faulty assumptions. I believe that this position is at best only partially correct for Sutherland's theory and that it is not all correct as a criticism of the social learning reformulation. I will come back to this as a major issue in Chapter 4.

Modifications and Extensions of Differential Association before the Social Learning Reformulation

CRESSEY: VERBALIZATIONS AND VOCABULARIES OF ADJUSTMENT

Donald R. Cressey was the first to undertake clarifications, modifications, and extensions of the concept of definitions favorable and unfavorable and to identify the empirical content of definitions favorable to specific crimes. He recognized that the brief statements in Sutherland's theory, especially the fourth and fifth, were somewhat ambiguous about the relationship between definitions and the concepts of rationalizations and attitudes. In his famous study of violations of financial trust, Cressey (1953) unambiguously categorized rationalizations and attitudes as subtypes of definitions favorable to crime. He found that none of the convicted embezzlers in his study committed the crime until he had reached the point of rationalizing it as justified or excusable. This rationalization was the last step in the process (after the formation of a nonshareable problem and the arising of an opportunity for embezzlement) by which persons in positions of financial trust betray it. In Cressey's terms, the embezzler applies "verbalizations," "rationalizations," and "vocabularies of adjustment and motives" such as "I am just borrowing the money, I will pay it back soon"; "The money is really mine"; "It is only fair that I get something more, I'm certainly not getting paid what I'm worth" (Cressey, 1953:93–138).

This type of definition is favorable to committing a crime because it "enables [the offender] to look upon trust violation as essentially non-criminal, as justified, or as part of a general irresponsibility for which he is not completely accountable" (Cressey, 1953:93). He (1954) also applied differential association theory to "compulsive crimes," which had usually been considered to be irrational, spontaneous, and unlearned manifestations of underlying pathology or uncontrollable impulses. Cressey showed that such violations are not exceptions to differential associations and that the very notion of being under some uncontrollable compulsion for which one cannot be held responsible can, itself, be learned as a definition justifying or excusing lawbreaking. To Cressey, the concept of verbalization or vocabulary of motives is not simply an ex post facto rationalization of behavior (although it may begin with that), but rather is part of the motivational process in carrying out behavior. Although he did not propose a specific modification of differential association theory, it should be apparent from Cressey's treatment of the rationalizations of embezzlers that he viewed them as concrete forms or operationalization of definitions favorable to crime.

SYKES AND MATZA: TECHNIQUES OF NEUTRALIZATION AS DEFINITIONS FAVORABLE TO DELINQUENCY

Cressey's development and application of the definitions concept became the foundation for later theoretical developments in differential association. The best known of these was by Sykes and Matza (1957), who laid out several "techniques of neutralization" learned by adolescents as justifications for delinquent behavior. As in Cressey's conception of the rationalization of embezzlement, these definitions are conducive to delinquent behavior because they allow the delinquent to "neutralize" anti-delinquent definitions and justify or make his delinquencies seem all right. Definitions favorable to delinquency do not stand in direct opposition to conventional norms by defining delinquency as a positive good. They are not the kind of "negativistic" subcultural delinquent values attributed to lower-class delinquents by Cohen (1955). Sykes and Matza found fault with the notion in theories of delinquent subcultures that account for "delinquent behavior as springing from a set of deviant values and norms—as arising, that is to say, from a situation in which the delinquent defines his delinquency as 'right' " (Sykes and Matza, 1957:664). Rather, the definitions favorable to delinquency offset conventional norms by functioning as excuses or justifications for delinquent acts. It is not that delinquency is "right"; it is that it is "all right" under certain conditions. Thus, one can violate norms in which he or she ostensibly believes by deflecting social and self-disapproval.

The concept of definitions favorable to delinquency does not require total rejection of conforming values. Deviant definitions need not, and usually do not, involve substitution of a complete set of counterculture values that ideologically compel or strongly motivate one to commit acts against the dominant culture in the manner of religious sects, conscientious objectors, or politically organized dissidents (see Chapter 4). Neutralizing definitions, rather, turn out to be peculiar extensions of "defenses to crime" already contained in the general culture (perhaps as "norms of evasion," Merton, 1957) and, indeed, embodied in the criminal law's allowing for pleas of "nonage, necessity, insanity, drunkenness, compulsion, self-defense, and so on."

> It is our argument that much delinquency is based on what is essentially an unrecognized extension of defenses to crimes, in the form of justifications for deviance that are seen as valid by the delinquent but not by the legal system or society at large. (Sykes and Matza, 1957:666)

The major forms that these neutralizing definitions take are "denial of responsibility," "denial of injury," "denial of the victim," "condemnation of the condemners," and "appeal to higher loyalties." Belief in these neutralizations need not be clearly articulated, and adherence to them does not mean they will always be acted upon in illegitimate behavior. Although they may be incorporated into and promoted by deviant subcultures, they do not by themselves constitute a separate set of oppositional deviant subcultural values. They are simply "subterranean values" that circumvent, and rationalize deviations from, conventional values that the adolescent has internalized to a greater or lesser degree (Matza and Sykes, 1961).

Sykes and Matza are sometimes interpreted as offering "neutralization theory" as a general theory of delinquency and deviance without reference to Sutherland. They, however, defined their list of techniques of neutralization as a modification or specification of differential association theory. Sykes and Matza begin by accepting Sutherland's differential association theory: "It is now largely agreed that delinquent behavior, like most social behavior, is learned and that it is learned in the process of social interaction" (Sykes and Matza, 1957:664). They left no doubt that techniques of neutralization are intended to be types of "definitions favorable" to crime that were left unspecified in Sutherland's theory. Thus, they did not propose their analysis of techniques of neutralization as a new and separate theory; it was intended as a modification and extension that is wholly congruent with and subsumable under the general theory of differential association.

In spite of this, a great many criminologists have retroactively interpreted Sykes and Matza as control theorists. Although they certainly had much to say that is relevant to control theory, Sykes and Matza did not take such a position on delinquency. In my opinion, this interpretation of their view came about principally because of two theoretical developments that took place after their original articles appeared—the publication of Matza's *Delinquency and Drift* (1964) and of Hirschi's *Causes of Delinquency* (1969).

Matza (1964) incorporated neutralization ideas into his "drift" theory. It proposes that the techniques of neutralization are ways in which adolescents can get "episodic release" from conventional moral constraints and thus represent a weakening of social control or a breaking of the bonds to society (Minor, 1980; 1981). Although Matza said very little about internal or external social control, his drift theory became almost universally accepted as a form of control theory; by extension, his earlier work with Sykes on the techniques of neutralization came to be classified in the same way.

The fact that Matza worked techniques of neutralization into his theory as ways by which adolescents are set "free to drift" into delinquency does not detract from their status as specific types of definitions favorable to delinquency as envisioned in differential association theory. Techniques of neutralization may be seen as a weakening of conventional controls only if conventional controls are defined as including general definitions unfavorable to delinquency and it is assumed that individuals will not commit delinquent acts unless these unfavorable definitions of delinquency are counteracted by techniques of neutralization. Thus, the point at which neutralizations offset conventional beliefs is simply a special case of the ratio of anti-delinquent and pro-delinquent definitions specified in differential association theory. The interpretation of techniques of neutralization as control theory, then, is an instance of renaming this ratio of definitions favorable and unfavorable and calling it a weakening of social control. This tendency to take differential association and other social learning concepts, rename them, and place them in the service of other theoretical formulations, particularly social control theory, continues today.

When Travis Hirschi later presented the pre-eminent version of control theory, social bonding theory, in *Causes of Delinquency*, he included techniques of neutralization under his discussion of the bonding element of belief and utilized them in his empirical operationalization of that concept. Surprisingly, Hirschi described both Cressey's concepts of verbalizations and rationalizations and Sykes and Matza's concept of techniques of neutralization as attempts by control theorists to answer the question of why a person can believe that an act is morally wrong and still commit it. He made no mention of the explicit link that the authors of both of these concepts made to differential association theory. Hirschi's book is among those at the top of the list of the most widely read and influential pieces of criminological literature in the past two decades (Cohn and Farrington, 1994a; 1994b; 1996a). Cressey was so closely identified with Sutherland throughout his career that almost no one believes him to have been a control theorist, in spite of Hirschi's characterization. In my opinion, however, Hirschi's inclusion of techniques of neutralization in the original statement and operationalization of his theory, without any reference to the links to differential association theory, was a major factor that led to the widespread perception that Sykes and Matza were control theorists, not differential association theorists. I believe this interpretation of neutralizations as central to control theory is mistaken, however, because it entirely overlooks the fact that, while he used techniques of neutralization as measures of the concept of belief in his theory, Hirschi rejected the notion that these techniques allowed delinquents to break away from strongly held conventional beliefs. Instead, he proposed that endorsement of the techniques of neutralization simply indicates that conventional beliefs are weakly held by delinquents in the first place because they failed to be strongly enough socialized into the conventional beliefs. Therefore, there is no strongly held prior conventional belief to be neutralized. In other words, to Hirschi, the techniques of neutralization do not neutralize.

Others (Ball, 1968) have viewed neutralization as part of control theory because it is interpreted as a weakening of "inner containment" in Reckless's (Reckless et al., 1956; Reckless, 1961) containment version of control theory. Internalizing neutralizations can be thought of as part of the kind of vulnerable self-concept posited in containment theory. However, Reckless himself considered both "good" and "bad" self-concept to be an outcome of socialization by age twelve and left no room for countervailing socialization into delinquent neutralizations. Both Hartung (1965) and Voss (1969) long ago made a persuasive case that self-concept (and whatever rationalizations or neutralizations are considered to be part of it) is itself a product of the childhood socialization process. These earlier efforts to use weak or vulnerable self-concept as the primary explanation of delinquency presaged the general self-control theory of crime proposed by Gottfredson and Hirschi (1990). They too view self-control as the result of childhood socialization. If socialization is not a social learning process, what is it? Therefore, it seems to be self-contradictory to claim, as Gottfredson and Hirschi do, that self-control explains crime in a way that is inconsistent with differential association and later learning theory (Akers, 1991). At any rate, in light of the intent of Cressey and of Sykes and Matza and the uses to which they put the concept, it is reasonable to view techniques of neutralizations as types of definitions favorable to deviance more than as components of self-concept or self-control. This provides at least a partial answer to the question of why some people violate the very norms that they ostensibly endorse, an answer that Kornhauser (1978) claims cannot be given within differential association or social learning theory. (For a fuller treatment of this issue, see my discussion in Chapter 4 of social learning as cultural deviance theory.)

HARTUNG: SOCIOCULTURAL LEARNING

This disconnecting of self-concept and self-control from the differential association tradition is even more puzzling in light of the modifications in the theory proposed by Frank Hartung. Hartung (1965) accepted the proposition that the self-concept is formed in the socialization process, which he characterized as a process of "sociocultural learning." His depiction of what takes place in sociocultural learning is basically a restatement of differential association theory, modified to include self-concept as a product of the process. He reiterated Sutherland's proposal that crime is learned through symbolic communication in primary groups (Hartung, 1965:37–51). Then he proposed that learning "criminal conceptions of thought and action" includes both a "vocabulary of motives" (drawing on Cressey and Sykes and on Matza) and "a self-conception that allows the individual to admit his criminal acts to himself without damage to his conception of himself as a worthy person" (Hartung, 1965:52). Hartung's modifications also included specification of types of definitions favorable to crime, in the process extending Cressey's analysis of "compulsive" violent crimes. He also generalized techniques of neutralization beyond delinquency to show how they are involved in many forms of adult crime and violence. He did this primarily by identifying denial of responsibility and the claim of uncontrollable compulsion or impulse as general excuses for deviant acts ("I just blew my top"; "I was drunk"; "I broke down"; "I didn't know what I was doing"). In agreement with Sykes and Matza, Hartung proposed that, while definitions justifying crime can be learned in contact with specifically deviant subcultures, they are also learned from the acceptable excuses or justifications already present in the general culture.

GLASER: DIFFERENTIAL IDENTIFICATION, ANTICIPATION, AND SOCIAL CONTROL

Daniel Glaser (1956) was not concerned about clarifying the concept of definitions, although he contended that "the phrase 'excess of definitions' . . . lacks clear denotation in human experience" (1956:438). He suggested, instead, that "we reconceptualize Sutherland's theory in terms which we call 'differential identification'" (1956:439), where the "person pursues criminal behavior to the extent that he identifies with real or imaginary persons from whose perspective his criminal behavior seems acceptable" (Glaser, 1956:439–40). These individuals may be close friends, members of more distant reference groups, or people presented in the mass media. Beyond putting a bit more emphasis than Sutherland did on groups (other than face-to-face associations) with which one identifies as sources of criminal and anti-criminal definitions, there is very little in the concept of identification with reference groups that is not already captured by the concept of differential association. Glaser acknowledged this, noting that Sutherland himself had previously been "dismayed by an assumption [found in a study cited by Sutherland] that 'association' is distinct from 'identification.'" He noted, further, that

Cressey had already argued that differential identification was subsumed under the concept of differential association (Glaser, 1956:439).

Later, Glaser (1960) briefly outlined the concept of "differential anticipation" of criminal and noncriminal opportunities as a modification of differential association. This became the basis for his later statement that "a person's crime or restraint from crime is determined by the consequences he anticipates from it" (Glaser, 1978:126–27). Glaser also suggested in 1960 that if control theory's emphasis on the breakdown of conventional personal and social controls could be combined with the "build-up of direct and indirect delinquent or criminal social control" it could lead to an integration of differential association and control theory as "differential social control" (Glaser, 1960:12). He acknowledged that control theorists of the past had not been interested in this kind of integration.

Nevertheless, Ross Matsueda (1988) and Karen Heimer (Heimer and Matsueda, 1994) in their later studies have attempted to develop this notion of differential social control as a modification of differential association. While I see value in integrating control and learning concepts, in my view "differential social control" adds nothing to differential association that is not already included in the social learning formulation to which we turn next. Differential social control simply recognizes that both conventional and criminal interactions can "control" or influence behavior (through socialization and the application of sanctions) and that the direction of behavior is determined by the "differential," or balance, of these pro- and anti-criminal influences. Glaser's hypothesis (and the similar one of Matsueda and Heimer) that the probability of criminal behavior is increased when the breakdown of conventional social control occurs in conjunction with the buildup of criminal control, then, is just another way of describing differential association/reinforcement favoring criminality.

The Burgess-Akers Social Learning Reformulation: Differential Association–Reinforcement

Sutherland believed that the process whereby one becomes a professional thief, as shown in his famous case study (1937), is consistent with differential association. He also contended that his later findings on white-collar crime could be explained by differential association theory (Sutherland, 1961:234–56). But neither the case study nor the study of corporate crime were designed specifically to test the theory. Moreover, both of these investigations were done before Sutherland formulated the final version of differential association, and they can be considered as consistent with his theory only in retrospect. He died so soon after publication of the final version of his theory that he did not have the opportunity to conduct his own publishable tests of it. Sutherland apparently did have some research under way, with some of his students interviewing incarcerated offenders in an attempt to apply the analytic induction technique in testing the theory (Schuessler, 1973). But the most that came of these efforts was the observation that only 1 case out of 125 had wound up in prison without prior association with other offenders. There is no indication that Sutherland rejected or modified his theory based on this one exception as required by analytic induction. The case histories of the inmates were consistent with the theory; we do not know, however, how many persons could be found who had associated with offenders just as frequently, intensely, and for as long a time as the inmates in the study but had not landed in prison. Also, such a finding contains nothing about the ratios of definitions or modalities of association. Other early efforts to test the theory directly (such as Lemert's and Clinard's) misunderstood and misspecified it. Even Cressey, in *Other People's Money* (1953; see also Cressey, 1952), suggested that differential association was best seen as a general organizing principle rather than a theoretical explanation to be tested directly.

However, by the 1960s there had been movement on operationalizing and testing the theory. DeFleur and Quinney (1966) demonstrated that differential association as set out by Sutherland is internally consistent, able to be stated in formal, set logic format, and capable of producing testable hypotheses. Their work assumes that the concepts can be operationalized in a way that allows the data to be brought to bear on the testable hypotheses. And hypotheses from the theory had, in fact, been tested in empirical research by James Short (1957; 1960). The evidence from that work was on balance favorable to the theory, although researchers, even those who found evidence supportive of the theory, continued to report difficulties in operationalizing it.

Most important, none of the empirical tests or the suggested modifications addressed the key question of the nature of the learning process on which the whole theory of differential association is based. Sutherland asserted in the eighth statement of his theory that all the same mechanisms of learning are involved in both criminal and noncriminal behavior. However, beyond a brief comment that more is involved than simple imitation, he made no attempt to explain what the mechanisms of learning are. Cressey and others recognized this lack of specificity about the basic learning process assumed to be operating in both criminal and noncriminal behavior as constituting the major shortcoming of the theory as Sutherland had finally phrased it in 1947. Indeed, Cressey felt the greatest challenge was to specify what should be included in "all of the mechanisms" of learning in any behavior:

> It is one thing to criticize the theory for failure to specify the learning process accurately and another to specify which aspects of the learning process should be included and in what way. (Cressey, 1960:54)

It was in response to this recognized need for specifying the learning process, and thereby enhancing the conceptualization and testability of the theory, that Burgess and I undertook a revision of differential association theory in 1965. At the time, we noted that

> [n]either the extant statement of the theory nor the [previous] reformulations of it make explicit the nature of the underlying learning process involved in differential association. In short, no major revisions have been made utilizing established learning principles. (Burgess and Akers, 1966b:130)

We began our revision by stating that the basic mechanisms are those identified by the principles of learning in psychological behaviorism and then fused Sutherland's theory with these principles. We called the revised theory a "differential association–reinforcement" theory of criminal behavior. The learning principles that we drew upon were mainly those of operant conditioning, identified primarily with the work of B. F. Skinner and his associates. We argued that Sutherland's basic notion of learning through association or interaction with others in a social environment was entirely compatible with the key notion in operant theory that the individual's behavior is shaped by interaction with the environment, which in operant theory could be either social or nonsocial. Therefore, in spite of their origin in different traditions, there should be no fundamental incompatibility of the symbolic interactionist concepts in the sociological approach to learning and socialization incorporated into Sutherland's theory and the behaviorism of operant conditioning theory. However, as I mentioned in Chapter 1 and shall show later in greater detail, the more I developed the theory after the initial reformulation, the greater the role that I gave to cognitive processes in line with symbolic interactionism in sociology and social behaviorism in psychology.

As Robert Burgess and I were working on this revision, C. Ray Jeffery (1965) proposed replacing Sutherland's entire theory with a single-sentence statement of the principle of differential reinforcement applied to criminal behavior:

> [A] criminal act occurs in an environment in which in the past the actor has been reinforced for behaving in this manner, and the aversive consequences attached to the behavior have been of such a nature that they do not control or prevent the response. (Jeffery, 1965:295)

Our judgment of Jeffery's statement was that it

> bears no obvious or direct relation to Sutherland's differential association, and nowhere else does Jeffery make it clear how differential reinforcement is a reformulation of differential association. Jeffery does discuss modern learning principles, but he does not show how these principles may be incorporated within the framework of Sutherland's theory.... (Burgess and Akers, 1966b:131)

In short, none of the previous efforts of Cressey, Sykes and Matza, Hartung, Glaser, or Jeffery offered a thorough and substantive revision of differential association. We believed such a revision could be done in a way that would integrate the explanatory variables of differential associa- tion, and all of the previous modifications of it, into a more general the- ory of human behavior. We pursued this objective by revising each of the nine statements in Sutherland's theory in light of behavioral theory. This was in line with DeFleur and Quinney's assertion that, even in the axi- omatic form in which they had restated differential association theory, it was still insufficiently specified because the learning mechanisms were not delineated. It was their opinion, however, that "modern reinforce- ment learning theory would handle this problem . . ." (DeFleur and Quin- ney, 1966:3).

In a separate paper, the two of us addressed the criticism of tautology that had been directed toward operant theory. We felt the criticism was valid because of how operant conditioners typically stated their prin- ciples and definitions of terms. They tended to define reinforcement as any event that resulted in the strengthening of a response, and thus the hypothesis that behavior is strengthened through reinforcement is true by definition and untestable. But we showed in the paper that there was nothing inherently tautological in operant principles and that they could be proposed in nontautological form (Burgess and Akers, 1966a). (For further discussion of this issue, see Chapter 5.)

Burgess and I revised Sutherland's nine-statement theory into seven statements by combining the first and eighth, dropping the ninth, and revising each original statement by using behavioral concepts and propositions. The seven-statement Burgess-Akers (1966b) theory reads:

1. Criminal behavior is learned according to the principles of operant conditioning.

2. Criminal behavior is learned both in nonsocial situations that are reinforcing or discriminative and through that social interaction in which the behavior of other persons is reinforcing or discriminative for criminal behavior.

3. The principal part of the learning of criminal behavior occurs in those groups which comprise the individual's major source of reinforcement.

4. The learning of criminal behavior, including specific techniques, attitudes, and avoidance procedures, is a function of the effective and available reinforcers, and the existing reinforcement contingencies.

5. The specific class of behaviors which are learned and their frequency of occurrence are a function of the reinforcers which are effective and available, and the rules or norms by which these reinforcers are applied.

6. Criminal behavior is a function of norms which are discriminative for criminal behavior, the learning of which takes place when such behavior is more highly reinforced than noncriminal behavior.

7. The strength of criminal behavior is a direct function of the amount, frequency, and probability of its reinforcement.

These statements were incorporated in modified form into each edition of my *Deviant Behavior* (1973; 1977; 1985). The modifications included substituting for "criminal behavior" the term "deviant behavior" as a general concept including criminal, delinquent, and other types of acts in violation of social and legal norms, and revising the wording of some of the statements. These seven statements were followed by a discussion of the concepts, propositions, and criticisms of the theory. The modifications and the presentation of the theory in narrative form were intended to both emphasize that the theory was rooted in differential association theory and that, although operant terminology was used, the theory was actually closer to social learning perspectives such as Bandura's.

As I noted in the Introduction, the relationship between Sutherland's differential association theory and my version of social learning theory is widely known and remarked upon in the literature. But I continue to come across discussions in textbooks and published research articles, and frequently in review papers submitted for journal publication, of differential association theory that either ignore the relationship or get it wrong. There are discussions and tests of differential association that proceed as if *nothing* has changed since 1947. Social learning theory is a revision that integrates *all* of what Sutherland set out in differential association theory (albeit in somewhat altered form); it is not a totally different or rival theory. Therefore, beginning with Chapter 3 I refer only to social learning theory. I do not distinguish it from differential association theory except when referring to others who make such a distinction or when I want to reiterate the changes made in differential association theory by the social learning revision. For this reason, I take the stance that every critique, discussion, or test of differential association must take the social learning reformulation into account. One may legitimately dispute and criticize the reformulation; it is also legitimate to differentiate between them to show how social learning modifies Sutherland. But it is not appropriate, I believe, simply to ignore the social learning revision and to refer only to the strengths and weaknesses of the original theory as if nothing has changed in fifty years. It is not appropriate because the reformulation claimed to be a revision, not an alternative to differential association, and because the revision rectifies some of the shortcomings of the original to produce an improved model that is not subject to some of the limitations of the original. In the next chapter I provide a new, updated statement of social learning theory that incorporates the Burgess-Akers reformulation and subsequent clarifications and modifications.

Note

1. I am grateful to Elaine Cressey Ohlin for her kind permission to reprint these nine statements and commentary in their entirety.

3
The Social Learning Theory of Criminal and Deviant Behavior

The term "social learning" was used only in passing in the Burgess-Akers article, but I began almost immediately to apply that label to the theory and used it in the first edition of *Deviant Behavior: A Social Learning Approach* (1973). The theory was specifically identified as a social learning theory by book title and by label and by chapter and section headings. I continue to use the social learning label almost exclusively, but it is still accurate to call the theory differential association–reinforcement. As I stressed in Chapter 2, social learning is not meant to be an alternative, competitive, or rival theory to Sutherland's position. It is, instead, a broader theory that integrates processes of differential association and definitions from Sutherland's theory, modified and clarified, with differential reinforcement and other principles of behavioral acquisition, continuation, and cessation from behavioral learning theory. It is aimed toward explaining criminal and deviant behavior more fully than did Sutherland's theory (and later research has shown that it does; see, for instance, Akers et al., 1979; Krohn et al., 1985; Warr and Stafford, 1991). But research findings in favor of differential association theory also support the integrated social learning theory, and support for social learning theory does not invalidate differential association. This was stated in Burgess and Akers (1966b) and reiterated in all editions of *Deviant Behavior:*

> It should be noted that the revision was not intended as an alternative theory, although of necessity some ideas not intrinsic to differential association were introduced and additions were made to the original propositions. Rather, the reformulation was a new theory which integrated differential association with

differential reinforcement; one could not arrive at it starting with reinforcement theory and ignoring differential association or by starting with differential association and ignoring reinforcement theory. (Akers, 1973:45)

This was the principal reason that the Burgess-Akers reformulation presented in Chapter 2 followed closely the format of numbered sequential statements that Sutherland used. We wanted to show a full statement-by-statement revision of differential association theory.

However, in presenting the theory to students and expounding on it in writing, I found the numbered statement format did not communicate the content of the theory as well as I would like. The key elements of the theory are differential association and definitions, taken from Sutherland's theory, and differential reinforcement and imitation (and also other behavioral elements, such as discriminative stimuli) taken from learning theory. All of these, as well as other concepts, were explicated in the Burgess-Akers article, but not all of the terms actually appeared in the seven numbered statements. I also became less satisfied with how social and nonsocial reinforcement was depicted in our second statement. Although the seven numbered statements were internally consistent, they did not lay out very well either the processual or situational logic of the theory. An expository narrative, concentrating on defining the four main concepts, making reference to other learning mechanisms when needed, and showing how they fit into the learning process, seemed to do a better job of elucidating the theory. In short, I leaned toward the system used by Hirschi (1969) in proposing social bonding theory, in which he systematically defined the core concepts of the theory and then, in the context of a general discussion of the concepts, presented specific propositions about their relationship to delinquency.[1]

In repeating the theory in *Deviant Behavior*, I retained the serial listing and wording of the statements as a readily visible link both to Sutherland's original and to the Burgess-Akers revision. The nine Sutherland statements were given, followed by a listing of the seven Burgess-Akers statements, with the modifications I had made in them for the book (Akers, 1973:35–47; 1977:39–43; 1985:39–42). These modifications included substituting, for "criminal behavior," the term "deviant behavior" to include criminal, delinquent, and other acts that violate social norms, along with rewording some of the statements to include specifically the terms "definitions" and "associations." It did not seem necessary to make drastic alterations in the seven statements because of the accompanying narrative in *Deviant Behavior*.

The seven statements were followed by the assertion that they "contain terms which need definition and present only an outline of the theory; reference to these seven statements will not give the full substance of the theory" (Akers, 1985:42). The theory was then expounded in a way that concentrated on identifying the major explanatory concepts, explicating its propositions, and summarizing the theory in order to apply it to the different forms of deviant behavior covered in the book. In my exposition, I seldom went back to or quoted directly from the seven statements.

I have continued to refine the statement of social learning theory. My efforts reflect attempts at conceptual clarification, experiences in devising operational measures of the theory's key concepts in order to test its central propositions, reactions to criticisms, developments in criminological knowledge, and the need to propose the theory as carefully and clearly as possible. In doing so I have continued to move away from the *ad seriatim* formulation keyed to the nine statements contained in Sutherland's 1947 theory or to the seven statements in the 1966 Burgess and Akers article. In this chapter, I provide a new statement of social learning theory in a more narrative format, while retaining what Gibbons (1994) has identified as the semiformalized nature of the theory. This new presentation builds on and remains true to, but goes beyond, earlier statements. Terms are clearly defined, assumptions stated, the logical structure of the theory is explicated, and empirically testable hypotheses are set out. I shall first give a concise statement of the theory, and then devote the remainder of the chapter to a detailed exposition of the major concepts, propositions, and processes specified in the theory.

The theory does well on all the major criteria by which sound theory is judged—logical consistency, scope, parsimony, testability, empirical validity, and usefulness (Akers, 1994). The main part of the book following this chapter is devoted to showing that social learning theory does especially well on what I consider to be the most important criterion for judging a theory—empirical validity.

Concise Statement of the Theory

The basic assumption in social learning theory is that the same learning process, operating in a context of social structure, interaction, and situation, produces both conforming and deviant behavior. The difference lies in the direction of the process in which these mechanisms operate. In both, it is seldom an either-or, all-or-nothing process; what is involved, rather, is the balance of influences on behavior. That balance usually exhibits some stability over time, but it can become unstable and change with time or circumstances. Conforming and deviant behavior is learned by all of the mechanisms in this process, but the theory proposes that the principal mechanisms are in that part of the process in which differential reinforcement (instrumental learning through rewards and punishers) and imitation (observational learning) produce both overt behavior and cognitive definitions that function as discriminative (cue) stimuli for the behavior. Always implied, and sometimes made explicit when these concepts are called upon to account for deviant/conforming behavior, is the understanding that the behavioral processes in operant and classical conditioning are in operation (see below). However, social learning theory focuses on four major concepts—differential association, differential reinforcement, imitation, and definitions. The central proposition of the social learning theory of criminal and deviant behavior can be stated as a long sentence proposing that criminal and deviant behavior is more likely when, on balance, the combined effects of these four main sets of variables instigate and strengthen nonconforming over conforming acts:

> The probability that persons will engage in criminal and deviant behavior is increased and the probability of their conforming to the norm is decreased when they differentially associate with others who commit criminal behavior and espouse definitions favorable to it, are relatively more exposed in-person or symbolically to salient criminal/deviant models, define it as desirable or justified in a situation discriminative for the behavior, and have received in the past and anticipate in the current or future situation relatively greater reward than punishment for the behavior.

The probability of conforming behavior is increased and the probability of deviant behavior is decreased when the balance of these variables moves in the reverse direction.

Each of the four main components of this statement can be presented as a separate testable hypothesis. The individual is more likely to commit violations when:

1. He or she differentially associates with others who commit, model, and support violations of social and legal norms.

2. The violative behavior is differentially reinforced over behavior in conformity to the norm.

3. He or she is more exposed to and observes more deviant than conforming models.

4. His or her own learned definitions are favorable toward committing the deviant acts.

General Principles of Social Learning Theory

Since it is a general explanation of crime and deviance of all kinds, social learning is not simply a theory about how novel criminal behavior is learned or a theory only of the positive causes of that behavior. It embraces variables that operate to both motivate and control delinquent and criminal behavior, to both promote and undermine conformity. It answers the questions of why people do and do not violate norms. The probability of criminal or conforming behavior occurring is a function of the variables operating in the underlying social learning process. The main concepts/variables and their respective empirical indicators have been identified and measured, but they can be viewed as indicators of a general latent construct, for which additional indicators can be devised (Akers and La Greca, 1991; Akers and Lee, 1996).

Social learning accounts for the individual becoming prone to deviant or criminal behavior and for stability or change in that propensity. Therefore, the theory is capable of accounting for the development of stable individual differences, as well as changes in the individual's behavioral patterns or tendencies to commit deviant and criminal acts, over time and in different situations (see Chapters 6 and 12). The social learning process operates in each individual's learning history and in the immediate situation in which the opportunity for a crime occurs.

Deviant and criminal behavior is learned and modified (acquired, performed, repeated, maintained, and changed) through all of the same cognitive and behavioral mechanisms as conforming behavior. They differ in the direction, content, and outcome of the behavior learned. Therefore, it is inaccurate to state, for instance, that peer influence does not explain adolescent deviant behavior since conforming behavior is also peer influenced in adolescence. The theory expects peer influences to be implicated in both; it is the content and direction of the influence that is the key.

The primary learning mechanisms are *differential reinforcement* (instrumental conditioning), in which behavior is a function of the frequency, amount, and probability of experienced and perceived contingent rewards and punishments, and *imitation*, in which the behavior of others and its consequences are observed and modeled. The process of *stimulus discrimination/generalization* is another important mechanism; here, overt and covert stimuli, verbal and cognitive, act as cues or signals for behavior to occur. As I point out below, there are other behavioral mechanisms in the learning process, but these are not as important and are usually left implied rather than explicated in the theory.

The content of the learning achieved by these mechanisms includes the simple and complex *behavioral* sequences and the *definitions* (beliefs, attitudes, justifications, orientations) that in turn become discriminative for engaging in deviant and criminal behavior. The probability that conforming or norm-violative behavior is learned and performed, and the frequency with which it is committed, are a function of the past, present, and anticipated differential reinforcement for the behavior and the deviant or nondeviant direction of the learned definitions and other discriminative stimuli present in a given situation.

These learning mechanisms operate in a process of *differential association*—direct and indirect, verbal and nonverbal communication, interaction, and identification with others. The relative frequency, intensity, duration, and priority of associations affect the relative amount, frequency, and probability of reinforcement of conforming or deviant behavior and exposure of individuals to deviant or conforming norms and behavioral models. To the extent that the individual can control with whom she or he associates, the frequency, intensity, and duration of those associations are themselves affected by how rewarding or aversive they are. The principal learning is through differential association with those persons and groups (primary, secondary, reference, and symbolic) that comprise or control the individual's major sources of reinforcement, most salient behavioral models, and most effective definitions and other discriminative stimuli for committing and repeating behavior. The reinforcement and discriminative stimuli are mainly social (such as socially valued rewards and punishers contingent on the behavior), but they are also nonsocial (such as unconditioned physiological reactions to environmental stimuli and physical effects of ingested substances and the physical environment).

SEQUENCE AND RECIPROCAL EFFECTS IN THE SOCIAL LEARNING PROCESS

Behavioral feedback effects are built into the concept of differential reinforcement—actual or perceived changes in the environment produced by the behavior feed back on that behavior to affect its repetition or extinction, and both prior and anticipated rewards and punishments influence present behavior. Reciprocal effects between the individual's behavior and definitions or differential association are also reflected in the social learning process. This process is one in which the probability of both the initiation and the repetition of a deviant or criminal act (or the initiation and repetition of conforming acts) is a function of the learning history of the individual and the set of reinforcement contingencies and discriminative stimuli in a given situation. The typical process of initiation, continuation, progression, and desistance is hypothesized to be as follows:

1. The balance of past and current associations, definitions, and imitation of deviant models, and the anticipated balance of reinforcement in particular situations, produces or inhibits the initial delinquent or deviant acts.

2. The effects of these variables continue in the repetition of acts, although imitation becomes less important than it was in the first commission of the act.

3. After initiation, the actual social and nonsocial reinforcers and punishers affect the probability that the acts will be or will not be repeated and at what level of frequency.

4. Not only the overt behavior, but also the definitions favorable or unfavorable to it, are affected by the positive and negative consequences of the initial acts. To the extent that they are more rewarded than alternative behavior, the favorable definitions will be strengthened and the unfavorable definitions will be weakened, and it becomes more likely that the deviant behavior will be repeated under similar circumstances.

5. Progression into more frequent or sustained patterns, rather than cessation or reduction, of criminal and deviant behavior is promoted to the extent

that reinforcement, exposure to deviant models, and norm-violating definitions are not offset by negative formal and informal sanctions and norm-abiding definitions.

The theory does not hypothesize that definitions favorable to law violation always precede and are unaffected by the commission of criminal acts. Although the probability of a criminal act increases in the presence of favorable definitions, acts in violation of the law do occur (through imitation and reinforcement) in the absence of any thought given to whether the acts are right or wrong. Furthermore, the individual may apply neutralizing definitions retroactively to excuse or justify an act without having contemplated them beforehand. To the extent that such excuses become associated with successfully mitigating others' negative sanctions or one's self-punishment, however, they become cues for the repetition of deviant acts. Such definitions, therefore, precede committing the same acts again or committing similar acts in the future.

Differential association with conforming and nonconforming others typically precedes the individual's committing crimes and delinquent acts. This sequence of events is sometimes disputed in the literature because it is mistakenly believed to apply only to differential peer association in general or to participation in delinquent gangs in particular without reference to family and other group associations. It is true that the theory recognizes peer associations as very important in adolescent deviance and that differential association is most often measured in research by peer associations. But the theory also hypothesizes that the family is a very important primary group in the differential association process, and it plainly stipulates that other primary and secondary groups besides peers are involved (see Sutherland, 1947:164–65). Accordingly, it is a mistake to interpret differential association as referring only to peer associations. The theoretical stipulation that differential association is causally prior to the commission of delinquent and criminal acts is not confined to the balance of peer associations; rather, it is the balance (as determined by the modalities) of family, peer, and other associations. According to the priority principle, association, reinforcement, modeling, and exposure to conforming and deviant definitions occurring within the family during childhood, and such antisocial conduct as aggressiveness, lying, and cheating learned in early childhood, occur prior to and have both direct and selective effects on later delinquent and criminal behavior and associations. (See the discussion of the priority principle in the subsection Modalities of Association below and in Chapter 6.)

The socializing behavior of parents, guardians, or caretakers is certainly reciprocally influenced by the deviant and unacceptable behavior of the child. However, it can never be true that the onset of delinquency precedes and initiates interaction in a particular family (except in the unlikely case of the late-stage adoption of a child who is already delinquent or who is drawn to and chosen by deviant parents). Thus, interaction in the family or family surrogate always precedes delinquency.

But this is not true for adolescent peer associations. One may choose to associate with peers based on similarity in deviant behavior that already exists. Some major portion of this behavioral similarity results from previous association with other delinquent peers or from anticipatory socialization undertaken to make one's behavior match more closely that of the deviant associates to whom one is attracted. For some adolescents, gravitation toward delinquent peers occurs after and as a result of the individual's involvement in delinquent behavior. However, peer associations are most often formed initially around interests, friendships, and such circumstances as neighborhood proximity, family similarities, values, beliefs, age, school attended, grade in school, and mutually attractive behavioral patterns that have little to do directly with co-involvement or similarity in specifically law-violating or serious deviant behavior. Many of these factors in peer association are not under the adolescents' control, and some are simply happenstance. The theory does not, contrary to the Gluecks' distorted characterization, propose that "accidental differential association of non-delinquents with delinquents is the basic cause of crime" (Glueck and Glueck, 1950:164). Interaction and socialization in the family precedes and affects choices of both conforming and deviant peer associations.

Those peer associations will affect the nature of models, definitions, and rewards/punishers to which the person is exposed. After the associations have been established, their reinforcing or punishing consequences as well as direct and vicarious consequences of the deviant behavior will affect both the continuation of old and the seeking of new associations (those over which one has any choice). One may choose further interaction with others based on whether they too are involved in deviant or criminal behavior; in such cases, the outcomes of that interaction are more rewarding than aversive and it is anticipated that the associates will more likely approve or be permissive toward one's own deviant behavior. Further interaction with delinquent peers, over which the individual has no choice, may also result from being apprehended and confined by the juvenile or criminal-justice system.

These reciprocal effects would predict that one's own deviant or conforming behavioral patterns can have effects on choice of friends; these are weaker in the earlier years, but should become stronger as one moves through adolescence and gains more control over friendship choices. The typical sequence outlined above would predict that deviant associations precede the onset of delinquent behavior more frequently than the sequence of events in which the delinquent associations begin only after the peers involved have already separately and individually established similar patterns of delinquent behavior. Further, these behavioral tendencies that develop prior to peer association will themselves be the result of previous associations, models, and reinforcement, primarily in the family. Regardless of the sequence in which onset occurs, and whatever the level of the individual's delinquent involvement, its frequency and seriousness will increase after the deviant associations have begun and decrease as the associations are reduced. That is, whatever the temporal ordering, differential association with deviant peers will have a causal effect on one's own delinquent behavior (just as his actions will have an effect on his peers).

Therefore, both "selection," or "flocking" (tendency for persons to choose interaction with others with behavioral similarities), and "socialization," or "feathering" (tendency for persons who interact to have mutual influence on one another's behavior), are part of the same overall social learning process and are explained by the same variables. A peer "socialization" process and a peer "selection" process in deviant behavior are not mutually exclusive, but are simply the social learning process operating at different times. Arguments that social learning posits only the latter, that any evidence of selective mechanisms in deviant interaction run counter to social learning theory (Strictland, 1982; Stafford and Ekland-Olson, 1982), or that social learning theory recognizes only a recursive, one-way causal effect of peers on delinquent behavior (Thornberry et al., 1994; Catalano et al., 1996) are wrong.[2]

BEHAVIORAL AND COGNITIVE MECHANISMS
IN SOCIAL LEARNING

The first statement in Sutherland's theory was a simple declarative sentence maintaining that criminal behavior is learned, and the eighth statement declared that this involved all the mechanisms involved in any learning. What little Sutherland added in his (1947:7) commentary downplayed imitation as a possible learning mechanism in criminal behavior. He mentioned "seduction" of a person into criminal behavior as something that is not covered by the concept of imitation. He defined neither imitation nor seduction and offered no further discussion of mechanisms of learning in any of his papers or publications. Recall that filling this major lacuna in Sutherland's theory was the principal goal of the 1966b Burgess-Akers reformulation. To this end we combined Sutherland's first and eighth statements into one: "Criminal behavior is learned according to the principles of operant conditioning." The phrase "principles of operant conditioning" was meant as a shorthand reference to all of the behavioral mechanisms of learning in operant theory that had been empirically validated.[3]

Burgess and I delineated, as much as space allowed, what these specific learning mechanisms were: (1) operant conditioning, differential reinforcement of voluntary behavior through positive and negative reinforcement and punishment; (2) respondent (involuntary reflexes), or "classical," conditioning; (3) unconditioned (primary) and conditioned (secondary) reinforcers and punishers; (4) shaping and response differentiation; (5) stimulus discrimination and generalization, the environmental and internal stimuli that provide cues or signals indicating differences and similarities across situations that help elicit, but do not directly reinforce, behavior; (6) types of reinforcement schedules, the rate and ratio in which rewards and punishers follow behavior; (7) stimulus-response constellations; and (8) stimulus satiation and deprivation. We also reported research showing the applicability of these mechanisms of learning to both conforming and deviant behavior.

Burgess and I used the term "operant conditioning" to emphasize that differential reinforcement (the balance of reward and punishment contingent upon behavioral responses) is the basic mechanism around which the others revolve and by which learning most relevant to conformity or violation of social and legal norms is produced. This was reflected in other statements in the theory in which the only learning mechanisms listed were differential reinforcement and stimulus discrimination.

We also subsumed imitation, or modeling, under these principles and argued that imitation "may be analyzed quite parsimoniously with the principles of modern behavior theory," namely, that it is simply a subclass of behavioral shaping through operant conditioning (Burgess and Akers, 1966b:138). For this reason we made no specific mention of imitation in any of the seven statements. Later, I became persuaded that the operant principle of gradual shaping of responses through "successive approximations" only incompletely and awkwardly incorporated the processes of observational learning and vicarious reinforcement that Bandura and Walters (1963) had identified. Therefore, without dismissing successive approximation as a way in which some imitative behavior could be shaped, I came to accept Bandura's conceptualization of imitation. That is, imitation is a separate learning mechanism characterized by modeling one's own actions on the observed behavior of others and on the consequences of that behavior (vicarious reinforcement) prior to performing the behavior and experiencing its consequences directly. Whether the observed acts will be performed and repeated depends less on the continuing presence of models and more on the actual or anticipated rewarding or aversive consequences of the behavior. I became satisfied that the principle of "observational learning" could account for the acquisition, and to some extent the performance, of behavior by a process that did not depend on operant conditioning or "instrumental learning." Therefore, in later discussions of the theory, while continuing to posit differential reinforcement as the core behavior-shaping mechanism, I included imitation as another primary mechanism in acquiring behavior. Where appropriate, discriminative stimuli were also specifically invoked as affecting behavior, while I made only general reference to other learning mechanisms.

Note that the term "operant conditioning" in the opening sentence of the Burgess-Akers revision reflected our great reliance on the orthodox behaviorism that assumed the empirical irrelevance of cognitive variables. Social behaviorism, on the other hand, recognizes "cognitive" as well as "behavioral" mechanisms (see Bandura, 1969; 1977a; 1977b; 1986a; 1989; Grusec, 1992; Staats, 1975; Baldwin and Baldwin, 1981). My social learning theory of criminal behavior retains a strong element of the symbolic interactionism found in Sutherland's theory (Akers, 1985:39–70). As a result, it is closer to cognitive learning theories, such as Albert Bandura's, than to the radical operant behaviorism of B. F. Skinner with which Burgess and I began. It is for this reason, and the reliance on such concepts as imitation, anticipated reinforcement, and self-reinforcement, that I have described social learning theory as "soft behaviorism" (Akers, 1985:65).

The unmodified term "learning" implies to many that the theory only explains the acquisition of novel behavior by the individual, in contrast to behavior that is committed at a given time and place or the maintenance of behavior over time (Cornish and Clarke, 1986). It has also been interpreted to mean only "positive" learning of novel behavior, with no relevance for inhibition of behavior or of learning failures (Gottfredson and Hirschi, 1990). As I have made clear above, neither of these interpretations is accurate. The phrase that Burgess and I used, "effective and available reinforcers and the existing reinforcement contingencies," and the discussion of reinforcement occurring under given situations (Burgess and Akers, 1966b:141, 134) make it obvious that we were not proposing a theory only of past reinforcement in the acquisition of a behavioral repertoire with no regard for the reward/cost balance obtaining at a given time and place. There is nothing in the learning principles that restrict them to prior socialization or past history of learning. Social learning encompasses both the acquisition and the performance of the behavior, both facilitation and inhibition of behavior, and both learning successes and learning failures. The learning mechanisms account not only for the initiation of behavior but also for repetition, maintenance, and desistance of behavior. They rely not only on prior behavioral processes but also on those operating at a given time in a given situation.

> These social learning variables are all part of an underlying process that is operative in each individual's learning history and in the immediate situation in which the opportunity for a crime occurs. . . . Whether a deviant act will be committed in a situation that presents the opportunity depends on the learning history of the individual and the set of reinforcement contingencies in that situation. (Akers, 1994:99)

Key Concepts and Propositions of Social Learning Theory

I turn now to a more thorough explication of the four major elements in social learning theory: differential association, differential reinforcement, imitation, and definitions (see Akers et al., 1979; Akers, 1985; Akers and Cochran, 1985; Akers, 1992b). In addition, I also mention frequently the behavioral concept of discriminative stimuli. It refers to the whole cross-situational discrimination/generalization process involving the presence or absence of certain people, symbols, and physical settings. But I have invoked it in explaining criminal behavior mainly with regard to conceptualizing definitions not only as the crime-relevant cognitive content of learning but as verbal and covert discriminative stimuli. The theory takes the concepts of differential association and definitions from Sutherland's work but it conceptualizes them in more behavioral terms and combines them with differential reinforcement, imitation, discriminative stimuli, and other concepts from behavioral learning theory. For this reason, I continue to discuss the role of discriminative stimuli in the learning process mainly in connection with definitions. However, both internal and external physical stimuli are incorporated into the concept of discriminative stimuli.

DIFFERENTIAL ASSOCIATION

Sutherland's emphasis on "intimate personal groups" is well founded because they are the ones that are most significant to the individual, especially the primary groups of family and friends. But secondary and reference groups can also be significant. Early on shaping of conforming and deviant behavior occurs principally in the family. In adolescence, school, leisure, recreational, and other peer groups become more important; later in life, the significant influences come from spouses, friendship groups, work groups, and so on. Neighbors, churches, schoolteachers, physicians, the law and authority figures, and other individuals and groups in the community, as well as mass media and other more remote sources of attitudes and models, have varying degrees of effect on the individual's propensity to commit criminal and delinquent behavior. Sutherland characterized media effects as "relatively unimportant" (Sutherland, 1947:6). Even though the media's effects remain less important and less direct than those of primary groups, their impact on behavior today is greater than it was in the 1940s when Sutherland formulated his theory. (See the discussion of imitation below.)

Interaction, Normative Definitions, and Learning Mechanisms. Differential association has both behavioral/interactional and normative dimensions. The former is the direct association and interaction with others and their conforming or deviant behavior; the latter is the different patterns of norms and values to which an individual is exposed through association. Sutherland (1947) viewed the normative content of what was shared through associations as the key part of the process by which the individual acquires his or her own conforming or law-violating attitudes. He concentrated on association with criminal and noncriminal "patterns," regardless of their source, rather than on criminals and noncriminals as different types of people (see Cressey, 1960). Thus, he understated the causative role of the additional effects of social interaction with others. Nevertheless, Sutherland's statements about "all the mechanisms" of learning, communication of gestures (as well as language) in intimate groups, and modalities of "associations with criminal behavior" (Sutherland, 1947:6–7) leave room in the theory for effects of differential association with persons and behavior beyond those coming only from exposure to cultural definitions.

Of course, aside from some dismissive remarks about imitation, Sutherland did not mention any learning mechanisms; nowhere in his theory are social reactions and sanctions, reward/punishing processes, vicarious reinforcement, discriminative stimuli, and other learning mechanisms recognized. Therefore, Sutherland's differential association theory did not address directly the issue of what these behavioral effects are; social learning theory, however, does. It proposes that the significance of primary groups comes not only from their role in exposing the individual to culturally transmitted and individually espoused definitions but also from the presence of behavioral models to imitate and their control over what rewards and punishers will likely be available and attached to criminal or conforming behavior.

Warr and Stafford (1991) raise the question of whether the impact of peers on one's own behavior comes from "what they think or what they do." They rightly understand social learning theory as supplying the answer to this question—namely, that it is both. Their findings dispute Orcutt's (1987) criticism that the behavioral mechanisms in social learning theory add no explanatory power to the effects of definitions. Peer influence comes from what peers think (or say) is right or wrong and from what they do, not only in the sense of committing or not committing delinquent acts but also in the sense of modeling, reacting to, instructing, and supporting that behavior. The same can be predicted for the influence of family and other groups.

In social learning theory, then, both the normative and behavioral dimensions are explicitly encompassed within the concept of differential association. The groups with which one is in differential association provide the major social contexts in which all the mechanisms of social learning operate. Not only do they expose one to definitions, they present models to imitate and mediate differential reinforcement (source, schedule, value, and amount) for criminal or conforming behavior.

The Modalities of Association. Sutherland identified four "modalities," or dimensions, along which associations may vary—frequency, duration, priority, and intensity. For him, the meaning of "frequency" and "duration" of associations are "obvious and need no explanations" (1947:7). Frequency is how often one interacts with a group or individual, while duration has to do with time spent in interactions with others. But Sutherland failed to note that there are really two dimensions to the modality of duration. The first is in the sense of length of time—the more longstanding the relationship, the more it will influence the person's behavior. The second involves absolute and relative amounts of time spent in different associations—other things being equal, the more time (and the greater the proportion of one's time) that is spent in the company of others, the more influence they will have on one's behavior (see Warr, 1993a).

By "priority" Sutherland did not mean relative ranking in importance. (The saliency of associations is captured in his concept of intensity.) Rather, he defined priority of associations in terms of "prior" in time:

> "Priority" is assumed to be important in the sense that lawful behavior developed in early childhood may persist throughout life, and also that delinquent behavior developed in early childhood may persist throughout life. This tendency, however, has not been adequately demonstrated and priority seems to be important principally through its selective influence. (Sutherland, 1947:7)

These two sentences offer a parsimonious explanation for differences (formed early in life) in individual propensity to be lawful or unlawful to persist over time. When other learning variables, beyond exposure to definitions, in the socialization processes are added, social learning offers a fairly complete explanation both for stabilized differences across individuals and for changes in the behavior of the same individual.

Therefore, this priority principle is part of the social learning explanation for the connection between early delinquency and later deviant behavior. (See Chapter 6 and the section in Chapter 12 on age and delinquency.) Patterns of behavior discernible early in life are important not only because they indicate priority in association. The family (or its surrogate) is the chief early socializer; it is there that fundamental associations, models, and training through rewards and punishments are to be found. For those in families with adequate conventional socialization, this early pattern is likely to set the stage for future conformity. For children reared in incomplete or inadequate families, in families with deviant members, or without families, the odds of developing predelinquent behavior early and delinquent and criminal behavior later increase.

But while recognizing the phenomenon of the tendency for behavior to persist once formed, Sutherland argues that it is more likely that the "selective influence" of prior association produces the stability and link to future behavior. He does not define what he means by selective influence, but it is congruent with the observation that if one begins to misbehave at any early age this sets up patterns through which later experiences are filtered. Behaviorally, this would be the development of habit strength, and prior behavior and experience with reinforcement produce expectations of what will pay off in the future. The term also refers to the expectation that early associations have a selective impact on later ones. A child reared conventionally in a law-abiding family, taught proper behavior, and exposed to conventional norms and values is less likely to associate with unconventional peers and more likely to come into contact with conventional ones early on in life. This will affect associations with peers later on. Thus, not only does early familial interaction act as a "selective influence" on peer associations but early peer associations have a selective influence on later ones.

The process of "selecting" delinquent or anti-delinquent companions depends in part, then, on the person's recreational interests and abilities. Yet it would be absurd to explain a person's delinquency or non-delinquency in terms of referring to his pool-playing or baseball-playing ability.

Further, selection or rejection of delinquent or anti-delinquent companions is itself a function of previous associations with anti-delinquent and delinquent behavior patterns. An excellent baseball player with strong anti-delinquent identification and intimate association with anti-delinquent behavior patterns may give up baseball rather than play with delinquents. A boy without such strong counter-acting values may join the team and become delinquent. . . . In this sense, an individual's "selection" of a delinquent, non-delinquent, or anti-delinquent play group depends on his prior associations with delinquent and anti-delinquent behavior patterns, just as does his delinquency itself. (Sutherland and Cressey, 1960:168)

Sutherland found "intensity" to be the most difficult of the modalities to define (Cohen et al., 1956; Sutherland, 1973), declaring it to be "not precisely defined" but having to do with the "prestige of the source of a criminal or anti-criminal pattern and with emotional reactions related to the associations" (Sutherland, 1947:7). Intensity also has to do with the significance, saliency, or importance of the association to the individual. One indicator of this is the closeness of the relationship with one's associates. In peer groups, for instance, relationships with "best" or "closest" friends are associations of high intensity. Intensity might also be a matter of "attachment," affectional ties and identity with peers (Hirschi, 1969), or of commitment and loyalty to friends (Warr, 1993a).

The proposition, then, is that those associations which occur earlier (priority), last longer and occupy more time (duration), occur more often (frequency), and involve others with whom one has the more important relationships (intensity) will have the greater effect on criminal or law-abiding behavior. The more frequent, intense, and long-lasting one's differential association with primary or secondary groups exposing him or her to reinforcement for criminal behavior, to salient criminal models, and to definitions favorable to criminal behavior, the more likely criminal behavior becomes.

In commentary on our reformulation of differential association theory, Burgess and I proposed that the modalities of association were important "to the extent" that they affected the modalities of reinforcement (Burgess and Akers, 1966b:144), and I carried this idea forward to later statements of the theory. The modalities of association affect differential reinforcement of criminal or conforming behavior because the socially rewarding or punishing outcomes of behavior depend on the extent to which they are socially defined as good, desirable, necessary, important, or approved by one's associates. The chance that a given act will be defined as desirable and rewarded or undesirable and punished by others with whom one customarily interacts depends in part on their values and norms.

However, associations are important not only because they relate to reinforcement patterns but because they also modulate exposure to definitions, to behavioral models, and to other discriminative stimuli. Interaction with others, moreover, has other behavioral effects that go beyond and are not fully captured by reinforcement, modeling, and definitions. This is especially true if these processes are underspecified or weakly measured in empirical research so that their unmeasured effects spill over into and are captured by measures of differential association. For that reason, empirical measures of one's differential association with family, peers, and others can serve as a kind of summary or global index of all the other unmeasured behavioral processes. I think this is one reason why in so much of the research where differential association is the only social learning variable measured it still has a very strong effect on the dependent variable.

Selection and continuation of associations, in turn, are functions not only of prior associations but of differential reinforcement. Interactions with others is itself behavior that is shaped through the social exchange of rewards and costs. Associations over which one has a choice will be more frequent and probably acquire greater importance if they are more highly rewarded in frequency (number and rate), amount (value), and probability (ratio of responses to reward). The more important the association, the more rewarding it is; the more rewarding it is, the more important it becomes. The relative reinforcement value of associations (as distinct from the relative reinforcement value of the individual's conforming or deviant acts), then, is conceptually related to the associational modality of intensity.

Peer Influence, Not Peer Pressure. The process of differential peer association is at variance with the popular image of "peer pressure." It is common to find this notion invoked as an explanation of adolescent deviance; in this view, young people are under unrelenting and coercive pressure from their peers to try drugs, engage in sex, commit delinquent acts, and do other rebellious and deviant things. The actual peer association process, however, is more correctly called peer influence, rather than peer pressure.

This is more than a semantic distinction. "Pressure" conjures up images of overt challenge, of forceful peers exhorting the naïve and fearful good kid and threatening him with ridicule or ostracism to compel him into deviance. Although teenagers do on occasion face this kind of pressure, and although social learning theory recognizes that such influence in this narrow sense does play some role in delinquency, it is seen as only a marginal factor. It is true that peers strongly affect one another's behavior, but the process is neither ubiquitous nor irresistible. The great majority of cases involve pressure only in a subtle, atmospheric sense. Its significance is often not recognized by the youngsters themselves, and whenever pressure is recognized it is usually not perceived as something that cannot be resisted. Furthermore, the influence is interactive—it is not simply a matter of good kids made to go bad by friends. They enter the interaction of peer groups with predispositions, past learning, family socialization, and other influences working together with peer influence. Moreover, the same youngster both influences and is influenced by his or her associates; even though some are more leaders than followers, who is leading whom may vary by situation. Nor does peer influence merely reinforce deviant behavior—for most teenagers, peers are more likely to endorse conforming definitions and to reinforce conforming behavior.

This influence is real, strong, and effective. But it does not fit the popular image of peer pressure. The image of the typical adolescent caught up in a youth culture and pressure by friends to violate adult norms simply does not apply to most teenagers. Therefore, while research showing that delinquency is not strongly related to "peer pressure" in this narrow sense undermines the popular image, it cannot be interpreted as contradicting social learning theory. Social learning pictures a more subtle and complex behavioral process that more accurately captures the real situation faced by teenagers.

DIFFERENTIAL REINFORCEMENT

Whether individuals will refrain from or initiate, continue committing, or desist from criminal and deviant acts depends on the relative frequency, amount, and probability of past, present, and anticipated rewards and punishments perceived to be attached to the behavior. Differential reinforcement refers to the balance of anticipated or actual rewards and punishments that follow or are consequences of behavior. The concept operates when two or more similar acts are differently rewarded, but the effects are more apparent when the alternatives are incompatible, with one being highly rewarded while the other is unrewarded or punished. This either-or, incompatible-choice instance of differential reinforcement is relevant for the explanation of criminal behavior because it applies to any given episode, event, or situation in which there is the opportunity either to violate the law or to refrain from doing so. However, the issue becomes more complex when one attempts to ascertain which of several behavioral options will be chosen at a particular time, as well as which of various conforming and deviant options will be taken up, committed with what frequency over time, and committed under different circumstances.

The process of behavioral changes from differential reinforcement is operant, or instrumental, conditioning. Operant behavior involves voluntary actions mediated by the central nervous system; respondent behavior, by contrast, is mediated by the autonomic nervous system. Respondents are reflexes that are unaffected by the outcome or change they produce in the individual's environment. Furthermore, operants are shaped by environmental consequences, while respondent behavior is reflex reaction elicited by a stimulus (although this distinction breaks down when autonomic processes like blood pressure respond to voluntary effort and are affected through biofeedback). In addition, the same stimulus can have the dual function of eliciting a reflex while reinforcing an operant (Staats, 1975:37–38).

Respondents occur automatically in reaction to certain unconditioned external and internal stimuli—heat, food, light, sound, and so on. Through Pavlovian, or "classical," conditioning, which involves associating the unconditioned stimulus with another stimulus, the same respondent can be conditioned to make a response to a new stimulus that would not naturally elicit it. Thus, at the sound of a bell the hand can be made to jerk back as it would from a hot stove, and the mouth can be made to water as it would by the sight of food. The stimuli, however, are not contingent on and do not function as consequences of the response; it is still autonomic, elicited by a prior stimulus. The form and rate of operant behavior, on the other hand, are a function of its consequences.

While any behavior may be a complex combination or chain of operants and respondents, criminal and deviant behavior is better understood as predominantly involving instrumental learning. Social learning theory recognizes, but only incidentally invokes, respondent conditioning to explain crime, although such processes are relevant in certain forms of deviance (e.g., sexual deviance). The theory invokes, rather, differential reinforcement as the most relevant behavioral mechanism.

Positive and Negative Reinforcement and Punishment. The probability that an act will be committed or repeated is increased directly by rewarding outcomes or reactions to it, for example, obtaining approval, status, money, awards, food, or pleasant feelings. This is the process of positive reinforcement. The likelihood that an action will be taken is also enhanced when the act allows the person to avoid or escape aversive or unpleasant events; this is negative reinforcement. Behavior is inhibited, reduced, or extinguished by punishment that may be direct (positive), in which painful or unpleasant consequences are attached to or result from a behavior, or indirect (negative), in which the consequence of the behavior is the removal of a reward or privilege. The terms "positive" and "negative" here are not evaluative, but simply mean that the behavior is followed, respectively, by the addition or removal of one or more stimuli (see Akers, 1985:45).

Schedules and the Modalities of Differential Reinforcement. Reinforcement and punishment vary in amount, frequency, and probability. The greater the value or amount (measurable quantities of social approval, money, prestige, food, etc.) of rewards for the person's behavior, the more frequently it is rewarded (holding constant the person's state of deprivation or satiation for the rewards), and the higher the probability that it will be rewarded (as balanced against alternative behavior), the greater the likelihood that it will occur and be repeated.

Frequency and probability of reinforcement are based on schedules of reinforcement. On a continuous schedule, each time a response is made it is followed quickly by one or more reinforcing (or punishing) stimuli. Intermittent schedules depart in some way from this continuous pattern. An interval schedule is one in which the intermittent pattern results from a lapse or interval of time (either fixed or variable) between the act and its reinforcement; the briefer the time interval, the higher the frequency of reward. The other type of intermittent schedule of reinforcement is the ratio schedule, in which there is variation in the number of times one must repeat an act before it is rewarded. Continuous schedules of reinforcement are rare in society; nearly all patterning of social reinforcement represents some variation on intermittent schedules. The diverse and uncertain intervals between, and ratios of, performance and social reward (or punishment) lie behind much of the variety, complexity, and stability of social behavior.

The Matching Function: Correlation-Based Effects of Reinforcement. Typically, social behavior is seldom a series of isolated acts proximally followed by contingent rewards or punishers. It is, rather, characterized by many different acts and by subtle variations of the same behavior, responding to simultaneous and complex schedules. The frequency of each of several different behaviors (e.g., committing or refraining from crime, or selecting from the variety of possible conforming or criminal acts) matches the frequency and value of reinforcement attached to each behavior. This process operates according to a "matching function" (rather than a simpler "step function"), in which the behavior most frequently, probably, and highly reinforced is chosen and performed to the exclusion of all other alternatives (Hamblin, 1979; Conger and Simons, 1995).

The "matching law," "quantitative law of effect," or "correlation-based law of effect" was first formulated by Herrnstein (1961; 1970). It has been described as

> considerably more descriptive of natural human environments than Skinner's earlier view of reinforcement. It is not always easy to isolate Skinnerian response-reinforcement units in the natural environment. Herrnstein's equation makes efforts to do so unnecessary. . . . (McDowell, 1982:778)

Briefly, the principle is that behavior responds not just to behavior-reward proximity at a given time and place but to the quantitative correlation between the two (Davey, 1988).

> This principle states that relative behavior (or time) matches relative rate of reinforcement delivered on two or more concurrent alternatives. The person distributes behavior in accord with the relative, rather than absolute, payoffs received over a period of time. (Epling and Pierce, 1988:48)

Therefore, a given behavior must be seen in the context of all other con-
currently available schedules and sources of reinforcement. The concept
of reinforcement does not require that behavior be shaped and maintained by rewards and punishers in a direct cause-effect way. Rather,
"only regular covariation, planned or adventitious, over time is necessary
to produce behavior change" (Epling and Pierce, 1988:48).

Social and Nonsocial Reinforcement. Sutherland referred only to learning in communication (both verbal and gestural) with others. Burgess and
I reviewed research showing that the presence and behavior of other
people were both reinforcing and discriminative for particular behavior,
but also that an individual can learn behavior purely through internal
physiological feedback or nonsocial feedback from the physical environment. We agreed with Sutherland that social contingencies are most important in human behavior, but we moved away from his exclusive concern with learning through communication in face-to-face groups.

In so doing, however, Burgess and I made a mistake in how we defined
nonsocial contingencies. We asserted that criminal behavior is learned
"both in nonsocial situations that are reinforcing or discriminating and
through that social interaction in which the behavior of other persons is
reinforcing or discriminating for such behavior." The latter part of this
statement adopted the Skinnerian notion of social behavior as only behavior for which direct reinforcement is mediated by another person. We
described nonsocial learning as any learning that takes place "without
any direct contact with another person" (Burgess and Akers, 1966b:138).
This was an error because it narrowly confines "social" reinforcement to
only those instances in which other people are present and play an active
role at the time the individual learns something. This restricts social
reinforcement of criminal acts only to those instances in which other
persons are physically present at the time and directly reward or punish
the behavior with words or gestures of approval or disapproval. In addition, we repeated Jeffery's (1965) error of defining as "material," rather
than "social," the reinforcement of criminal behavior that comes from
acquiring money or material goods by breaking the law in those situations where others are not present to reinforce the behavior directly
through social approval.

This is obviously a too restrictive, and I believe mistaken, conception of social reinforcement. It makes little sense to think of money, for instance, as a nonsocial reward (it is a secondary reinforcer conditioned by its association with approval, power, status, and other socially valued stimuli), and most of a person's learning, even when he or she is alone, is still quite "social" because of prior learning. Certainly, individuals can learn by trial and error or "pick it up on their own" or "figure it out on their own" without direct tutelage or prior experience with other people. Some of this process could be described as "nonsocial"—individuals can learn without contact, directly or indirectly, with social reinforcers and punishers.

Nevertheless, even the behavior of someone who is alone is predicated on or mediated by the implied or symbolic presence of others, since such actions may well stem from past observation of behavioral models. Learning something new on one's own is very often based on skills, insights, and behavior previously learned from others. Self-reinforcement usually involves application of social reward, that others might deliver if present, by the person to his or her own behavior.

In other words, "social" includes much more than what Burgess and I implied. I partially corrected the error in the first edition, and fully corrected it in the second and third editions, of *Deviant Behavior*. I continue to define social reinforcement as "involving not just the direct reactions of others present while an act is performed, but also the whole range of tangible and intangible rewards valued in society and its subgroups" (Akers, 1977:55). Nonsocial reinforcement in social learning theory, then, is more narrowly defined.

Nonsocial reinforcement includes experiencing unconditioned positive and negative effects of physiological and physical stimuli—for example, from the direct neurological effects of drugs and alcohol. But even in this case, whether or not these effects are experienced positively or negatively is partially contingent upon previously learned expectations. Through social consequences, one learns to interpret the effects as pleasurable and enjoyable or as frightening and unpleasant. For this reason, it is difficult without specific, laboratory-controlled measures to separate the purely unconditioned nonsocial from the socially conditioned effects of substances. Nonsocial reinforcement also includes those instances in which committing or anticipating some deviant action invokes an internal physiological or emotional arousal (e.g., sexual) that is intrinsically rewarding to the individual. Some criminal and deviant acts, for instance, may elicit internal sensations of excitement or thrill without any prior social conditioning of those reactions. Wood and his associates (1995) provide evidence that some kinds of deviant behavior may be intrinsically rewarding because "voluntary risk-taking and thrillseeking behavior provide sensory or physiological stimulation which is highly rewarding to the individual" (Wood et al., 1995:174). To the extent that some individuals are physiologically predisposed to experience greater sensation-seeking rewards from deviant acts, this can be seen as nonsocial reinforcement. Again, even in these instances, experiencing or interpreting these sensations as pleasurable may be based as much on past social conditioning as on strictly physiological reactions.

Social rewards can be highly symbolic. Their reinforcing effects come from their fulfilling ideological, religious, political, or other goals. Even those rewards that we consider to be very tangible, such as money and material possessions, gain their reinforcing worth from the symbolic prestige and approval value they have in society. Social reinforcement is also typically involved in the response hierarchies stated in the Premack (1965) principle—behavior that the person engages in most frequently can be used itself to reinforce less probable behavior.

Even though learning does occur in connection with nonsocial rewards and punishments, it is the power and centrality of the direct, indirect, and symbolic social rewards in society that sustain labeling the theory "social learning." The theory proposes that the groups and individuals who comprise or control the major sources of social reinforcement for the individual will have the greatest influence on his or her behavior. Usually these are primary groups with which one is in differential association, but as I have stressed before they are also secondary or more distant reference groups. They might include imaginary or real groups, persons, and situations portrayed through the various media, as well as more formal bureaucratic organizations such as those encountered on the job or in school or agencies of social control, law enforcement, and criminal justice.

Social Control, Self-Control, Self-Reinforcement, and Self-Efficacy. The social control system provides differential social rewards and punishers for conforming behavior by invoking formal and informal social sanctions as external controls and socializes individuals to become conforming societal members. Socialization is social learning in which individuals learn from parents, peers, and others, and take on as their own concepts of the right and wrong things to say and do in given contexts. They assume these views by being subjected in the socialization process to external social sanctions (rewards and punishers) in conjunction with behavioral examples, verbalizations, and instructions. It is through the process of sanctioning and modeling that people learn, as they mature, the cultural expectations (rights and obligations) that go along with their age, sex, marital, occupational, and other social roles.

As individuals become more socialized, they develop self-control. They conform to expectations by controlling their own behavior without directly or consistently applied social sanctions. Socialization is never perfect or complete, and there is variation in the extent to which individuals learn self-control. Although there may be some inherent temperamental inclination toward self-control, this quality is largely social in the sense that it is based on prior socialization. The individual exercises self-control through self-reinforcement by reinforcing or punishing his or her own behavior (usually in a covert and subtle fashion), often taking the role of others, even when alone. Or, when others are present, the person regulates his or her own behavior as if the others will apply social sanctions, even though they have not and will not.

Every social system relies to a great degree on socialization to develop self-control among the population. But no society relies entirely on childhood socialization; social control continues to be exercised through the application of external social sanctions, and the law itself can have a socializing effect. Therefore, when self-control fails and the person violates the rules, even after undergoing the relevant socialization, there is some chance that he or she will face external sanctions. Applying sanctions, at least intermittently, remains the prime mechanism in social control. Rewarding proper and punishing improper behavior does not only correct people's conduct at a given time and place; it also acquaints them with what is expected and helps them to learn to direct their own behavior. Bandura (1977a; 1977b; 1986b) and other social learning theorists conceptualize self-control as a "self-regulative" mechanism.

> The source of self-regulative functions lies in modeling and in direct tuition. Adults respond differentially to children's behaviors, and this differential re-

sponsivity is one kind of information children take into account when formulating personal standards or ideas about which behaviors are worthy of self-blame or self-praise. . . . In addition to imitating the evaluative behavior of others, children are also reinforced by agents of socialization for engaging in self-regulation. *In the end, self-regulation depends, then, on external forces.* (Grusec, 1992; emphasis added)

Self-control, then, is a product of the social learning process that may become stabilized across a variety of situations. Although learning occurs throughout life, basic socialization (varying in degree of success from close to zero to close to complete) into the values and norms of conventional society takes places mainly in the early years of life and is mostly over by some point in the adolescent or pre-adolescent years. Therefore, there is also some stability of self-regulative mechanisms over time.

Since the mid-1970s the notion of self-regulative processes in behavioral control has become increasingly central to Bandura's social-cognitive learning theory. He has proposed the perceived level of self-efficacy as the central mechanism accounting for the effectiveness of different treatment procedures in modifying behavior (Bandura, 1977b; 1986a; 1986b; 1989). Self-efficacy is itself the outcome of direct and vicarious reinforcement, modeling, verbal persuasion, and arousal states. Self-efficacy expectations are not the same as anticipated reinforcement or expectations of the outcome of particular behavior. The concept refers to self-appraisal of the ability to master a task, achieve a goal, or deal with a problem:

> An outcome expectancy is defined as a person's estimate that a given behavior will lead to certain outcomes. An efficacy expectation is the conviction that one can successfully execute the behavior required to produce the outcome. . . . [I]ndividuals can believe that a particular course of action will produce certain outcomes, but if they entertain serious doubts about whether they can perform the necessary activities such information does not influence their behavior. (Bandura, 1977b)

Self-efficacy is also distinguished from Rotter's (1954) earlier concept of "locus of control"—the general expectation that one has power over what happens in life (internal locus of control) or the belief that one's behavior and its consequences are determined by forces beyond one's power (external locus of control). A person may have a high internal locus of control but still score low on self-efficacy in the belief that he or she does not have the ability or skills to be effective in a given behavior. Self-efficacy, therefore, is not a general personality trait but one that varies by behavior and circumstances. Since self-efficacy is directed toward accounting for the initiation and persistence of "coping" behavior, its application to the explanation of law and norm violation is not clear and would appear to be restricted only to that part of deviant and criminal behavior in which self-assessment of coping ability is a factor.[4] But as part of the general process of self-regulation it demonstrates one of the ways in which social learning theory incorporates the process and content of self-control.

IMITATION

Committing behavior modeled on, and following the observation of, similar behavior in others is called imitation. Whether the behavior modeled by others will be imitated is affected by the characteristics of the models, the behavior observed, and the observed consequences (vicarious reinforcement) of the behavior, as well as by other variables (Bandura, 1977a; 1986a):

> Observers tend to imitate modeled behavior if they like or respect the model, see the model receive reinforcement, see the model give off signs of pleasure, or are in an environment where imitating the model's performance is reinforced. . . . [I]nverse imitation is common when an observer does not like the model, sees the model get punished, or is in an environment where conformity is being punished. (Baldwin and Baldwin, 1981:187)

Modeling is more important in the initial acquisition and performance of novel behavior than in the maintenance or cessation of behavioral patterns once established, but it continues to have some facilitative effect in maintaining or changing behavior.

Orthodox operant theory viewed imitation as itself a learned behavior shaped by direct reinforcement or the chaining together at a given time of a series of acts present in the imitator's behavioral repertoire that had been gradually shaped up through previous differential reinforcement. As noted above, social learning theory recognizes this mechanism but views it as inadequate by itself to account for modeling effects (Bandura, 1969:118–203; Staats, 1975:161–200; Baldwin and Baldwin, 1981:186–206; Bandura, 1986a:75–80). "Prior reward increases performance of modeled behavior, but tests of acquisition reveal equivalent observational learning regardless of whether or not imitativeness has been previously rewarded" (Bandura, 1986a:78).

Since all the modalities of associations are likely to be present to a greater degree in primary groups, Sutherland's hypothesis of a greater effect from direct interaction than from media is on solid theoretical ground. Yet, technological and social changes have meant that the mass media have a greater impact on individuals and society than they did in his time. The priority, duration, frequency, and perhaps intensity of exposure to patterns presented in the media for an increasing proportion of the population have become so strong that they can overwhelm counteracting but less frequent, intense, and lasting primary group relations. For some individuals the most salient models and definitions are to be found in television, movies, and video games. Behaviorally, the main media effects are modeling, vicarious reinforcement, and moral desensitization for criminal behavior. Imitation effects are weaker than reinforcement effects even in face-to-face interaction, and therefore the theoretical expectation is that media effects in general will be weaker than direct group effects. However, the effects may still be persistent, and, combined with desensitizing conditioning with regard to such behavior as violence and sexual deviance, they may counteract conventional negative definitions and provide additional neutralizing and positive definitions of the behavior.

The media, therefore, can be conceptualized as providing additional reference groups and sources of exposure to criminal and noncriminal patterns and behavioral models. Their effect will be a function of the relative frequency, intensity, duration, and priority of association with media depictions; the relative frequency, amount, and probability of reinforcement; and the saliency, importance, or prestige of models and vicarious reinforcement. Media impact will vary by type of behavior, the relevancy of the exposure for that behavior, and the extent to which it is a "group" or "solitary" behavior. Donnerstein and Linz (1986; 1995) report television viewing of violence has a desensitizing effect and is related to aggression in children and teenagers. Whether persons will commit aggressive acts following media exposure depends on efficacy (rewarded or punished), normative justification, the similarity to real life of the media depiction, and the prior susceptibility of the viewer.

The most salient models for behavior are persons with whom one is in direct contact in primary groups, but models are also found in pictorial, verbal, and visual depictions in the media.

> Modeling refers to the observed behavior of others whether presented through direct demonstrations or through films, television, or stories which are heard or read. When modeling cues are presented by direct exposure to other persons, the phenomenon has typically been referred to as *live modeling*, while the behavior of others as observed in movies, television, and other representative media is usually considered to fall in the general category of *symbolic modeling*. (Liebert, 1972:3; emphasis in original)

> Models can be real (bodily present) or symbolic (presented via books, movies, TV, or verbal descriptions). (Baldwin and Baldwin, 1981:187)

> The basic conception-matching process [in imitation] is the same, regardless of whether the conception of the behavior has been constructed from words, pictures, or actions. (Bandura, 1986a:71)

Research has shown growing exposure to deviance and violence on television and its probable effects, particularly on children (Comstock and Rubinstein, 1972; Murray et al., 1972; Pearl et al., 1982; Donnerstein and Linz, 1995). Imitative effects have been found in exposure to rape, homicide, and other mass-media violence (Boeringer et al., 1991; Phillips, 1982; 1983; Baron and Reiss, 1985; Phillips and Hensley, 1984); such effects on pro-social behavior have been found as well (Rushton, 1980; 1982).

DEFINITIONS AND DISCRIMINATIVE STIMULI

The Concept of Definitions. Sutherland asserted that learning criminal behavior includes "techniques of committing the crime which are sometimes very complicated, sometimes very simple" and the "specific direction of motives, drives, rationalizations, and attitudes" (1947:6). I have retained both definitions and techniques in social learning theory, with clarified and modified conceptual meanings and with hypothesized relationships to criminal behavior. The qualification that "techniques" may be simple or complex shows plainly that Sutherland did not mean to include only crime-specific skills learned in order to break the law successfully. Techniques also clearly include ordinary, everyday abilities. This same notion is retained in social learning theory.

By definition, a person must be capable of performing the necessary sequence of actions before he or she can carry out either criminal or conforming behavior—inability to perform the behavior precludes committing the crime. Since many of the behavioral techniques for both conforming and criminal acts are the same, not only the simple but even some of the complex skills involved in carrying out crime are not novel to most or many of us. The required component parts of the complete skill are acquired in essentially conforming or neutral contexts to which we have been exposed—driving a car, shooting a gun, fighting with fists, signing checks, using a computer, and so on. In most white-collar crime, the same skills needed to carry out a job legitimately are put to illegitimate use. Other skills are specific to given deviant acts—safe cracking, counterfeiting, pocket picking, jimmying doors and picking locks, bringing off a con game, and so on. Without tutelage in these crime-specific techniques, most people would not be able to perform them, or at least would be initially very inept.

Sutherland took the concept of "definitions" in his theory from W. I. Thomas's "definition of the situation" (Thomas and Thomas, 1928) and generalized it to orienting attitudes toward different behavior. It is true that "Sutherland did not identify what constitutes a definition 'favorable to' or 'unfavorable to' the violation of law" (Cressey, 1960:53). Nevertheless, as I pointed out in Chapter 2, there is little doubt that "rationalizations" and "attitudes" are subsumed under the general concept of definitions—normative attitudes or evaluative meanings attached to given behavior. Exposure to others' shared definitions is a key (but not the only) part of the process by which the individual acquires or internalizes his or her own definitions. They are orientations, rationalizations, definitions of the situation, and other attitudes that label the commission of an act as right or wrong, good or bad, desirable or undesirable, justified or unjustified.

In social learning theory, these definitions are both general and specific. General beliefs include religious, moral, and other conventional values and norms that are favorable to conforming behavior and unfavorable to committing any of a range of deviant or criminal acts. Specific definitions orient the person to particular acts or series of acts. Thus, there are people who believe that it is morally wrong to steal and that laws against theft should be obeyed, but at the same time see little wrong with smoking marijuana and rationalize that it is all right to violate laws against drug possession. The greater the extent to which one holds attitudes that disapprove of certain acts, the less likely one is to engage in them. Conventional beliefs are negative toward criminal behavior. The more strongly one has learned and personally believes in the ideals of honesty, integrity, civility, kindness, and other general standards of morality that condemn lying, cheating, stealing, and harming others, the less likely he or she is to commit acts that violate social and legal norms. Conversely, the more one's own attitudes approve of, or fail to condemn, a behavior, the greater the chances are that he or she will engage in it. For obvious reasons, the theory would predict that definitions in the form of general beliefs will have less effect than specific definitions on the commission of specific criminal acts.

Definitions that favor criminal or deviant behavior are basically positive or neutralizing. Positive definitions are beliefs or attitudes that make the behavior morally desirable or wholly permissible. They are most likely to be learned through positive reinforcement in a deviant group or subculture that carries values conflicting with those of conventional society. Some of these positive verbalizations may be part of a full-blown ideology of politically dissident, criminal, or deviant groups. Although such ideologies and groups can be identified, the theory does not rest only on this type of definition favorable to deviance; indeed, it proposes that such positive definitions occur less frequently than neutralizing ones.

Neutralizing definitions favor violating the law or other norms not because they take the acts to be positively desirable but because they justify or excuse them. Even those who commit deviant acts are aware that others condemn the behavior and may themselves define the behavior as bad. The neutralizing definitions view the act as something that is probably undesirable but, given the situation, is nonetheless justified, excusable, necessary, all right, or not really bad after all. The process of acquiring neutralizing definitions is more likely to involve negative reinforcement; that is, they are verbalizations that accompany escape or avoidance of negative consequences like disapproval by one's self or by society.

While these definitions may become part of a deviant or criminal subculture, acquiring them does not require participation in such subcultures. They are learned from carriers of conventional culture, including many of those in social control and treatment agencies. The notions of techniques of neutralization and subterranean values (Sykes and Matza, 1957; Matza and Sykes, 1961; Matza, 1964) come from the observation that for nearly every social norm there is a norm of evasion. That is, there are recognized exceptions or ways of getting around the moral imperatives in the norms and the reproach expected for violating them. Thus, the general prohibition "Thou shalt not kill" is accompanied by such implicit or explicit exceptions as "unless in time of war," "unless the victim is the enemy," "unless in self-defense," "unless in the line of duty," "unless to protect others." The moral injunctions against physical violence are suspended if the victim can be defined as the initial aggressor or is guilty of some transgression and therefore deserves to be attacked.

The concept of neutralizing definitions in social learning theory incorporates not only notions of verbalizations and rationalizations (Cressey, 1953) and techniques of neutralization (Sykes and Matza, 1957) but also conceptually similar if not equivalent notions of "accounts" (Lyman and Scott, 1970), "disclaimers" (Hewitt and Stokes, 1975), and "moral disengagement" (Bandura, 1976; 1990). Neutralizing attitudes include such beliefs as "Everybody has a racket"; "I can't help myself, I was born this way"; "It's not my fault"; "I am not responsible"; "I was drunk and didn't know what I was doing"; "I just blew my top"; "They can afford it"; "He deserved it." Some neutralizations (e.g., nonresponsibility) can be generalized to a wide range of disapproved and criminal behavior. These and other excuses and justifications for committing deviant acts and victimizing others are definitions favorable to criminal and deviant behavior.

Exposure to these rationalizations and excuses may be through afterthe-fact justifications for one's own or others' norm violations that help to deflect or lessen punishment that would be expected to follow. The individual then learns the excuses either directly or through imitation and uses them to lessen self-reproach and social disapproval. Therefore, the definitions are themselves behavior that can be imitated and reinforced and then in turn serve as discriminative stimuli accompanying reinforcement of overt behavior. Deviant and criminal acts do occur without being accompanied by positive or neutralizing definitions, but the acts are more likely to occur and recur in situations the same as or similar to those in which the definitions have already been learned and applied. The extent to which one adheres to or rejects the definitions favorable to crime is itself affected by the rewarding or punishing consequences that follow the act.

Definitions and Motivation for Criminal Behavior. Sutherland's inclusion of the terms "rationalizations" and "attitudes" in his fourth statement is straightforward. On the other hand, some confusion is introduced by his also listing in the same clause the "direction" of "motives" and "drives" without specifying what he meant by these terms. "Motives" ordinarily refers to anything that moves or induces a person to do something; "drives" is often used to denote strong pushes to satisfy emotional or innate needs. They are more apt to label independent rather than dependent variables. Apparently Sutherland wanted to stress that motives and drives for crimes (even those frequently ascribed to psychological or physiological origins), as well as the criminal acts themselves, are learned. But did he view motives and drives as alternative names for, or something very different from, rationalizations and attitudes? Why did he list them serially in the same clause? Are motives and drives also subsumed under the concept of definitions? Are all the terms equivalent alternatives for the same thing, or are they separate and distinguishable factors in criminal behavior?

Sutherland offered no comment at all on his fourth statement, and we do not know what he intended by placing these terms in the same sentence. But in his fifth statement Sutherland proposed that the "specific direction of motives and drives is learned *from* definitions" (1947:6; emphasis added). Here he seems to view motives and drives not as independent variables but as separate dependent variables "caused" by definitions, or perhaps as intervening variables between learned definitions and criminal behavior. Yet, how can definitions of behavior as right or wrong by themselves motivate one to engage in the behavior, or how can they constitute drives that produce behavior? Sutherland does not tell us. Especially when the balance or ratio of pro-criminal and anti-criminal attitudes approaches unity (Orcutt, 1987), but also at all points on the balance scale, it is not clear how one's attitudes toward crime, by themselves, could provide the impetus or motivation to break the law.

In addition to the uncertainties surrounding the precise meaning of the terms, some part of this ambiguity is based on Sutherland's insertion of the preposition "from" in the fifth statement. It could be that he meant that one's own definitions are learned (but not necessarily or even typically in a perfect or complete form) "from" exposure to others' definitions in the socialization process; once learned, these definitions motivate the person to commit or refrain from law violations. The concept of definitions refers not only to definitions shared by others (norms) to which one is exposed but also to which of them the individual learns and takes on as his or her own. In this sense of internalized definitions, then, it is not so much that motives and drives are learned "from" definitions as it is that the definitions are the cognitive *content* of what is learned (in addition to the overt behavioral content of the learning) as found in Sutherland's fourth statement. These definitions are attitudinal sets that are brought to a situation that make lawbreaking seem appropriate or inappropriate in that situation. But does this cognitive set, which provides a readiness or a willingness to commit crime, itself provide the motivation to undertake the acts? Is having a negative attitude toward a particular crime all that is needed to deter it?

Sutherland did not provide good answers to these questions. He left unspecified how learned definitions provide motivation for criminal behavior, and, as I have pointed out a number of times, he did not delineate other mechanisms that could motivate behavior. One can extrapolate from the concept of definitions that strongly held beliefs may "motivate" crime in the sense that they direct one to what "ought" to be done or not to be done in certain situations. Indeed, some of the definitions favorable to deviance are so intensely held that they almost seem to "require" the one faithfully holding them to violate the law. For instance, the ideologies of some revolutionary groups positively prescribe terrorist acts, just as the fervent moral stance of some anti-abortion groups justifies in their minds the need to engage in civil disobedience, property damage, or violence. But the process envisioned in the theory would place these cases toward the end of a continuum in which the very definitions or beliefs one holds play a decisive role in criminal motivation. For the most part, definitions favorable to crime and delinquency do not require or compel action in this sense. Rather, they are conventional beliefs so weakly held that they provide little or no unfavorable orientation to crime, or else they are positive or neutralizing attitudes that facilitate lawbreaking in the right set of circumstances. Social learning theory proposes that there are variations in the extent to which persons hold to both deviant and pro-social definitions, values, and beliefs. These differences in what is believed and how strongly it is believed can develop within the same normative system; they do not require the existence of or participation in an organized deviant subculture that is in conflict with the larger normative system of society.

Definitions favorable to deviance include weakly held general beliefs and more strongly held deviant justifications and definitions of the situation; those unfavorable to deviance include more strongly held conventional beliefs and deviant definitions that are weakly subscribed to. Both the concept of beliefs in social bonding theory (Hirschi, 1969) and of definitions in social learning theory refer to the moral content of evaluative cognitions, with social learning theory also referring to discriminative stimulus behavioral effects.

Think of two parallel continua running in opposite directions:

1. General and Specific *Conforming* Beliefs/Definitions

|——————————————————————————————|

| Strongly held | Absent or weakly held |
| Unfavorable to Deviance | Favorable to Deviance |

2. General and Specific *Non-Conforming* Beliefs/Definitions

|——————————————————————————————|

| Strongly held | Absent or weakly held |
| Favorable to Deviance | Unfavorable to Deviance |

Individual beliefs and definitions can lie at any point on either continuum. Any location or movement away from the left side of the first continuum and the right side of the second continuum increases the odds that one will commit deviant acts, given opportunities or situations that fit the definitions and the anticipation of reward. Those persons whose beliefs lie at the far left of the second continuum may feel compelled toward deviant behavior, but this will not be true for those whose beliefs lie at other points on either continuum. Both strongly held conventional beliefs and strongly held deviant beliefs can be weakened or fail to develop. This happens through differential association, in which one learns conflicting definitions, and through changes in reinforcement patterns for the beliefs.

Social learning theory proposes that the definitions themselves are learned through reinforcement contingencies operating in the socialization process and function less as direct motivators than as facilitative or inhibitory "discriminative stimuli," cues signaling that certain behavior is appropriate and likely to be rewarded or inappropriate and likely to be punished. It is this anticipated reinforcement/punishment (based on direct or vicarious reinforcement in the past) that motivates the behavior, independent of whatever motivation to engage in or refrain from an act comes from its conformity to or violation of a person's beliefs.[5] One may be willing to commit a crime in the sense of holding a favorable definition of the behavior, but one is less likely to act on that favorable inclination if the situation does not allow for expectations of a payoff and low risk of punishment. Thus, the concept of instrumental learning posits a precise role for definitions in motivation for crime that goes beyond Sutherland's notion that drives and motives are learned "from" definitions.

Sutherland's sixth statement posits "excess" of definitions as the basic differential association process, as was discussed extensively in Chapter 2. In revising the theory, Burgess and I proposed that the basic process is one of differential reinforcement, the balance of positive and negative consequences of behavior. Definitions remained central to the theory as part of the content of what is learned through differential reinforcement and as discriminative stimuli for the performance of behavior.

The definitions favorable and unfavorable to criminal and delinquent behavior are developed through imitation and differential reinforcement. Once learned, the definitions then may become implicated in differential reinforcement of future behavior, in that adhering to or violating them may act as positive rewards or moral costs attached to behavior. Cognitively, they provide a mind-set that makes one more willing to engage in deviancy or crime when the opportunity occurs. Behaviorally, they affect the commission of deviant or criminal behavior by serving as internal discriminative stimuli that cue certain actions.

These definitions are only one set of stimuli that discriminate among responses. Present in the environment in which behavior is reinforced are the physical surroundings, other people, one's own feelings, others' behavior, one's own and others' spoken words, and other animate and inanimate stimuli. Those that customarily accompany or are present in reinforcement (or punishment) of particular behavior come to be associated with it and become conditioned cues indicating that reinforcement is to be expected. Such stimuli help the person to "discriminate" among different situations and sets of circumstances or, conversely, to "generalize" from one similar situation to another. In a sense, discriminative stimuli signal the actor that certain behavior is appropriate or inappropriate, and likely or not likely to be rewarded, in a given situation or set of circumstances. These stimuli thereby increase the probability that the behavior will recur beyond the probability provided by previous or anticipated reinforcement. The greater the extent to which stimuli in one situation are the same as or similar to those in another situation where the person has been reinforced for some behavior, the higher the probability that the behavior will be repeated in that situation.

In addition to the presence of other people, the most important stimuli that become discriminative for social behavior are verbal symbols. Social reinforcers typically consist of or are delivered through words, and verbal interaction often accompanies nonverbal reinforcement. A significant portion of these verbal stimuli are made up of normative or evaluative definitions of the behavior as good or bad, right or wrong, justified or unjustified, words that accompany positive and negative social sanctions. This is a basic mechanism in socialization, wherein norms and values are internalized. These verbalized evaluative definitions associated with reward and punishment of behavior become overtly discriminative for the behavior, and, as the individual learns them, they function as subvocal, internal discriminative stimuli.

Conceptualizing definitions as verbalizations that are reinforced and behaviorally discriminative links the concept of definitions to behavioral learning theory. However, as noted above, social learning theory retains cognitive dimensions of definitions that are not captured entirely by the concept of discriminative stimuli. The concept of definitions favorable and unfavorable in social learning theory owes more to the meaning given them in Sutherland's theory than to how human verbal behavior is treated in operant behavior theory. Operant theory recognizes overt verbal responses as audible, verbal discriminative stimuli. But the concept of definitions in social learning theory retains the notion that a person may apply them to his own behavior in a sort of conversation with himself. Moreover, the notion that one cognitively engages in self-reinforcement guided by internalized norms and by other covert or mentalistic events, although given little place in orthodox operant theory, is quite consistent with the symbolic interactionism in Sutherland's original differential association theory.

It is also quite consistent with modern social behaviorism, which has moved away from the injunctions against the use of any mentalistic concepts. Indeed, Bandura has gone from social "learning" to social "cognitive" theory (1986a), and it has become increasingly difficult to distinguish his theory from symbolic interactionism in sociology or from social learning theory, as developed in the Sutherland tradition, in criminology. For instance, his conceptualization of the different ways in which "disengagement of self-deterring consequences" affect self-rewards or self-punishments for aggression (Bandura, 1976), which he later described as a process of "selective activation and moral disengagement of moral control" (Bandura, 1990), is virtually a clone of Sykes and Matza's (1957) "techniques of neutralization" (although Bandura makes no citation to and is apparently unaware of their work). Bandura (1976; 1990) argues that "self-regulatory mechanisms" and "self-sanctions" can be disengaged by various mechanisms, such as "moral justification," "justification of aggression in terms of higher principles," "advantageous comparisons," "displacement of responsibility," "diffusion of responsibility," "disregard of harmful consequences," "blaming and dehumanizing victims," and "attribution of blame." These concepts as used by Bandura are no more than variants of neutralizing definitions as I have long incorporated them into the social learning theory of crime and deviance.

Both Sutherland and Cressey (as well as many of their critics, like the Gluecks) believed that if definitions are learned from past associations, then the excess of definitions favorable and unfavorable must be measured by recounting and totaling up all previous exposures to definitions to reach some sort of grand sum, or "ratio," of favorable and unfavorable definitions. No such effort is needed. One can simply measure the balance of general and specific definitions at a given time, as is true for the balance of reinforcement for behavior. It is not necessary to reconstruct accurately a person's history of definitions, reinforcement, and discriminative stimuli and come up with an exact ratio of favorable and unfavorable definitions or an exact cumulative record of reinforcement balance. One need only measure the perceived or anticipated balance of reinforcement and the relative discriminative stimulus values of one set of verbalizations or definitions over another. This balance can become relatively stable over time and across situations. But as both Sutherland and Cressey pointed out, the definitions are activated by time, place, circumstances, and type of offense—"stable" does not mean "unchangeable." This discussion of the concept and function of definitions in the social learning process relates to the issue of differential association/social learning theory as a "cultural deviance" theory, a subject to which I turn in the next chapter.

I then present empirical tests of the theory to demonstrate that a large body of research evidence has accumulated favoring social learning. I go into considerable detail on the methodology of my own research because I want to show precisely how the major concepts explicated in this chapter can be put into operation and how some of the measures can be improved.

Notes

1. Further, I became convinced that the way Hirschi presented his theory in the context of operationalization and direct empirical test of its key propositions with survey data was much better than the way most criminological theory had been presented in the past and the way in which Burgess and I proposed differential association–reinforcement theory—state the theory and let others worry about testing it. Therefore, as described in Chapter 1, in anticipation of restating the theory in the book, I secured a small grant to collect data and test the theory with adolescent alcohol and drug use in 1969. That effort fell through when previous administrative permission to conduct the study in Seattle area schools was withdrawn. It was not until 1976 that the opportunity to test the theory in this way became available. I also considered reducing the theory into axiomatic format, following the efforts of DeFleur and Quinney and of Gibbs. Indeed, at one point during the Boys Town Study I attempted to state the theory in the form of an algebraic equation. I was not at all satisfied with these efforts and gave up on them.

2. To interpret social learning theory as positing only socialization and no selection effects is clearly mistaken. My presentations of the theory have long stipulated reciprocal and feedback effects, operative in each individual's learning history and in the immediate situation in which an opportunity for a crime occurs. Behavioral theory is based on a response-stimulus-response sequence. That is, operant conditioning (instrumental learning) is a process in which behavior (response) produces consequences (stimuli), and in turn the recurrence of that behavior is a function of those rewarding or aversive consequences. The reciprocal or feedback effects of consequences on behavior, therefore, have been a visible part of the theory from the beginning.

My earlier discussion of the theory, however, may have partly contributed to the misinterpretation that it posits only recursive relationships. In the original Burgess and Akers article and the first edition of *Deviant Behavior*, the reciprocal relationships between definitions and behavior and between peer associations and behavior were left implicit rather than explicitly stated (Akers, 1973). In the second edition, I provided a brief statement on feedback effects, especially with regard to definitions and reinforcement. But in the Akers et al. (1979) article testing social learning theory, the discussion stressed the causal effect of prior associations on delinquent behavior without paying much attention to how delinquent behavior could then affect future associations. That this inattention in the empirical test of the theory did not negate the nonrecursive aspects of the theory was pointed out in response to criticism of the article. We objected that the critics *"ignore the feedback effects which are an inherent part of the theory,* oversimplify the process, and *force it into a recursive linear model."* We pointed out that the theory predicts that the consequences of behavior will feed back and reinforce its future occurrence, and that "the consequences of use also will affect whether or not one continues to define use favorably and whether or not one continues to associate more with other users." Finally, we stressed that it was incorrect to pit the "social selection" model against the "socialization" model as competing explanations of the relationship between peer associations and one's own deviance because the two models "provide less in the way of competing explanations of the findings than they illustrate subtle complexities within the social learning process" (Lanza-Kaduce et al., 1982). A fuller, explicit statement of time sequences and reciprocal effects was subsequently incorporated into the theory (Akers, 1985; 1994). That explicit theme has been reiterated in empirical articles (Akers et al., 1989; Akers and La Greca, 1991), essays (Akers, 1991), and books (Akers, 1994). Yet, theorists and researchers continue to interpret the theory as if none of this had been written (e.g., various articles in the Spring 1996 issue of *Journal of Drug Issues,* especially). See Chapter 5 for results of others' research and Chapter 8 for my own research findings on sequences and reciprocal effects that are consistent with social learning theory.

3. That statement combined and restated Sutherland's first and eighth propositions that "criminal behavior is learned" and that it "involves all of the mechanisms" of learning any behavior. The principles are found in the literature as social learning theory, operant theory, reinforcement theory, behavior analysis, and behavior modification. See B. F. Skinner (1953; 1959; 1971; 1974), Staats (1964; 1975), Ullman and Krasner (1969), Bandura (1969; 1973; 1977a; 1986a), Bandura and Walters (1963), Thompson and Grabowski (1972), Blackman (1974), Mahoney (1974), Craighead et al. (1976), Millenson and Leslie (1979), Catania (1979), Chance (1979), Swenson (1980), Davey and Cullen (1988), Klein and Mowrer (1989), and Grusec (1992). See also the *Journal of Experimental Analysis of Behavior, Journal of Applied Behavior Analysis, Behavior Modification,* and *Behavior Research and Therapy.* For behavioral principles in sociology see Homans (1974), Burgess and Bushell (1969), Scott (1971), Kunkel (1970), Hamblin and Kunkel (1977), Emerson (1981), Baldwin and Baldwin (1981), and Tarter (1979).

4. A number of studies have been done on self-efficacy and treatment outcome, but the empirical verification of self-efficacy has not yet been firmly established. Moreover, Bandura seems to have wavered somewhat over the years, blurring the distinction between self-efficacy and such concepts as locus of control. I have not specifically incorporated self-efficacy into my social learning theory of crime and deviance. I view it as

simply a variation on self-control or self-reinforcement and do not accept it as the "unifying theory of behavioral change" that Bandura (1977b) claims it to be.

5. In the absence of reinforcement or unity in the balance of reward and punishment (just as is true in the case of unity of favorable and unfavorable definitions), differential reinforcement becomes nonpredictive. Another way to view this unity either for definitions or reinforcement is that when the sum is zero or the ratio is one, the variable is held constant or controlled. Of course, when a variable is controlled or held constant it can have no effect.

4

Social Learning and Cultural Deviance Theory

In Chapter 3, I pointed out that Cressey (1960) argued persuasively that many of the critiques of Sutherland's differential association theory were "literary errors," or misinterpretations by the critics. These have largely been laid to rest, and one seldom sees reference to them in the literature. Subsequently, however, the theory has been subjected to other criticisms. One is that it cannot accommodate reciprocal relationships between social learning variables and deviant or criminal behavior; I will examine this issue in Chapter 5. Here, I will concentrate on the critique of differential association/social learning as the archetypal "cultural deviance" theory. Appearing in the 1960s and still perhaps the major criticism of the theory, this view attends less to what the theory has to say than to what some see as its underlying assumptions about human nature. Matsueda (1988) argued that the critics' attribution of cultural deviance assumptions to differential association theory grossly distorted it. Similarly, Bernard has taken exception to how the cultural deviance label has been applied both to the original differential association formulation and to the social learning revision (Vold and Bernard, 1986:227–29; Bernard and Snipes, 1995). I will show in this chapter that the theory is not one of "cultural deviance" in the critical sense that this label has been applied to it. In the process, I will clarify in what sense cultural elements are incorporated into the differential association/social learning explanation of crime and deviance.[1]

The Cultural Deviance Critique

According to this view, differential association/social learning theory rests on the inherently untenable assumptions that "man has no nature, socialization is perfectly successful, and cultural variability is unlimited" (Kornhauser, 1978:34). These premises lead the theory into a dead end where it cannot explain individual differences; it is doomed to apply *only* to those group differences in crime that rest on adherence to a criminal or deviant subculture opposed to conventional culture. Although several subcultural theories are included in this view of cultural deviance theory, the principal example of such a theory is said to be differential association/social learning.

This characterization of Sutherland's theory apparently began with an unpublished essay by Ruth Kornhauser in 1963. (I say "apparently" because I have not read her paper.) But Hirschi referred to it as "a truly devastating critique of theories of cultural deviance" (Hirschi, 1969:12). Later, Kornhauser (1978) expanded on the theme of differential association as the quintessential "cultural deviance" theory and included in her analysis the social learning reformulation. Shortly thereafter, Hirschi and Gottfredson (1979) repeated the cultural deviance criticism of the theory, a stance taken also by Wilson and Herrnstein (1985). The critique of differential association as a cultural deviance theory was reiterated more recently by Gottfredson and Hirschi (1990) in their contrasting of positivistic theories with their own general self-control theory of crime. Later critics continue to repeat the assertions about the theory made by Kornhauser and Hirschi (see, for instance, Messner and Rosenfeld, 1994), although the objections by Matsueda and Bernard to this approach are sometimes also noted (Shoham and Hoffman, 1991).

According to Kornhauser (1978:34), the theory's assumption that "socialization is perfectly successful" leads to the further supposition that individuals are incapable of violating the cultural norms of any group to which they belong. The theory is said to rest on the assumption that everyone completely internalizes social norms and obeys them; belief in the norms of the group to which one belongs is in itself sufficient to ensure behavioral conformity. Since individuals will always be in perfect conformity with the cultural expectations of their own groups, if these particular cultures are deviant by the standards of conventional society then the individuals comprising the groups will automatically be deviant or criminal. Behavioral adherence to unconventional culture places one in direct violation of conventional norms. In Kornhauser's view, then, cultural deviance theory assumes that subscribing to deviant values "requires" the individual to violate the norms of other groups if these conflict with his or her own group's norms. If the values of these other groups are incorporated into the law, then the violations will be criminal. According to the assumptions imputed to cultural deviance theory, *individuals* cannot be deviant. Only the *cultures* or *subcultures* in which criminal values are transmitted can be deviant with regard to the culture of the larger society or with regard to groups sustaining different subcultures. The theory is incapable of explaining any deviation from the culture into which one is socialized or any behavior that is inconsistent with one's professed values. Hirschi reiterates this criticism:

> A third set of theories [of cultural deviance] assumes that men are incapable of committing "deviant" acts. A person may indeed commit acts deviant by the standards of, say, middle-class society, but he cannot commit acts deviant by his own standards. In other words, theorists from this school see deviant behavior as *conformity* to a set of standards not accepted by a larger (that is, more powerful) society. (Hirschi, 1969:11)

> In simplest terms, cultural deviance theory assumes that cultures, not persons, are deviant. It assumes that in living up to the demands of his own culture, the person automatically comes into conflict with the law. (Hirschi, 1969:229)

Although Kornhauser makes some reference to other theories, she presents differential association/social learning as the "pure" model of cultural deviance theory. Upon closer examination, however, it can be seen that this characterization is based on gross misinterpretations. Although there are certainly cultural factors implicated in the theory, differential association/social learning is not the pure model of a cultural deviance theory, and it does not at all fit the category as defined by Kornhauser.[2]

Misinterpretations of Extreme Cases in Differential Association

Sutherland's theory is explicitly designed to account for variations in criminal behavior by individuals, not differences in group rates of crime.

As I noted in Chapter 2, Sutherland made an unequivocal distinction between differential association as a theory of individual behavior and social disorganization (or differential social organization) as a theory of group differences. To claim that differential association theory applies only to deviant cultures, and not at all to individual deviance, is to impute assumptions to it that are directly contradictory to propositions clearly stated in the theory and to distinctions expressly maintained by Sutherland (1947:5–6).

The theory posits individual deviance as coming from the person's holding definitions favorable to norm-violating acts that are shaped by relatively greater exposure to deviant than to conventional normative definitions. Therefore, the extreme case in which an individual's deviance is based entirely on his or her having been socialized solely in, and having completely internalized the dictates of, a deviant subculture without contact with conventional society is consistent with differential association theory. But this is the extreme case and is not proposed as the only or even the typical case accounted for by the theory. Differential association assumes neither that all (or even many) cases of deviance fall into this extreme category nor that everyone reared within the same subculture will conform perfectly to its norms. The theory does not propose that there is no possibility that individuals will violate internal group norms. Therefore, the defining characteristics attributed to "cultural deviance" by Kornhauser, Hirschi, and others apply to differential association theory only if one limits its scope to the most extreme cases within the purview of the theory. Similarly, nowhere does Sutherland state that his theory rests on the assumptions of perfect socialization and no possibility of within-group deviance by individuals. Further, there is nothing in his statement of differential association that asserts that persons are incapable of violating the very group norms to which they express allegiance. Yet, these are the assumptions that Kornhauser lists as the sine qua non of cultural deviance theory.

If the author of differential association theory does not state assumptions attributed to cultural deviance theory and, indeed, incorporates propositions in the theory that are contradictory to such assumptions, then how can the theory be characterized as the prime cultural deviance theory? It appears that the attribution of such assumptions to differential association theory is based on references to other theories, to works by other authors, or to ancillary comments by Sutherland, rather than on an analysis of the statements found in the theory itself. For instance, Hirschi (1969:11) offers a quotation from a 1929 book on delinquency areas by Shaw and others to substantiate his claim that cultural deviance theories assume that only cultures, not individuals, can deviate. Similarly, Kornhauser (1978) includes no specific discussion or analysis of the nine propositions in differential association theory to support her description of it as the model of cultural deviance theory. She relies, instead, on interpretations of passages from Sutherland, Cressey, Sellin, and others in which culture conflict, social disorganization, and differential social organization—but not differential association—are discussed (Matsueda, 1988).

To support her contention that differential association theory rests entirely on the assumption of conflict between cultures and that one always obeys the norms of one's group, Kornhauser (1978:37–38) quotes from remarks that Sutherland made in 1942 that he intended to illustrate culture conflict. The paragraph from which she quotes relates how some members of the historically criminal tribes of India steal and commit acts of violence in obedience to tribal codes. This automatically brings them into conflict with the laws of a larger unit, the state:

> This lack of homogeneity is illustrated . . . in the criminal tribes of India. Two cultures are in sharp conflict there. One is the tribal culture which prescribes certain types of assault on persons outside the tribe, in some cases with religious compulsions. The other is the legal culture as stated by the Indian . . . governments. . . . When members of the tribe commit crimes, they act in accordance with one code and in opposition to the other. According to my theory, the same principle or process exists in all criminal behavior. . . . (Sutherland, 1956:20, as quoted in Kornhauser, 1978:37–38)

Compare this with Sutherland's full paragraph (with the crucial phrases left out by Kornhauser restored in brackets):

> This lack of homogeneity is illustrated [in extreme form] in the criminal tribes of India. Two cultures are in sharp conflict there. One is the tribal culture which prescribes certain types of assault on persons outside the tribe, in some cases with religious compulsions. The other is the legal culture as stated by the Indian and provincial governments and made applicable to the criminal tribes. . . . When members of the tribe commit crimes, they act in accordance with one code and in opposition to the other. According to my theory, the same principle or process exists in all criminal behavior, [although the conflict may

not be widely organized or sharply defined as in the Indian tribe]. (Sutherland, 1956:20)

In her quotation, Kornhauser deletes the key qualifying phrase that Sutherland used to introduce the point, namely, that it is "illustrated *in extreme form*" (Sutherland, 1956:20, emphasis added). Although he did assert at the end of the paragraph that the "principle" of culture conflict operates to some extent in all criminal behavior, Sutherland qualified this by noting that it may not operate in the "sharply defined" or "organized" way given in the illustration. That is, it is the general principle or process of relatively greater exposure to definitions favorable to crime that is operative in committing criminal behavior, not the specific way in which the process operates in this extreme case. But again, Kornhauser drops this essential qualifying phrase from her quotation.

With the qualifying phrases omitted, the meaning of culture conflict is not presented as Sutherland intended. The theory is also inaccurately represented because the quotation is taken out of the context of purpose and time in which it was written. Sutherland's reference to "my theory" does not refer at all to differential association as found in his 1947 statement of the final version of the theory. Kornhauser took this quotation from a 1942 paper (which was included in a 1956 posthumous collection of Sutherland's work by Cohen et al.) that referred to Sutherland's 1939 version of the theory (see also Sutherland, 1973.) That earlier version contained statements about both culture conflict and differential association. Moreover, in the same passage Sutherland (1956:20–21) makes a clear distinction between culture conflict as a group principle and differential association as a principle of individual behavior.

Nevertheless, Kornhauser takes this example as demonstrating the "basic paradigm" of Sutherland's theory:

> According to Sutherland, originator of the *pure cultural deviance* model, the *basic paradigm* of this approach is given by the fabled "criminal tribes of India," whose culture mandates crimes abhorred in the so-called legal culture. (Kornhauser, 1978:26; emphasis added)

But it can be taken as such only by disregarding the original date of the paper, Sutherland's qualifier that the Indian tribes represented an extreme case, his statement that the example illustrates but does not fully state the principle of culture conflict, and his distinction between culture conflict and differential association. Obviously, it is inaccurate for Kornhauser to ignore Sutherland's own restrictions on the illustration and then claim that it forms the basic assumption in his theory. Nor is it accurate to assert, as Kornhauser does, that the scope of differential association theory published in 1947 is limited to the type of subcultural criminal behavior found in an anecdotal illustration published several years earlier. Sutherland's theory does include cultural factors in its main proposition that norm-violating behavior of individuals is learned through their differential association with others supporting definitions favorable to criminal and deviant behavior. Differential association does not rest, however, on any of the main assumptions attributed to cultural deviance theory by the critics.

Kornhauser (1978) also gives a mistaken interpretation to the proposition that differential association mediates sociodemographic variations in criminal behavior by hypothesizing that rules, norms, and role expectations differ by age, race, sex, class, and so on (Sutherland and Cressey, 1955). She believes that Sutherland and Cressey are thereby assuming that there is a separate criminogenic culture or subculture to account for each of these differences. But their hypothesis is simply that one's location in the social system, as indicated by such characteristics as race, sex, and age, means that one will be differentially exposed to and learn definitions favorable and unfavorable to law violation (whatever the source of those definitions). Such a hypothesis does not require that each of these sociodemographic categories constitute an interacting group with a singular culture into which men, young people, or blacks are obediently enculturated. Cressey (1960) made it clear that the conflict can come from normative variations and discontinuities in the same social system to which both sexes, all ages, and all races are exposed, as well as from differences among subcultures.

Definitions and Motivation for Criminal Behavior

The cultural deviance critique depicts the differential association process in criminal behavior as one in which internalizing definitions favorable to crime (1) "requires" the person to behave in violation of conventional norms and (2) provides the "sole" motivation for behavior.

> Theories in the cultural deviance tradition suggest that in committing his acts the delinquent is living up to the norms of his culture. These theories *usually*

suggest the existence of beliefs that *positively require* delinquent acts. (Hirschi, 1969:197; emphasis added)

Internalized cultural values [according to differential association theory] provide the *sole* basis of motivation. . . .
   This view [Sutherland's] assumes first that there are *no other* determinants of human behavior than values. (Kornhauser, 1978:195–96; emphasis added)

Since cultural definitions are wholly determinative, and no other source of motivation is allowed to counteract them, all socialization is "perfectly successful," and all members of the group are rendered incapable of acting in any way contrary to the deviant norms. Therefore, only the group's culture can be deviant, since no one within the group can deviate from it.

Neither Kornhauser nor Hirschi identifies what specific statement(s) in differential association theory leads them to interpret the theory in this way. And there is nothing in any of the statements of the theory that restricts the concept of definitions favorable to crime to norms that "positively require" deviant acts. Nor is the claim made anywhere in the theory that definitions are the only cause of crime. However, the theory is more vulnerable to this critique because of uncertainties as to exactly what Sutherland meant by "definitions" and the role they play in motivating law violations. The fourth statement of differential association theory refers to learning both "techniques" and "[t]he specific direction of motives, drives, rationalizations, and attitudes," while the fifth hypothesizes that "[t]he specific direction of motives and drives is learned *from* definitions of the legal codes as favorable or unfavorable" (Sutherland, 1947:6; emphasis added).

As I noted in Chapter 3, Sutherland introduced some conceptual confusion in the meaning of "definitions" and its role in criminal motivation in these two statements. Nevertheless, when read in the context of the whole theory, the statements run counter to the cultural deviance interpretation, which holds that the theory proposes that internalizing definitions favorable to crime motivate criminal behavior by compelling obedience to them. But committing a crime solely on the basis of adherence to a set of values or beliefs would occur only in extreme cases of highly ideologically motivated offenses or of intense group loyalty. Nowhere does Sutherland state that all or most definitions favorable to crime and delinquency strongly require, compel, or motivate action in this sense. Definitions may motivate criminal behavior, but Sutherland does not hypothesize that they are the only source of motivation. His reference to "all" learning mechanisms elsewhere in the theory indicates that he did not conceptualize definitions as the sole causal stimuli. However, he did not delineate what these other learning mechanisms were that could motivate behavior or how they relate to favorable/unfavorable definitions in motivating criminal acts.

The presentation of social learning theory in Chapter 3 should demonstrate that whatever confusion remained in Sutherland's original statements on this point was rectified by social learning theory. Hirschi is correct in holding that differential association/social learning theory "suggests" the existence of definitions that require violation of some norms. But it is a misinterpretation to contend that the theory thereby proposes that the mere existence of such definitions is the principal way that they provide motivation. The theory does not posit such motivation for deviance except in cases of strongly ideologically based deviance. Definitions are conceptualized in social learning theory as referring most often to the weakly held conventional beliefs (general definitions unfavorable to deviance that are conceptually the same as the concept of belief in Hirschi's, 1969, social bonding theory) or to the behavior-specific positive or neutralizing definitions that may favorably dispose, but do not provide the only motivation for, one to commit a crime. Probabilities of committing criminal or deviant acts are affected by individual variations in endorsement of pro-social and pro-deviant definitions within the same general culture or in different subcultures.

Moreover, social learning theory proposes that the definitions themselves are differentially reinforced and function as discriminative stimuli, vocal and internal cues signaling that certain behavior is appropriate or inappropriate, right or wrong. Differential reinforcement is a separate source of motivation for behavior that operates with and without accompanying definitions favorable or unfavorable to the behavior. Social learning theory answers questions about social and nonsocial sources of variations in behavior beyond variations in definitions. There is no mystery about how individuals may violate the very norms to which they subscribe, and there is no room for the cultural deviance interpretation that the theory sees cultural norms as the sole cause of criminal behavior.

Social learning theory proposes that reward/punishment contingencies shape both one's attitudes and overt behavioral repertoire over time and provide the motivation to engage in or refrain from action at a given time and place. It is quite in line with the theory to assert that one may violate group norms because of failures of socialization or because he or she has insufficiently learned the moral dictates of the group's norms. Embedded in the same general normative system may be both the prohibition of an act and definitions that justify the act (Sykes and Matza, 1957). Parents and other socializers may make inefficient or inconsistent use of rewarding and punishing sanctions and create the unintended outcome of reinforcing behavior that is contrary to their own normative standards. They may fail to serve as effective models (Patterson et al., 1975). Deviant models are available outside the family and other conventional socializing institutions, in the media, and among peers. One's own learned normative definitions may be violated because the rewards for the behavior outbalance the normative inhibitions. One may refrain from law violation, in spite of having learned definitions favorable to violation, because he or she anticipates more cost than reward attached to the violation.

Social learning theory posits that, in addition to or counter to a favorable attitude toward criminal behavior, one is motivated to break the law by the expected reward and is inhibited by the expected aversive consequences. Definitions are implicated in the reinforcement balance because part of the package of rewards and punishments is the congruence or discrepancy between one's beliefs and deeds. If the act is congruent with or allows one to demonstrate adherence to a certain norm or set of values, that may provide enough positive motivation to do it. If the act is not congruent with one's beliefs, the attendant guilt and self-reproach will often be sufficiently aversive to deter committing it. But positive or negative attitudes are only part of the motivational package inducing or inhibiting behavior. Social learning theory proposes that the relative reinforcement from other known or anticipated rewards and costs motivates a person to commit an act even in the face of negative attitudes. An individual may believe that it is wrong to lie, but lie anyway if it will get her off the hook when accused of a misdeed or if it will put a lot of money in his pocket. That a person may be motivated to violate even those normative standards to which he subscribes is clearly explained by the balance of other social and nonsocial rewards and punishers attached to the behavior.

Of course, subscribing to those normative standards is itself responsive to, and over time will be modified by, the rewarding or punishing consequences of the behavior to which they refer. That is, not only the overt behavior itself but also the definitions favorable or unfavorable to it are affected by the positive and negative consequences of the initial acts. To the extent that they are more rewarded than alternative behavior, the favorable definitions attached to the acts will be strengthened and the unfavorable definitions will be weakened, and it becomes more likely that the deviant behavior will be repeated under similar circumstances.

> That is, the using of the definitions is an operant behavior which can be reinforced, but the definitions may in turn serve as discriminative stimuli for other behavior, provided that they accompany (at least occasionally) reinforcement of the behavior. Of course, deviant actions may be reinforced and may recur without being accompanied by definitions. However, . . . it is more likely that the behavior will recur in situations to which the definitions can be applied. (Akers, 1973:57)

The operation of motivating factors beyond definitions that were implicit in Sutherland's reference to all the mechanisms of learning has been made explicit in social learning theory. The explanatory shortfall left by the ambiguity in his statements regarding "motives" and cultural definitions as the "sole" factor in criminal behavior has been made up by social learning theory. One may reject the answer, but one cannot deny that the theory provides an answer by stipulating that social and nonsocial reinforcement, modeling, discriminative stimuli, and other behavioral processes motivate behavior independently of, and in interaction with, the effect of cultural definitions. This incorporation of behavioral reinforcement and punishment (social and nonsocial) and other learning mechanisms into the equation plainly answers the question of how a person can engage in behavior that is not congruent with his or her own normative definitions. But Kornhauser rejects this answer and classifies social learning as a cultural deviance theory because including nonsocial reinforcement in the social learning reformulation "certainly violates Sutherland's principle of cultural definitions as the sole causal stimuli" (Kornhauser, 1978:198–99). If the principle of definitions as the sole causal stimuli is crucial to cultural deviance theory as defined by Kornhauser, and if social learning propositions violate that principle, then how can social learning be called a cultural deviance theory?

Kornhauser's reasoning is circular. She begins by imputing to cultural deviance theory the assumption that cultural definitions are the sole cause of criminal behavior. Then she rejects any learning theory concept or proposition that would explicitly contradict the assumption, precisely because it does not fit the imputed assumption with which she began. Thus, any theory can be classified as a cultural deviance theory simply by ignoring what it actually assumes and proposes and by imputing to it assumptions and propositions that fit what one has defined as a cultural deviance theory.

Kornhauser also misinterprets the fact that social learning theory contains such reinforcement processes in other ways. For instance, although she clearly places not only Sutherland's differential association theory but Akers's social learning theory at the center of the cultural deviance theories, Kornhauser still maintains that *any* "[c]ultural deviance theory denies that men ever violate norms out of considerations of reward and punishment" (1978:44). While it is true that Sutherland's theory does not refer to the impact of reward and punishment on individual behavior, this is precisely what social learning theory proposes. How can a theory in which differential reinforcement plays such a central role be declared to ignore rewards and punishment? As noted above, Kornhauser dismisses the inclusion of nonsocial reinforcers in the theory as a way of providing noncultural motivation to crime because she believes that including such reinforcers contradicts the assumption she ascribes to cultural deviance theory, namely, that only cultural definitions can cause crime. Then, paradoxically, she claims that "since it is entirely possible for criminal behavior to be learned and maintained in the absence of social reinforcements" social learning theory is no more able than Sutherland's differential association to explain individual deviant behavior (Kornhauser, 1978:199). Perhaps it is this reasoning that leads Kornhauser to view both Sutherland's and Akers's theories as conforming to the assumptions she attributes to cultural deviance theory.

Cultural Elements in Definitions and Differential Association

None of the foregoing should be taken to mean that culture is unimportant in differential association/social learning theory. Cultural elements were central in Sutherland's differential association and remain, albeit less prominently, in Akers's social learning theory. The main point is that neither approach meets the criteria for a cultural deviance theory ascribed to it by Kornhauser, Hirschi, and others. If the traditional cultural deviance critique is not accurate, what is the proper way to describe the role of culture in the theory? The question has already been partially answered, but it can be clarified further through a closer examination of the concepts of "culture," "definitions," and "differential association."

Culture is commonly defined along the lines proffered by Kroeber and Parsons (1958:583) as "transmitted and created content and patterns of values, ideas, and other symbolic-meaningful systems as factors in the shaping of human behavior." Aside from material culture, it is conceptualized generally as conduct codes and "symbols and symbol-making" (Gilmore, 1992:409). This would include the values, norms, beliefs, moral evaluations, symbolic meanings, and normative orientations shared or professed by members of a social system (society, community, or subgroup). Values, beliefs, and norms are incorporated into differential association/social learning theory in the concepts of definitions and differential association.

The concept of definitions in the theory includes: (1) group-shared definitions expressed or exhibited by others favorable or unfavorable to deviant or conforming behavior to which the individual is exposed through the family, peers, and other primary and secondary sources, and (2) the individual's own internalized or professed definitions/attitudes favorable or unfavorable to the behavior. The theory predicts that (2), one's own definitions, are positively correlated with (1), others' definitions. But as I have shown above, it does not predict that the correlation will be 1.0.

Since the general conventional culture in modern society is not uniform and there are conflicts and variations among subgroups in society, the individual is likely to be exposed to different and perhaps conflicting cultural definitions of specific acts as good or bad. The theory does not assume that one's own attitudes are a perfect replication of those cultural patterns or that exposure to them is the sole source of a person's taking on and changing his or her own definitions favorable or unfavorable to deviance. And, as shown above, once learned these definitions are not the sole motivation in the process whereby individuals come to the point of committing criminal and deviant acts.

As I demonstrated in Chapter 3, the favorable and unfavorable definitions shared by others constitute the normative, or cultural, dimension of the process of differential association. But the concept of differential association also has a social, behavioral/interactional, dimension that is made up of the direct and indirect associations with others who are engaging in conforming or deviant behavior (see Akers, 1985; 1994). While this was less clear in Sutherland's statements, both dimensions are clearly included in my presentation of social learning theory. It is a distortion of Sutherland's position to claim that it allowed only for a normative dimension in differential association and recognized no impact of others' behavior. The idea that exposure to criminal definitions in more likely to occur in differential interaction with people who themselves not only present such definitions but also commit deviant acts is found in Sutherland's comments on learning in intimate, primary groups and to his notion that it involves the communication of gestures as well as language. Further, in comments on the seventh statement of his theory, Sutherland explicitly listed "associations with criminal behavior." Also, if "all the mechanisms of learning" are involved, then the theory necessarily implies that the interaction with others should have effects beyond the normative content of that interaction. In this chapter I have indicated how social learning theory stipulates what these other effects are and how both dimensions are involved in motivating people to engage in criminal and deviant behavior. This goes back to the question of how persons may behave in violation of the tenets of their culture or subculture or even of the very values they personally advocate. A child reared in a community espousing nonviolent values and living in a family that professes nonviolent attitudes may nonetheless come to engage in and justify violence because he has witnessed abusive behavior in the home, has been the object of abuse himself, or has otherwise learned violent behavior in spite of the nonviolent cultural norms to which he has been exposed.

Summary and Conclusion

According to Kornhauser and others, differential association/social learning theory epitomizes "cultural deviance" theory. Several assumptions are attributed to such a theory: Pro-deviant definitions are perfectly transmitted subcultural values held so strongly that they positively compel the person to violate the law. It is impossible for individuals to deviate from the culture or subculture to which they have been exposed; thus, there can only be deviant groups or cultures, not deviant individuals. There are no other individual or independent sources of variations in these definitions beyond exposure to the culture of subgroups, and, therefore, cultural definitions are the sole cause of criminal behavior.

The critics do not cite any part of Sutherland's 1947 theory to substantiate their ascription of these assumptions to differential association theory or to support their view that it is the purest form of what they call "cultural deviance" theory. And one searches Sutherland's nine statements in vain to find anything explicit in them that would lead to the conclusion that they necessarily rely on these assumptions. The theory does not state that definitions favorable to deviance operate only by compelling norm violation, that it is impossible for individuals to violate the norms of groups with which they are in association, that there can only be deviant cultures, or that learned definitions constitute the only motivations to crime.

It may be that critics have attributed these cultural deviance assumptions to Sutherland's theory not because of what he specifically stated, but because of something he wrote in his commentary on the theoretical propositions or comments he made elsewhere. For instance, Sutherland used a phrase in his commentary on the sixth statement of his theory that may imply that there are no individual variations in learning definitions—"any person inevitably assimilates the surrounding culture unless other patterns are in conflict" (1947:6). But this refers only to the general idea that what an individual learns depends on the extent to which he or she is exposed to only one set or to conflicting sets of values. It does not state that socialization is completely successful or that there is no individual variation in assimilation of culture. Moreover, neither Kornhauser nor others cite this statement as the reason for assigning cultural deviance assumptions to differential association theory. Therefore, it might be some other feature of Sutherland's theory that leads the critics to call it cultural deviance.

Perhaps it is the vagueness (that I pointed out in Chapter 3) in Sutherland's stipulation of how definitions can provide the motivation for committing criminal acts on which the cultural deviance critique is based. But again, none of the critics claims that his or her arguments rest on this ambiguity. And it is unlikely that this is the basis for the critics' claim that the theory posits definitions as the only possible motivation for crime, because they do not accept the social learning resolution of the ambiguity. Indeed, the critics do not make clear distinctions between Sutherland's theory and social learning theory as I have presented it. Therefore, the same cultural deviance assumptions are ascribed to social learning theory that are imputed to Sutherland's differential association theory. I have shown here that this imputation is based on a misinterpretation both of the original differential association theory and of social learning theory.

This conclusion does not forbid any reference to the theory as cultural deviance if that label simply means that an important role is given to cultural factors in explaining deviance. Sutherland's differential association theory would fit that description, and although the cultural elements are less important to social learning theory, it too would fit. Therefore, by objecting to the label "cultural deviance" I do not mean that all references to cultural deviance elements in the theory are inapplicable. I do mean that if there is a class of cultural deviance theories as traditionally defined by Kornhauser, Hirschi, Gottfredson, and others, differential association/social learning theory does not belong in it.[3]

Notes

This chapter and parts of Chapter 3 are taken from my article "Is differential association/social learning cultural deviance theory?" which appeared in Criminology: An Interdisciplinary Journal, 34:229–247, May 1966. I gratefully acknowledge the reprint permission of the American Society of Criminology.

1. The shortcomings attributed to cultural deviance theory continue to be used as a critique not only of Sutherland's differential association theory but also of the social learning theory reformulation presented in highly influential criminological works (Gottfredson and Hirschi, 1990). This chapter is based on an article in which I attempted to show, as Cressey had done with earlier criticisms, that this characterization of differential association/social learning as the principal cultural deviance theory is based on misreading and misinterpretation (Akers, 1996). Hirschi (1996) contested this and continues to believe that the cultural deviance criticism accurately applies to the theory. In turn, I do not believe that his reply provides answers to the questions I raised about Kornhauser's critique and fails to demonstrate that either Sutherland's or my theory is truly a cultural deviance theory. The issue is probably not settled, and I expect to see additional discussions in the literature.

2. In fact, I am not sure that any criminological theory fits into this category. Which

theory of crime is clearly predicated on assumptions such as these attributed to cultural deviance theory? Vold's (1958) group conflict theory comes close by hypothesizing (not assuming) that much (but not all) crime results from individuals behaving as good members of their respective interest groups. But Vold does not rely on the concept of culture and does not assume that all persons in the group will support the group interest. Sellin's (1938) early notions of culture conflict might have implied, but did not expressly state, the assumptions Kornhauser attributed to cultural deviance theory. Shaw and McKay's (1942) notions of cultural transmission of delinquent values in urban areas, Miller's (1958) theory of lower-class culture, Wolfgang and Ferracuti's (1967) subcultural theory of violence, and theories of delinquent subcultures such as Cohen's (1955) and Cloward and Ohlin's (1960) have some elements of these assumptions imputed to cultural deviance theory (see Barlow and Ferdinand, 1992).

3. In his reply to the article on which this chapter is based, Travis Hirschi (1996) reported that after a long and courageous struggle against major illness, Ruth Kornhauser died. I was saddened to learn of her passing. I never met her or had communication with her, but from what Travis said, she must have been a remarkable person. My objections in this chapter are to the mistaken ideas about differential association and social learning theory she espoused and imply absolutely nothing personal about her.

5

Research on Social Learning Variables in Crime and Delinquency

Social learning principles are useful in designing treatment and prevention programs and in setting other policies. Indeed, these principles, often in combination with guidelines from other theories, have become the basis for group counseling and self-help programs, positive peer counseling programs, gang interventions, family and school programs, teenage drug, alcohol, and delinquency prevention programs, and other private and public initiatives aimed at delinquents and adult offenders in institutions and in the community. A broad range of behavior modification programs that follow social learning principles operate in correctional, treatment, and community facilities for juveniles and adults (see Bandura, 1969; Stumphauzer, 1986; Bynum and Thompson, 1992; Akers, 1992a; Lundman, 1993). Having had some successes, these programs can be taken as additional support for the social learning approach, broadly conceived. But the empirical validity of a theory can be judged only indirectly by its practical applications; it needs to be evaluated by the criteria of testability and empirical evidence (Akers, 1997). By these criteria, social learning fares well. It is a testable theory that is supported by the preponderance of empirical evidence and has stood up well to major logical and methodological critiques.

The basic processes of instrumental and classical conditioning, observational learning, discriminative stimuli, schedules of reinforcement, the matching law, and other behavioral principles specified in Chapter 3 have received empirical support from systematic experimental studies with both animal and human subjects. Studies in more natural settings and the application of learning principles in behavior modification projects continue to support confidence in the basic propositions of learning theory and its extension into social exchange theory. Rather than reviewing that research, I refer the reader to the references in behavioral psychology cited in Chapter 3 and to the large body of research literature in behavioral psychology and behavior modification in psychology and social exchange in sociology. Similarly, I take it as given that the principles of symbolic interactionism, the other major theoretical paradigm on which social learning is based, are empirically sound (see Ritzer, 1992).

The first purpose of this chapter is to review the research, other than my own (which is presented in detail in later chapters), on crime and delinquency relevant to one or more of the four principal social learning concepts of differential association, definitions, differential reinforcement, and modeling. Few findings in any of the research contradict or are inconsistent with the theory, and most of the research provides strong to moderate support for social learning hypotheses. The chapter's second purpose is to address some important methodological, conceptual, and theoretical controversies that have arisen in that research.

Testability of Social Learning Theory

Some critics have alleged that the basic behavioral learning principles incorporated into social learning theory cannot be tested because they may be tautological. Burgess and I examined this issue early in our efforts to integrate differential association with behavioral theory (Burgess and Akers, 1966a). It became clear to us that the way in which a basic principle of operant conditioning was (and to some extent still is) often stated by behavioral psychologists rendered it true by definition and thus tautological. We found that Skinner and other behaviorists would define reinforcement by stating that reinforcement occurs when a response has been strengthened, that is, when its rate of commission has been increased. Then they would state propositions like, "If behavior is reinforced, it will be strengthened." Given the definition of reinforcement, this sentence is tautological. If reinforcement means that behavior has been strengthened, then the hypothesis states simply, "If behavior is reinforced, it is reinforced." The repetition of the dependent variable, the behavior that is supposed to be explained, is taken as evidence that reinforcement has occurred. If the behavior is not strengthened, then by definition it has not been reinforced; therefore, no instance of behavior that is not being strengthened can be used to falsify the hypothesis. It is nontestable.

The solution that Burgess and I offered was to separate the definitions of reinforcement (and related behavioral concepts) from nontautological, testable propositions in operant theory and to propose criteria for falsifying those propositions. Although we did not offer concrete guidelines beyond "extended and systematic analysis" for deciding when enough exceptions to the reinforcement principle had been found to falsify it, our resolution of the tautology issue was accepted as a reasonable approach (Chadwick-Jones, 1976; Molm, 1981). Others have proposed somewhat different, but still satisfactory solutions (Liska, 1969; Chadwick-Jones, 1976). Liska (1969) argued that while the basic operant conditioning principle may at bottom remain tautological, this does not prevent deriving testable hypotheses from it. Operant principles are "open concepts" from which nontautological propositions and hypotheses about the effects of positive and aversive stimuli on behavior can be derived. Emerson (1972a) takes a similar approach in arguing that operant conditioning principles should be taken as nonproblematic assumptions from which testable propositions can be devised. The tautology problem is avoidable in experimental laboratory studies because there is clear separation of the manipulation of reinforcement contingencies by the experimenter from changes in the behavior of the subject(s). Also, as Molm (1981) notes, the reinforcing or punishing stimuli can be established from previous experiments before the current experimental study begins, allowing for refutable prediction about the effects of those stimuli on different behavior.

Tautology has not been a problem for social learning theory as I have developed it. As Chapter 3 shows, differential reinforcement is clearly distinguished conceptually from its contingent behavior. Moreover, the operational definitions of reinforcement are independent of the operational definitions of the occurrence and frequency of the delinquent or criminal behavior it is meant to explain. Thus, the variables in the process of reinforcement are always measured separately (and hence nontautologically) from crime and deviance in research on social learning theory. The theory would be falsified if it is typically the case that positive social approval or other rewards for delinquency (that are not offset by punishment) or the person's report of a positive balance of rewards for behavior fail to increase, or more often reduce, its recurrence. These answers to the tautology question and the formulation of a testable social learning theory seem to have been accepted in the sociology of deviance and criminology. One seldom sees the question raised anymore.

Overview of Research on Social Learning Variables in Crime and Delinquency

A large body of literature has accumulated reporting research that tests full or partial social learning models or other models of deviance and crime that include one or more of the social learning concepts, sometimes comparing social learning to, or combining or integrating it into, models with variables from other theories. The preponderance of evidence from that research favors the major propositions from social learning theory that differential reinforcement, differential association, definitions, and modeling, mainly involving peer groups and the family, account for individual differences in criminal, delinquent, and deviant behavior. I will not discuss all of this literature, nor will I examine it in detail as I do the delinquency prediction literature in Chapter 6. I will begin, rather, with an extensive listing of research literature, followed by a discussion of some specific dimensions of the research. Later, I take up some controversial methodological and theoretical issues raised in that literature.

Although no research had tested a fully specified model of the differential association–reinforcement theory until the Boys Town Study that I did with Marvin Krohn and others in the mid-1970s (see Chapter 7), supportive research reporting the effects of differential association and definitions can be traced back at least to the early self-report delinquency studies on differential association theory by Short (1957; 1958; 1960), Nye (1958), Voss (1964), Matthews (1968), and others. Since then, a large number of studies using measures of one or more of the social learning variables of differential association, imitation, definitions, and differential reinforcement have continued to report findings that uphold the theory's hypotheses. Studies in the 1970s include Jensen (1972), Krohn (1974), Kandel (1974), Burkett and Jensen (1975), Conger (1976), and Jessor and Jessor (1977). A large number of studies appeared in the 1980s that offered evidence directly relevant to the claims of social learning theory. A lengthy but not exhaustive chronological listing of these includes Minor (1980), Andrews (1980), Matsueda (1982), Dull (1983), Winfree and Griffiths (1983), Meier et al. (1984), Patterson and Dishion (1985), LaGrange and White (1985), Elliott et al. (1985), Massey and Krohn (1986), Dembo et al. (1986), White et al. (1986; 1987), Marcos et al. (1986), Kandel and Andrews (1987), Fagan and Wexler (1987), Matsueda and Heimer (1987), Johnson et al. (1987), Orcutt (1987), Burkett and Warren (1987), White et al. (1987), and Winfree et al. (1989).

Research reporting findings supportive of social learning continues in the 1990s, as shown by Sellers and Winfree (1990), Loeber et al. (1991), Kandel and Davies (1991), Agnew (1991a; 1993; 1994), McGee (1992), Warr and Stafford (1991), Rowe and Gulley (1992), Winfree et al. (1993; 1994), Lauritsen (1993), Warr (1993a; 1993b; 1996), Inciardi et al. (1993), Benda (1994), Burton et al. (1994), Elliott (1994), Simons et al. (1994), Dabney (1995), Conger and Simons (1995), and Wood et al. (1995). As is true for most of the research testing criminological theories, the bulk of this work in social learning has been done with samples of adolescents. The dependent variable in this research ranges from minor forms of adolescent deviance, to teenage substance use or abuse, to serious delinquent and criminal behavior. Some of the investigations have been conducted among adults, with substance use and abuse or various types of criminal behavior as the dependent variable. The most commonly measured social learning variable is differential peer association (although it is sometimes given a different label, such as "deviant peer bonding"). Typically, it is measured by number or proportion of friends who are involved in delinquent or deviant behavior, although the modalities of associations are sometimes measured. Definitions favorable and unfavorable, most often calculated by respondents' endorsement of positive/negative attitudes or beliefs and neutralizing definitions toward given deviant behavior, are also often found in this research as independent variables (again, often given labels other than "definitions"). Differential reinforcement is also measured in various ways (and given various labels), such as reports of peer approval or disapproval, parental sanctions, or other actual or rewarding and punishing consequences of one's deviant behavior. Modeling, or imitation, is least often included in this research; not surprisingly, such imitative effects are most likely to involve adolescent or younger population samples. Modeling is sometimes measured directly, but it is also inferred from parental behavior or from exposure to media portrayals.

Most of the research is presented as a test of (or otherwise acknowledges) variables and hypotheses derived from social learning and/or differential association theory. Oddly, a number of the research reports make no direct reference to differential association or to social learning theory, even though they measure, and demonstrate the strong effects on crime and delinquency of, peer associations, parental models, pro-social and deviant attitudes, informal social sanctions and reactions to deviance, and other relationships that are obviously supportive of social learning theory. Therefore, I count the research as providing relevant evidence on social learning theory if its independent variables plainly are or can easily be interpreted as empirical measures of one or more social learning concepts, whether the authors of the research specifically identify their work as a test of differential association, social learning, or some other theory.

The magnitude of the relationships reported between these social learning variables and delinquent, criminal, and deviant behavior is seldom weak. The typical finding is one of strong to moderate effects, differing somewhat by which social learning variable is considered, by type of deviance under study, or by sample. The relationships have generally been far stronger and found more consistently than any other set of social psychological or sociodemographic variables included in the research, and there has been very little negative or counter evidence reported in the literature.

Many of the studies include one or more indicators of definitions favorable and unfavorable to criminal or deviant behavior; a segment of this literature specifically tests the effects of neutralizations, a subcategory of deviance-favorable definitions, on criminal or delinquent behavior. The evidence supports the social learning hypothesis that holding definitions favorable to deviance is related to committing delinquent and criminal behavior. Neutralizations both excuse and encourage deviance; they both precede it and are retrospectively applied to behavior and then perpetuate the further development of deviance. Neutralizing, justifying definitions influence various kinds of adolescent deviance, violence, and white-collar crime. Sometimes the research is interpreted as testing a separate "neutralization theory," and much of the research measures Sykes and Matza's "techniques of neutralization" or some modification of them. The earlier studies either referred only to Sykes and Matza or to Sutherland (Ball, 1968; Austin, 1977; Minor, 1980; 1984). The later research conceptualizes neutralization as part of social learning theory (Hollinger, 1991; Agnew, 1994; Dabney, 1995). Bandura's (1977b) social learning "mechanisms of moral disengagement," which are essentially synonymous with neutralizing definitions favorable to deviance, have also been found to have significant effects on delinquent behavior.

A number of researchers have directly compared or tested social learning theory against other theories (usually social bonding and strain theories) using the same data collected from the same samples. All of this research finds that the social learning variables have stronger direct and net effects on criminal or delinquent behavior than variables taken from the other theories (Conger, 1976; Johnson, 1979; Matsueda, 1982; Matsueda and Heimer, 1987; White et al., 1986; Kandel and Davies, 1991; McGee, 1992; Benda, 1994; and Burton et al., 1994; see also my research directly comparing social learning and other theories in Chapters 7 and 10). Similarly, when social learning variables are included in integrated or combined models that incorporate variables from different theories, it is the social learning variables that have the strongest main and net effects (Elliott et al., 1985; Kaplan et al., 1987; Kaplan, 1996; Thornberry et al., 1994; Catalano and Hawkins, in press; Catalano et al., 1996). Research on expanded deterrence models, showing the strong effects of moral evaluations (definitions favorable and unfavorable toward deviance), actual or anticipated informal social sanctions, and measures of anticipated reward as well as risk of penalty (differential social reinforcement) on an individual's commission of crime or delinquency, also provides support for social learning theory (Anderson et al. 1977; Meier and Johnson, 1977; Jensen et al., 1978; Grasmick and Green, 1980; Paternoster et al., 1983; Lanza-Kaduce, 1988; Stafford and Warr, 1993; Decker et al., 1993).

It is most common in the research to concentrate on the social learning variables operative in peer interactions (as discussed below). But there is also abundant evidence to show the significant impact on deviant behavior of learning in the family, especially in the early years but also during adolescence (Kandel, 1996). The family usually serves as a conventional socializer against delinquency and crime. It provides anti-criminal definitions, conforming models, and the reinforcement of conformity through parental discipline; it promotes the development of self-control. In the differential association process in primary groups, the family most often weighs in on the side of conformity. But deviant behavior may be the outcome of internal family interaction, and parental deviance and criminality is predictive of the children's future delinquency and crime (McCord, 1991a; McCord, 1991b). (See Chapter 6 on delinquency prediction.) Antisocial, troublesome, and delinquent behavior on the part of children is directly affected by deviant parental models, ineffective and erratic parental supervision, inconsistent discipline in the use of positive and negative sanctions, and the endorsement of values and attitudes favorable to deviance. Patterson and his associates have shown that the operation of social learning mechanisms in parent-child interaction is a strong predictor of conforming/deviant behavior. Their research supports Patterson's "coercion" model, which proposes that aggressiveness and coercive techniques in interpersonal relationships are learned in the family primarily through negative reinforcement that operates according to the matching law of reinforcement. The antisocial patterns carry over into later delinquent and deviant behavior, and are especially likely to occur when reinforced in a peer context (Patterson, 1975; 1995; Patterson et al., 1992; Snyder and Patterson, 1995; Dishion et al., 1992). In some cases, parents directly train their children to engage in deviant behavior (Adler and Adler, 1978).

Moreover, youngsters with delinquent siblings in the family are more likely to be delinquent, even when parental and other family characteristics are taken into account. Brothers and sisters are involved in differential association as family members and, if the age difference is not too great, as peers (Rowe and Gulley, 1992; Lauritsen, 1993). The effect of parents is often tested in conjunction with the effect of peers. There is some evidence that low levels of parental support are conducive to a greater influence of delinquent peers (Conger, 1976; Poole and Regoli, 1979; Patterson and Dishion, 1985) and that delinquent tendencies learned in the family are exacerbated by differential association with delinquent peers (Simons et al., 1994; Lauritsen, 1993).

In addition to imitation of parents, peers, and other primary-group models, research has shown a growing exposure to deviance and violence on television, and the probable effects of this in society, particularly on children (Comstock and Rubinstein, 1972; Murray et al., 1972; Pearl et al., 1982; Bandura, 1983; Donnerstein and Linz, 1995). The effect of the media is often indirect, through family, peer, and school variables (Bandura, 1983), and through the extent to which the imitated behavior has been or is likely to be directly reinforced:

> Laboratory studies have demonstrated many times that children imitate aggressive behavior immediately after they have seen it on film or television. . . . Several . . . field studies [provide] important support for the learning of behaviors from the observation of models. . . . [V]icarious reinforcements—either reward or punishment—can influence the behavior's occurrence. The persistence of the behavior, however, seems to be related to the children's own reinforcement. (Pearl et al., 1982:38)

Research on the imitative and other effects of televised violence has found that "(a) it teaches aggressive styles of conduct; (b) it alters restraints over aggressive behavior; (c) it desensitizes and habituates people to violence; and (d) it shapes people's image of reality, upon which they base many of their actions" (Bandura, 1983:8). Exposure to violent rape depictions in magazines, videos, and books have a strong effect on rape (Boeringer et al., 1991), and imitative effects on homicide arise from violent events portrayed in the media (Phillips, 1982; 1983). Observing salient models in primary groups and in the media affects both deviant behavior and such pro-social behavior as altruism, friendliness, cooperation, self-control, and delaying gratification (Rushton, 1980; 1982).

The vast majority of the relevant studies have been conducted in the United States. That social learning is not a culture-bound or society-specific explanation of deviance, however, is attested to by confirming cross-cultural research in Israel, Ireland, Europe, Taiwan, and China (Kandel and Adler, 1982; Lee, 1989; Junger-Tas, 1992; Bruinsma, 1992; Nolan, 1994; Zhang and Messner, 1995).

Differential peer association is the social learning variable that is most commonly measured in crime and delinquency research. Most of the work cited above includes some measure of peer association as an independent variable. While it is often the only social learning variable in a study, research reported in the past decade is more likely to include measures of other social learning variables as well. Most often, peer association has the strongest effect of any single variable on crime and deviance,

especially adolescent deviance. Other than one's own prior deviant behavior, the best single predictor of the onset and the continuance or desistance of criminal and delinquent activity is differential association
with conforming or law-violating peers. (See Chapter 6 on delinquency
prediction.) More frequent, longer-term, and closer association with
peers who do not commit or support deviant behavior is strongly correlated with conformity, while a greater ratio of associations with peers
who engage in and approve of delinquency is predictive of one's own delinquent behavior. It is in peer groups that the first availability of drugs
and opportunity for delinquent acts are typically provided, and delinquency is most frequently committed in the company of peers. Virtually
every study that includes a peer association variable finds it to be significantly and strongly related to delinquency, alcohol and drug use and
abuse, crime, and other forms of deviant behavior.

> Perhaps the most consistent finding in the literature on the causes of delin-
> quency is that adolescents with delinquent peers are more likely to be delin-
> quent themselves. In most research, the relationship of delinquent peers to
> delinquency exceeds that of any other independent variable. And in certain of
> the longitudinal research, delinquent peers is the only independent variable—
> other than prior delinquency—to have a nontrivial effect on subsequent delin-
> quency. . . . As a result of this effect, it is now a matter of routine for research-
> ers to include a measure of delinquent peers in their studies. And much of the
> research designed to prevent and control delinquency has come to focus on
> this variable. (Agnew, 1991a:47)

This impact of differential peer association is found so routinely that
it is no overstatement to say that it is among the most fully substantiated
and replicated findings in criminological research. Only the well-known
relationships of crime rates to basic sociodemographic variables like age
and sex are as consistently reported in the literature. While any research
finding a relationship between differential association with conforming
and deviant peers supports social learning theory, the theory is bolstered
further by findings that the effects of peer association are not limited to
exposure to delinquent definitions, but involve their additive and inter-
active behavior effects with imitation and reinforcement (Agnew, 1991a;
Warr and Stafford, 1991).

> Although Sutherland did not limit his theory to peer influence, tests of the
> theory have conventionally examined the correlation between self-reported de-
> linquency and the number of delinquent friends reported by adolescents. That

association has proven to be among the most consistently reported findings in the delinquency literature. . . . Tests of the theory also consistently indicate, however, that attitude transference is not the sole or even primary mechanism of transmission (see Warr and Stafford, 1991), lending support to the behaviorist or social learning reformulation of the theory developed by Burgess and Akers (1966: see also Akers, 1985). (Warr, 1993b:19)

While this relationship between peer association and delinquency is seldom disputed, some have attempted to explain it away or to downplay its significance. One approach is to assert that it is simply a methodological artifact; another is to dismiss any causal significance of peer associations. The latter argument holds that the relationship results only from deviant peers seeking out other deviant peers with whom to associate. This criticism is typically stated as "Birds of a feather flock together" (Glueck and Glueck, 1950; Hirschi, 1969; Gottfredson and Hirschi, 1990; Sampson and Laub, 1993). It is sometimes broadened to declare that social learning theory proposes only one-way linear causation, not only for the peer association variable but for the other social learning variables as well (Thornberry, 1989; Thornberry et al., 1994; Krohn et al., 1996).

Is the Delinquency–Differential Peer Association Relationship No More Than a Methodological Artifact?

Some commentators dismiss the strong relationship between self-reported delinquency and peer associations as arising entirely or mainly from the fact that these associations are often measured by the individual's report of the delinquency of his or her friends. Since the respondents also report their own behavior, the two questions essentially measure the same phenomenon twice. The researcher is measuring the respondents' own delinquent involvement, whether they are asked about the delinquency of their friends or about their own delinquency. But research shows that the two are not the same and that a respondent's reports of friends' behavior does not simply reflect his or her own delinquent behavior; the relationship is not just the result of correlating two indicators of the same dependent variable (Menard and Elliott, 1990; Elliott and Menard, 1991; Agnew, 1991b; Warr, 1993b; Thornberry et al., 1994).

Gottfredson and Hirschi (1990:157) claimed that asking respondents to report peer delinquency is nothing more than "another measure of self-reported delinquency." Warr (1993b:37) specifically examined this position and gave the following response:

> A careful examination casts doubt on the validity of these arguments, especially as they pertain to the NYS [National Youth Survey]. First, it may well be true that respondents are frequently witnesses to or participants in the delinquent acts of their friends. But how does this undermine the accuracy of respondents' reports? If the contention is true, it would seem to substantiate rather than undermine the validity of peer measures. Then, too, it is difficult to understand why respondents in the NYS would feel a need to impute their own behavior to their peers when respondents were asked about their own behavior at a point in the interview *well after* they have been questioned about their peers.... Finally, it is not clear why respondents' reports about their peers should be any less reliable than their reports about their teachers or parents, information that is routinely utilized by control theorists.

Thornberry and his colleagues (1994) have also considered in detail the issue of tautological measurement producing the strong relationship between one's own and peers' behavior; they reach similar conclusions:

> Gottfredson and Hirschi (1990:156–57) suggest that the observed correlation between peer delinquency and self-reported delinquency may exist because respondents' reports of their friends' delinquency is another measure of self-reported delinquency, since the two measures typically contain questions about the same behaviors. If their argument is correct, then factor analyzing the items used to create the indices should result in the identification of one factor with all or most of the items loading on that item. This is not the case for our data, however; as a result of a factor analysis using maximum-likelihood estimation procedures with oblique rotation, all the peer delinquency items loaded on one factor, and the self-reported delinquency items either loaded on a second factor or did not meet the criterion level (.40) on either factor. As further evidence that the two measures are not measuring the same construct, the correlation coefficients range from .50 to .59 over the three times. Although strong, these coefficients do not suggest that the two measures are identical. Similar findings have been reported by Agnew (1991a:56; 1991b:144) and by Reed and Rose (1991:16). An alternative way to address Gottfredson and Hirschi's argument is to use a measure reflecting peer misbehavior that does not contain items overlapping with those of the self-reported delinquency measure in the analysis. (Thornberry et al., 1994:62)

> The central point, however, is that this analysis does not support Gottfredson and Hirschi's contention that the relationship between delinquent peers and self-reported delinquency is simply a methodological artifact. When the behavioral overlap is eliminated, the hypothesized structural effects are still observed. (Thornberry et al., 1994:70)

Kandel (1996) points to some evidence that the strength of the relationship between one's own and one's friends' delinquency may be overestimated (and parental effects on delinquency underestimated) by how the variables are measured. She proposes that the magnitude of the correlations between differential peer association and one's own delinquency is increased by perceptual and attributional effects in the measures that depend on the respondents' reports of peer behavior. The relationship is weaker when the behavior of peers is measured separately from the respondent's perception of peer behavior, but it still remains the strongest predictor of delinquency (Kandel, 1978).

There is a certain amount of pluralistic ignorance in peers' perceptions of one another's behavior and attitudes, and one's own behavioral tendency will color observation and interpretation of what others do and say. Even close friends do not spend all their time in each other's company, and what one observes others doing and hears them say in that context may be overgeneralized to extend to how they behave when alone or away from their friends and what values they espouse. If delinquent behavior and expressions of approving or permissive attitudes toward it are more probable in the company of peers, then one's perceptions that grow out of that experience may overestimate the level of peer involvement in delinquent patterns. But this perception is itself important in the peer effect on delinquent behavior. Even if peer behavior is misperceived as more (or less) delinquent than it actually is, the peer influence will still come through that perception. The actual behavior and values of peers is important, but in the impact on the youth's deviant or conforming tendencies it may be no more important than his or her perception of peer behavior and values.

In deterrence research, we have learned that the perception of the level of risk of apprehension and the severity of legal sanctions for criminal behavior is usually inaccurate. Behavior matches the perception more closely than objective indicators of legal risk and sanctions. In research on strain theory, the perceptions of blocked opportunity and relative deprivation are more significant than actual or absolute opportunities and deprivation. In the same vein, Jussim and Osgood (1989), in a study of incarcerated delinquents, found that respondents did not accurately estimate their friends' attitudes and values as reported by the friends themselves and that respondents overestimated their similarity with friends. But they also found strong evidence of the influence of those subjective perceptions on one's own attitudes.

Research on Reciprocal and Feedback Effects in the Social Learning Process

Gottfredson and Hirschi (1990:154–59), following earlier statements by the Gluecks and Hirschi, also dismiss the findings on peer associations by asserting that prolonged contact with deviant peers simply confirms the old adage "Birds of a feather flock together" (see similar assertions by Sampson and Laub, 1993). If this assertion is intended only to note that similarity in delinquent or conforming behavior plays a role in choices adolescents make about their associates, it is self-evident, non-controversial, and not in the least inconsistent with social learning theory. But this does not appear to be the intent; rather, it is to discount all but trivial effects of peer association on delinquent behavior. The implication is that such associations are typically (if not always) a consequence rather than a cause of one's own deviant behavior—that any relationship of the behavior of peers to one's own actions comes from the effects of choice of friends rather than from the influence of friends on one's actions. Young people become delinquent first, and then seek out other delinquent youths; they continue or discontinue those relationships depending on whether they continue in criminal pursuits regardless of peers' behavior. It is not that delinquent associations cause delinquency, but that delinquency causes delinquent associations. The only, or at least main, function of the peer group is to "ease" or "facilitate acts that would be too difficult or dangerous to do alone" (Gottfredson and Hirschi, 1990:159). If it were not for this easing and facilitating function of the group, deviant acts would be largely committed alone and without reference to friends' behavior. This denies that deviance-relevant learning takes place in peer groups. Individuals do not learn attitudes or behavior in peer groups, and the effects of modeling or peer reinforcement of behavior are insignificant. The clear implication of this position is that peer associations take place only or largely after adolescents have already separately and individually established a pattern of deviant behavior and then choose delinquent peers simply because they have the same behavior in common. The peer associations, therefore, have no independent or causal effect on the individual's behavioral patterns anywhere in the process. Association with delinquent friends does not affect either the onset or the acceleration, the continuation or the cessation, of delinquent behavior.

Stated in this rather stark fashion, the birds-of-a-feather argument is out of line with the empirical evidence. If it is not taken in this unequivocal sense, but understood only as a colorful way of saying that peer associations involve both selection by behavioral homophily and peer influence on behavior, then it is inconsistent neither with the empirical evidence nor with social learning theory. As I demonstrated in Chapter 3, the reciprocal relationship between one's own conduct and association with friends is recognized in social learning theory. Therefore, the fact that delinquent behavior may precede the association with delinquent peers does not contradict the theory, provided that there is evidence of modeling, reinforcement, and behavioral or normative peer influence after the association has begun. "Social learning admits that birds of a feather do flock together, but it also admits that if the birds are humans, they also will influence one another's behavior, in both conforming and deviant directions" (Akers, 1991:210).

As I pointed out in Chapter 3, it would contradict the theory if research demonstrates that the onset of a pattern of delinquency always or almost always antedates interaction with peers who have engaged in delinquent acts or have adhered to delinquency-favorable definitions. It would not support the theory if the research evidence were to show that whatever level of involvement in delinquent behavior preceded association with delinquent peers stayed the same or decreased rather than increased after the association. Research has not yet found any of this to be the case. Instead, the findings from several studies favor the recursive and nonrecursive process proposed by social learning theory. That is, a youngster (based on prior family, residential, behavioral, attitudinal, and other variables) associates differentially with (both influencing and being influenced by) peers who commit or are tolerant of deviant acts, learns new definitions favorable to delinquent behavior or strengthens adherence to existing ones, is exposed to deviant models that reinforce delinquency, and then initiates or increases involvement in that behavior, which goes on to influence further associations and definitions (Jessor et al., 1973; Krohn, 1974; Kandel, 1978; Andrews and Kandel, 1979; Sellers and Winfree, 1990; Agnew 1991a; Empey and Stafford, 1991; Elliott and Menard, 1991; Kandel and Davies, 1991; Warr, 1993b; Esbensen and Huizinga, 1993; Menard and Elliott, 1994; Kaplan, 1996). (See also Chapter 8, and Akers and Lee, 1996.)

Kandel and Davies (1991:442) note that "although assortive pairing plays a role in similarity among friends observed at a single point in time, longitudinal research that we and others have carried out clearly documents the etiological importance of peers in the initiation and persistence of substance use." Thornberry and his colleagues (1994:70) found that

> associating with delinquent peers tends to increase delinquency, and at least part of that effect is mediated through perceptions of positive reinforcement for delinquency. In turn, engaging in delinquency exerts a positive effect on associating with delinquent peers . . .[;] both socialization and selection processes are at play in accounting for the development of delinquency over time.

Warr (1993b) also refers to the considerable amount of research evidence that has accumulated showing that peer associations precede the development of deviant patterns (or increase the frequency and seriousness of deviant behavior once it has begun) more often than involvement in deviant behavior produces associations with deviant peers or that such associations are the result of escalations in individually developed delinquent behavior. The sequence in which delinquent behavior precedes and influences delinquent peer association does occur, however, and Warr proposes that it is "a more complex, sequential, reciprocal process: Adolescents are commonly introduced to delinquency by their friends and subsequently become more selective in their choices of friends. The 'feathering' and 'flocking' . . . are not mutually exclusive and may instead be part of a unified process" (Warr, 1993b:39). This is, of course, completely consistent with social learning theory. Menard and Elliott (1994:174) also support the process as predicted by social learning theory:

> [I]n the typical sequence of initiation of delinquent bonding and illegal behavior, delinquent bonding (again, more specifically, association with delinquent friends) usually precedes illegal behavior for those individuals for whom one can ascertain the temporal order. . . . similarly . . . weakening of belief typically preceded the initiation of illegal behavior.

The preponderance of findings thus far shows a stronger effect of peer associations on the individual's delinquent behavior. However, some research finds the stronger effects running in the other direction, while other investigations hold the relationship to be about equal, depending on measures of the independent and dependent variable and other aspects of the research methodology (see Kandel, 1996; Krohn et al., 1996).

It bears repeating that, contrary to how social learning theory has sometimes been interpreted, both peer "socialization" and "selection" effects are expected in the theory as part of the ongoing social learning process. However, a finding that there is no, or weak, "socialization" and that associations have no effect beyond "selection" would be nonsupportive of social learning theory. To a lesser extent, a finding of no selection effect in those associations over which one has some control would also be inconsistent with the theory. At this point, the evidence favors the typical process of peer associations most often preceding the onset and escalation of delinquency, rather than the process of delinquent behavior most often preceding the onset or escalation of peer association. Bear in mind that the "selection" process in choosing and interacting with friends is itself part of the social learning process. Friendships that are anticipated to be more rewarding than punishing are more apt to be initiated; those that continue on balance to be more rewarding will be sustained. Choice of friends is based on prior differential association in the family and other primary groups, which yields definitions favorable and unfavorable toward interacting with some and not others.

Thus, I take strong exception to statements like the following:

> [T]he socialization perspective, which derives from differential association and social learning theory, grants causal priority to peer associations. The selection perspective, which derives from social control theory, grants causal priority to delinquent behavior. . . . To look solely at either one of these processes as if it offered a complete explanation for human behavior is incomplete and misleading. (Thornberry et al., 1994:74–75)

In my opinion, this statement is itself incomplete and misleading.

First, it is only the critics of social learning theory who describe it as proposing a one-way, socialization-only model of delinquent behavior. The authors of the theory have never taken this position. It is fair to say that the emphasis in presentations of the theory has been on the effects of differential association on deviant behavior, and that in the research the focus has been on the impact of differential peer association on one's own delinquency. Nevertheless, Sutherland never stated, and I have never stated, that one's own delinquent behavior has no effect on one's delinquent associations. There is nothing in the theory that necessarily leads to hypothesizing only recursive effects of peer associations on the individual's behavior. In fact, as I have shown in Chapter 3 and elsewhere (Akers, 1994; 1997), social learning theory posits sequential and reciprocal effects, with the causal and temporal ordering depending on what stage of the behavioral sequence one observes. Therefore, while the expectation that peer socialization has casual effects on delinquent behavior can certainly be derived from social learning theory, it is incorrect to state that the socialization-only model has been derived from the theory "as if it offered a complete explanation for human behavior."

Those who would argue that it is simply a matter of "birds of a feather flock[ing] together" seem to be saying that it is a one-way causal process in which peer behavior or attitudes are said to have no causal effect on delinquency. The behavior is acquired and performed by individuals independently of all but incidental peer-group effects. Therefore, research finding both "selection" and "socialization" effects, rather than running counter to social learning theory, directly disputes the explanation contained in this popular aphorism.

Second, it would appear that the selection-only stance is mainly a way of making a critical counterpoint to social learning theory, rather than being driven by or directly derived from social control theory. It is clear that the selection-only model has been most often used by control theorists as a critique of social learning theory. Nonetheless, it has yet to be shown just how the selection model has been logically "derived" from or predicted by control theory. The Gluecks' birds-of-a-feather criticism of differential association was characterized by Hirschi (1969:136–37) as an "apt formulation of a central assumption of control theories." Hirschi may have seen it as central to control theories, but the Gluecks took an eclectic approach, and one is hard-pressed to characterize their comments as constituting or reflecting any particular theory. Further, he saw the assumption of "a causal ordering opposite to that assumed by differential association theorists" as only one of "two approaches to this question within control theory." Hirschi's version of control theory prefers the second approach, which is to "take the question of causal ordering

as less crucial, suggesting that the relationship between gang membership (or the delinquency of companions) and delinquency is *spurious"*
because both are the result of the same cause—loss of stakes in conformity (Hirschi, 1969:138; emphasis added). Thus, social bonding theory
sees no causal effects either way, whether of one's own delinquency on
peer associations or of peer associations on one's own delinquency. The
theory would predict that there is no more than a correlational relationship between peer association and delinquency. Whether such a relationship comes from selection or socialization, then, is a moot issue in social
bonding theory.

The two approaches Hirschi identified as both falling within control
theory, therefore, seem logically contradictory. The proposition that one's
individually developed delinquency causes peer associations is directly
contrary to the proposition that any relationship between the two is
"spurious," without any causal significance. Both cannot be true, and
both cannot be derived from the same theory. Gottfredson and Hirschi's
(1990) self-control theory also takes the spuriousness approach to the
question; both delinquent behavior and delinquent associations emanate
from the same low-self-control cause. If a theory rules that a relationship
between two variables is spurious, how can one derive causal-order
hypotheses from that theory?

The emphasis in social learning theory is on differential association
and exposure to deviant and conforming models, definitions, and reinforcement as causes of individual conforming or deviant behavior. At the
same time, the deviant behavior itself is not viewed as all effect and no
cause. In differential reinforcement, the behavior is conceptualized as
provoking or inducing reinforcing or negative consequences that in turn
have a feedback effect on the future repetition of the behavior. One's own
behavior and attitudes are conceptualized as not only being affected by,
but also having an effect on, the behavior and attitudes of one's friends.
The effects of conforming or deviant behavior on the social learning variables are specifically included in the theory.

It is fair to say that the social learning theory of deviance is not focused on what causes selection of friends. Therefore, research finding
only or principally peer "socialization" effects with little or no "selection" effects would be more supportive of the theory than research finding the opposite. On the other hand, if research were to find that the

relationship between one's own behavior and that of one's peers resulted only or primarily from the tendency of deviant individuals to seek one another out, with little or no peer-group effect on the behavior itself, it could not be taken as evidence in favor of social bonding or self-control theory, since both would explain the relationship as spurious. I am not sure what theory of crime and deviance would be supported by such a finding.

Thus, as I have stated for many years and have shown precisely in Chapter 4, social learning theory is *not* simply a theory of one-way causation of peer influence or other variables. The impact of other primary and reference groups is taken into account, as is the life-cycle stage (see Chapter 12). The shaping of one's behavior by the behavior and reactions of peers should occur most evidently during the adolescent years. Earlier, the primary group of most importance should be the family. Later, as one grows older and gains more control over his or her environment, including selection of residence, spouse, occupation, organizations, and friends, the more likely it is that associations will reflect homophily of behavior than the similarity of behavior growing out of the associations.

Conclusion

The research record so far provides empirical verification of social learning theory. It may be that significant counterevidence will be found in future reasearch that requires the theory be abandoned or substantively modified. This has not happened yet. As I have shown both here and in Chapter 4, the criticisms of the theory have not been substantiated logically or empirically. Almost all of the studies done so far that include adequate measures of social learning variables have produced favorable findings. I stand ready to be corrected, but I do not believe that there is any other general explanation of criminal, delinquent, and deviant behavior that has been so consistently and strongly supported by the empirical evidence over so long a period. This conclusion is based on the large number of studies cited in this chapter, on the research on delinquency prediction reviewed in Chapter 6, and on my own research, which will be presented in the following chapters.

6

Social Learning Variables in Delinquency Prediction

Introduction

DELINQUENCY PREDICTION AND SOCIAL LEARNING THEORY

As was shown in Chapter 5 and as will be pointed out in subsequent chapters, a body of cross-sectional and longitudinal research (both my own and that conducted by others) has developed that, both directly and indirectly, tests the tenets of the social learning theory of crime and deviance. The preponderance of evidence from this research supports the hypotheses that differential reinforcement, differential association, definitions, and modeling, mainly involving peer groups and the family, are strongly related to delinquency. Little negative or counterevidence has been found in these investigations.

Some of the research, including my own, is longitudinal. From that research, one could conclude that social learning variables are relatively good predictors of future delinquency. However, there has been little effort in my own or others' research on social learning to fit the findings specifically into the long-standing and substantial body of "delinquency prediction" research that had developed specifically to predict delinquency in adolescence from variables measured in earlier years.

Further, little of the prediction literature refers specifically to learning theory. Indeed, although some of the prediction studies have started from fairly strong theoretical bases, much of the work has involved essentially atheoretical efforts to locate whatever predictors can be found in the data (most of the time official) at hand. No theory can take great comfort from the findings of prediction research, because even the best predictive models contain a sizable amount of predictive error. Nonetheless, I propose that among the best delinquency predictors are variables that obviously are, or can be shown to be, reasonably valid indicators of social learning theory.

More than thirty years ago, Daniel Glaser (1960:7) was able to show that the most accurate predictors of parole outcome and criminal recidivism were "reasonable indices" of the modalities of differential association. Among the most accurate predictors were predominance of criminal or delinquent associates (as measured by prior delinquent companions and gang membership) and relative isolation from pro-social or anti-delinquent associations (as measured by alienation from parents and schools). Also, priority of delinquent associations (as measured by age of first arrest), and frequency, duration, and intensity of delinquent/criminal associations (as measured by number of previous arrests, convictions, and incarcerations), were at the top of the list of predictors of future delinquency and crime.

Having reviewed the classical and most recent studies in delinquency prediction, I propose that Glaser's conclusions of many years ago apply to all of the principal components of social learning theory—differential association, differential reinforcement, imitation, and definitions. I do not claim here that the predictive variables were intended by the original researchers to be indicators of learning variables. Nor do I claim that all of the best predictive variables fit uniquely into a social learning framework. The claim only is that the prediction findings fit very well into the social learning model, as well or better than any alternative theory.

The focus of this review is on research designed specifically to use variables measured at an earlier time, in either a retrospective or prospective longitudinal design, to predict the onset, frequency, or continuation of delinquent behavior at a later time. I am not asserting that longitudinal research is the only, or even the best, methodology for testing explanations of delinquency. Longitudinal data will not necessarily resolve the theoretical and causal issues left unsolved by cross-sectional data. Gottfredson and Hirschi (1987; 1990) have presented cogent analyses of problems with longitudinal and career-research strategies on crime and delinquency. Nonetheless, when we say "prediction" we generally mean predicting behavior before it occurs, and this implies some measure of explanatory variables taken at one point and some measure of the outcome variables at a later time. In this chapter I concentrate on studies predicting delinquency during the adolescent years, although some of the studies carry over into the adult years.

THE EARLY IDENTIFICATION AND PREVENTION PHILOSOPHY

The basic idea that it is possible, and indeed practical, to identify the potential for delinquency and crime at an early age, predict future deviancy from that identification, and effectively intervene to forestall, delay, or prevent it altogether has a long history. Both early identification and prevention were proposed long ago and have been attempted many times since (Horn, 1986; McCord and Tremblay, 1992). While progress has been made, neither prediction nor prevention efforts have produced a clear record of achievement.

> Although as early as 1920 it was recognized that behavior problems in school-aged children predict criminal behavior in adults, researchers have yet to develop effective strategies for intervening in childhood to prevent later delinquency and crime. . . . This limited success in preventing crime reflects no lack of interest in the issue in the first half of this century. . . . In spite of enthusiastic interest from the 1910's through the 1930's in applying the knowledge that the misbehaving child might grow up to be the criminal of the future, preventing delinquency proved to be a thorny problem, and one not easily nipped in the bud. (Horn, 1986:57)

> [There] is the affirmative postulate that the discovery of and early intervention in the lives of children at risk can reduce delinquency and later criminality. . . . [But] how does one discover children who are either overtly manifesting delinquency tilt or are in peril of delinquency as indicated through identifiable signals? . . . Who discovers these children and by what criteria? Once at-risk children are discovered, who can intervene and with what remedial strategies, raising what legal and constitutional questions? (Dutile et al., 1982:7)

Delinquency prediction studies, from the earliest to the most recent, have had to confront methodological and theoretical issues that are not yet resolved. What is to be predicted and which predictors are the most valid? How do we explain change and stability in delinquency over time? What methodological strategies (sampling, data collection, and analysis) are best suited to validating predictors, and at what cost? Similarly, both early and more recent prevention/intervention programs have had to confront difficult ethical, legal, and political issues. What are the most effective intervention/prevention techniques? Is it ethical or constitutional to intervene in individuals' lives to prevent them from committing illegal acts that they have yet to commit? Can behaviorally effective and cost-effective strategies be devised that provide positive, noncoercive programs for populations, programs that do not negatively label or identify individuals? Monahan (1982) noted some years ago that selecting possible predictive factors and intervention techniques is more a matter of public policy than of science. He maintained at the time that we probably have good enough knowledge to justify and support positive, voluntary pre-emptive intervention, but probably not knowledge good enough for coercive, involuntary intervention. Research and experience with prevention programs since then only serves to confirm that this conclusion is still applicable today (McCord and Tremblay, 1992; Hawkins et al., 1992b).

FALSE POSITIVES, FALSE NEGATIVES, AND DOING BETTER THAN CHANCE IN DELINQUENCY PREDICTION

The outcome predicted may be general delinquency, serious delinquency, recidivism (stable delinquency), reduction, or desistance (cessation). At one time the outcome was ordinarily gauged by official contact with the juvenile or criminal-justice system, but it has become common to measure self-reported delinquency; in a few cases the delinquent outcome variable is indexed by both official and unofficial measures (e.g., West and Farrington, 1973; Dunford and Elliott, 1984; Elliott, 1994). The best predictors of delinquency should be able to differentiate between those persons who are at high risk and those who are at low risk, with a minimum of errors both in false positives (individuals predicted to be delinquent who do not become so) and in false negatives (individuals predicted not to be delinquent who become delinquent). Also, the higher the base rate (proportion of the sample actually having been arrested or having committed delinquent acts within the period of the study), the better the chance that any variable or set of variables will correctly predict a delinquent outcome in that sample. That is, the same variables will score as more accurate predictors in a sample with a high base rate than in a sample with a low base rate. The proportion of the sample predicted to be delinquent is the selection rate (or selection ratio).

The RIOC. A technique called the Relative Improvement Over Chance (RIOC) developed by Loeber and his associates (Loeber and Stouthamer-Loeber, 1986; 1987; Loeber and Dishion, 1983; 1987) allows evaluation of the accuracy of a predictor variable that takes into account valid and false predictions, base rate, and selection rate. The RIOC approach offers an accurate and intuitively interpretable way of calculating the predictive efficacy of individual variables or factors beyond what would be expected simply by chance as determined by the base and selection rates. Poor predictors will have an RIOC coefficient of close to 0, while the better predictors will have an RIOC coefficient closer to 1.

The RIOC can always be figured from raw data, but it can be calculated from published tabular data only when the numerical or percentage frequencies on both the predictive and delinquency outcome variables are reported. These are placed in a two-by-two table with a dichotomous predictor (predicted to be delinquent or nondelinquent) and a dichotomous outcome measure (actually delinquent or nondelinquent). It is from this table that false and valid positive and negative predictions and the other values needed to solve the RIOC equation are computed. The RIOC is calculated by subtracting the percentage of all predictions that would be correct by random chance from the percentage of predictions that were actually correct, then dividing that result by the difference between the maximum percentage of the predictions that could be correct and the percentage that would be correct by random chance. The maximum and random probabilities are calculated from the base rate (actual percentage of delinquents in the sample) and the selection rate (percentage of those in the sample predicted to be delinquent).

Pioneering Delinquency Prediction Studies

During the post-depression era, there were several attempts to identify children who were at risk of becoming delinquent in order to target them for prevention or intervention programs. The most notable of these early efforts at delinquency prediction were the Gluecks' studies, the Cambridge-Somerville Youth Study, and Hathaway's MMPI studies. The outcomes of these pioneering efforts to predict delinquency remain significant today because they both identified some of the same important variables and adumbrated some of the same significant problems that have characterized almost all subsequent prediction research.

The most cited and widely known, yet most criticized, of the early investigations were Sheldon and Eleanor Glueck's work in delinquency research (Glueck and Glueck, 1950; Glueck and Glueck, 1959; Glueck and Glueck, 1968; Glueck and Glueck, 1970; Glueck and Glueck, 1974). Over four decades, the Gluecks studied retroactively 500 institutionalized delinquents and a comparison group of 500 nondelinquents. Working from the observed differences in the groups, they developed a Social Prediction Table containing five (later three) family variables "with a view to determining the bases for truly crime-preventive programs and effective therapy" (Glueck and Glueck, 1950:ix) by identifying potential delinquents at five or six years of age (Glueck and Glueck, 1970). The five-factor prediction scale was (1) affection of the mother for her son, (2) affection of the father for his son, (3) discipline of the boy by his father, (4) supervision of the boy by his mother, and (5) family cohesiveness. (Their revised scale consisted only of the last three factors.) At a later stage of their studies, the Gluecks used this three-factor prediction device for transforming the delinquency risk categories into clinical types.

Their research was sponsored by Harvard Law School and funded by several foundations. It was an expensive multidisciplinary project that involved "no fewer than ten trained social investigators, a psychiatrist-physician, two physical anthropologists, six psychologists, two Rorschach Test analysts, two statisticians, a secretarial staff of eight, and an editorial assistant" (Glueck and Glueck, 1974:15). In short, it was a large-scale, in-depth study needing a level of funding that very few researchers could secure at the time.

The prestige of their backers, the depth of financial support for their work, and the intensive nature of their research did not prevent problems, however. The Gluecks' studies were severely criticized at the time and later for conceptual and methodological shortcomings (Reiss, 1951b; Rubin, 1951; Shaplin and Tiedman, 1951; Toby, 1965; Voss, 1963; Hirschi and Selvin, 1967; Monahan, 1981; Gottfredson and Hirschi, 1987). The selection of the delinquent sample from an incarcerated population was not representative of delinquents in general, nor was the selection of nondelinquents in the comparison group representative of that general population. Matching the number of delinquents with an equal number of nondelinquents ignored the base-rate factor (10% is closer to the actual distribution of habitual delinquency in the general population than is the 50% rate in the Gluecks' study) and overestimated the efficacy of the prediction factors. It is also problematic to generalize retroactively from differences obtained between delinquents and nondelinquents at age 14 to factors operating among children at the ages of 5 or 6. That is, the Gluecks' studies have the same problem as any retrospective research—namely, trying to identify which of the features of family life, parental discipline, and present characteristics of incarcerated delinquents preceded, and which of the features resulted from, their involvement in delinquency.

The most telling criticisms were directed toward the fairly low predictive utility of the Social Prediction Scale. The Gluecks included only family variables in the scale because they believed that it was important to measure predictors as early as possible (at least by the first grade) and that the family variables were the only important ones at so young an age. The problem is that this strategy has predictive utility only if one assumes no subsequent changes take place in the child's life closer to the time of the onset of delinquency that would alter the prediction based on his or her family circumstances at an early age (Toby, 1963). Indeed, there are delinquency-related events like association with deviant peers and negative school experiences that typically occur well after the first grade. Thus, the Gluecks' scale omitted the strongest correlates of delinquency found in their own research, all of which come into effect after age 5 or 6. The variable most strongly related to delinquent behavior in their sample was association with delinquent companions, followed by truancy and misbehaving in school (Glaser, 1960). The Gluecks did not include these variables in their prediction table because they could not be measured at age 5 or 6 and because they believed them to be only effects, not causes, of delinquency.

Perhaps owing to the failure to consider important events that occur later in childhood, prospective studies have had limited success in demonstrating that scores on the Social Prediction Scale obtained at the age recommended by the Gluecks actually predict subsequent delinquent behavior (Craig and Glick, 1963; Toby, 1965; Voss, 1963; Tait and Hodges,

1972). The problems are probably best illustrated by the results of the prediction study carried out by the New York City Youth Board between 1952 and 1959 (Toby, 1965; Voss, 1963).

This study was conducted on a sample of 223 boys selected from the first grade in two schools located in high delinquency areas, with predominantly black and Puerto Rican populations. The home life of the boys (parental affection, discipline, cohesion) in the first year of the study was assessed by social workers making in-home visits. The boys were followed for seven years, and any official known delinquency was recorded. At first, the predictions were based on the original five-factor Glueck scale (which predicted that 67 boys would be delinquent by age 13); later, the scales were revised to include two or three factors, which lowered the number of boys predicted to be delinquent to 37. The five-factor scale was wrong (false positives) in 75% of the cases predicted to be delinquent, and it led to more errors than when predictions were based only on the single factor of the welfare status of the boys' families. The revised two-factor and three-factor scales did better, mistakenly predicting delinquency (false positives) in 65% of the cases (Toby, 1965). But even these reduced-factor scales did no better than simply making the general prediction that all of the boys in the study would be nondelinquent (Voss, 1963).

In spite of its methodological problems, and the low effectiveness of the Gluecks' prediction scales, their research has been widely recognized as the first major step in delinquency prediction and has influenced virtually all subsequent prediction studies. *Unraveling Juvenile Delinquency* became the second most frequently cited book in criminology published between 1945 and 1972 (Wolfgang et al., 1978:38), and the data collected fifty years ago are still being used in various ways today (Sampson and Laub, 1993). More recent longitudinal research, while not supporting the Gluecks' prediction scale as such, have found family variables to be significant predictors of delinquency.

THE CAMBRIDGE-SOMERVILLE YOUTH STUDY

While the Gluecks were conducting their research, a project to prevent delinquency by offering troubled children the opportunity to develop a friendship with an adult counselor, the Cambridge-Somerville Youth Study, was under way. A total of 650 boys—325 in the treatment group and 325 in the control group—participated in the project, beginning in

1937. The groups were matched according to physical health, intelligence, emotional adjustment, home background, neighborhood, and "delinquency prognosis"—the latter determined by ratings made by teachers, psychologists, psychiatrists, and social workers for each boy. Both the initial evaluation and a long-term evaluation ten years after the project ended (Powers and Witmer, 1951; McCord and McCord, 1959) found that it did not prevent delinquency.

The analysis of the project by the McCords included a major evaluation of the "origins" of crime. It used data collected on the treatment and control groups at the time the boys came into the project and measured their delinquent/criminal outcomes up to 17 years later. Thus, it was a prospective study, perhaps the first such comprehensive work in delinquency research. Follow-up outcome data were collected on official delinquent/criminal convictions or incarceration (ages 13–22+) for 253 subjects in the control and treatment groups. Information on intelligence, social environment, family variables, and parents' character was recorded for each boy at the time of his participation in the project.

The McCords found no significant relationship between measured childhood intelligence and subsequent delinquent behavior nor between the child's general health and criminal tendencies. They found, moreover, that other cultural factors, such as parents' level of education or degree of religiosity, did not have a significant relation to the boys' delinquency. The McCords did find, however, that participating in youth gangs was a major factor in predicting crime. They concluded that "it is the basic socialization process in the early years of life which determines whether a boy will be prone to criminal acts" (McCord and McCord, 1959:73).

Following the Gluecks' lead, the McCords examined parental discipline as one of the factors in the basic socialization process. They found that consistent parental discipline, whether administered lovingly or punitively, decreased the chances of criminality, while erratic discipline proved harmful. Both paternal and maternal attitudes, as well as the parents' behavior as criminal or deviant role models, was significantly related to the boys' later proclivity to delinquency. Consistent discipline and maternal affection can negate the influence of the deviant parental models, while erratic-punitive discipline enhances the effect of deviant/criminal parental role models. Sons of criminals with loving mothers are less likely to become criminal than sons of criminals with nonloving mothers. Thus, any combination of two negative factors (nonloving parent or deviant parental model) results in sharply increased criminal rates.

The predictive utility of these variables is compromised, however, because the Cambridge-Somerville Youth Study encountered the same problem found in the Gluecks' research, namely, overprediction of delinquency. Of those predicted to be delinquent, only 37% actually turned out that way (a false positive rate of 63%). As was true for the Gluecks, the forecasts in the Cambridge-Somerville project were most accurate when predicting nondelinquent outcomes (only 12% false negatives). The overall error rate for both delinquent and nondelinquent predictions was 46%. In slum neighborhoods, prediction errors decreased (to 58%) for delinquency, but they increased (to 16%) for nondelinquency (Toby, 1965).

McCord (1991a) followed 223 boys born between 1926 and 1933 who were participants in the Cambridge-Somerville Youth Study, collecting data on them in 1948 and again between 1975 and 1980. Criminality was measured by court convictions, and only family variables were studied. Mother's competence (consistently nonpunitive, confident, and affectionate child rearing), father's interaction, and family expectations (supervision and control) were the important family factors. Poor child rearing in any of these areas increased the risk of delinquency, but the explained variance using all of the predictive factors was not high, about 12%. The same variables, but in a somewhat different configuration, were predictive of adult criminality (again with fairly low explained variance). Among sons with criminal fathers, family socialization includes both "protective" factors that work to mitigate and "instigating" factors that promote whatever tendency toward crime comes from having a criminal father (McCord, 1991b).

THE MINNESOTA MULTIPHASIC PERSONALITY INVENTORY (MMPI) PREDICTION STUDY

Both the Gluecks' and the Cambridge-Somerville studies had a decided tilt toward psychiatric assumptions about the formation of pathologies in the family and relied heavily on psychologists and psychiatric social workers. However, the studies did not depend on psychological measures; rather, they concentrated on measuring social factors in the family and, to some extent, social characteristics and interaction of the boys. The MMPI is based entirely on the assumption that delinquency is caused by psychiatric or personality problems. Originally designed in 1939 by Starke Hathaway to detect deviant personality patterns in mentally ill adults, the MMPI is a paper-and-pencil instrument made up of 550 statements that identify personality characteristics. The items retained on the instrument are those that distinguished, in the original samples, between hospitalized mental patients and nonhospitalized adults in Minnesota. Extending the use of the MMPI to analyze and predict deviant personality patterns in delinquents was based on the somewhat dubious assumption that delinquency is symptomatic of mental illness similar to adult psychiatric impairment (Hathaway and Monachesi, 1953). The MMPI uses several scales to measure "abnormal" personality traits, such as depression, hysteria, paranoia, psychopathology, introversion/extroversion, and compulsiveness (Hathaway and Meehl, 1951).

Research by Hathaway and Monachesi (1953) found that institutionalized delinquents scored higher on the scales of asocial, amoral, and psychopathic behavior, while nondelinquents tended to be more introverted. However, when they later administered the MMPI to ninth graders and followed up with a check of official records for detected delinquents among the juveniles, they found that the instrument was not very successful in predicting delinquency. Using single-scale scores, even the most predictive scale was incorrect in 76% of the cases predicted to be delinquent; combining scores from two scales produced 65% false positive predictions. Moreover, the most predictive scale, the "F" scale, was not a measure of personality at all. Rather, it scored inconsistent or careless response patterns to the MMPI items or poor reading ability in completing the instrument. The overall base rate of delinquency in the sample was 20% (80% nondelinquent), and none of the scales improved prediction over this base rate by more than 4% (Hathaway and Monachesi, 1957; 1963).

Major Prediction Research of the 1960s and 1970s

THE ST. LOUIS STUDY OF DEVIANT CHILDREN GROWN UP

This thirty-year follow-up study, by Lee Robins, Patricia O'Neal, and others, of persons who were referred to a municipal psychiatric clinic as children is not a delinquency prediction study as such and is only incidentally concerned with predicting adult crime. However, it has come to be regarded as one of the classic prospective, longitudinal studies in deviance and is frequently referred to by delinquency prediction researchers. Robins and her associates matched a sample of 524 young people from the files of a defunct psychiatric clinic with a sample of 100 normal schoolchildren. Then, through interviews and official records (police, hospital, social agencies), they collected data on both groups as adults to determine their social and psychiatric status and deviant behavior (see Robins, 1966; Robins and Hill, 1966; Robins et al., 1962). The purpose was to test the notion that "problem behavior as a child strongly predicts problem behavior as an adult" (Robins, 1966:11).

The various childhood problem behaviors considered included theft, aggression, sexual deviance, truancy, lying, and other "anti-social symptoms." Several of these behaviors and other factors were related to an adult diagnosis of sociopathic personality, but the best overall predictor was having ten or more anti-social symptoms as a juvenile (43% of the persons in this category were later diagnosed as sociopathic).

THE BIRTH COHORT STUDIES

The major investigation of the incidence and prevalence of delinquency in a birth cohort was done in Philadelphia by Wolfgang and his associates (Wolfgang et al., 1972; Wolfgang, 1983; Wolfgang et al., 1987). The cohort (born in 1945) was followed up between the ages of 10 and 18 using public school records and police contact data. The chief concerns were to track the development of delinquent behavior over time and to determine the incidence and prevalence of delinquency in the cohort.

The earlier the age at first arrest, the greater the likelihood that the young person would become a chronic offender. Race and social class were most strongly related to delinquency, to serious delinquency, and to recidivism. The other variables, among them mobility, school achievement, IQ, and type of school attended, were not related when race and class were controlled. A sample of the cohort was later followed up at age 26 with an interview and check of police records and at age 30 with a check of police records (Wolfgang et al., 1987), in which prediction of adult criminal behavior from juvenile delinquency and characteristics was of interest. First arrests and number of offenders peaked at age 16. Socioeconomic status (SES), race, and dropping out of school were strong factors in future criminality (Thornberry et al., 1985). Wolfgang and his associates studied a later Philadelphia birth cohort (born in 1958) that included both males and females and self-reported as well as official delinquency. Findings on this cohort do little to change conclusions based on the 1945 cohort (Wolfgang, 1983). There have also been cohort studies by Lyle Shannon in Racine, Wisconsin; these are less well known than the Philadelphia studies, but they bear many similarities to Wolfgang's investigations and reach similar conclusions (see Shannon, 1978; 1980; 1982).

THE CAMBRIDGE (U.K.) STUDY IN DELINQUENT DEVELOPMENT

One of the most thorough and widely cited delinquency prediction studies is that conducted in London by Donald J. West, David P. Farrington, and others. This was a long-term, prospective longitudinal investigation of urban lower-class boys, aged 8 to 14, beginning in 1961–62 and continuing with periodic data collection until 1980 (see West, 1969; West and Farrington, 1973; 1977; Farrington and West, 1981; West, 1982; Farrington, 1983; 1985). The study began with a sample of 411, and at various points in the research included interviews with the boys (at ages 21 and 24 only subsamples were studied), interviews in the home (mainly with the mother), interviews with peers, completion of questionnaires on the boys by their teachers, and search of official records. In the early stages the boys were given various ratings by peers, teachers, and social workers and were administered psychological and personality tests. West and Farrington were interested in predicting delinquency and nondelinquency in general, timing of onset, and recidivism in adolescent delinquency, as well as the relationship between delinquency and later adult offending. The study included both official (conviction) and self-report measures of delinquency and used a number of home, school, community, and behavioral variables as predictors.

A long list of variables was considered, but the main predictive factors emerging from the research were low family income, large family size, poor parental child-rearing practices, below average intelligence and school achievement, criminality by parents, delinquency by peers, and a high rating on "troublesomeness" by teachers and peers. This troublesome, acting-out behavior noted at an early age turned out to be the single best predictor for both self-reported and official delinquency. Measures of delinquent personality characteristics, neurotic tendencies, and extroverted personality types did not predict later delinquency or crime. By age 25, one-third of those in the sample had acquired a criminal conviction. Early age at first conviction was predictive of later persistent offending. Blumstein and his associates (1985) later constructed a seven-point predictive scale from the London study (early conviction, low family income, troublesomeness, low school attainment, psychomotor clumsiness, low verbal IQ, and delinquent sibling) that did a reasonable job of distinguishing between the chronic "persisters" and the desisters and innocents. West and Farrington note that even a combination of good predictors still leaves much room for prediction errors. Of the 63 boys in the study with several "adverse" factors predicting later delinquency, 31 actually became delinquent and 32 stayed out of trouble. Moreover, of the 84 boys who actually became officially delinquent by age 18, the majority (53) did not belong to the high-risk group based on the measures used and were not predicted to be delinquent.

Major Recent and Ongoing Longitudinal Research Projects

THE NATIONAL YOUTH SURVEY

The only longitudinal panel study of delinquency with a national probability sample of adolescents aged 11 to 17 in the United States was begun by Delbert Elliott and his associates in 1976 and continued at one-year intervals for five years ($N = 1,725$). (See Elliott et al., 1985; Elliott et al., 1987; Dunford and Elliott, 1984.) The cohort was picked up again later, and a total of nine waves of data were collected by 1993, when the respondents were aged 27 to 33 (Elliott, 1994; Esbensen and Elliott, 1994). Both self-report and official measures of delinquency were used. The main purpose of the study was to test causal theories of delinquency. The model that best fit the data was derived from social learning theory, doing as well as an "integrated" model that added variables from social control and anomie theory to the social learning model. The researchers also used self-reported delinquency and other measures from the first year to predict delinquent career patterns (nonoffenders, noncareer, nonserious career, and serious career) over the next four years.

Elliott's models were able to predict more than 70% of the career offenders, but they contained a high level of false positive predictions; only 22% of those predicted to be career offenders actually became so. The kind of variables that might be known to the police at time of arrest (such as age, class, place of residence, grades in school, and offense seriousness) did not produce any increase in predictive accuracy over the base rate. On the other hand, variables like peer associations, parental relationships, norms, and attitudes, taken from social learning and social control theories, did increase predictive accuracy. However, all of the variables are measured during adolescence; we do not know if the same variables measured at earlier ages would predict teenage delinquency patterns.

The National Youth Survey (NYS) research has shown that family, peer, and attitudinal measures taken in one year are predictive of the subsequent onset of violent behavior. The NYS findings reveal that minor forms of delinquent behavior and substance use precede serious criminal acts of theft and violence, with the typical behavioral sequence moving from aggravated assault to robbery and rape. Family bonding, parental sanctioning practices, and early exposure to violence (including victimization) in the family foreshadow subsequent violence primarily through their relationship to the individual's own attitudes toward deviance, peer norms, peer sanctions, and exposure to delinquent peers. These attitudinal and peer variables were the best predictors of the onset of serious violent offending in adolescence (Elliott, 1994). A similar "block" of social learning variables (exposure to drug-using friends, involvement with such friends, peer approval/disapproval of drug use, and parental approval/disapproval of drug/delinquent behavior) also are better predictors of the initiation of the use of alcohol, marijuana, and other drugs than age and demographic variables. The social learning variables are less successful in predicting desistance from use (probably because there were very few drug-using respondents who actually terminated use during the period under study). But association with drug-using peers is the single best predictor for both initiation and discontinuation of drug use (Esbensen and Elliott, 1994).

THE SEATTLE SOCIAL DEVELOPMENT MODEL

A large-scale, comprehensive longitudinal effort involving research and the prevention of delinquency and drug use was begun in Seattle in 1981 by J. David Hawkins and Joseph G. Weis. The theoretical basis for the project was labeled the Social Development Model. Subsequently, Hawkins organized and continues to direct a Social Development Research Group at the University of Washington that has carried on longitudinal research on predicting and preventing adolescent deviance. All of this has been done within the framework of the social development model that combines social learning and social bonding variables (Weis and Hawkins, 1981; Hawkins and Weis, 1985; Hawkins and Lam, 1987; Hawkins et al., 1992a; O'Donnell et al., 1993; Catalano and Hawkins, in press). The goals of the project are to explain the onset, escalation, maintenance, and cessation of delinquency and drug use and to provide intervention programs that prevent onset or facilitate de-escalation and desistance. The theoretical variables in the model are reinforcement, skills, family and peer interaction, opportunities, and pro-social and anti-social attachments, commitments, and beliefs. The intervention strategies for the early grade school years involve teacher training to modify teaching practices and parent training to produce pro-social attitudes and behavior. The school and family programs are meant to enhance social bonding and to promote opportunities, skills, and reinforcement for pro-social behavior and activities in the classroom and at home.

The intervention strategies in the family focused on management, re-strained punishment, communication, and attachment. In the school, the effort was to modify, in a pro-social direction, rewards, attachment, and commitment, and to reduce trouble in school. The strategies were directed toward changing the children's beliefs, perceptions of rewards and punishment for delinquent behavior, and pro-delinquent attitudes. By the fifth grade, the cumulative effects of having worked with the intervention group since the first grade produced significant changes in the family and school variables, compared to the control group. Furthermore, by grade five the intervention group had significantly lower levels of initiation of alcohol use and minor delinquency, although the actual percentage differences (of about 7% lower alcohol use and minor delinquency) were not large.

These findings indicate that school and family interaction, rewards and punishment, and attachment are moderately predictive of the onset of drug use and delinquency and that doing something to modify them in a pro-social direction has some measurable effect on preventing that onset. The project has provided more direct tests of the capacity of social learning and bonding variables (both protective and risk variables) measured at ages 10 to 11 to predict the onset of various forms of adolescent deviance by ages 13 to 14 among a group of boys identified as aggressive in the fifth grade. The variables were school bonding, family bonding, drug use norms, pro-social skills, association with deviant peers, and association with deviant adults. Models of these variables successfully classified three-fourths or more of the boys who subsequently became involved in and who refrained from five categories of delinquency—serious delinquency, violent behavior, theft, drug use, and sexual behavior. Family bonding variables were not related to the onset of any of these delinquent outcomes. School bonding and social skill variables were related to three of them. Drug use norms, association with deviant adults, and association with deviant peers were each significantly related to four of the five behaviors.

THE DENVER YOUTH SURVEY AND THE PITTSBURGH YOUTH STUDY

Three major longitudinal studies of correlates and predictors of delinquency in high-risk areas are under way; the investigations are funded by the Office of Juvenile Justice and Delinquency Prevention of the National Institute of Justice and by the National Institute on Drug Abuse. Two of these have reported findings that focus on predictive factors in delinquency. The first is a report by Huizinga and his associates (1991) on a project in Denver; the second is a report by Loeber and his associates (1991) on a project in Pittsburgh. Each is a multiyear project, and the results given below are based on the first two years. Findings have also appeared from the third major project, the Rochester Youth Development Study, but these reports have concentrated on the issue of reciprocal effects between social control or social learning variables and delinquent behavior, rather than on the predictive efficacy of theoretical variables (Thornberry et al., 1991; 1994).

David Huizinga and his colleagues (1991) selected a random sample of 802 boys and 728 girls from five birth cohorts (aged 7, 9, 11, 13, and 15) residing in "high risk" areas of Denver. Their report includes measures from Year 1 and Year 2 of the study. Interviews were conducted with parents/guardians and with children in the sampled households. Delinquency was measured by a standard self-reported checklist. The researchers developed a typology of family/peer environments and personal characteristics that relate to delinquency. Although delinquents come from each type of environment, some factors carry greater risk of delinquency than others, and I have combined and simplified the typology somewhat. For children 7 to 9 years old at Year 1, the typology is as follows:

1. Pro-social. This type combines two very similar groups in the Huizinga scheme. It includes those children with few or no delinquent friends who were socialized in strongly pro-social families in which parents' attitudes and socialization do not support delinquent behavior and those children who have no delinquent friends but whose parents are somewhat permissive about deviance and misconduct.

2. Pro-delinquent attitudes and beliefs. This type also combines two clusters (one appearing with very low frequency) in the Huizinga scheme. It refers to pro-social home environment of average strength or less in which the child has already developed pro-delinquent attitudes and beliefs.

3. Impulsive/hyperactive. This is a cluster of children who were reared in an average home environment but who are above average on impulsivity/hyperactivity measures.

4. Delinquent friends. The children classified in this type are from average home environments but have friends who are above average in delinquent involvement.

The clusters, or types, for young people (aged 11 to 15) defined by Huizinga and his colleagues were similar to these categories, except that the pro-delinquent attitudes clustered with delinquent friends and one type was identified that was essentially average on all variables (home, friends, attitudes, and impulsivity).

The findings for the younger age group are presented in Table 6.1a, those for the older group in Table 6.1b. The data here indicate that among children and teenagers who were not delinquent in Year 1 of the survey (Y1), those with delinquency-prone friends and holding delinquent attitudes and beliefs ran a much higher risk of becoming delinquent themselves by Year 2 (Y2). Even when the home situation was conducive to conformity, of the younger respondents who had friends who were involved in delinquency (Type 4) in Y1, 37% had committed delinquency in Y2 (40% becoming involved in low-level delinquency, 23% in high-level delinquency). Those in pro-social home environments (Type 1) were much less likely to become delinquent (with 71% remaining nondelinquent by Y2). As for the older children, although the numbers are small, 14% of those with pro-delinquent attitudes and friends were in the high-delinquency category by Y2.

Similar differences are reported for the respondents who had already become involved in delinquency in Y1. Within each type, those who had developed delinquent behavior patterns by Y1 were likely to remain involved at some level at Y2. However, they were much more likely to remain delinquent at a high level, and less likely to have reduced or desisted delinquency, by Y2 if they had delinquent friends and attitudes at Y1. Of the younger children who were higher in delinquent involvement and who also had delinquent friends in Year 1, 93% were still involved in delinquency in Y2, and more than half remained highly involved in delinquency. Similarly, 86% of the older children who were delinquent in Y1 and who held pro-delinquent attitudes and associated with delinquent friends remained delinquent at Y2; 60% remained highly involved.

Table 6.1a   Findings on Younger Group in the Denver Youth Survey

Of those aged 7–9 who were *nondelinquent* in Y1, by Y2 the percentage who were:

Year 1 Type	Not Delinquent	Low Delinquency	High Delinquency	N =
1. Pro-social home, no delinquent friends	71%	21%	9%	124
2. Pro-delinquent attitudes/beliefs	67	23	11	57
3. Impulsive/hyperactive	57	41	2	44
4. Delinquent friends	37	40	23	35

N = 260

Of those aged 7–9 who were *higher in delinquency* in Y1, by Y2 the percentage who were:

Year 2 Type	Not Delinquent	Low Delinquency	High Delinquency	N =
1. Pro-social home, no delinquent friends	22%	43%	34%	49
2. Pro-delinquent attitudes/beliefs	27	34	38	29
3. Impulsive/hyperactive	37	13	50	30
4. Delinquent friends	7	39	54	26

N = 134

SOURCE: Adapted from Huizinga et al. (1991).

In the Pittsburgh Youth Study, Loeber and his associates (1991) sampled 850 boys in each of grades 1, 4, and 7 from the city's public schools. The boys and a parent, guardian, or caretaker (almost all women, and 40% single parents) were interviewed at home. A follow-up sample weighted toward high-risk youth, with 500 in each group (equally divided between white and black children), was interviewed three times over the next year.

Relative Improvement Over Chance (RIOC) coefficients were calculated for a large number of factors correlated with the onset or continua-

Table 6.1b   Findings on Older Group in the Denver Youth Survey

Of those aged 11–15 who were *nondelinquent* at Y1, by Y2 the percentage who were:

Year 1 Type	Not Delinquent	Low Delinquency	High Delinquency	N =
1. Pro-social	69%	29%	2%	164
2. Average	58	31	10	67
3. Impulsive/hyperactive	57	33	10	51
4. Pro-delinquent attitudes and delinquent friends	57	28	14	7

N = 289

Of those aged 11–15 who were *higher in delinquency* at Y1, by Y2 the percentage who were:

Year 2 Type	Not Delinquent	Low Delinquency	High Delinquency	N =
1. Pro-social	17%	48%	35%	23
2. Average	9	35	56	78
3. Impulsive/hyperactive	10	49	41	39
4. Pro-delinquent attitudes and delinquent friends	14	26	60	57

N = 198

SOURCE: Adapted from Huizinga et al. (1991).

tion of delinquency in groups Y (age 8), M (age 11), and O (age 14). I have selected the most predictive of the factors for the M and O groups and reproduced them in Table 6.3 so that they can be more readily compared to the average RIOC coefficients from previous research shown in Table 6.2. Again, the findings are that the best predictors are peer, family, and school variables in the onset and the continuation or desistance of delin-

Table 6.2   List of Delinquency Predictor Variables and Average RIOC from Delinquency Prediction Studies

Variables	Average RIOC
General Delinquency	
Composite prediction scales	.64
Drug use	.53
Composite scale of family management variables	.50
Childhood problem behavior and aggression	.32
Deviant peers	.32
Stealing, lying, truancy	.26
Criminal or deviant behavior in family	.24
Poor educational achievement	.23
Family management (discipline)	.23
Separation from parents	.20
Socioeconomic status	.18
Delinquent Recidivism	
Composite prediction scales	.87
Stealing, lying, truancy	.46
Poor educational achievement	.43
Drug use	.42
Childhood problem behavior and aggression	.38
Criminal or deviant behavior in family	.36
Level of prior delinquency	.36
Composite scale of family management variables	.26
Socioeconomic status	.14

SOURCE: Adapted from Loeber and Dishion (1987) and Loeber and Stouthamer-Loeber (1987).

quency. This study also shows again that prior childhood misbehavior and developing pro-delinquency and pro-deviance attitudes and beliefs considerably improve prediction over chance. Class (SES) and race by themselves are somewhat weaker predictors, important primarily through their relationships to the peer, family, school, and other variables.

Table 6.3   Variables Predictive of Initiation and Desistance of Delinquency for Youth Up to Age 11 (M) and Youth Up to Age 14 (O) in the Pittsburgh Youth Study

Variables	RIOC		RIOC	
	M	O	M	O
	Initiation		Desistance	
Peers				
Delinquent peers	.75	.09	.53	.58
Deviant peers	.35	.30	.42	.61
Family				
Negative relationships	.60	.49	.38	.47
Single parent	.24	.12	–	–
Poor supervision	.25	.42	.11	.40
Not getting along	.28	.14	.40	.36
Prior behavior problems				
Physical agression	.48	.75	.47	.41
Truancy	.37	.35	.45	.57
Hyperactivity	.37	.85	.46	.64
Attitudes				
Pro-deviancy attitudes	.31	.24	.38	.64
Pro-delinquency attitudes	.08	.17	.39	.24
School				
Low educational achievement	.25	.20	.63	.38
Low school motivation	.19	.49	.57	.58
Sociodemographic				
SES	.28	–	–	.13
Race	.17	.35	–	–

SOURCE: Adapted from Loeber et al. (1991).

Other Delinquency Prediction Research

Reckless and his associates studied "good" and "bad" boys in a high-delinquency area in Columbus, Ohio, from 1955 to 1959. Using teacher nominations, they selected a group of sixth-grade (12-year-olds) "good" boys considered unlikely to become delinquent and another group of "bad" boys considered likely to become delinquent. The boys were given California Personality Inventory schedules and other questionnaire items to measure "self-concept" and were interviewed about family life, relationship with peers, satisfaction with school, and other variables (Reckless et al., 1956; 1957; Scarpitti et al., 1960). The "good" boys (without any delinquent record at age 12) were followed up four years later to see to what extent their self-concept and the other variables measured earlier had "insulated" them from engaging in delinquent behavior, even though they continued to live in a high-delinquency area. Of the 103 "good" boys followed up, only four had become involved with the police or juvenile court, and the group as a whole scored very low on self-reported delinquency.

Werner and others followed a cohort of 698 newborns (actually starting with data on their pregnant mothers) in Hawaii beginning in 1954 (Werner and Smith, 1982; Werner, 1987). Data were collected at ages 1, 2, 10, and 18 including pediatric evaluations, maternal ratings, physical and psychological examinations, evaluations by teachers and parents, mental ability tests, and family interviews. Later delinquency was related to medical, sociological, and behavioral variables at three age levels— infancy to 2 years of age, 2 to 10, and 11 and older. The small number of delinquents in the sample (67 boys and 35 girls) led to caution in interpreting the findings, and none of the predictors was strong. Low socioeconomic status, low family stability, low IQ, and very low or very high levels of activity in infancy were among the risk factors. Being first born, and having verbal skills, social skills, high self-esteem, and good parental relationships, served as "protective" factors reducing the vulnerability to delinquency of those at risk.

As I have pointed out, research has tended to support the idea that behavior patterns emerging in grade school may predict later delinquency and that teachers' rating of behavior at the time are pretty good predictors. This was the focus of a longitudinal study of 660 kindergarten and elementary-school children begun in Philadelphia in 1968 (Spivack and Cianci, 1987). Teacher ratings were obtained on the Devereux Elementary School Behavior rating scale (DESB) in kindergarten and the first three grades. Official police contacts were recorded for ages 6 to 17. The DESB ratings were somewhat predictive of police contact up to ten years later for both girls and boys, with the ratings done in the third grade slightly more predictive.

Kaplan collected data in Houston on a sample of seventh grade students in 1971, and again in 1972 and 1973 when they were eighth and ninth graders. The primary aim of the research was to test his self-attitudes theory of delinquency, but the longitudinal design allows the findings to be used predictively (Kaplan, 1975; Kaplan and Robbins, 1983). Self-derogation and felt rejection by peers, family, and school were measured in a self-report questionnaire in the first year of the study and were used to predict delinquency in the next two years. All of the data are from adolescence, and the period of prediction is short. The relationships were not strong, but generally the self-attitude model was supported.

Simcha-Fagan (1979), as part of a larger Family Research Project, collected data on a sample of 1,034 Manhattan children at Time I and on a sample of 729 five years later at Time II. Five sets of predictor variables (social characteristics, parental behavior, parent-child relationship, child behavior, and school behavior) were obtained from Time I data. The findings in this study indicated that social, familial, and early childhood behaviors are highly predictive of later delinquency, while, in contrast to findings from other research, school behavior did not appear to be as important.

White and her associates (1987) sampled 882 adolescents (aged 12, 15, and 18) in New Jersey through random-digit telephoning in 1979–80 and then re-tested the panel three years later, measuring drug use and delinquency by self-reports. While false negatives were high, the researchers were able to predict correctly up to 84% of serious substance use and up to 96% of serious delinquency; these predictions, however, must be viewed in light of the fact that between 65% and 80% accuracy could have been obtained from base rates alone. The investigators found that family variables like parental control and some school-related variables like grades and commitment to studies predicted serious drug and delinquent behavior from Time 1 to Time 2. However, the strongest predictors were friends' attitudes toward and involvement in drug and delinquent behavior at Time 1. There was support for the hypothesis that the connection between drug use and delinquency arises from a common-cause set of family, school, and peer factors.

In another panel study, Burkett and Warren (1987) followed 264 adolescents through the last three years of high school. They found religiosity (religious commitment and belief) to be related to later marijuana use, although this effect was mediated through peer associations with using and non-using friends. In fact, the peer association variable was the strongest predictor of subsequent use. Employing data from the national Youth in Transition study, Wells and Rankin (1988) followed a panel of tenth graders, beginning in 1966, for four years. They found that "direct parental control" (normative regulation, monitoring, and punishment) had a greater impact on delinquency than indirect parental attachment.

Informative longitudinal studies of delinquency and crime have also been conducted in Scandinavian countries, although their findings are of limited applicability to more heterogeneous and culturally diverse societies. The most extensive of these is the Danish study by Mednick and his colleagues (Mednick and Christiansen, 1977; Mednick et al., 1983; Van Dusen et al., 1983). Because the study focuses primarily on biological and genetic factors (although social variables are also included), it concentrated on comparisons of twins and of adoptive versus biological parents, using official agency and court records ($N = 14,427$). The illegal behavior of adoptees was somewhat better predicted from knowledge of biological parents' criminality (20% of the adoptees with biological parents with criminal records themselves had a conviction) than from knowledge of the criminality of the adoptive parents (15% of the adoptees with adoptive parents with criminal records themselves had a conviction). These findings suggest possible genetic factors in illegal behavior, but there were high proportions of false negatives and false positives (80% and 85%, respectively). The Danish study also found that subsequent delinquency is related to the social class of both the biological and adoptive parents. The actual predictive ability of these variables may be considerably less than the modest effects originally reported because of sample contamination and other problems with the data (see Gottfredson and Hirschi, 1990).

Other Scandinavian studies have not shared this emphasis on biological factors. One investigation in Sweden (Janson, 1983) is of a birth cohort living in Stockholm in 1963 (N = 15,117), following through to age 30. The researchers found school misbehavior, social class, criminality in the family, school achievement, and individual characteristics to be predictive of delinquency, but they could achieve only modest amounts of explained variance in delinquency. In another Stockholm study (Magnusson et al., 1983) of a 1955 cohort, the investigators obtained teachers' rating of aggressiveness on 412 boys at ages 10 and 13; they obtained official arrest data on all subjects up to age 26. High aggressiveness scores were predictive of subsequent juvenile offenses.

White and her associates (1990) studied the characteristics of preschoolers in New Zealand (N = 1,037), following them up to ages 11 and 15. They found that the best single predictor of anti-social behavior at age 11 was preschool behavior problems, confirming again that past misbehavior is one of the best predictor of similar misbehavior in the future, even when measured early in life. But the findings also point up again the limitations of predicting from these early signs of childhood misconduct to delinquent or criminal careers later in life, because childhood misbehavior does not involve exactly the same set of acts as adolescent criminal and delinquent behavior. In this study, the preschool variables had only limited predictive validity for delinquency at age 15. I calculated the RIOC predicting police contact by age 15 from preschool variables (based on the data reported by White et al.) to be a weak .11. The anti-social behavior at age 11 was closer in kind and in time to law violations found in later adolescence, but the data reported did not allow calculation of the RIOC. Therefore, anti-social behavior at age 11 was much more predictive of self-reported delinquency and police contacts at age 15 than were preschool problem behaviors. Moreover, the findings from this study contained a high level of false positives:

> Of the 209 children predicted to have antisocial outcomes at age 11, *84.7% did not develop stable and pervasive antisocial behavior.* (White et al., 1990:521; emphasis added)

In other words, the preschool predictors were correct in only 15% of the cases. These results led the authors to conclude that because of

> the high rate of false positives among those children predicted to have antisocial outcomes, the usefulness of preschool behavioral predictors for selecting

children for intensive early intervention efforts may be limited at present. (White et al., 1990:523)

Kandel and Mednick (1991) attempted to learn if researchers could push the predictive variables even further back into childhood—past infancy, to birth. They found that could not be done at least with the measures they had. They examined the medical records on complications and trauma in mother's pregnancy and subject's birth for 15 convicted violent criminals and 24 convicted property offenders (aged 20 to 22); then they compared these findings with 177 nonoffenders in a Danish birth cohort. Although two-thirds of the children studied had a parent with a psychiatric problem, essentially no relationship was found between pregnancy and delivery problems and later criminal behavior. Most relationships were not statistically significant. And where there were significant relationships, the magnitude of explained variance was tiny (less than 1.6%). There was virtually no difference in the proportions of those with high complications in pregnancy or delivery and those without in the percentages who were later convicted of a crime. About 80% in both groups had no convictions.

Tremblay and his colleagues (1992) surveyed 324 French-Canadian children in the first grade. Among the measures used was an index of peer-assessed and self-assessed "disruptive behavior" taken from the PEI (Pupil Evaluation Inventory). The children were followed up in grade 4 (age 10) and grade 8 (age 14). For the boys, but not the girls, both assessments of disruptiveness in the first grade were significantly correlated with self-reported aggression (r = .32 and .39) and with self-reported delinquency (r = .41 and .46) at age 14. Also, the disruptive behavior at age 7 had a strong direct effect on delinquent and aggressive behavior at age 14 in a LISREL model that included indicators of school achievement.

What Variables Predict Delinquency?

This review of research going all the way back to the classical studies shows that we have some ability to predict adolescent deviance from measures taken before young people enter high school. The most accurate predictors, of course, are those measured closer to the high school years, but in some of the research predictors have been identified as early as elementary school. Still, the earlier in life the measures are taken, the poorer their predictive efficacy for adolescent or adult deviance. Attempts to predict from genetic, prenatal, or postnatal factors have not been very successful, although few of these studies have been done. This is not to say that the predictions are highly accurate even when the research identifies variables that are successful predictors. Some of the studies, even among the best known and most frequently cited, report false positive rates as high as 89%. The average false positives (those persons predicted to be delinquent who do not become so) in the various studies is about 50%, and on average even the best single predictors do not exceed an RIOC coefficient of .50.

The pioneering studies (Glueck and Glueck, 1950; McCord and McCord, 1959) reported family structure, parental disciplinary techniques, parent-child relationships, criminality or deviance by parents and others in the family, deviant peer associations, and gang membership measured in pre-teen or early teen years to predict subsequent delinquency and, to some extent, adult crime. More recent research has turned up similar findings, wherein risk factors in the family, sociodemographic correlates, school-related variables (e.g., IQ, academic achievement, school commitment), peer group variables, adult role models, and various indicators of overtly aggressive, deviant, and delinquent behavior evidenced at one point predict later delinquency (Wolfgang et al., 1972; 1987; West and Farrington, 1973; Farrington, 1983; 1985; Elliott et al., 1985; 1987; Elliott, 1994; Spivack and Cianci, 1987; White et al., 1987; Burkett and Warren, 1987; White et al., 1990; McCord, 1991a; Loeber et al., 1991; Huizinga et al., 1991; Hawkins et al., 1992a; O'Donnell et al., 1993).

The factors have been defined and classified in a number of different ways, and there have been efforts to summarize or codify findings from the prediction studies. The best of these is by Loeber and his colleagues. Using the RIOC as a guide (calculated from the published data), they identify factors from the literature that have some predictive validity for general delinquency and for delinquent recidivism. Table 6.2 presents the best predictors from the Loeber lists.

His compilation included only those studies reporting data in such a way that the RIOC could be calculated. The average coefficients for some variables are based on a fairly low number of studies. Some of these are sampled from specially selected populations, and there is a dearth of studies with samples of minority group members. Nevertheless, the factors in the table are the type that are likely candidates for inclusion in any accurate risk profile. Obviously, an index, scale, or composite of factors will be more predictive than single variables, but the identification of single variables remains important for both theoretical and practical purposes.

Loeber's own data from his longitudinal research produce similar lists of variables (with some significant additions that were not measured in previous studies) that are able to predict future delinquency significantly beyond chance. Table 6.3 presents a selection of the better predictors from the first two years of the research by Loeber and his colleagues in Pittsburgh. Compare the similarity of factors in Table 6.2 and Table 6.3.

Hawkins and his associates (1992b), after conducting an exhaustive review and analysis of the prediction literature on the risk and protective factors for substance use and abuse in adolescence and early adulthood, prepared a similar compilation of predictive variables. They did not develop RIOC or other quantitative measures of effect, but based their conclusions on a substantive analysis of a very large body of longitudinal and cross-sectional studies on alcohol and drug problems. Their list includes such sociolegal contextual factors as laws and norms favorable to substance use and availability, economic deprivation, and neighborhood disorganization, as well as biochemical/genetic factors. The major risk factors, however, are other "individual and interpersonal" variables of early childhood misbehavior, variables involving peers and family, pro-social or anti-social attitudes, and school and intelligence factors. Notice the similarity of this list with the items in Tables 6.1–6.3.

Social Learning Concepts and Variables Predicting Delinquency

Although a great many factors have been tested for efficacy in predicting delinquency, the number of variables that has proven consistently to be good predictors is not large. In addition to sociodemographic and contextual variables like class, race, and societal norms, five major variables have consistently been empirically validated in the delinquency prediction literature:

I.　Prior problem, anti-social, or deviant behavior
　　Early drug/alcohol use
　　Early arrest or delinquent involvement
　　Childhood aggression, lying, stealing, or troublesomeness

Truancy
Impulsivity/hyperactivity

II. Deviant peer associations
Deviant or delinquent friends and peers
Delinquent gang membership

III. Parental and family factors
Lack of pro-social, or presence of anti-social, family values and social-ization
Criminality or deviance by parents and siblings
Parental control, discipline, and management deficiencies
Family conflict and negative relationships

IV. Deviant attitudes and beliefs

V. School factors
Low school achievement

I contend that each of these can reasonably be defined as an operational indicator of social learning concepts. Therefore, it is sensible to interpret the findings on delinquency prediction as giving additional empirical support to the social learning theory of crime and delinquency. It should be noted that many of these, especially in III, parental and family factors, and in V, school factors, may also be taken as reasonable indicators of concepts in social bonding theory.

I. PRIOR PROBLEM, ANTI-SOCIAL, OR DEVIANT BEHAVIOR: THE PRIORITY PRINCIPLE AND BEHAVIORAL STABILITY IN SOCIAL LEARNING

As I have noted, one of the most common findings in prediction studies is that past behavior relates to current behavior, which in turn relates to future behavior. Early delinquency predicts later delinquency, and early conformity predicts later conformity. Good kids tend to remain good kids; bad kids who get into trouble early in life tend, more than kids who stay out of trouble early on, to keep on getting into trouble. In studies predicting behavior during the adolescent years, drug use and the onset of delinquent involvement like stealing, status offenses like truancy, and contact with the police early on predict later and more serious delinquent and drug involvement. Those prediction studies beginning in the pre-adolescent years have found that rule breaking and deviant behavior in childhood, even in fairly early childhood, is predictive of delinquency in adolescence. Such things as highly troublesome or disruptive behavior at home or in school, lying, cheating, aggressiveness, and stealing in the earlier years are the "behavior problems" or "anti-social behavior" that predict later delinquency. The more closely the early behavior resembles the later behavior, the better the early episodes predict the later ones. The closer in time the two are measured, the stronger the relationship. Thus, not all of the indicators of prior behavior are strong predictors, but they are among the most consistent.

Before examining the congruence between social learning theory and the findings that prior deviance predicts later deviance, I will discuss the general issue of whether this well-established finding of behavioral persistency and consistency can be captured and claimed by any particular theory. It comes as no surprise to a social learning theorist, of course, that the best predictor of future behavior is one's current behavioral patterns. But in truth it comes as a surprise to almost no one, regardless of theoretical orientation. "Nobody is surprised to learn that children who begin their anti-social conduct at a very early age are the most troublesome youth and likely to become the most serious delinquents" (Wilson, 1991:121). This commonplace finding that behavior at T1 is related to behavior at T2 and, with decreasing strength, to behavior at Tn cannot be taken as uniquely supporting any theoretical perspective. Although it is quite congruent with and expected from social learning theory, it is also congruent with any number of other theoretical perspectives.

Virtually any theory can claim that the behavior at T1 is a function or manifestation of the causal variables it specifies and that the measures of some form of that behavior at T1 are, therefore, an index of the theoretical variables; consequently, the relationship between measures of the behavior at T1 and T2 demonstrates the empirical efficacy of the theory. Such an argument is hard to support, however, because to predict from these behaviors at T1 to the same or similar behavior at T2 is simply predicting that behavior A is related to behavior A, even when separated in time. The relationship of childhood aggression, lying, cheating, and so on to later delinquency is not surprising, since many of these are the same as or behaviorally very similar to deviant acts that we define as delinquent behavior when they occur in adolescence. The relationship of delinquent acts in the pre-teen or early teen years to delinquent and criminal acts in the later teen and adult years is even less surprising, since it is the same behavior. If this is stated as a causal relationship, it is tautological. It is quite acceptable to use T1 behavior, as is often done in prediction research, as a noncausal, empirical predictor or "marker" variable; it is proper to use it as a control variable to see how much change in that same behavior at T2 is accounted for by the independent variables in the prediction model. But it is not acceptable to attribute causal significance simply to a correlation between behavior A at T1 and behavior A at T2, or to assert that the correlation is supportive of only one theory and disconfirming of all other theories.[1]

For these reasons the claims by Gottfredson and Hirschi (1990) that measures of previous misbehavior are uniquely measures of self-control and that the stability of behavior over time can be explained only by self-control theory cannot be sustained. A similar claim for social learning theory or any other theory also cannot be sustained. Simply observing that the average difference among individuals in propensity to commit or refrain from committing crime is fairly stable over time or that the individual's behavior tends toward consistency over time does not, ipso facto, demonstrate the effects of self-control, peer associations, reinforcement, genetic factors, or any other independent variable. (As I will point out in Chapter 12, the issue also involves behavioral change and inconsistencies over time.) It is merely the observation with which one begins. The question, then, is how well a particular theory explains the relationship and how well this explanation conforms to the other empirical predictors. What theoretical links between T1 and T2 behavior reasonably account for the empirical links? I will confine my remarks here to showing how social learning theory would explain the relationship, with some comments about self-control theory, since it is the theory about which the strongest claims regarding the persistence of behavior have been made.

I begin with the priority principle in social learning theory, developed in Chapter 3. According to this principle, not only associations but also reinforcement, modeling, exposure to conforming and deviant definitions occurring within the family during childhood, and such anti-social conduct as aggressiveness, lying, and cheating learned in early childhood can be expected to affect later delinquent and criminal behavior and associations. Recall that social learning theory proposes that behavior learned earlier, and the operation of the learning mechanisms earlier in life, have both continuity and selective effects on the operation of the learning mechanisms and the persistence of behavior patterns into later years. If the learning variables change later, perhaps because of changes in life circumstances, the behavior is likely to undergo change.

Thus, social learning theory can account in large part for the link between early and later behavior. It involves more than just the selective effects of associations on later associations and behavior as posited by Sutherland. The priority of the behavior itself—the models, values, socialization, and rewards and punishments earlier—has a selective and conditioning effect on later behavior. The more behavior has been shaped through differential reinforcement in the past, the more likely it is that it has developed habit strength, and the more likely it is to be repeated in the future. Behavior learned on intermittent schedules, the most common type of social reinforcement schedule, is especially persistent. Thus, patterns of troublesome behavior earlier in life (indicative of priority of association, modeling, definitions, and reinforcements) is expected to have an effect on conforming or deviant behavior later in life. This effect is not immutable, however, and is subject to more recent and time-proximate changes in the social learning variables. (See Chapter 12.)

From this perspective, then, above and beyond any direct effect of previous behavior on later behavior, the relationship is accounted for by intervening social learning variables. Recent findings from the National Youth Survey support this hypothesis. A model of family, peer, and attitudinal variables predicts the onset of serious violence; of these, social learning variables have the most powerful direct effects and mediate the effects of family bonding and stress variables. They also mediate the predictive effects of earlier involvement in minor delinquency and in drug use on later serious delinquency.

> Earlier involvement in minor offending (including minor forms of violence) has no significant effect on the subsequent onset of serious violence. This finding, together with earlier findings that used this model to predict involvement in minor delinquency, suggests a common etiology for minor delinquency, alcohol use, and serious violence. It does *not offer much support for a causal interpretation of early aggression or delinquency leading to later serious violence;* rather, it suggests that *the stability of aggressiveness-violence over the lifespan is due more to a stability in the nature of social relationships and social contextual factors than to some underlying individual predisposition.* (Elliott, 1994:16; emphasis added)

Gottfredson and Hirschi propose that such behavioral stability is based on an underlying, unmeasured, stable predisposition that they prefer to designate as self-control. Although I have stated reservations about the tautological character of this explanation and its applicability to all forms of crime and deviance (Akers, 1991), it seems a plausible and parsimonious account of behavioral persistence. The validity of the argument would not at all exclude the kind of social learning explanation that I am offering here. Gottfredson and Hirschi (1990) conceive of self-control as the product of childhood socialization processes. This is wholly compatible with the way in which social learning views self-control. That is, socialization is part of the social learning process, and the patterns of behavior and cognition to which we give the label of self-control are the product of that process. But it is not only for this reason that I assert that social learning theory explains differences in individual propensity to be lawful or unlawful that were formed early in life and persist over time. Aside from any reference to a summary concept such as self-control, social learning theory uses reinforcement, associations, and definitions to explain stabilized differences and similarities between individuals' patterns of deviance and conformity while also accounting for changes in the behavior of the same individual over time and in varied circumstances.

Moreover, I contend that social learning theory, again aside from any overlapping of concepts, explains the connection between early misbehavior and later delinquency more accurately than either social bonding (Hirschi, 1969) or self-control theory (Gottfredson and Hirschi, 1990). The measures of prior behavior found in delinquency prediction research are more accurately viewed as indicators of previously learned behavior patterns than as indicators of high or low self-control. Psychological research has shown that even infants respond and adapt to pleasurable and uncomfortable events in the environment and make initiative responses. Differences in behavior patterns can be found early in life. General misbehavior, self-interested fraud, and resort to force occur long before childhood socialization is complete or has had the chance to produce stable self-control or an internalized conscience. If self-control is the product of social control in the socialization process, then it is difficult to sustain the contention that behavior patterns formed before socialization is complete indicate an already developed stable self-control. The individual's growing self-control is shaped by social learning. Previously learned behavior that violates social expectations and norms, in the absence of conditioning and situational factors redirecting it, produces tendencies to behave in similar ways later. Thus, social learning variables link past and current behavior.

Moreover, as noted above, the question of behavioral persistence is not the only one that must fit into the theoretical perspective; behavioral discontinuities must also be explained. While research has shown that later behavior is linked to earlier behavior, it has also shown that the link is often broken. As I have pointed out, research often finds only weak correlations between early childhood misconduct and later delinquency, and the positive and negative prediction errors based on early misbehavior are often quite high. Many youngsters who get into trouble early desist later (Loeber et al., 1991). The concept of the stable self-control expects mainly stability of differences in self-control across time; thus, it is hard pressed to account for instability. On the other hand, social learning theory expects priority and selective effects to produce persistence of behavior, but it allows for modifications of behavioral responses by changing circumstances and conditions. (Again, this anticipates the discussion of the relationship between delinquency and age in Chapter 12.) In social learning theory, congruency of behavior is expected because, once learned as part of the individual behavioral repertoire, the behavior will persist unless there is sufficient change in the contingencies shaping and sustaining it. Behavioral patterns learned early and repeated in rewarding circumstances develop habit strength and act as a selective mechanism filtering later experiences. But these effects can be offset by new experiences, punishing consequences that offset the rewards to such an extent that the behavior is extinguished, and experiences that develop new behavior. The stability of behavior through time and across situations comes from stimulus generalization processes; the diversity and versatility of behavior from one situation to another comes from discriminative processes. In brief, the presence of variations and stabilities in the social learning mechanisms accounts for both change and stability in behavior.

Once learned and strengthened, neither habits nor self-control is immutable, although each may be resistant to change. Social learning posits that behavior may be changed through the same process by which it was acquired. The same variables are operative in the effect that situational variables like "opportunity" have on the commission of crime. While self-control theory (Gottfredson and Hirschi, 1990) sees these as separate events unrelated to self-control, social learning theory sees both self-control and opportunity as operating through the social learning process. Past behavior is a function of prior socialization, modeling, reinforcement/punishment, and exposure to definitions/verbalizations. The relationship that the behavior has acquired to these past events is brought to the present situation, which has a configuration of actual or potential rewards/costs and other learning variables that interact with previously learned behavioral tendencies to produce the response to it. This involves, of course, the classic question of the person versus the situation. Social learning principles unify these by postulating the same set of variables to explain the effect of both the person (and his or her behavioral and cognitive repertoire) and the current situation.

The foregoing should make it plain that I disagree with the assertion by Gottfredson and Hirschi (1990) that *only* self-control theory can adequately explain stable difference across individuals in the propensity to commit criminal acts. I also disagree that the question of stable differences between individuals is more important than the question of changes in behavior by the same person. Self-control is itself a product of social learning, and therefore any variation that it accounts for ultimately depends on social learning. Neither I nor other social learning theorists have treated the question of stable differences in individual propensities to commit delinquency as a major issue. Nevertheless, I have shown here and in Chapter 3 that Sutherland offered the modality of priority in his theory fifty years ago as an explanation for the link between early and later behavior. I have also shown here that variations in the social learning process readily account for behavioral persistence and individual differences in behavioral tendencies over time, both by conceptualizing self-control as a product of social learning and by reference to the operation of learning variables, a process that begins at an early age and continues through time.

For instance, once one develops a cigarette habit there is obviously a stable individual difference in her propensity to smoke compared to someone who has not developed such a habit. The earlier it begins and the longer it is sustained, the more likely it is that the habit will persist in the future. The nonsmoker can be said to have strong self-control and the smoker to have low self-control. It is quite easy to show, however, that beginning and continuing to smoke are learned in the process of differential association with smokers, imitation of parental, peer, and media models, and social and nonsocial reinforcement. It is also easy to show that when the smoker comes to perceive that the negative consequences outweigh the pleasures of continued smoking she will very likely stop. Indeed, millions of confirmed smokers have quit; 95% have stopped "on their own" without recourse to treatment or therapy (Akers, 1992b). The self-control of the smoker, the stable propensity to smoke, has changed to become behaviorally the same as the self-control of the nonsmoker. How can this happen if the differences between individual propensity toward "analogous" behavior like smoking are stable across time, circumstances, and consequences? Gottfredson and Hirschi assert that the differences between individuals cannot be accounted for by variations in their motivation to continue in the behavior, only by differences in self-control or ability to refrain from the behavior that remain stable. Yet with smokers who stop, changes in both motivation and self-control take place.

I have concentrated so far on how social learning theory can account for the basic "behavior predicts behavior" generalization from prediction research. I turn now to supporting the argument that many of the other indicators that have been found to be major predictors of delinquency— such as peer, family, attitudinal, and school variables—are valid measures of the key social learning concepts of differential association, differential reinforcement, imitation/modeling, and definitions favorable and unfavorable.

II. DEVIANT PEER ASSOCIATIONS:
PEER ATTITUDES, MODELS, AND REINFORCEMENT

Both in the behavioral-interactive sense of associating with those who behave similarly and in the normative sense of exposure to definitions favorable or unfavorable to delinquency, peer associations are, of course, a central part of the differential association process in social learning. The number or proportion of delinquent friends has long been a favorite among researchers as a measure of differential peer association. Not only is this or other measures of association with delinquent or deviant peers strongly related to delinquent behavior cross-sectionally—it is also a strong predictor of later delinquency and crime. Other than one's own prior deviant behavior, the best single predictor of the onset, continuance, or desistance of delinquency is differential association with law-violating or norm-violating peers (as the data in the tables above show). Indeed, in some studies, peer association is a stronger predictor of the onset and persistence of delinquency than one's own previous behavior patterns. More frequent and closer association with conventional peers who do not support deviant behavior is strongly predictive of conformity, while greater association with peers who commit and approve of delinquency is predictive of one's own delinquent behavior. It is typically in peer-group contexts that illicit substances first become available, and it is in the company of peers that young people first act upon opportunities for delinquency. Furthermore, the repetition of such acts most often occurs in peer groups. Virtually every cross-sectional and longitudinal study that incorporates one or more peer association variables finds them to be significantly and strongly related to delinquency and other forms of deviance. That such findings tend to support social learning theory is obvious.

Interacting with peers who behave in certain ways provides behavioral models to be imitated and exposes the youngster to normative acceptance, tolerance, or disapproval of deviant acts. The importance of the peer association variable in delinquency prediction also reflects the social reactions and sanctions of peers as powerful sources of differential social reinforcement for beginning or continuing delinquency. This differential reinforcement for conforming or deviant behavior occurs within the family as well. The counterpart in the peer group to parental control in the family is peer sanctions and reactions to behavior. But while this social reinforcement dimension of family socialization is often measured directly as parental control and discipline (see below), it is seldom measured directly by indicators of peer influence in prediction research. When it is taken into account (Loeber et al., 1991), it is a good predictor variable. If modeling and reinforcing processes were to be measured more adequately in future research, rather than inferring them from the usual peer association measures of numbers, proportion, or closeness of deviant/delinquent friends, the peer variable would become an even more potent delinquency predictor.

III. PARENTAL AND FAMILY FACTORS:

PARENTAL ATTITUDES, MODELS, AND REINFORCEMENT

The family factors predictive of delinquency, such as discipline, control, and cohesive relationships, are typically claimed as measures of family attachment or other social bonding concepts. This is very reasonable, in that control theory has long stressed socialization in the family and parental practices in discipline. It is just as reasonable, however, to view these family factors as indicators of the social learning process. Social learning and social bonding make exactly the same predictions about the effect of family variables on delinquency. Social learning theory claims greatest saliency for learning in primary groups—the family as well as friendship groups. There is no doubt that the family is the major agency of early socialization, learning right from wrong, and behaving accordingly. As noted above, social learning theory expects associations and behavior acquired early in the home to have selective and other effects on subsequent behavior patterns. The typical variables used in the prediction research to measure parental control, discipline, and management are transparently indicators of differential social reinforcement (rewarding and punitive social sanctions) by parents for conforming or nonconforming behavior. Informal sanctioning and control in the family has long been conceptualized as part of the social learning process in producing deviance or conformity (Akers, 1985:34–35, 67–68), and empirical investigations of family discipline and control processes in producing delinquency have long been conducted within a social learning perspective (Conger, 1976; Patterson, 1982; Dishion et al., 1992).

As the main conventional socializer against delinquency and crime, the family provides anti-criminal definitions, conforming models, and reinforcement for conformity through parental discipline. Parents who do not apply consistent or effective discipline fail in producing conforming social skills or in extinguishing troublesome behavior. It is not only the direct parental reinforcement of conforming, and punishing of deviant, acts, but also parental models and the normative climate of the home that affect the learning of conforming and deviant behavior in the family. In the early years, differential association is centered in the family and is balanced largely in a pro-social direction; later, family association must compete against association with peers. For some, the balance of peer associations leans in a deviant direction. Parental attitudes as the child grows up toward lying, cheating, stealing, truancy, and other acts that predict, or in fact constitute, delinquency obviously are a source of definitions favorable or unfavorable to misbehaving in the home, school, or community.

When parents, older siblings, or other family members engage in deviant or criminal behavior, then the family's effectiveness in conventional socialization is undermined, and differential association, modeling, and reinforcement of delinquent tendencies are more apt to occur. There are documented cases in which parents directly socialize and reinforce their children to engage in deviant behavior (Adler and Adler, 1978; Bandura and Walters, 1963). In this sense, delinquent family members behave similarly to delinquent peers. To return to a point made in Chapter 3, it is an error to regard family variables as "belonging" only to control theory and peer variables as "belonging" only to social learning theory. The variables found in research to be most predictive of delinquency in both family and peer contexts are social learning variables.

IV. DEVIANT ATTITUDES AND BELIEFS:
DEFINITIONS FAVORABLE TO DELINQUENCY

Pro-deviant or anti-social attitudes and beliefs that are predictive of delinquency obviously are measures of definitions favorable and unfavorable to delinquency, one of the four main concepts in social learning theory. I have measured them (Krohn et al., 1985) directly; some other studies, such as those using self-concept or attitudinal scales (Scarpitti et al., 1960; White et al., 1987), have measured them indirectly in longitudinal investigations. More recent prediction research (Loeber et al., 1991; Huizinga et al., 1991) has included direct measures of pro- and anti-delinquent attitudes and beliefs. The attitudinal measures are not as consistently good predictors as the peer and family variables, but they are among the variables that significantly improve prediction above chance and are considerably more successful in predicting onset and recidivism than most other variables. The recent studies provide evidence that one's pro-delinquency definitions are precursors to later delinquent acts. Such measures unequivocally index the concept of definitions favorable and unfavorable to deviance in social learning theory and require no further comment.

V. SCHOOL FACTORS:

DIFFERENTIAL REINFORCEMENT

Although many school variables have been studied as predictive of delinquency, the one that appears most often as a strong factor in onset and persistence is some variation of poor school performance. As with family variables, school achievement variables are typically defined as measures of control theory concepts. This is reasonable, because Hirschi (1969) and many others following him used educational aspirations and grades in school as empirical indicators of the commitment concept in social bonding. On the other hand, school achievement is not a direct measure of any of the major social learning concepts, and it has seldom been used in tests of social learning theory. Nevertheless, one does not have to stretch much to relate such measures to social learning concepts and predictions.

Social bonding theory hypothesizes that the good student has a high commitment to conformity through investments in conventional lines of action. Therefore, involvement in deviance carries higher costs (punishing consequences) for the good student than for the poor student, who risks less by engaging in delinquent behavior. As I have argued elsewhere (Akers, 1989; 1990), this "rational" element of commitment is only a special case of negative punishment in learning theory, that is, of refraining from an act because of actual or anticipated loss or cost. As such, it is wholly subsumable under the general differential reinforcement concept in social learning. Moreover, from a social learning view, that one does poorly in school is an indication of other learning mechanisms beyond negative punishment. It is a sign of low (or no) reward for good schoolwork or, more generally, for conformity to conventional school expectations. Poor scholarship is also associated with lack of participation in extracurricular activities and other pro-social behavior. The poor student receives less reward from engaging in conventional actions that are incompatible with serious involvement in deviance; this increases the probability that the youngster will turn to, and gain rewards from, delinquency. Doing poor academic work alienates the young person from school and is more likely to foster association with deviant than with conforming youth. Thus, the social learning theory can account for the predictive link between school performance and delinquency.

Conclusion

I have reviewed delinquency prediction studies, some in considerable detail, highlighting variables that have shown to be among the best predictors of onset and recidivism in delinquency (although even the best make a sizable number of prediction errors). There is a remarkable amount of congruence between social learning theory and the published findings in the classical and the more recent delinquency prediction studies. Virtually all of the major predictor variables fit into a social learning model. The match between the theory and the prediction findings is even more remarkable when one recalls that the studies have most often been conducted without any reference to social learning theory. If the researchers had begun with social learning theory and designed careful, valid, and direct operationalizations of its key concepts, the consistency between the theory and the empirical results would have been even closer. If social learning variables had been directly measured and used as predictors of delinquency in more studies, additional social learning measures could be added to the short list of consistently predictive variables. For this reason, I hypothesize that the best prediction models in future research projects will be those that most adequately incorporate direct measures of social learning concepts.

Note

I thank Linda Smith, who collaborated with me (together with Thomas Blomberg and Gordon Waldo) on the portion of a delinquency risk-profile report to the Florida Department of Education on which parts of this chapter are based.

1. Catalano and Hawkins (in press: 34) argue that if the specific behavior measured in early childhood (e.g., the "problem behavior" of aggressiveness) is not precisely the same as later delinquent and drug-using behavior, "behavioral continuity" can be included in causal theoretical models such as their Social Development Model, while avoiding the "tautological and theoretically trivial claim that antisocial behavior predicts later involvement in the same antisocial behavior."

I find this argument only partially persuasive. It is true that the greater the difference in the empirical indicators taken at two times, the less danger there is that one is simply correlating behavior A to behavior A. However, specific forms of problematic or deviant behavior typically occur as part of a pattern or syndrome, and any behavior within that context could be taken as an empirical measure of the pattern. Does it avoid the triviality and tautology problem if one takes the measure of behavior A from that pattern and uses it to predict behavior B from the same overall pattern? This is the same issue raised by using measures of adolescent drug use to predict delinquent behavior (and measures of delinquent behavior to predict drug use). Drug use is certainly not exactly the same behavior as vandalism, theft, violence, or burglary, and each of these is different from the others. Nonetheless, all of them are, by definition, delinquent behavior, and often measures of them are combined into a single delinquency scale. Does predicting from one of the items on this scale to another avoid the triviality issue? Is predicting from vandalism to burglary different than predicting from delinquency to delinquency? Can one attribute causal significance to findings of a strong relationship between one subtype of delinquent behavior to another? Ultimately, no two episodes of the same behavior, say, burglary, are exactly the same. But does this make it appropriate to predict from an act of burglary at T1 to an act of burglary at T2? Does treating the time difference as if it were a difference in behavior avoid tautology and triviality? Perhaps it is justified solely for the purpose of predicting repetition, but it would not avoid tautology to treat behavior at one time as the cause of the same behavior at another time. The two acts of burglary are simply different empirical indicators of the same dependent variable taken at two different times.

7

Adolescent Drug and Drinking Behavior: The Boys Town Study

In the two preceding chapters I have reviewed the body of research testing the cross-sectional and longitudinal relationships between various social learning variables and criminal, delinquent, and deviant behavior, as well as those predicting delinquent behavior. In doing so, I relied primarily on investigations conducted by others. In this and the next three chapters, I concentrate on research I have conducted (in collaboration with students and colleagues) over many years to test full models of social learning theory directly with both cross-sectional and longitudinal data collected specifically for that purpose. This chapter will report my research on adolescent drug and alcohol behavior. Known as the Boys Town Study, it was conducted with Marvin D. Krohn, Lonn Lanza-Kaduce, and Marcia J. Radosevich. This was a large-scale, self-report questionnaire survey of substance abuse involving students in grades 7 through 12 in the Midwest (Akers et al., 1979; Krohn et al., 1982; Krohn et al., 1984; Lanza-Kaduce et al., 1984; Akers and Cochran, 1985; Cochran and Akers, 1989). (For additional information, see Chapter 1.)

First opportunities to use drugs and initiation of drug use both typically occur during adolescence. Certainly onset can and does occur later, but it is quite unusual for first use of any substance, legal or illegal, to occur after the young adult years. First use sometimes occurs in childhood, but this is not common. Therefore, the statement and test of the social learning theory of drug and alcohol behavior in this chapter concentrates on adolescent use and abuse. The general explanation, however, is applicable to such behavior regardless of the age of onset. Similarly, although my emphasis here is on marijuana and alcohol use, the social learning process is hypothesized to be essentially the same no matter what the substance. Therefore, the social learning process applies to any age group and to any substance, although the nature of the relevant social groups and settings for use may differ.

Social Learning Theory of Drug Behavior

Whether individuals will abstain from or take drugs (and whether they will continue or desist) depends on the past, present, and anticipated future rewards and punishments perceived to be attached to abstinence and use (differential reinforcement). The physiological effects of alcohol and other drugs on the nervous system can function as direct nonsocial reinforcers and punishers. These primary effects also acquire secondary, or conditioned, reinforcing effects (even though they may be initially aversive) by being experienced in the context of group approval and other sources of social reinforcement for use. Individual variations in the probability of social reinforcement, exposure to definitions favorable or unfavorable to drug use, and observation of using and abstinent behavioral models (imitation) come from differential association with primary groups of family and friends, various reference groups, and significant others, (including to some extent distal groups and models portrayed in the mass media). Through these processes the individual learns attitudes, orientations, or evaluative knowledge that are favorable or unfavorable to using drugs (definitions), as well as the behavior needed to acquire and ingest drugs in a way that produces effects. The more individuals define use as good, permissible, or excusable, rather than holding to general or specific negative attitudes toward drugs, the more likely they are to become users.

The typical social learning process in which the person comes to the points of using or not using some substance, of ceasing or continuing use, and of progressing to serious abuse is hypothesized to be as follows.

Differential association with family (parents, siblings, and others), peers and friends, and others in the community provides the adolescent with the social environments for exposure to definitions, imitation of models, and differential reinforcement (source, schedule, and value), as well as for the operation of other behavioral learning variables conducive to use or abstinence. Typically, the family acts as a conventional socializer against drug use and underage drinking and supports the child's and adolescent's conforming behavior. However, family socialization will sometimes result in the young person's initiation of substance use. That is, initial underage use of alcohol and tobacco (and, in fewer cases, of marijuana and other illegal drugs) occurs when the child has learned such behavior at home. Although parents may deliberately and directly socialize their children into deviant substance use, such direct tutelage is not necessary. It is more likely that family-fostered deviant use of alcohol, tobacco, marijuana, or other drugs grows out of inadequately socializing the children into conventional definitions and abstinent behavior.

Social learning theory posits the family as a very important primary group with which individuals are differentially associated. However, it also proposes that the most important of the primary groups in the initiation and continuation of substance use among adolescents are peers, particularly close friends. The hypothesis is that differential association with peer users and nonusers is a strong—typically the strongest—correlate and predictor of whether the individual will use drugs. More frequent, longer term, and closer association with peers who do not support drug use is hypothesized to result in abstinence, while greater association on balance with peers who approve of or use drugs increases the probability of use. The outcome of the process is not simply taking drugs or abstaining; frequency and quantity of use are predicted to be related to the number and type of users and nonusers one has as friends. Nor is differential association with peers and parents the only influence. Other family members, neighbors, church and religious groups, schoolteachers, physicians, law-enforcement figures, and other individuals and groups in the community, as well as mass media and other more remote sources of attitudes and models, have varying degrees of effect on use and abstinence. Typically, these other actors have less influence than do friends and family.

These group influences most often act in harmony to move the youngster toward abstinence and away from drug use, maximizing the chances of conformity to conventional norms regarding drug and alcohol behavior. And, of course, family socialization, values residence, and other circumstances play a powerful role in determining with which peers the youth of that family associate and know as friends. But when family and peer influences conflict, adolescents will most often behave similarly to close peers, that is, to those who are their best friends and with whom they are in most frequent, most intense, and longest association. Social learning theory does not propose that only drug-using behavior is learned in peer groups; indeed, drug-abstinent behavior is more likely to be learned in such groups. Nonetheless, it is in peer groups that drugs typically are first made available to the adolescent, and support and social reinforcement for learning the techniques and definitions of drug taking is more likely to be found with peers than with parents. The process is one of peer influence, however, and does not usually involve peer "pressure." (See the discussion of this issue in Chapter 3 and the more detailed discussions in Akers, 1985; 1992b.)

INITIATION OF USE

The normative definitions (attitudes, rationalizations, beliefs) that are positive, neutralizing, or negative toward drugs are learned through imitation and social reinforcement of them in peer and other groups. Once learned, the definitions serve as discriminative stimuli (along with stimuli like physical setting, occasion, and place) for using or abstaining. According to social learning theory, the definitions combine with imitation of admired or valued behavioral models and the anticipated balance of reinforcement to produce initial episodes of drug use or to inhibit such experimentation and sustain continued abstinence.

CONTINUATION OR CESSATION OF USE

Once the person has experienced drug taking, the actual consequences of use (social and nonsocial rewards and punishers) come into play to affect the probability that use will be discontinued or continued and at what level. If initial drug effects are pleasant or desirable, it is likely that drug use will be positively reinforced. If the drug effects or other consequences of taking drugs are more aversive than rewarding, the person is likely to refrain from doing it again unless the effects can be reinterpreted or conditioned to become positive. After the onset of substance use, imitation effects, while still operating to facilitate experimentation, become less important than they were in bringing the person to the point of first trying drugs. The effects of definitions and anticipated social and physical consequences of use continue at this stage of the process. The experience of drug taking will, however, affect one's attitudes toward drug use, expected social reactions, and even the perceived physical effects of the drugs. If the drug effects are intrinsically rewarding to the person or become so through conditioning, the chances of continuing to use are greater than for stopping.

In the process one learns to take the drug for optimal effect. Ingesting some substances, such as alcoholic beverages, requires nothing beyond learning to drink any beverage from a glass, bottle, or can, something we all learn in an entirely conventional setting. But smoking marijuana, injecting drugs intravenously, smoking crack, and taking other substances for maximizing the desired effects means learning certain techniques of preparation and ingestion usually not previously known by the person and not commonly learned in the course of conventional socialization. These are not complex techniques, and they are easily learned; it is quite possible to pick them up by individual trial and error. But typically they are learned from observing and imitating other persons' drug taking and from receiving direct tutelage in the techniques.

The effects of use may be positively reinforcing and motivate the individual to use further, or they may be unpleasant and inhibit using again. Some drugs, such as cocaine, seem to induce positive effects in the great majority of new users; others, such as the opiates and alcohol, while inducing enjoyable initial effects for most, have a higher proportion of new users reporting aversive or upsetting reactions (Young and Seymore, 1986; Beschner and Bovelle, 1985). Substances like tobacco and marijuana have even more variable effects. Persons with a predisposition toward thrill- or sensation-seeking behavior may be more likely to react positively to drug effects (Wood et al., 1995). Not all of the effects are purely intrinsic or physiologically reinforcing or punishing. The positive or negative effects of the drugs are themselves subject to expectations learned before trying them, and, through association with social reinforcement, the effects become conditioned reinforcing stimuli. That is, one learns to interpret or perceive the effects as pleasurable and enjoyable. The social rewards and punishing consequences of drug use come from the actual and anticipated approving or disapproving reactions of others, one's self-approval or self-disapproval, and other sources of tangible and intangible social rewards actually or perceived to be attached to use. Drug taking and its consequences now begin to have an effect on choice of friends and association with abstaining or using friends.

PROGRESSION INTO GREATER FREQUENCY, QUANTITY OF USE, AND ABUSE

Movement into regular patterns of use, heavy use, and abuse of illegal drugs means developing connections for purchase beyond a small group of trusted friends. This gets the person involved with others who control availability and provides additional opportunities and associations in support of drug use of various kinds. Indeed, more extensive involvement in most drug patterns is often accompanied by buying and reselling on an informal or money-making basis. This presents a great risk of disclosure to the authorities by associates and customers, discovery by nonusers, and police action and legal penalties. These and other probable negative social and physical consequences mean that only some of those who continue use beyond the initial stages will go on to more frequent, or habitual, drug use. Those who do move on to greater involvement will have had these counterdrug consequences offset by positively or negatively reinforcing consequences, become more differentially associated with other abusers, and learned and applied definitions favorable to abuse. Cessation of abuse and movement back to abstinence or lower levels of drug use occur when this balance of associations, rewards/punishers, and definitions shift back in the other direction.

Use of drugs like heroin and other opiates, as well as other central nervous system depressants, also fits into this general social psychological process. In the pre-addictive stage there is no difference. But since habituation to drugs like heroin involves physical dependence, additional processes of physiological withdrawal and negative reinforcement (ingestion of the drug to alleviate or avoid withdrawal pains) are present that are not involved for marijuana and other drugs that do not cause physical dependence (see Akers, 1992b).

SUMMARY OF THE SOCIAL LEARNING PROCESS OF SUBSTANCE USE/ABUSE

The probability of beginning and continuing to use some substance increases when (1) there is greater exposure to using than to abstaining persons who serve as behavioral models, (2) there is more association with using than with abstaining peers and others, (3) use is differentially reinforced over abstinence, and (4) the individual has come to define use in more positive or neutralizing terms. Among users, the probability of developing drug patterns of greater quantity/frequency or of abuse (rather than quitting or developing light or moderate patterns) increases significantly with (1) more association with heavy users, (2) differential reinforcement of abusive patterns over more moderate use, (3) continued adherence to positive or neutralizing rather than negative definitions, and, to some extent, (4) more exposure to rewarding and rewarded abusive models.

The Social Learning Process and Testing Empirical Models of the Theory

This application of social learning theory to the process of substance use and abuse points again to what I argued in Chapter 3—that social learning theory is a processual theory in which feedback and nonrecursive relationships are accommodated and expected. It is an ongoing behavioral process of interdependence and interaction that cannot be fully captured or disentangled by observation or measurement in natural settings. Linear models of covariance, even models capable of handling nonrecursive relationships and using longitudinal data, cannot fully reproduce the behavioral process envisioned in social learning theory. At the same time, such empirical models are appropriate, because the principal independent variables in this process have been identified (differential association, modeling, definitions, reinforcement, discriminative stimuli) as causally linked to deviant behavior.

Therefore, if the theory is correct, empirical structural models derived from it that approximate the process or provide a snapshot of the underlying process, should be supported by the data when subjected to proper statistical analysis. If such data do not conform to the expectations of the theory, then it is not confirmed, and the underlying social learning process does not operate as hypothesized. Therefore, it is reasonable to expect the theory to withstand empirical scrutiny with cross-sectional and longitudinal survey data even though they do not fully reproduce the ongoing process. The relationships between measures of social learning variables and measures of deviant behavior predicted by the theory can be tested with the same sort of statistical modeling used in testing other criminological theories that are not predicated on an underlying inter-active social process. If the relationships are as predicted, then the theory is supported; if not, the theory is undermined. The greater the magnitude of the observed relationships, the stronger the support for the theory. Weaker relationships raise questions about the power of the theory, and relationships in the direction opposite from theoretical expectations dis-confirm the theory.

Moreover, using the same type of data and empirical models for testing other theories allows direct comparisons of the effects of social learning variables with the effects of variables taken from other theories. No the-ory of crime and deviance has been able to explain all instances of or variation in such behavior. The question, therefore, is not only one of how well the empirical models of the theory fare when considered on their own, but, more importantly, how well they fare when compared to different, alternative, or competing models. It was with the intent of test-ing social learning models in both ways that I undertook the Boys Town Study of adolescent substance use.

Methodology of the Boys Town Study

SAMPLING AND ADMINISTRATION OF THE SURVEY

The original design of the research to test social learning theory on ado-lescent substance use and abuse envisioned a general community sample of young people and a sample of residents at Boys Town. Indeed, one of the chief reasons for going to the Boys Town Center for Study of Youth Development was the opportunity to conduct research with those housed at Boys Town. In addition, I proposed to include a sample of delinquents incarcerated in a secure state training school (St. Charles Reformatory for Boys in Illinois). The intent was to include as wide a range of behavior as possible, from total abstinence to the most serious cases of adolescent substance use, among both the general and incarcerated populations. Substance use among youngsters was at historic levels then, and I was confident that a general adolescent sample would pick up sufficient numbers of high-frequency/quantity users and abusers to produce suffi-cient variance in the dependent variable for reliable statistical testing. However, the most serious drug users are more apt to be found in institu-tionalized populations of teenage deviants, and the idea was to include them by sampling from the less serious delinquents from Boys Town and from the most serious delinquents at St. Charles Reformatory.

This design was approved by the Boys Town Center for Study of Youth Development and by the board overseeing both the center and the Boys Town institution. I was enormously surprised and disappointed, then, to arrive at the center and learn that the director of the institution, acting on the advice of the director of child care, denied me any research access whatsoever to the population at Boys Town. Therefore, the research was conducted entirely on a sample from the general adolescent population drawn from various school districts in the Midwest. Since it was the Boys Town Center that funded the research, I have continued to refer to it as the Boys Town Study even though not a single respondent in the study came from that institution. I am satisfied that it was good study, and its quality has been verified by peer-viewed publication of its findings. I continue to believe, nonetheless, that it would have been even better if it had included a sample from the population of youngsters living in Boys Town.

We began the sampling by mailing a brief description of the proposed study and a request for access to school districts in Nebraska, Iowa, and Wisconsin in communities ranging from urban to rural. These were mostly public schools, although one was parochial. Restricting the research to these states and starting our sampling frame with school districts was based both on methodological grounds and on practical limitations of time and resources. Since the main goal of the research was to test social learning theory as an explanation of adolescent drug and drinking behavior, rather than to generalize from the sample to the prevalence and the sociodemographic variations in the nation or the region, we felt that a probability sample of households or individuals was not needed. I basically had only one year to do the study, and, although the Boys Town Center was generous in its funding, the total monies available for the project did not allow hiring enough personnel to do a wider study in that time. We needed to get as large a sample as possible in order to pick up enough cases of frequent and serious drug use, and we needed to do so at the least cost and within the time constraints. This meant beginning where the vast majority of adolescents can be found and where surveys can be administered in groups—in schools.

We followed up the mailing to the school districts with telephone calls and went in person to meet with the appropriate officials or committees (superintendents, principals, and research committees). We stopped soliciting when we had an urban-to-rural range of districts and it was clear that we could get a sample that would produce at least 2,000 respondents by our planned procedure of selecting required classes at each grade level from 7 to 12. This point was reached when seven school districts agreed to participate in the survey. Within each of these, we selected schools based on size and location. We sampled two or three required classes within each school and administered the questionnaire to all of the consenting students in attendance on that day for whom we had obtained parental permission to participate in the survey. We obtained student and parental permission by having our researchers come to the classes and tell the students about the survey, and then sending letters addressed to the parents home with the students. A parental permission form to be signed and returned to the school was enclosed with the letter. One more visit to the class was made before the survey date to remind students to return the permission forms. Of the returned forms, 95% granted parental permission, and 95% of the students with such permission were present and completed the questionnaire on the day of the survey. The total number of completed and usable questionnaires was 3,065, representing 67% of the total number of students enrolled in the selected classes.

Because the respondents had the option to place their names on a tear-out sheet (number-coded to match the respondents' questionnaire) that they removed from the questionnaire, it was possible to identify respondents for a small subsample ($n = 106$) for follow-up interviews. We did these from two to eight weeks after the survey, asking the students to answer the same set of frequency and quantity questions on marijuana, alcohol, and other drugs that they had answered before on the questionnaire. The consistency between the two sets of answers was very high (gammas equaled .89 or greater), indicating that the test/re-test reliability was quite good. Also, responses to interlocking items on the questionnaire showed high internal consistency (gamma = .91). All the interviewees reported that they believed in the assurances of confidentiality and that they had responded to both the questionnaire and the interview honestly and truthfully. There was every reason to believe that the responses were reliable and valid. (I will again take up the issue of reliability and validity of adolescents' responses to questions about engaging in deviant behavior in my discussion of teenaged smoking in Chapter 8.)

MEASUREMENT OF SOCIAL LEARNING VARIABLES

Imitation/Modeling. The Boys Town Study questionnaire contained a series of items asking both users and nonusers (of alcohol, marijuana, stimulants, depressants, and stronger drugs) if they had ever "observed or watched anyone whom *you admire* using [the substance]." The response categories were the media ("on TV or in the movies"), parents, someone else in the family, peers ("someone about your own age"), and older persons outside the family. The same series of questions was asked only of users about "before you started using [the substance]." We did not employ this latter measure, since it included only users. Rather, an *Imitation Index* was devised for each substance by summing the number of categories checked by the respondent for that substance.

Differential Association. To measure the normative dimension of differential association, respondents were asked to report the norm qualities, the degree of attitudinal approval or disapproval, that they perceived were held by important reference groups toward each of the substances. The question was asked separately for significant adults in the adolescent's life ("adults whose opinions you value or think are important," which we assumed included parents), for peers ("teenagers whose opinions you value or think are important"), and for religious groups ("what your religion or church teaches"). These became, respectively, single-item measures for *Exposure* to *Adult Norm Qualities, Peer Norm Qualities,* and *Religious Norm Qualities* for each substance.

We did not ask specifically about the using or nonusing behavior of parents and other adults. We were forced into this omission because three of the school districts would not allow us to ask respondents about their parents' drug and drinking behavior. Our measure of imitation referred only to watching admired adults using; it was not designed to measure differential association with using and abstinent parents or other adults. To gauge the interactional dimension of differential association, we concentrated on differential peer association, specifically the modalities of association with using and abstaining friends. This methodological and practical decision does not mean that the concept of differential association refers only to peer associations. It also includes associations with family and adults. But in adolescence the most important associational context is the peer group.

Intensity of peer association was measured by asking respondents to report for each substance the proportion of their best friends (none or almost none, less than half, more than half, almost all) who used it. Frequency and duration of peer association were measured by asking the same question regarding friends with whom the respondent associated most often and those with whom he had associated for the longest time. We did not measure priority of associations. From these items we constructed reliable scales of *Differential Peer Association* for each substance (with item-to-scale correlations ranging from .83 to .96).

One's Own Definitions Favorable and Unfavorable to Substance Use.
These were measured by items on one's own *Neutralizing Definitions, Law-Abiding/Violating Definitions,* and *Positive/Negative Definitions.* The neutralizing definitions were three items each for drugs and alcohol measuring strength of agreement with three "techniques of neutralization." These are condemning the condemners (e.g., "Adults have no right to condemn teenagers for using alcohol since they have more problems with drinking or drugs than teenagers do"), denial of injury (e.g., "People shouldn't condemn teenagers for using drugs since it doesn't really hurt anyone"), and denial of responsibility (e.g., "Teenagers who use drugs really shouldn't be held responsible since they are under too much pressure to resist"). The three items for each substance formed a scale with good item-to-scale correlations in the .7 to .8 range.

Law-abiding/violating definitions were measured by a scale of attitudes toward obeying the law in general and alcohol and drug laws in particular (e.g., "We all have a moral duty to obey the law"). One's own positive or negative attitudes toward alcohol, marijuana, stimulants, depressants, and stronger drugs were measured by a single item on each questionnaire that asked, "What is *your attitude* toward using [the substance]?" The response categories ranged from approval, through mixed or ambivalent attitudes, to disapproval.

Differential Reinforcement. Recall that social reinforcement is broadly defined. It includes not only face-to-face exchange of social rewards and punishments but a whole range of material, tangible, symbolic, and intangible stimuli. Nonsocial reinforcement is more narrowly restricted to the physiological effects of drugs and alcohol and to other unconditioned physiological or physical stimuli. It would also include the extreme feral case of learning without any human contact.

We had no direct measures of physiological drug effects, but we did include some items on perceived overall effects and consequences of taking drugs that encompass perceived physical effects. We also had a list of "good" and "bad" things that happen when drugs are taken; it contained items that could include physical effects, such as a good or bad high. Responses to both the general outcomes measures and the checklist of good and bad consequences can reasonably be seen as tapping both social and nonsocial dimensions. Including these items did not permit us to draw a clear distinction between social and nonsocial reinforcing or punishing stimuli, but it did allow us to make an operational distinction between differential social reinforcement and differential reinforcement based on a combination of social and nonsocial consequences of drug and alcohol use.

Differential Social Reinforcement. This concept involves a process wherein the probability of an act depends not only upon the balance of rewards/costs for that act but also upon the relative balance for alternative acts. One of the methodological difficulties in measuring this process with deviant behavior is that the alternative is to refrain from doing something. Ordinarily, refraining from deviant acts is seen as having been deterred by aversive outcomes (costs), and we included perceptions of the certainty of getting caught (and by implication punished) by the police (*Formal Deterrence*) or by parents (*Informal Deterrence*). But not only do deterrence measures leave out rewarding consequences of committing an act, they also leave out rewarding consequences of refraining from it. Therefore, we included both deterrence measures of inhibition and measures of positive encouragement for staying off drugs and alcohol. Specifically, *Praise for not Using* was measured by asking the respondents to report for each substance (alcohol, marijuana, stimulants, depressants, and stronger drugs) whether friends, parents, both, or neither had encouraged them not to use it.

Friends' Reactions to One's Use and *Parents' Reactions to One's Use* were based on the respondents' reports of anticipated or actual positive or negative sanctions of friends and parents to the respondents' use (or potential use, in the case of nonusers). For friends these ranged from the positive ("become closer friends," "encourage your using"), to the permissive ("do nothing"), to the negative ("criticize your using," "tell your parents," "stop being your friend," "turn you in to the authorities"). For parents the options were "encourage your using," "disapprove but do nothing," "scold or punish you," "kick you out of the house," "turn you in to the authorities."

Another factor involved in engaging in a particular act is the extent to which it is compatible with engaging in other behavior that is important or rewarding to the person. If it is compatible it will be rewarded; if not, it carries the cost of interfering with other valued behavior. *Interference with Other Important Activities* was measured first by asking how important participating in a list of conventional activities is for the respondent. This was followed by a question for each of the substances ("How likely is it that using it regularly would interfere with your participation in . . . activities checked above or other activities which are important to you?").

COMBINED SOCIAL/NONSOCIAL DIFFERENTIAL REINFORCEMENT

Rewards-Costs of Use, an index of rewards minus costs of use, was calculated by adding up the total "good things" perceived to happen from using each of the substances and subtracting the corresponding total of "bad things." The list of four good things included "fit into groups better" and "a good high." The list of bad things initially included five outcomes, but one of these was dropped to make the two lists numerically equal. The bad outcomes included "drop in school grades," "loss of health," and "a bad high." The *Overall Reinforcement Balance* was measured by respondents' assessment of whether, on balance, "mainly good," "mainly bad," or "about as much good as bad" would result (as perceived by nonusers) or usually has happened (as reported by users). Finally, a measure of *Usual Effects* felt by users of each of the substances was obtained.

Since this was measured only for users, it was included only in the analysis of abuse among users.

Frequency of Use. We measured nonmedicinal drug use in the Boys Town Study primarily with a frequency scale that ranged from abstinence through five levels of use up to "nearly every day." The same question was asked for tobacco, beer, wine, liquor, marijuana, stimulants, depressants, strong psychedelics, and strong narcotics. We included both opiates and cocaine in this last category (even though cocaine is a stimulant) because it was at the time and still is socially defined as a "hard" drug that is about as dangerous as heroin. We also had a quantity-of-use measure that we combined with the frequency scale to produce the usual Q-F scale, but this latter scale was not used because it was almost perfectly correlated with the frequency scale. For similar reasons (separate or combined scales of wine, liquor, and beer drinking measured essentially the same thing), we employed only the frequency scale for the use of beer (the most frequently consumed alcoholic beverage) as the measure of alcohol behavior.

Abuse. For this measure we dropped the abstainers and asked the users a fairly standard series of questions about problems associated with their use of alcohol, marijuana, stimulants, or stronger drugs. To avoid including one-time-only episodes, we asked for problems that had occurred "on more than one occasion" while or soon after using each of the substances. We ran a cross-tab on each of these items with the corresponding frequency scale, and then categorized and ranked the various frequency-by-problems cells into four levels of abuse, ranging from no abuse to heavy abuse.

Findings from the Boys Town Study

The cultural milieu in which abstainers, drinkers, and abusers of alcohol are differentially located has long been a central concern of sociological and anthropological studies of alcohol behavior. Individuals' drinking attitudes and behaviors are congruent with the normative climate to which they are exposed through primary reference groups (see reviews in Pittman, 1967; Akers, 1985; Pittman and White, 1991). One particular form that this explanation has taken is that rates of drinking and alcoholism reflect the "norm qualities" of the group, that is, the proscriptive, prescriptive, permissive, or ambivalent content of its norms regarding alcohol (Mizruchi and Perruci, 1962; Larsen and Abu-Laban, 1968). The norm-qualities explanation applied to alcohol behavior is one in which individuals are exposed to the conflicting or congruent normative proscriptions and prescriptions about alcohol of their reference groups and learn their own positive, negative, ambivalent, or confused attitudes. Their normative orientations will then be reflected in decisions about abstaining from alcohol or when and how much to drink. A logical extension of this explanation is that the effect of norm qualities depends on the attitudes of the particular group—family, friends, religious, or other. It is also a logical extension of the argument to apply it to substances other than alcohol.

This explanation obviously portrays the normative dimension of differential association as proposed by Sutherland and as integrated into social learning theory. That is, norm qualities constitutes one type of group definitions favorable and unfavorable to substance use. Social learning hypothesizes that the group definitions will influence one's own favorable and unfavorable definitions of using alcohol and other drugs, which in turn will affect one's behavior with regard to the substances.

The data in Table 7.1 show that, as expected, there is a strong relationship between one's own definitions and the adult, peer, and religious norm qualities (permissive, prescriptive, ascriptive, or proscriptive) to which they have been exposed. The measures of norm qualities refer specifically to the adults and peers whose opinions the respondent highly valued, including (but not limited to) parents and close friends. Group norm qualities explain 40% of the variance in one's own attitudes about alcohol and marijuana.

This substantiates the first part of the process, whereby one's own definitions are related to group definitions. Table 7.2 presents findings on the next step in the process, where alcohol and drug behavior are related to the groups' and one's own norm qualities. Not shown in the table is the finding that group norm qualities by themselves, without measures of one's own definitions in the equation, have a modest direct effect on alcohol behavior (explaining 19% of the variance in use and 9% of the variance in abuse) and marijuana behavior (explaining 14% of the variance in use and 8% of the variance in abuse). The process whereby the various primary groups' norm qualities affect substance use is hypothesized to be one in which the groups' norms are learned and taken on by the individual as his or her own normative attitudes toward the substance. If the adolescents' friends, family, and religion disapprove of alcohol or marijuana, there is a lower probability that young people will come to approve of drug taking or drinking and will act accordingly. Therefore, we would expect to find, as we have, not only that one's own normative orientation tends to be congruent with that of his or her primary groups but also that there is a relationship between one's own attitudes and substance use and abuse. Further, we would expect that one's own definitions should mediate the relationship between norm qualities and behavior, a finding supported by the data in Table 7. 2. There is a strong zero-order relationship between one's own normative orientation and behavior

Table 7.1   The Relationships between One's Own Attitudes toward Alcohol Use and Marijuana Use and Reference Group Norm Qualities: Zero-Order Correlations and Partial Regression (standardized beta) Coefficients

| | Own Definitions of | | | |
| | Alcohol | | Marijuana | |
	$r=$	$B=$	$r=$	$B=$
Adult norm qualities	.37	.19	.26	.15
Peer norm qualities	.59	.52	.61	.57
Religious norm qualities	.18	.05	.08	.04
Religious affiliation[a]	.11	.06	.08	.04
$R^2 =$	.40		.40	
$N =$	2,473		2,463	

[a]Ordinal scale of no religion, Catholics and Jews, nonfundamentalist Protestants, fundamentalist Protestants.
SOURCE: Adapted from Krohn, et al. (1982).

($r = .54$ for alcohol and $r = .70$ for marijuana). And with one's own definitions in the equation the direct effects of the group norm qualities are significantly reduced, down to essentially zero effect for religious and adult norm qualities.

Also, the total amount of explained variance of use and abuse increases very substantially when one's own definitions are entered into the equation. For alcohol use, explained variance is nearly doubled, and it is increased by more than three times for marijuana use. Similarly, the variance explained in alcohol abuse is nearly doubled, and the variance explained in marijuana abuse is doubled.

ADOLESCENT USE AND ABUSE OF ALCOHOL AND MARIJUANA

To test the full social learning model of differential association, imitation, definitions, and differential reinforcement, the main analyses of data from the study concentrated on the individual variations in abstaining from or drinking alcoholic beverages and smoking marijuana, including variations among users in abuse of these substances. Table 7.3 reports findings that offer strong support for the theory. The bivariate and the multivariate coefficients show that both teenage drinking and mari-

Table 7.2   The Relationship of Alcohol and Marijuana Use and Abuse with Group Norm Qualities and One's Own Definitions of Alcohol and Marijuana: Zero-Order Correlations and Partial Regression (standardized beta) Coefficients

| | Alcohol | | | | Marijuana | | | |
| | Use | | Abuse | | Use | | Abuse | |
	$r=$	$B=$	$r=$	$B=$	$r=$	$B=$	$r=$	$B=$
Own definitions	.54	.45	.33	.25	.70	.65	.40	.36
Religious affiliation	.16	.10	.10	.08	.08	.03	.10	.07
Peer norm qualities	.40	.13	.27	.12	.47	.09	.25	.06
Religious norm qualities	.11	−.02	.04	−.02	.11	−.05	.10	.05
Adult norm qualities	.23	.02	.14	.03	.20	.02	.11	.02
$R^2 =$		.32		.13		.49		.17

SOURCE: Adapted from Krohn et al. (1982).

Table 7.3   Zero-Order Correlation and Partial Regression (standardized beta) Coefficients of Social Learning Variables for Alcohol and Marijuana Use

	Alcohol		Marijuana	
	$r=$	$B=$	$r=$	$B=$
Imitation				
Imitation index	.16	.01	.38	.03
Definitions				
Neutralizing definitions	.34	.04	.48	.02
Law-Abiding/violating definitions	.47	.14	.40	.05
Positive/negative definitions	.52	.16	.72	.26
Differential Association				
Exposure to adult norms	.20	.00	.24	.02
Exposure to peer norms	.40	.05	.50	.08
Differential peer association	.68	.46	.79	.55
Differential Reinforcement				
Social				
Praise for not using	.28	.03	.29	.00
Friends' reactions to one's use	.40	.01	.50	.02
Parents' reactions to one's use	.29	.06	.18	.01
Informal deterrence	.13	.03	.31	.01
Formal deterrence	.04	.02	.15	.03
Interference with activities	.21	.00	.36	.03
Social/Nonsocial Combined				
Rewards-costs of use	.44	.07	.15	.02
Reinforcement balance	.46	.09	.52	.08
$R^2 =$	.54		.68	

Alcohol use $N = 2{,}414$; marijuana use $N = 2{,}395$. Differences in N result from listwise deletion of missing values. Similar results are found with pairwise deletion.
SOURCE: Adapted from Akers et al. (1979).

juana use are related to all of the social learning variables (with the exception of formal deterrence of drinking). Very strong bivariate relationships are found with peer associations and attitudes, one's own positive/negative definitions, reinforcement balance, and the rewards-costs of use. The other coefficients show moderate to strong effects. The results of the multiple regression analysis show that more than one-half of the total variance ($R^2 = .54$) in frequency of drinking and more than two-thirds of the variance ($R^2 = .68$) in marijuana use were accounted for by the theoretical variables.

The strength of the standardized partial regression coefficients in the table indicates that both the full model and each of the five major subsets of variables (measuring the major social learning concepts of imitation, definitions, differential association, and social and nonsocial differential reinforcement) are significantly related to alcohol and marijuana use. This is confirmed when multiple regression models are run separately for each subset of variables, as shown in Table 7.4. Moreover, with the exception of the measure of imitation, each of the subsets explains a substantial portion of variance in the dependent variables. Thus, the

Table 7.4   Multiple Regression of Alcohol and Marijuana Use and Abuse on the Major Subsets of Social Learning Variables

	Alcohol $R^2 =$		Marijuana $R^2 =$	
	Use	Abuse	Use	Abuse
Imitation	.16	.02	.14	.01
Definitions	.36	.11	.53	.19
Differential association	.47	.25	.58	.31
Differential reinforcement				
Social	.23	.07	.33	.15
Social/nonsocial	.28	.13	.38	.15
R^2 for all variables =	.54	.31	.68	.39

Ns for use same as in Table 7.3. Alcohol abuse $N = 1,764$; marijuana abuse $N = 948$. A variable measuring the balance of positive and negative usual effects felt when ingesting alcohol or marijuana was added to the equations for abuse.
Source: Adapted from Akers et al. (1979).

power of the social learning model does not depend on only one component. Although interrelationships among the independent variables are expected, they still should have separable effects on the dependent variables, and that is what was found. The strongest subset of variables is the measures of differential association, and within this the measure of differential peer association is the most important variable.

The findings from the Boys Town Study support the social learning hypothesis about the mechanisms by which peer influence is exercised—friends (and to some extent parents) reinforce or punish, provide normative definitions of, and to a lesser extent serve as admired models for use or abstinence. When the effects of the differential peer association variable are removed, the remaining social learning variables still explain substantial amounts of variance in marijuana and alcohol behavior. The weaker effects of imitation are to be expected. Imitation refers to the narrowest range of empirical phenomena, and the interrelationships among the independent variables expected in the theory mean that much of the concept's impact is absorbed by the other, broader measures; furthermore, its operationalization is probably the least satisfactory of all of the measures in this study. More importantly, the role of imitation in social learning theory is considered greatest in the acquisition or initiation stages. Imitation is expected to be more significant in first starting to use than in frequency of use, in maintenance of use, and in abuse, which were the dependent variables in the Boys Town Study.

One may conclude from these findings that social learning theory is a powerful explanation of whether youngsters abstain from using and of the frequency with which they use these substances. As the theory predicts, they use drugs or drink alcohol to the extent that the behavior has been differentially reinforced through association in primary groups and defined more favorably than abstinence. Moreover, the findings in Table 7.4 support the hypothesis that the same social learning variables substantially affect the probability that the adolescent who begins use will move on to more serious involvement in drugs and alcohol. The analysis of abuse included only users, but the findings are similar to those for differences between users and nonusers. The explained variance in abuse is lower (partly a function of the more truncated variance in the abuse variables), but it is still substantial.

CESSATION OR CONTINUATION OF DRUG USE

As I have shown, social learning theory addresses the entire use process of abstinence, frequency of use, abuse, cessation, and relapse. The next step in the Boys Town Study was to test the hypothesis that the social learning variables will differentiate between those who begin and then stop using drugs and those who begin and continue using. To do this we went beyond looking at drinking alcohol and smoking marijuana to measure cessation not only of the use of these drugs but of stimulants, depressants, and stronger drugs like heroin and cocaine as well.

The measurement of the social learning variables has already been described. Nine were employed in the analysis of cessation: Imitation Index, Specific Positive/Negative Definitions, Differential Peer Association, Friends' Reactions to One's Use, Parents' Reactions to One's Use, Informal Deterrence, Formal Deterrence, Reinforcement Balance, and Usual Effects Felt When the Substance Is Used. Each of these was measured for each category of substance use. Because the issue is whether social learning can discriminate between those who continue to use and those who have ceased using a particular substance, we felt that employing discriminant function analysis was more appropriate than the multiple regression techniques used in analyzing the frequency of use and abuse. In the two-group discriminant function analysis, one group is defined as the adolescents in the sample who started using but stopped, while the other group is defined as those who report current use. The first group is made up of respondents who reported that they used a given substance "some but have stopped" or "quite a bit but stopped." The latter group is composed of those who reported that they "have not stopped; still use" a given substance. The analysis does not include anyone who has never used a given substance or has used it only once.

If social learning theory is correct, cessation should be related to a preponderance of nonusing associations, aversive drug experiences, negative social sanctions, exposure to abstinent models, and definitions unfavorable to continued substance use. This, indeed, is what was found. The squared canonical correlations ranged from .18 for cessation of alcohol, to .35 for marijuana, to .36 for stronger drugs (Lanza-Kaduce et al., 1984).

Why some adolescents stop using and others continue depends to a large extent on where they stand with regard to the social learning factors. As predicted by the theory, teenagers who take up drinking or other drug use will stop when they associate less with using than with nonusing friends, develop definitions counter to continuing use, and find the drug experience no longer rewarding (or less rewarding or more costly than giving it up). As is true for abstinence and frequency of use, cessation or continuation is most influenced by peer associations.

EMPIRICAL COMPARISON OF SOCIAL LEARNING

WITH OTHER THEORIES

We designed the Boys Town project to test not only social learning theory but other theories as well, particularly social bonding theory and anomie/strain theory. The plan was to apply them singly and in comparison with one another to adolescent alcohol and drug behavior. As far as we could tell at the time, this was the first attempt to collect data utilizing direct measures, designed as such from the beginning, of the major concepts of all three theories and to test their explanatory power with the same dependent variables and population. We subsequently learned that Delbert Elliott and his associates at the University of Colorado were doing very much the same thing (but with a goal of theory integration) about that time with a national sample.

The first step in judging the relative efficacy of the three theories in explaining adolescent drug use and abuse was to test each theory separately. The findings reported thus far have shown social learning to be an empirically valid explanation of adolescent abstinence, frequency of substance use, and cessation or continuation of the use of alcohol, marijuana, and other drugs. The empirical models from strain theory we tested were quite weak but in the direction expected. We found more support for social bonding models of alcohol and marijuana use and minor delinquency. There was weaker but still positive support for social bonding models of harder drug use and more serious delinquency (Krohn and Massey, 1980). The next step, and the one I will focus on here, is to compare empirical models of the three theories directly. That requires specifying how the social bonding and anomie/strain theories would explain adolescent substance use.

Social Bonding Theory. Hirschi's social bonding theory explains adolescent delinquency as resulting "when an individual's bond to society is weak or broken," (1969:16). There are four principal "elements" that make up this bond—attachment, commitment, involvement, and beliefs. The weaker these elements are with regard to adults (e.g., parents and schoolteachers) and peers, the less the individual's behavior is controlled, and the more likely it is that he or she will violate the law or social norms.

Attachment is the extent to which we have close affectional ties to others, admire them, and identify with them so that we care about their expectations. The more insensitive we are to others' opinions, the less we are constrained by the norms that we share with them; therefore, the more likely we are to violate these norms. To Hirschi, such concepts as self-control, internalization of norms, internal control, indirect control, personal control, and conscience are too subjective. They cannot be observed and measured. "The essence of internalization of norms, conscience, or superego thus lies in the attachment of the individual to others" (Hirschi, 1969:18).

Hirschi emphasizes that attachment to parents and parental supervision are important in controlling delinquency and maintaining conformity. But he also stresses that attachment to peers can control delinquent tendencies. Although he often uses the phrase "attachment to conventional others," Hirschi maintains it is the fact of attachment to other people itself, not the character of the people to whom one is attached, that determines adherence to or violation of conventional rules. "We honor those we admire not by imitation, but by adherence to conventional standards" (Hirschi, 1969:152). Therefore, the more adolescents are attached to parents and friends, the less likely they are to be delinquent, even if the parents and friends are themselves deviant.

Commitment refers to the extent to which individuals have built up an investment in conventionality, or a "stake in conformity" (Toby, 1957), such as investment in educational or occupational endeavors, that would be jeopardized or lost by engaging in lawbreaking or other forms of deviance. The cost of losing one's investment in conformity prevents one from violating norms. Commitment, therefore, refers to a more or less rational element in the decision to perpetrate crime.

Involvement refers to one's absorption in conventional pursuits like studying, extracurricular activities, and spending time with the family. One is restrained from delinquent behavior because one is too busy, too preoccupied, or too consumed in conforming activities to become involved in nonconforming pursuits.

Belief is defined as the endorsement of general conventional values and norms, especially the belief that laws and society's rules in general are morally correct and should be obeyed. The concept does not necessarily refer to beliefs about specific laws or acts, nor does it imply that people hold specifically deviant beliefs. "[T]he less a person believes he should obey the rules, the more likely he is to violate them" (Hirschi, 1969:26).

The theory, then, would predict a negative relationship between drug use and each element of the social bond. It would explain adolescents' drug use as resulting from weak attachment, commitment, involvement, and beliefs.

Hirschi (1969) provided clear measures for the four principal elements of the social bond. Although most research projects on this theory have not used the same standards he employed, the bulk of the research has employed either Hirschi's or similar measures (Kempf, 1993). Reviewing the measures of the four main elements will help clarify the results of the research on social bonding theory.

An adolescent's attachment to parents is measured by close parental supervision and discipline, good communication and relationships, and his or her close affectional identification with them (e.g., he or she would like to be the same kind of person as the parent). Academic achievement (as demonstrated by grades, test scores, and self-perception of scholastic ability) is taken to indicate attachment to school, but it also indicates to some extent commitment and involvement. Attachment to school is directly measured by positive attitudes toward school, a concern for teachers' opinions of oneself, and an acceptance of the school's authority. Attachment to peers is measured by affectional identification with and respect for the opinions of best friends. Recall that in social bonding theory it is the strength of this attachment to parents and peers itself, not the conforming or nonconforming behavior and attitudes of these significant others, that is predicted to have effect.

Adolescents' commitment to conventional lines of action refers to their desire and pursuit of conventional goals. Premature engagement in adult activities like smoking, drinking, or owning a car indicates a lack of commitment to achieving educational goals and to conformity as an adolescent. Commitment to education is measured by both educational aspirations (e.g., earning a college degree) and achievement orientation. Commitment is also measured by occupational aspirations. Adolescent involvement in conventional activities includes working part time, dating, sports, recreation, hobbies, doing homework, and spending time with friends.

Belief is measured by reference to values relative to the law and the criminal-justice system. These include the extent to which an adolescent has general respect for the police and the law, believes that the law should be obeyed, adheres to the techniques of neutralization, and endorses middle-class values like the importance of education.

Hirschi's own investigations (1969) supported the theory, and a large body of research on social bonding theory has developed (Kempf, 1993) that, on the whole, has been supportive (e.g., Hindelang, 1973; Austin, 1977; Johnson, 1979; Wiatrowski et al., 1981; Krohn et al., 1983; Lasley, 1988), although at least one review article concludes that "[b]y this important measure of scientific merit, social control theory has not fared well" (Kempf, 1993:167).

In the Boys Town Study we measured attachment by a maternal attachment scale and a paternal attachment scale, each containing six items (e.g., "seems to understand you," "makes you feel close to her,"), and by a five-item peer attachment scale. We reasoned that measures of school attachment used by Hirschi and others, such as grade point average, come closer to measuring the concept of commitment. Also measures of involvement in conventional activities used by Hirschi (particularly measures of time involved in such activities) more clearly indicate commitment than involvement (Krohn and Massey, 1980). Therefore, we combined commitment and involvement into one element measured by four variables: commitment to conventional activities (athletics, music, church, etc.), educational aspirations, occupational aspirations, and grade point average. Beliefs were measured by three items asking the respondents' agreement or disagreement with values of parents, the law, and education.

Strain Theory. This concept is derived from Merton's (1938; 1957) well-known anomie theory, a macro-level explanation of the concentration of officially recorded crime in lower-class urban areas, as well as of the high overall crime rate in U.S. society. Anomie is the form that societal malintegration takes when there is a dissociation between valued cultural ends and legitimate societal means to those ends. The cultural emphasis on success goals in the United States is not matched by an equally strong emphasis on socially approved means. Further, there is a discrepancy between means and ends perpetuated by the class system in the United States and, to a lesser degree, in other industrialized societies. The success ethic permeates all levels of the class structure and is embodied in the educational system, to which persons of all social classes are exposed. The American dream promotes the ideal that equal opportunity for success is available to everyone. In reality, however, disadvantaged groups do not have equal access to such legitimate opportunities. They are socialized to hold high aspirations, yet they are relatively blocked off from the conventional educational and occupational opportunities needed to realize those ambitions. This anomic condition produces "strain," or pressure, on these groups to take advantage of whatever effective means to success they can find, even if these means are illegitimate or illegal.

In Cohen's (1955) version, this anomic condition arises because lower-class boys are judged by unattainable middle-class criteria. In Cloward and Ohlin's (1960) version (differential opportunity theory), the discrepancy between goal and means relates to both legitimate and illegitimate opportunities. Whatever the source of the strain, the expectation is that individuals will become alienated and either seek deviant means to success or retreat into drug abuse. The sociological concept of anomie as alienation and powerlessness is similar to the psychological concept of locus of control (Rotter, 1954), in which individuals either feel that they have mastery over events or that control lies in the hands of others or of fate.

As Thomas Bernard (1987) and Steven F. Messner (1988) argue, Merton's anomie theory is a structural one that makes no direct predictions about individual behavior. Nevertheless, the gap between the cultural ends and the social means that it proposes at the structural level implies that there must be some perception of this discrepancy at the individual level. At the social psychological level, then, strain may be experienced as a discrepancy between an individual's aspirations and expectations about access to appropriate means. Aspirations involve what one hopes to achieve in life, economically, educationally, or occupationally (e.g., how much schooling one would like to complete). Expectations refer to what one believes is realistically possible to achieve (e.g., how much education one could expect to get). Strain theory predicts that the greater the perceived discrepancy between aspirations and expectations, the higher the probability of deviant behavior. A considerable amount of research has tested this "strain" hypothesis (Hirschi, 1969; Liska, 1971; Elliott et al., 1985; Farnworth and Leiber, 1989; McGee, 1992).

We measured the discrepancy between aspirations and expectations in the Boys Town Study for both education (how far the respondent would like to go in school versus how far he or she actually expected to go) and occupation (how important is it to get a good job after finishing education versus the expectation that one will get that kind of job). Alienation was measured within the context of the school with three items—learning in school is relevant to getting a job, students are involved in decisions at school, and students have influence in running the school. Locus of control was measured by one item indicating internal locus of control and one item indicating external locus of control.

FINDINGS ON THE RELATIVE EMPIRICAL VALIDITY OF THE THREE THEORIES

The dependent variable in this analysis was marijuana use. On its own, the fifteen-variable social learning model explained 68% of the variance in the dependent variable. The social bonding model, with ten variables, accounted for 30% of the variance. The four-variable strain model accounted for 3% of the variance. Therefore, each theoretical model has some empirical validity. But these findings show that the strength of that empirical validity differs greatly. There is strong empirical support for social learning, moderately strong support for social bonding, and positive but weak support for the strain model of adolescent marijuana use. The social learning variables account for more than twice as much variance as social bonding variables and for more than twenty times as much variance as the strain variables.

This kind of direct comparison of explained variance by different regression models is possible in a study like this one in which the dependent variable and its variance is measured in the same way, in the same population with the same instrument. This also allows for an even more revealing comparison by putting the variables from all three theories into the same regression model and directly comparing which variables have the strongest net effects on the dependent variable, an outcome shown in Table 7.5.

To equalize the number of independent variables in each model, the variables in Table 7.5 include only three social learning, four social bonding, and four strain variables. These are the strongest variables from each theory. From the findings in this table it is clear that only the social

---

Table 7.5 Comparison of Relative Efficacy of Social Learning, Social Bonding, and Strain Variables in Explaining Adolescent Marijuana Use: Standardized Partial Regression (beta) Coefficients

	$B=$
Social Learning Variables	
Positive/negative definitions	.24
Differential peer associations	.44
Friend's reactions to one's use	.15
Social Bonding Variables	
Commitment to conventional activities	−.07
Grade point average	−.05
Belief in parents' values	−.02
Belief in the law	−.04
Strain Variables	
Discrepancy in educational aspirations/ expectations	.01
Discrepancy in occupational aspirations/expectations	−.00
Contextual alienation	.00
Locus of control	.02
$R^2 =$	.69
$N =$	3,055

SOURCE: Adapted from Akers and Cochran (1985).

learning variables have substantial net relationships with marijuana use. In fact, all of the social bonding effects are reduced to nonsignificance and all of the effects of strain variables are reduced to zero.

Thus, when the variables from all three theories are placed into the same regression equation (based on the same sample, instrument, and measure of the dependent variable) so that net effects can be discerned, it is clear that whatever effects the bonding and strain variables have are absorbed or mediated by the social learning variables. This combined model with variables from all three theories added only 1% ($R^2 = .69$) to the variance explained by the social learning model alone ($R^2 = .68$). The strong empirical support for social learning becomes even stronger when it is put in direct empirical competition with other theories.

This finding from the Boys Town Study that social learning theory does especially well when compared directly to other theoretical models has been confirmed by subsequent research. Whenever social learning theory is tested against other theories using the same data collected from the same samples with good measures of all variables it has been found to account for more variance in the dependent variables than the theories with which it is being compared (Elliott et al., 1985; White et al., 1986; McGee, 1992; Benda, 1994).

Summary and Conclusion

Social learning theory proposes a process whereby the probability of beginning and continuing to use some substance is a function of the four main variables of differential association, imitation, definitions, and differential reinforcement. That is, onset and continuation or cessation comes from a process in which there is greater exposure to using than to abstaining norms and models, more association with using than with abstaining peers and others, differential reinforcement of use over abstinence, and adherence to definitions of use in positive or neutralizing terms. Among users the probability of developing excessive or abusive drug patterns increases when they come to associate more with high-frequency users, find more rewarding than aversive consequences attached to their abusive patterns, continue to define use in positive or neutralizing ways, and become more exposed to rewarding and rewarded models of drug abuse behavior.

The Boys Town Study was the first major project to test the full social learning model. It was designed to collect primary data in the field, using good measures of all theoretical variables, in order to test social learning on its own and in comparison with other major theories of deviance. The classic steps in theory testing were followed in the right sequence. The theory was formulated, hypotheses were derived predicting expected relationships, measures of the principal theoretical concepts were devised, the data were collected, and the hypotheses were tested against the data. The findings from the Boys Town Study strongly support the theoretical model. The main variables from social learning theory have strong effects and are able to account for high levels of explained variance (up to 68%) in adolescent alcohol and drug behavior. Each set of variables measuring the four main concepts on its own also accounts for substantial amounts of explained variance in these forms of adolescent deviance. Although the strength of relationships for the full model and for variable subsets, as well as for different stages of use and different substances, varies, the social learning model works well for use/nonuse, heavy use and abuse, and cessation of use for both minor and serious drug behavior (Akers et al., 1979; Krohn et al., 1982; Lanza-Kaduce et al., 1984; Krohn et al., 1984; Akers and Cochran, 1985).

A great deal of other research on adolescent substance use has produced findings that are very consistent with those from the Boys Town Study, further supporting the social learning theory of substance use. Some of this research preceded the Boys Town Study and, while not specifically testing the Akers' social learning model, did find support for theoretical models that overlapped with or shared a common perspective with social learning (see, for instance, Jessor and Jessor, 1977; Kandel, 1974). But most of the supportive research has been done after the Boys Town Study and specifically included direct measures of social learning concepts (see, for instance, Dull, 1983; Winfree and Griffiths, 1983; Dembo et al., 1986; Marcos et al., 1986; Burkett and Warren, 1987; Orcutt, 1987; White et al., 1987; Winfree et al., 1989; McGeee, 1992; Benda, 1994).

We ended the first article published from the Boys Town Study (Akers et al., 1979) with the statement that longitudinal data would allow a more adequate test of the underlying process and ordering of variables in the theory than the cross-sectional data we had already collected. Other research prior to our study had reported findings consistent with the typical history of coming to use drugs, in which the youngster associates differentially with peers, family members, and others who are users or tolerant of use, learns definitions favorable to use, and then uses (Jessor et al., 1973; Krohn, 1974); subsequent research has produced similar findings (Andrews and Kandel, 1979; Sellers and Winfree, 1991; Elliott and Menard, 1991; Elliott, 1994). I hoped at the time that longitudinal data would resolve most of the issues of causal orderings and the hypothesized typical process. Therefore, the next project I undertook to test social learning theory, on teenage smoking, was longitudinal.

That study is reported in Chapter 8. As I have argued throughout, social learning is a general theory of crime and deviance. Adolescent substance use and abuse is but one specific type of deviance on which to test the theory. Therefore, I turned to tests of the theory using other types of behavior as the dependent variable. These projects will be reported in subsequent chapters.

Adolescent Smoking Behavior: The Iowa Study

After the Boys Town Study, the next opportunity to test social learning theory came when I began a five-year longitudinal study of teenage smoking in an Iowa community with Ronald Lauer, a pediatric cardiologist at the University of Iowa medical school (Sherilyn Spear, James Massey, and William Skinner served as our research assistants). I remained with the project after moving to Florida, but my direct involvement diminished after the first two years, and I was succeeded as co–principal investigator by Marvin Krohn, who stayed with the project through to its completion. Lauer had been doing research on risk factors in pediatric heart disease for several years in a community in Iowa; and the smoking study was also carried out there (Lauer et al., 1982; Akers et al., 1983; Krohn et al., 1983; Krohn et al., 1985; Spear and Akers, 1988; Akers and Lee, 1996).

Tobacco use has increasingly come to be seen as part of the overall problem of substance use and abuse in society. Smoking at all ages, but especially during adolescence, has come to be defined as deviant behavior, and habitual smoking as an addiction. The evidence on the health hazards of smoking is clear, and this social disapproval is based not only on smoking as a violation of norms of healthful behavior but also as a violation of norms of good and acceptable behavior. The disapproval has become more strident as smokers of all ages are increasingly defined as pariahs and morally condemned. The restrictive nature of legal regulation has made smoking in most public accommodations illegal. Organized interest groups have been working for many years to secure ever more restrictive regulations on smoking and to ban all tobacco advertising (Troyer and Markle, 1983).

The notion that smokers are drug-dependent has been formalized in declarations by the U.S. surgeon general and the Food and Drug Administration that nicotine is an addictive drug; it is proported to produce an addiction that is more difficult to overcome than heroin addiction. Even tobacco companies have stipulated, in an effort to settle lawsuits, that tobacco is addictive. Prevention and treatment of smoking has become a major industry, and nicotine addiction, relapse, and treatment have come to be viewed in the literature as essentially the same as the processes involved with any other drug. The textbooks on drug use and abuse routinely include sections or chapters on tobacco (Akers, 1992b; Goode, 1993; Ray and Ksir, 1993; Fishbein and Pease, 1996), and journals on alcohol and drug behavior regularly carry articles on the etiology, prevention, and treatment of nicotine addiction (Carmody, 1992), including adolescent smoking (Urberg et al., 1991).

Smoking, even by adolescents, is still apt to be seen as less serious than using illegal drugs, but there can be little doubt that nicotine is now considered by public opinion and in the research community to be a drug that is used and abused with serious negative consequences. Among teenagers, smoking is correlated with the use of alcohol, marijuana, and other drugs and bears a substantial relationship to involvement in serious delinquency (Jessor and Jessor, 1977; Akers, 1992b). As with all drug use, most of those who smoke begin in the adolescent years, and there have been recent increases in tobacco smoking among teenagers (along with increases in the use of other substances). The issue of explaining and predicting smoking among adolescents, then, is related to that of drug use of all kinds, and general models of substance use should apply to smoking as well as to consumption of other substances. Tobacco use among adolescents, therefore, is a relevant type of behavior on which to test the social learning theory of deviant behavior. It was with this in mind that we undertook the teenage smoking project.

The Iowa study was also intended to develop and implement a smoking-prevention project based on social learning theory. However, this model was never put into place as envisioned. The prevention program was designed to be implemented in the seventh grade during the second year of the project, with findings on smoking behavior in the first year serving as the baseline. It targeted one junior high school as the treatment group and used the other as the control group. In the treatment school, an in-class anti-smoking program would be instituted. Students in classes that showed reductions in proportions and frequency of smoking during and following the program or that showed lower levels of onset of smoking than those experienced by students the year before would receive special rewards. These included such activities as early-out days, being released from some exams, special field trips, and free travel and admission to a University of Iowa football game. The program was to teach social skills and ways of countering pro-smoking influence, attitudes, and models from peers and media through role playing and sociodrama. We also planned to introduce athletes and other high-prestige high school students into junior high classes and activities as nonsmoking models. The program would involve initial sessions and later booster sessions for several days. However, most of the plan was not implemented because of difficulties in getting school officials to approve the rewards activities, to allow high school students released time to come to the junior high schools, or to commit as much time to the program as planned. A smoking-education program was instituted for seventh grade students in certain classes, but it simply amounted to a few class periods studying anti-smoking materials and thus had very little to do with social learning theory. Not surprisingly, it had little discernible preventive effect on taking up smoking.

Social Learning Theory of Adolescent Smoking

This approach draws on the four principal sets of independent variables in social learning—differential association, differential reinforcement, definitions, and imitation. Through differential association, varying in frequency, intensity, duration, and priority, with those who smoke and those who do not smoke in family and peer groups (as well as by contact with secondary reference groups and by behavioral and normative patterns portrayed in the media) children and youth learn definitions favorable or unfavorable to smoking and are exposed to behavioral models that may be imitated. Differential reinforcement refers to the process whereby behavior is acquired and persists or does not develop depending on the anticipated, past, and present rewards and punishments attached to it and to alternative behavior. These may be social (direct social reactions to smoking or other direct and indirect social consequences attached to it) or nonsocial (from the direct physiological and health effects of smoking).

These variables are part of an ongoing behavioral process. Although the sequence of empirical events may change, depending on the particular behavior and individuals in question, the typical process envisioned by the theory is that individuals interact and identify with different groups in which they are exposed to behavioral models, norms, and reinforcement patterns tending toward abstinence or smoking. The balance of definitions favorable and unfavorable to smoking combines with imitation and the anticipated balance of reinforcement to produce or inhibit initial smoking. After one starts to smoke, imitation becomes less important (although facilitative effects of modeling may remain), while the influences of norms and definitions (themselves now affected by the consequences of initial smoking) continue to have an effect on the development of stable or habitual use. Differential association is hypothesized to have a strong impact on both initiation and maintenance of smoking. Those associations are most often formed initially on bases other than co-involvement in smoking. This is obviously true within the family, and it is also hypothesized to be the typical case with peer associations. However, forming or continuing peer friendships will be affected in part by one's own attitudes and by parental and peer reinforcement. Further, after the young person has begun smoking and has experienced the social and nonsocial consequences accompanying it, the associational patterns (those over which one has any choice) may themselves be altered.

Pomerleau and Pomerleau point to both social reinforcement and the physiologically reinforcing effects of nicotine in sustaining smoking behavior:

> Some of these phenomena can be explained in a straightforward manner within the context of social learning theory. Acquisition of the habit is known to occur under conditions of social reinforcement. . . . Smoking can thus be conceptualized as a generalized primary and secondary reinforcer, providing both positive and negative reinforcement over a remarkably wide array of life situations. Smoking is also powerfully entrained because of its ability to provide immediate reinforcement: Nicotine from an inhaled cigarette reaches the brain in seven seconds. . . . Furthermore, the habit is greatly over learned: at ten puffs per cigarette, the pack-a-day smoker gets more than 70,000 puffing

reinforcements in a year—a frequency unmatched by any other form of drug taking. Although most smokers recognize that sustained smoking can lead to a variety of unpleasant consequences, . . . these aversive consequences are delayed and therefore have less influence over ongoing smoking behavior than immediate consequences—a situation common to a number of substances of abuse. Unlike alcohol and many other dependence-producing substances, however, not only does nicotine *not* impair performance, but it seems to enhance the capacity of normal people to work and to socialize. There are thus few immediate noticeable negative consequences to interfere with entertainment. (Pomerleau and Pomerleau, 1988:122–23)

Methodology of the Iowa Study

SAMPLE AND PROCEDURE

The project to test this theory of adolescent smoking was a longitudinal study of secondary school students in a community in Iowa with a population of about 23,000. The research was a self-report questionnaire survey of students attending the two junior high schools (grades 7 through 9) and the one senior high school (grades 10 through 12) in the town. The sample each year (about 2,000) included students who had already participated for one or more years, new respondents in the seventh grade, and new students coming into any grade who had not taken part the year before. Of course, graduating seniors and students in lower grades who left the school system the next year or who were not in attendance on the day of the annual survey were lost to further study. Embedded within this overall sample is a panel of 1,068 students who completed the questionnaire for three consecutive years and a panel of 454 students (in grades 7 and 8 in the first year of the project) who participated in the study for all five years. The findings in this chapter are based on the whole sample of the first year ($N = 2,194$), the three-year panel, and the five-year panel of respondents.

The sample approximated a complete enumeration of all students in the junior and senior high schools. All the junior-high students who were present on the day the questionnaire was administered were surveyed in their homerooms. This was done each year except for the final year of the study. Scheduling problems prohibited a complete enumeration of high school students in the first year, and the questionnaires were administered on two days in mandatory physical education classes (producing a representative sample of 74.5% of the high school student body in the first year). Subsequently, a complete enumeration of high school students was surveyed. The average completion rate for all students initially targeted at each data collection point was 91.3%. (For additional description of the study see Lauer et al., 1982; Akers et al., 1983; Krohn et al., 1985; Akers et al., 1987; Spear and Akers, 1988).

VALIDATION OF SELF-REPORTED SMOKING BEHAVIOR
WITH BIOCHEMICAL MEASURES AND RANDOMIZED RESPONSE

The truthfulness of oral or written reports of behavior is an issue regardless of what is being measured, but it is especially salient if the information asked for in the interview or survey questionnaire is sensitive, potentially incriminating, or embarrassing. As I have argued above, smoking by teenagers is socially disapproved; thus, when teenagers smoke, they do so knowing that it is generally disapproved. Moreover, many use tobacco specifically without parental knowledge, permission, or approval. Therefore, one can assume that there will be some motivation for many respondents to conceal or under-report smoking out of fear of disclosure, even as others may be motivated by a desire to be different or to show willingness to flout parental and societal rules to report themselves falsely as smokers or to over-report how much they smoke. The widespread use of self-reported behavior in studies of deviance has been accompanied by a keen awareness of both of these types of response-validity problems and attempts to get the truth about behavior that is socially defined as undesirable. Hence, a number of techniques of gauging response validity were developed long ago for self-reports of drug use, such as including a bogus drug in the list of substances and comparisons of self-reports with clinical records (Whitehead and Smart, 1972), and for other forms of self-reports of delinquent behavior, such as comparing questionnaire responses with polygraph findings and with official records (Hardt and Peterson-Hardt, 1977; Hindelang et al., 1981). On balance, the research findings from these checks on truthfulness of responses give us some confidence in the validity of self-report measures of deviance in samples of adolescents (Radosevich et al., 1979). When the reported acts involve consumption of some substance, we have the opportunity to use another type of validity check by measuring the metabolized residues of the substance in body fluids and comparing this with self-reported measures of consumption. This provides an independent biochemical indicator of behavior, one that there is no, or a very low, probability of respondents modifying successfully to produce a false reading of results.

In the Iowa study (Lauer et al., 1982; Akers et al., 1983) we gauged the truthfulness of responses to our questions about smoking by matching the answers with the level of thiocyanate (a chemical residue of nicotine) found in saliva samples taken from the same respondents. One may under-report or over-report his or her own smoking behavior, but one cannot deliberately falsify the level of thiocyanate or other residues of nicotine in body fluids. Through matching code numbers assigned to each respondent and placed on the questionnaire and the vial containing the saliva sample (5 milliliters), we were able to match the individual's self-report response to a series of questions about smoking with the amount of thiocyanate in his or her saliva.

We also checked response validity with a technique known as randomized response. Here, the group rate of self-reported smoking given by respondents on the confidential questionnaire was checked against the rate obtained from an anonymous response to one question randomly selected from two questions. One question concerns something innocuous (e.g., My birthday is in April) and the other concerns the more sensitive question of interest (e.g., I have smoked cigarettes yesterday or today). The response is given on a single sheet with nothing on it except the two questions and a place to check the response (in this case Yes or No). Since there is no way for anyone except the respondent to know which question was randomly selected to be answered by that individual, and since even the respondent's reply does not identity which question has been selected, the procedure makes it obvious to the respondent that anonymity cannot be compromised. The assumption is that any tendency to over-report or under-report that may arise from uncertainties about whether confidential responses might be revealed, and fear of any negative consequences stemming from such a revelation, would be completely assuaged by this totally anonymous procedure. Therefore, group proportions measured by the randomized response can be used as a validity check by comparing them with group proportions obtained from responses to the confidential questionnaire.

The levels of thiocyanate found in the saliva of the teenagers in the study corresponded closely to their self-reports about smoking within the last forty-eight hours, how frequently they smoked, how many cigarettes they smoked each day, and their self-descriptions as nonsmokers, moderate smokers, or heavy smokers. Using this procedure, we were able to estimate that only about 1% to 2% of the self-report responses were invalid either because of over-reporting or under-reporting. The randomized response procedure also showed a high level of validity in the respondents' answers. The proportion reporting smoking at least once on the questionnaire and the proportion reporting smoking at least once on the randomized response instrument were essentially the same (within the 95% confidence level). Both the biochemical measure of nicotine residues and the randomized response procedure clearly indicated the validity of the self-report measures of smoking behavior in the Iowa study.

Measurement of Social Learning Variables

All of the social learning variables measured with multiple questionnaire items were produced from factor analysis; the scales were created by summing responses for items for which the standardized score loaded .40 or above on the factor. The reliability of each scale was established by Cronbach alpha coefficients of .50 to .91 (see Krohn et al., 1985; Spear and Akers, 1988).

IMITATION/MODELING

Theoretically, imitation and association are part of the same underlying process of behavioral acquisition and maintenance, as is also true for acquiring favorable and unfavorable definitions and for the processes of reinforcement. But associations, definitions, and reinforcement can be fairly cleanly differentiated with empirical measures. It is more difficult through self-reports to disentangle imitation processes from association processes. Imitation is predicated on observing or being aware of the behavior of admired or significant models. In the Boys Town Study we asked about "observing or watching" parents, people on television or in movies, other family members, others about the respondent's own age, and older persons. The responses for all of these were combined into an overall index of imitation. This is a good measure of imitation because it taps the observation of models, but it does not allow for measuring variations in frequency of behavior by the models or for differentiating between parental and peer models. It also does not allow for measuring general imitative effects based on awareness of others' smoking beyond that gained from direct observation while in the company of smokers.

In the Iowa study we measured imitation in the general sense of being aware of smoking or nonsmoking by significant others. The assumption was that this awareness could be based on direct observation or simply on knowing about the behavior of significant models. Therefore, instead of asking only about those whom one has observed smoking, we asked, "As far as you know, about how much does each of the following people smoke?" Those listed were mother, father, best female friend, best male friend, brother, and sister. The response categories were never, once in a while, at least once a week, nearly every day or every day, and used to smoke but not now. We used the responses for mother and father as measures of *Parental Modeling* and the responses for friends as measures of *Friends' Modeling*. Parental and friends' modeling were also combined into an overall *Index of Imitation*. (We did not utilize sibling modeling.)

We gain something with this measure, since it allows for gauging parental and peer imitation in the same way. But it overlaps, more than the Boys Town measure, with indicators of peer association. The two processes of imitation and association can be separated in a controlled laboratory setting where the one observing can be separated from models and when the models are displayed on the screen or other media where the models are observed but one cannot interact with them or be personally in their presence. The influence of behavioral models shown in the media should not be underestimated, but they are secondary to in-person modeling in primary groups of family and friends.

Therefore, it is important to delineate modeling processes in family and peer groups. Even though the measure of association is often simply a question about the behavior of others with whom one is in interaction, it is easier to argue that questions about being aware of or directly observing the behavior of others have face validity as measures of imitation, rather than as measures of association, when the models are parents or other adults (and perhaps older adolescents) than when the models are same-age peers. Children "look up" to parents as models, and, especially in the younger years, the adolescent is watching, observing, and modeling parents in a way that is substantively different from the same processes in association with peers. Further, it is accepted that socialization in the family involves training by parental example. Therefore, asking adolescents whether one or both parents use tobacco or other substances is a valid way of measuring parental modeling. It is more difficult to devise measures that distinguish between imitation and associations in peer groups; asking about awareness or observation of friends' behavior taps empirical events that also are, and have been used by researchers as, indicators of peer associational patterns. How does one measure the different dimensions of association and imitation in the field when they are occurring simultaneously? This was the challenge facing us in both the Boys Town and Iowa studies. I believe we were successful, but only up to a point.

ASSOCIATION/IMITATION

We also attempted to measure imitation in the Iowa study by asking those who had already begun smoking, "How often have you smoked in front of the following?" (mother, father, brother, sister, other relatives, friends, other peers). Nonsmokers were asked the same question, phrased as, "If you were to start smoking, how often would you smoke in front of the following . . .?" Since imitation is a process in which one observes others' behavior and then performs that behavior, we reasoned that asking about smoking in the presence of the models would tap both the observational and performance elements of imitation. For those who are nonsmokers at the time, such a measure indicates readiness to imitate observed models in their presence.

I think this is a reasonable approach to measuring imitation in natural settings, but it does not distinguish clearly between imitation and associational processes. This measure of imitation clearly differs from our main measure of differential peer association as a scale of the modalities of association with smokers and nonsmokers (see below). Nevertheless, smoking in the presence of others, even when they are parents or other adults rather than peers, necessarily implies association at least during those episodes, and such episodes are more likely to take place if one has associated with those persons in the past. It is not exactly the same as asking about the behavior of others with whom one is interacting (the usual measure of differential association), because it asks about one's own behavior in the company of others. It is also not exactly the same as measuring imitation by asking about observation or awareness of others' smoking. Earlier, we labeled this variable "integration" of smoking into one's lifestyle (Spear and Akers, 1988), on the grounds that it indicates the extent to which smoking has become an ordinary and overt part of the adolescent's everyday activities. But in recognizing that, in effect, both imitation and association are measured by the questions, I label the variable here as association/imitation.

The measure has another problem, however. Since it asks directly about how often one smokes in a particular situation (e.g., in the presence of others), it is indirectly a measure of smoking frequency. Therefore, it is confounded to some extent with the dependent variable that is a direct measure of smoking frequency, making the empirical relationship between the two at least partly tautological. This means that the correlation would be inflated to some extent, and depictions of association/imitation (measured in this way) as an independent variable producing smoking frequency must be interpreted with caution. Therefore, after the first year, we stopped using this variable in data analysis. In the second year of the study, we added (asking both smokers and nonsmokers), "Have any of the following people smoked in front of you?" This measure does a better job of distinguishing modeling from association and avoids the empirical tautology.

DIFFERENTIAL ASSOCIATION

The measure of differential peer association in the Iowa smoking study repeated the measure used in the Boys Town Study. Three of the modalities of association were measured by asking, "How many of your friends smoke?" for friends known the longest time (duration), friends most often together with (frequency), and best friends (intensity). The response categories were none, less than half, more than half, and all or almost all. These three modalities are highly intercorrelated and were formed into a scale of *Differential Peer Association.* Although it differs from our measure of peer modeling, which simply asked about awareness of friends' smoking behavior, this latter measure has been used in some of the research literature as a peer association variable. Moreover, in our study the measures of differential peer association and modeling are intercorrelated ($r = .63$), indicating that we were only partially successful in measuring imitation as a separate process that occurs during differential association. There is no comparable measure for "differential parental association" that would make any sense, and we did not try to construct one.

However, for the normative dimension of differential association, we devised directly comparable measures for both parents and friends as the most important primary groups. We did this by asking, "What is the general attitude of each of the following toward teenagers smoking?" The list included mother, father, brother, sister, other relative, best male friends, best female friends, and others about your own age. The response categories were approve, sometimes approve and sometimes disapprove, disapprove, and strongly disapprove. From this list we devised scale measures of *Parents' Definitions* and *Friends' Definitions*.

DEFINITIONS

The individual's definitions of smoking behavior were measured by a general question on his or her *Positive/Negative Definitions* (general approval or disapproval of teenage smoking). Definitions were also measured by a series of attitudinal questions to which the respondents responded on a four-point Likert scale of strong agreement to strong disagreement. Three of these attitudinal questions formed a scale of *Neutralizing Definitions* favorable to smoking (takes many years for bad health effects from smoking, smoking is all right if you do not get the habit, and is all right with parental permission). Two of the items were summed to form a scale of *Negative Definitions* counter to smoking (cigarette advertising should be stopped, and sales should be outlawed).

DIFFERENTIAL REINFORCEMENT

The measures of differential reinforcement involved asking about both positive and negative consequences. Some of these are social, while others have to do with the physical effects of smoking, both immediate and over the longer term. The same caveats given in Chapter 7 on our inability to measure directly physical, nonsocial reinforcement and to separate that from purely social reinforcement in survey research must be made again here. Nonetheless, we were better able than in the Boys Town Study to devise questions indexing experienced or anticipated physical effects differentiated from experienced or anticipated social effects.

The first sets of reinforcement measures were *Parental Reinforcement* and *Friends' Reinforcement*, positive or negative reactions of father and mother and of two best friends, respectively, to the adolescent's smoking, ranging from strongly encouraging to strongly discouraging. The other measures of differential reinforcement come from a list of "good things" and a list of "bad things" that "happen or you think would happen to you from smoking cigarettes." All of the items in the first list were summed to measure combined social and nonsocial *Positive Consequences;* all of the items in the second list were used as a general measure of social and nonsocial *Negative Consequences.* Then, from the same lists, items were selected through factor analysis to construct scales of *Positive Physical Effects* of smoking ("calming," "satisfying," "controls weight," "enjoyable," "relaxing," and "stimulating") and *Negative Physical Effects* of smoking ("tastes bad," "feel bad," "upset stomach," "get sick"). The latter factor also included one item ("hurts schoolwork") that is not a physical effect of smoking; its central meaning, however, is unpleasant physical reactions to smoking, and the label given the factor here is appropriate. Finally, two items from the list of positive consequences of smoking formed a factor labeled *Positive Social Effects* ("look sophisticated" and "feel like an adult").

MEASUREMENT OF SMOKING

The main dependent variable in the Iowa study was *Frequency of Smoking* cigarettes, measured on a six-point scale from never smoked to smoke every day or nearly every day. We also measured the number of cigarettes smoked daily (from none to more than one pack). In addition, the respondents were asked to report whether they had smoked one or more cigarettes in the past month, past week, yesterday, and today. Finally, we asked the respondents to describe themselves as a nonsmoker, ex-smoker, light smoker, moderate smoker, or heavy smoker. These other measures were taken primarily to aid in analyzing reliability and validity of self-reported smoking behavior (see Akers et al., 1983).

First-Year Cross-Sectional Findings

The social learning theory was initially tested on teenage smoking by analyzing data from the first-year survey. A six-variable social learning model was found to be strongly related cross-sectionally to frequency of smoking. As shown in Table 8.1, measures of each of the four major social learning concepts are moderately to strongly correlated with smoking frequency, and in the expected direction; taken together, these explain more than half of the variance in smoking behavior.

As the data in the table make plain, the findings from the Boys Town Study of adolescent substance abuse were essentially replicated in the results from the Iowa study of adolescent smoking. The level of explained variance in smoking ($R^2 = .54$) in the latter is exactly the same as the level we found for alcohol behavior in the earlier work. Just as in the Boys Town Study, the imitation variable in the Iowa smoking study is correlated with the dependent variable, but its main zero-order and net regression effects are less than those of the other social learning variables. The new variable of association/imitation has very strong effects, but the reader should recall my earlier caveats about confounding it with the dependent variable. As was found in the Boys Town research, differential association is the strongest social learning variable set, with both definitions and reinforcement variables also having strong effects.

Table 8.1   Social Learning and Frequency of Teenage Smoking: Zero-Order Correlation and Standardized Partial Regression Coefficients

	$r=$	$B=$
Imitation		
Index of imitation	.20	.03
Definitions		
Positive/negative definitions	.56	.20
Differential Association		
Association/imitation	.63	.38
Differential peer association	.58	.17
Differential Reinforcement		
Negative consequences	−.50	−.06
Positive consequences	.38	.11
$R^2 =$	.54[a]	
$N =$	2,156	

---

[a]This R^2 includes a seventh variable, age at onset of experimentation, $r = .07$ and $B = .02$.
SOURCE: Adapted from Spear and Akers (1988).

The influence of peers can be seen clearly in the differential peer association variable, while the influence of parents on teenage smoking is encapsulated primarily in the imitation index (and also to some extent in the association/imitation variable). Although the modeling and associational influences of parents and peers often counteract one another, they also may point in the same direction. When this happens, the combined effect on the adolescent reaches its greatest power, as shown in Table 8.2. When neither parents nor friends smoke, the individual is very likely not even to try cigarettes and is almost certain (99% of the time) not to be a regular smoker. On the other hand, when both parents and friends smoke, 84% of the youngsters have smoked at least experimentally, and 44% are regular smokers.

These findings from the Iowa study provide strong evidence favoring the social learning explanation of teenage smoking. They also add weight to the Boys Town findings that social learning is a valid explanation of

Table 8.2   The Combination Effects of Parents and Friends on Teenage Smoking

Smoking by Parents and Friends of Respondents	Smoking by Respondents		
	Never	Regularly	N =
Neither parents nor best friend smoke	75%	1%	522
Parents smoke but best friend doesn't	63	6	543
Best friend smokes but parents don't	27	26	120
Both parents and best friend smoke	16	44	458

Occasional smokers not shown.
$X^2 = 509$; $p < .001$.
SOURCE: Adapted from Lauer et al. (1982).

adolescent deviance. The next step in the Iowa study was to test this model longitudinally. We did this initially with a panel of respondents who were in the study for the first three years, and then again with a panel who participated for five years. Among those in the study who were abstainers in grades 7 and 8 in the first year of the survey, 16% tried cigarettes the next year. By the last year of the study (when these respondents were juniors and seniors in high school), half of them had at least experimented with smoking. On the other hand, 20% of those who reported smoking in grades 7 and 8 stopped the next year. After that, a decreasing percentage in subsequent years reported not smoking, indicating a tendency for smoking to stabilize over time.

Findings from the Three-Year Panel

In this analysis, two path models of smoking were constructed, one for *Initiation* and one for *Maintenance.*

The Initiation Model included only those respondents who were not smoking in the first year or second year; the goal was to predict who in this cohort would still be abstinent and who would smoke at least once or twice in the third year of the study ($N = 523$). The Initiation Model begins the paths with T1 (Year 1) measures of imitation (Parents' and Friends' Modeling) and the normative dimension of differential association (Parents' and Friends' Definitions). These were hypothesized to have only indirect effects on T3 (Year 3) smoking by affecting social reinforcement for smoking through the anticipated encouraging or discouraging reactions of parents and friends measured at T2 (Year 2). These, in turn, were hypothesized to have direct effects on T3 smoking, as well as indirect effects through other social learning variables measured at T2—own Positive/Negative Definitions, Neutralizing Definitions, Negative Definitions, Positive Physical Effects, Negative Physical Effects, and Positive Social Effects.

All of these variables were included in a fully specified initiation model, but when nonsignificant path coefficients were deleted to produce a respecified model only six remained. Parental and peer modeling variables in the first year (T1) had the expected effects on parental and friends' reinforcement in the second year (T2), explaining moderate levels of variance (7% in parental reinforcement and 16% in friends' reinforcement). However, the direct and indirect effects of the two T1 and the two T2 social learning variables on smoking at T3 in the respecified model accounted for low levels of variance ($R^2 = .03$). Therefore, the social learning variables included in the Initiation Model did a poor job of predicting the onset of smoking by T3 among respondents who had been abstainers at T1 and T2. While the main relationships were as predicted, most of the social learning variables had nonsignificant indirect or direct effects on initiation of smoking, and the magnitude of the remaining significant relationships provides only weak support for the model (see Table 8.3).

At the same time, Table 8.3 shows that the social learning theory was strongly supported in the respecified Maintenance Model (retaining only statistically significant path coefficients) that predicted the continuation or cessation of smoking among those who had already started smoking. The variables measured at T1 and T2 accounted for 41% of the variance in smoking or quitting by T3. The Maintenance Model included only those respondents who were smoking in the first year of the study, and the dependent variable measured whether their smoking had been maintained, had increased, had decreased, or had stopped in the third year ($N = 379$). Therefore, their level of T1 smoking is in the equation. However, recall that smoking and differential peer association are highly intercorrelated in the first year, and removal of the T1 smoking variable from the equation, leaving only social learning variables, reduces only slightly the explained variance in the maintenance model.

Findings from the Five-Year Panel

THE INITIATION MODEL IN THE FIVE-YEAR PANEL

The findings from the three-year panel on the weak effects in the initiation model were somewhat surprising. Of course the initiation of some new behavior pattern may be inherently more difficult to predict than the continuation of a pattern already in place. Thus, any set of variables from any theoretical perspective may be less able to predict onset than maintenance of some behavior pattern. Still, an initiation model based on social learning should do better in predicting the new behavior than was revealed in the three-year panel. In the article where these findings

Table 8.3   Longitudinal Social Learning Models of Initiation and Maintenance of Smoking in the Three-Year Panel

Initiation Model. Direct and Indirect Effects of T1 and T2 Variables on T3 Initiation of Smoking

	Indirect Effects	Direct Effects
T1 Variables		
Friends' modeling	.01	
Friends' definitions	.03	
T2 Variables		
Friends' reinforcement	.04	.09
Neutralizing definitions		.12

$R^2 = .03$
$N = 523$

Maintenance Model. Direct and Indirect Effects of T1 and T2 Variables on T3 Maintenance of Smoking

T1 Variables		
Smoking	.11	.39
Friends' definitions	.01	
Differential peer association	.09	
T2 Variables		
Positive physical effects		.20
Negative physical effects		−.23

$R^2 = .41$
$N = 379$

Only standardized coefficients significant at .05 level shown. Effects of T1 variables on T2 variables not shown.
SOURCE: Adapted from Krohn et al. (1985).

were first reported (Krohn et al., 1985), we speculated that the results may have been due to the fact that cigarette smoking is a minor form of deviance for which "motivational factors" (favorable definitions, antici- pated reinforcement, association with smokers) may be less important among the initiators for whom the experience is only experimental. That is, it may be that among initial abstainers who experiment with smoking the balances of pro-smoking and anti-smoking associations, definitions, and reinforcements are close to unity; therefore, they are essentially con- stants and not predictive. If so, then we would hypothesize stronger ef- fects of social learning variables for that group for whom initiation of smoking marks the beginning of "real" smoking behavior that will con- tinue. It was also my opinion, not necessarily shared by my co-authors, that the measures and models used in the three-year panel could be im- proved. I felt we had misspecified to some extent the social learning con- structs.

This reasoning guided the next step in testing longitudinal models of smoking with five-year data. In the Initiation Model for the five-year panel the goal is to predict the onset of teenage smoking by the third to fifth year of the study for respondents who reported themselves as nonsmokers in both the first and second year. Peer and family modeling and definitions at T1, and anticipated reinforcement and one's own defi- nitions at T2, are expected to have direct and indirect effects on initiation of smoking, while the main direct effects on smoking should come from T3 differential peer association.

The variables were measured as described above. In the model, initial family and peer influences are represented by three concepts measured in the first year of the study, T1—parental models (smoking and non- smoking), parental normative definitions of teenage smoking, and favor- able or unfavorable peer definitions of teenage smoking. Parental Model- ing was measured by forming a scale from both mother's and father's smoking behavior as reported by the respondent (alpha = .66). Parents' Definitions was measured by perception of mother's and father's general attitude of approval or disapproval of smoking by teenagers (alpha = .84). Similarly, Friends' Definitions was measured by the approving or disap- proving attitudes toward teenage smoking perceived to be held by the respondent's best male and female friends (alpha = .82). To avoid some of the questions discussed above about measuring both peer association and peer imitation by responses regarding friends' behavior, measures of Friends' Modeling were excluded from the initiation models.

At T2 there are three reinforcement constructs. Parental Reinforcement and Friends' Reinforcement are the anticipated positive or negative reactions of parents and friends if one were to start smoking (Parental Reinforcement alpha = .91; Friends' Reinforcement alpha = .84). Differential reinforcement is also measured at T2 by Anticipated Effects of smoking in a five-item scale of Positive and Negative Consequences as defined above (alpha = .83). One's own definitions favorable or unfavorable to smoking are also included at T2, using only the Neutralizing Definitions measure. The direct measure of one's personal approval or disapproval of smoking by teenagers, Positive or Negative Definitions, was not included because there was essentially no variation in response to this item. Recall that all respondents in this sample were total abstainers at both T1 and T2. It is not surprising, then, that nearly everyone held only negative attitudes toward smoking at both T1 and T2. Given this, the only definitions measures that could make a difference are those held by abstainers that may neutralize or counteract their general anti-smoking attitudes. As described above, Neutralizing Definitions is a scale composed of three items measuring beliefs that the health effects from smoking will not really occur for many years, that it is all right for a teenager to smoke if he has parental permission, and that it is all right to smoke if one does not get a habit (alpha = .50). The final component of the model is Differential Peer Association at T3. This measure adds two scales of the frequency, intensity, and duration of associations with smoking and non-smoking male friends (alpha = .88) and female friends (alpha = .91).

For reasons already mentioned and to be discussed in more detail below, the initiation of smoking was measured in two ways, and two longitudinal models were tested. First, the smoking variable was dichotomized, with those who were abstinent at both T1 and T2 and continued to be abstinent through T5 scoring 0, and those who reported smoking at least once at any time during the three years (but not all three years) of T3, T4, or T5 scoring 1 (N = 206). I label the dependent variable measured this way *Initiation of Experimental Smoking*. Second, a dichotomous variable was created with total abstainers for all five years scoring 0 and those who had first begun smoking at T3 and T4 and were still smoking at T5 scoring 1 (N = 162). This is called *Onset of Stable Smoking.*

The finding from the three-wave study that the social learning model could account for substantial amounts of the variance in continuing or ceasing to smoke by T3 among those who were already smoking at T1, but only for a small amount of the variance in onset of smoking among those who were nonsmokers at T1, was puzzling. The theory should be able to explain the onset of some behavior pattern as well as its maintenance. It appears the low level of explained variance in the three-year initiation model arose partly because we had somewhat misspecified the empirical indicators and the sequencing of the social learning variables. Indeed, a re-analysis of the three-wave data using somewhat different measures of the social learning variables shows that the power of the social learning model to account for onset of smoking at Year 3 among the abstainers at Year 1 can be dramatically enhanced (from R^2 = .03 to R^2 = .15).

This offers greater support for the social learning initiation model, but it is a moderately, not strongly, predictive model. Even at its best, any empirical model will usually have weaker relationships with dependent variables longitudinally than cross-sectionally, but the difference should not be so large. The power of the longitudinal model on maintenance (41% of the variance explained) was somewhat lower than that found for cross-sectional relationships with social learning variables (54% of the variance explained). The much lower magnitude of relationships in the longitudinal initiation model, even when better measures of the social learning variable raise explained variance from 3% to 15%, would suggest that the difference has to do with more than simply cross-sectional versus longitudinal relationships. It may have more to do with measures of smoking behavior.

As noted above, the power of the longitudinal model may have been hampered by how initiation was conceptualized and measured in the three-year model. In that model even experimental, tentative tries at smoking during the third year were counted as initiation of smoking. The findings might have been affected by the presence of these "dabblers," who may be less affected by the social learning variables than either those who remained totally abstinent or those who began smoking in a serious way in the third year.

The presence of smoking experimenters who do not become regular smokers presents measurement problems in determining who has and who has not in fact initiated smoking. In one sense they are more like abstainers, since they remain basically nonsmokers even though they have given it a try or two. One could argue that they have not really initiated anything. The fact that they have crossed over the line from total abstinence to at least try cigarettes, on the other hand, means that they have something in common with smokers. A measure of initiation that includes these experimenters, then, may incorrectly classify them as having started smoking when they have not really begun to smoke, or it may incorrectly classify them with total abstainers when, in fact, they are not. The model may be less able to predict initiation as we measured it in the three-year analysis because the differences between those who become experimental initiators and those who stay abstinent may be too subtle for the year-interval measures to pick up. If so, then the social learning variables, or any set of independent variables, would be less able to differentiate between the two.

Thus, for both conceptual and methodological reasons, it is reasonable to test the hypothesis that the social learning variables would predict the onset of smoking better when experimental starters are excluded from the sample than when they are included. The additional years of data allow this to be done and still measure social learning variables one and two years before onset. With three years of data we could only measure whether smoking had been tried at all during T3, the year following the T1 and T2 measures of the predictive variables, without knowing whether that signaled the initiation of a stable pattern of smoking or signaled nothing more than adolescent experimentation with different kinds of behavior.

First, we estimated a path model for the Initiation of Experimental Smoking in the five-year panel. In this model the dependent variable is initiation of smoking at any time from T3 to T5, however tentative and fleeting that initiation was, versus remaining abstinent through the fifth year. A path analysis was done, producing a model that retained only those paths that were statistically significant at the .05 level. None of the T1 and T2 variables in the model had significant direct effect on initiation; the only direct effects came from T3 peer association. The model accounted for 13% of the variance in initiation of experimental smoking (model not shown). Our notion that the "motivational" factors in social learning cannot predict who among a group of abstainers will later experiment with smoking is not sustained by these findings. Social learning variables can predict this, but apparently with only moderate success.

Next, we moved to see if expectations were met regarding better prediction by social learning variables of Onset of Stable Smoking. In this model, the dependent variable is the measure of smoking that eliminated experimental initiation, leaving only the adolescents who remained abstinent throughout the five-year period, compared with those who initiated smoking at T3 or at T4 that was still in evidence at T5. Figure 8.1 presents a respecified model retaining only significant paths. That model explains a substantial amount, 43%, of the variance in the onset of stable smoking. The power of this five-year initiation model is, as expected, less than the cross-sectional model, but it is comparable to the successful three-year maintenance model.

The expected strong effect of T3 Differential Peer Association is found. Parental Modeling and Parents' Definitions at T1, and one's own Neutralizing Definitions at T2, also have significant direct effects on T3–T5 smoking, but it should be noted that these coefficients are based on variables with skewed distributions and small cell frequencies and may not be reliable. Friends' Definitions at T1 have some direct effect on the onset of stable smoking, and we have left this path in the model even though the path is not significant. It also has some indirect effect through Anticipated Friends' Reinforcement at T2, which in turn is related to Differential Peer Association at T3.

The predictive power of the model regarding Onset of Stable Smoking is not simply an artifact of dropping out the experiments and comparing only the two extreme groups of total abstainers over all five years with those who began and continued smoking after the first two years of the study. We know from analysis of the Boys Town data on teenage drinking and drug use that dichotomizing the dependent variable so that only extreme types are compared does not increase explained variance; in fact, dropping out the middle range of scores served to decrease explained variance (Akers et al., 1980).

In addition to the differences in the dependent variable and the longer time period, the five-year path model of smoking initiation differs from

Figure 8.1 Social Learning Path Model for Onset of Stable Adolescent Smoking

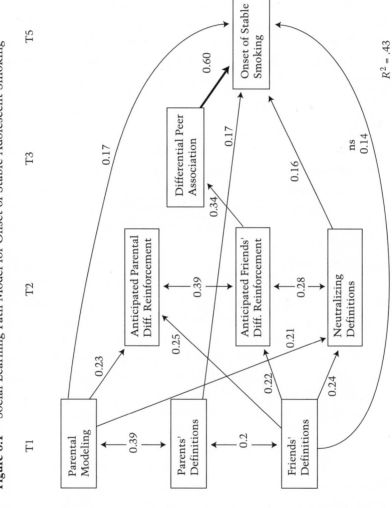

the three-year initiation and maintenance models somewhat in the social learning variables that it incorporates. The social learning variables at T1 and T2 are about the same, but in the five-year model we insert peer association at T3 and do not repeat reinforcement variables or definitions at T4 (although the assumption is that they are affected by T3 differential association). Since only respondents who had totally abstained from tobacco in both T1 and T2 are in the analysis, the models make a prospective prediction of who among a group of adolescent nonsmokers will in the course of three subsequent years become smokers. The models in the five-year analysis, therefore, are for initiation only, one for the onset of experimental smoking and one for the onset of smoking that continues into Year 5. In each case, the findings show the social learning variables do a much better job of predicting initiation than we found in the analysis of the three-year data.

These findings on the five-year longitudinal model of initiation of smoking, then, support social learning theory. There are some caveats, however. First, by dividing the five-year initiation panels between onset of experimental and onset of stable smoking, the sample sizes for each model become fairly small, and this may have affected the reliability of the coefficients. Second, in one sense, the model for the onset of stable smoking is a mixed one, rather than purely a model of initiation; it predicts initiation among those youngsters who, once they begin, continue their smoking over time, and some of that onset is contemporaneous with the differential peer association at T3. Thus, it contains an element of maintenance of smoking. Nevertheless, it is an initiation model that differentiates between those young people abstinent at one point in time who remain so and those who are abstinent at one point but later start and continue to smoke.

SEQUENTIAL AND RECIPROCAL EFFECTS
IN ADOLESCENT SMOKING IN THE FIVE-YEAR PANEL

The five-year panel in the Iowa study also allowed a test of the sequential and feedback effects in the social learning process spelled out in Chapter 3. As I noted in Chapter 5, previous research findings are generally consistent with the theory, but none of that research on sequential and reciprocal relationships directly tests full models of the theory, usually concentrating instead on the "selection" versus "socialization" effects in peer associations.

The model that Gang Lee, one of my doctoral students, and I (Akers and Lee, 1996) tested incorporates social learning variables and smoking behavior in the first, third, and fifth years of the survey, designated here, respectively, as Time 1 (T1), Time 3 (T3), and Time 5 (T5). Therefore, it is a model of abstinence and continuation or cessation of cigarette smoking rather than a model of the initiation of smoking. We measured both the social learning and smoking variables at each time in order to examine the cross-lagged effects as a way of approximating the process specified in the theory. This avoids a problem with the common model of change in which behavior at one time is explained by certain variables after controlling for earlier measures of the same behavior. This model is especially inappropriate for testing social learning that addresses both behavioral continuities and behavioral changes, because, as succinctly described by Lanza-Kaduce and Hollinger (1994:13) in their study of college cheating, one is left only with a model of change (see Chapter 11).

The model of social learning in teenage smoking behavior we proposed incorporates both change and stability in behavior. The overall model included measures of reinforcement, differential association, and definitions as the indicators of a latent construct of the general social learning process. We also tested a series of three-wave, two-variable models separately for differential association, differential reinforcement, and definitions. The findings were essentially the same as for the general model, and I will not show them here.

Smoking behavior and each of the social learning variables were measured in the first year (T1), the third year (T3), and the fifth year (T5). The variables have parallel form across time, since the same items were used through the five years. Therefore, in the analysis of the models, we assume that the parallel forms of each indicator have equal factor loadings and equal error variances by equating both coefficients and error terms across time (Jöreskog, 1971). The model posits covariances between two different latent variables across time ($\phi21$, $\phi43$, $\phi65$). The model estimates cross-lagged paths of adolescent's smoking at T1 to social learning at T3, social learning at T1 to adolescent's smoking at T3, adolescent's smoking at T3 to social learning at T5, and social learning at T3 to adolescent's smoking at T5.

The social learning variables measured at T1 and T3 were substantially related in the expected direction to subsequent smoking behavior. As expected, the smoking at T1 is related to smoking at T3 (.547) and smoking at T3 with smoking at T5 (.527). These two-year lag relation-ships are stronger than the four-year lag relationship of smoking in the first year with smoking by the fifth year (.340). Not surprisingly, smoking behavior at one time is predictive of smoking behavior at a later time, but it becomes progressively less predictive the farther into the future one goes (see Chapter 6 and Akers et al., 1987).

The measures of the social learning variables across the years are also positively correlated. Their magnitude ranged from .18 for parents' defi-nitions at T1 and T3 to .45 for adolescents' negative definitions at T3 and T5. Thus, social learning variables are related, but the relationships are not at a level to suggest problems of multicollinearity (less than 21% of shared variance).

The overall social learning LISREL model, with beta coefficients and factor loadings, is shown in Figure 8. 2. Separate models were also run for each of the major social learning dimensions of differential reinforce-ment, definitions, and differential association, but those figures are not reported here. The estimation of these models was calculated with the LISREL VII statistical program (Jöreskog and Sörbom, 1989). Based on maximum-likelihood statistical theory, it allows for multiple indicators of constructs, adjusts parameter estimates for the unreliability of mea-surement when multiple indicators are used, permits correlated residu-als, and provides a test of the extent to which overidentified models fit the data. LISREL is well suited to testing longitudinal models, because it takes into account correlated measurement errors that are usually pres-ent when the same measure is used at two or more points in time.

Figure 8.2 shows that the overall social learning model of adolescent smoking is supported. The model fits the data well (X^2 with 41 degrees of freedom = 60.88, p = .023). Although the X^2 is significant at the .05 level, its ratio to degrees of freedom (1.5) is low (Carmines and McIver, 1981). The goodness-of-fit index and adjusted goodness-of-fit index are greater than .90 (Jöreskog and Sörbom, 1989). Factor loadings of social learning variables are relatively high and stable across indicators.

The stability path coefficients for adolescents' smoking and social learning show that adolescents' earlier smoking is associated with later smoking (.36 and .32) and that the social learning variables at one time are highly associated with the same variables at a subsequent time (.73 and .56). This strong influence of variables at an earlier stage on the same

Figure 8.2 Sequential Effects in Adolescent Smoking and Social Learning ($N = 440$, $^*p < .05$)

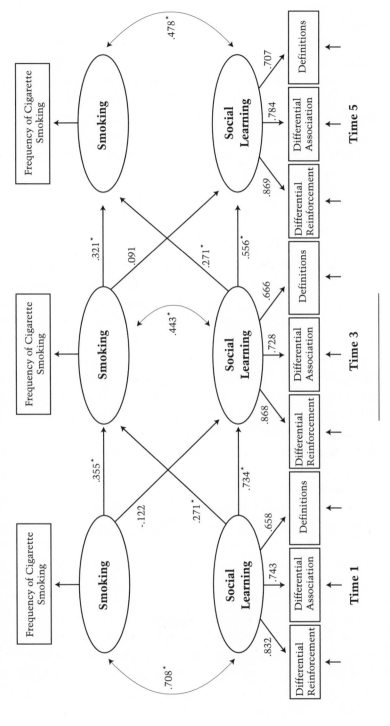

SOURCE: Adapted from Akers and Lee (1996).

229

variables at a later stage, especially for the social learning variables, suggests that the stability is relatively autonomous (Hertzog and Nesselroade, 1987). The model allows T1 latent variables to influence other T3 variables, and T3 variables to influence other T5 variables; it also includes estimates of our cross-lagged paths to address the issue of change. Effects of social learning at T1 and T3 on adolescents' smoking at T3 and T5, respectively, are measured, as are the effects of smoking at T1 and T3 on social learning at T3 and T5.

The cross-sectional relationship between social learning and smoking at T1 is strong; the later cross-sectional relationships are not as strong, but remain high. The model accounts for 33% of the variance in smoking at T3, and for 31% at T5. The magnitude of effects (in the .3 range) of the model variables on smoking shows that prior social learning predicts later smoking almost as well as does prior smoking behavior itself. The model also accounts for 43% of the variance in social learning at T3 and 39% of the variance at T5. Unlike smoking behavior, however, most of the effect on the social learning construct comes from the same social learning construct at an earlier time, rather than from prior smoking behavior. Social learning at T1 is significantly and positively associated with adolescent smoking behavior at T3 (.27), and smoking behavior at T3 is positively, but not significantly, associated with social learning at T5. In turn, adolescent smoking behavior at T1 is nonsignificantly, and unexpectedly negatively, associated with social learning at T3, and social learning at T3 was significantly, positively associated with smoking behavior at T5 (.27). Only the variables measuring social learning have significant effect on adolescents' smoking behavior, while individuals' abstinence or frequency of smoking has some, but nonsignificant, lagged effects on social learning variables. There is, therefore, some evidence of reciprocal effects between the social learning variables and smoking, but the lagged effects of social learning on smoking are stronger than those of smoking behavior on social learning.

The findings on the other models for each of three major dimensions of social learning—differential reinforcement, definitions, and differential association—are similar to those for the overall model and are supportive of the theory. The variance explained in smoking learning ranges from 28% to 47%. However, the findings show that the reciprocal effects of smoking behavior on social learning is clearer for peer associations than for the other learning variables of reinforcement and definitions.

Adolescents' smoking at T1 is not significantly related to differential reinforcement for smoking at T3, but smoking at T3 is associated with differential reinforcement for smoking at T5. The lagged effects of differential reinforcement on smoking are positive and significant for all time periods. Results of testing the definitions model show that while one's attitudes toward smoking have a clear influence on abstaining from the practice or taking it up, one's behavior in this regard does not have much of a subsequent effect on his or her positive/negative or neutralizing attitudes toward smoking. In the differential association model, the lagged effects of differential peer association (peer behavior and definitions) on smoking are strong and significant at each time interval. Smoking at T1 has only weak lagged effects on differential association at T3. However, one's own smoking behavior at T3 has a significant impact on differential association at T5, and the magnitude of the effect are similar to that of differential peer association at T3 on smoking at T5. These findings would indicate that as smoking behavior develops it is shaped by association with peers, exposure to their normative definitions of smoking, and social reinforcement. Over time, though, one's own smoking behavior comes to exert some influence over patterns of association with friends and, to a lesser extent, over the other social learning variables.

This pattern of peer association → smoking behavior → peer association → smoking behavior supports the sequential process in social learning theory spelled out in Chapter 3. The behavioral process in smoking remains relatively stable through time, and the social learning variables continue to have an effect on smoking behavior through the years, even when taking into account behavioral stability and the effect of prior smoking behavior on such variables.

Summary and Conclusions

The social learning theory was first tested on teenage smoking in the Iowa study by analyzing cross-sectional data from the first-year survey. All of the social learning variables were strongly related to frequency of smoking ($R^2 = .54$). Next, the social learning model was tested with the first three years of the longitudinal data to see to what extent social learning variables could predict who among abstainers would begin to smoke and who among smokers would continue or stop. We found that among those adolescents who were smoking in the first year of the survey (T1) the social learning variables measured at T1 and T2 successfully predicted (41% of the variance explained) who was still smoking and who had quit at T3, the third year of the survey. Thus, the theory was well supported by findings on the three-year Maintenance Model. The social learning model did not predict well which abstainers in the first and second years would begin smoking cigarettes at T3.

However, when these abstainers were followed until the fifth year, the social learning model did a better job of predicting the onset of experimental smoking and an even better job of predicting the onset of stable smoking among abstainers. Indeed, the relationships are of about the same magnitude as for predicting continuation or cessation among smokers. Peer association was found to be the best predictor. In fact, knowing the smoking behavior of one's best friends in the first year of the study is about as good a predictor of one's smoking behavior in the fourth and fifth years as knowing one's own smoking behavior in the first year. The imitation of parental smoking models, parental attitudes toward smoking, and one's own definitions favorable to smoking also had significant direct effects.

There were, however, some statistical problems with the path model of the onset of stable smoking. The sample size is considerably reduced by including only those in the five-year panel who were abstaining in the first two years and then by excluding those who started in year three or four but were not still smoking by year five. Further, there are problems of multicollinearity among some of the independent variables in this reduced subsample.

There were no such multicollinearity problems in the LISREL models we used to test the sequential and feedback effects of smoking behavior and the social learning variables in the five-year panel. The general social learning model and each of the specific models on definitions, differential reinforcement, and differential association found the expected two-year lagged effects, with the stronger effects running from the social learning variables to smoking behavior rather than vice versa. The reciprocal lagged effects between peer associations and one's own smoking behavior from the third to the fifth year, however, were about the same.

The same variables found to be important in the Boys Town Study of drug use and drinking are also important in adolescent smoking, and the cross-sectional correlations are as high. Moreover, the evidence shows that knowing where the students stand with regard to the social learning variables of differential association, reinforcement, definitions, and imitation in one year allows one to predict whether they will be smokers in later years. The findings from the Iowa study of teenage smoking, therefore, provide additional support for social learning theory.

Elderly Drinking Behavior: The Florida Study

The primary research and development of social learning theory has been on samples of teenagers, as in the Boys Town and Iowa studies. Of course, all of the other major social psychological theories of crime and delinquency causation also have been tested mainly on juvenile delinquency. But social learning theory, as well as other major perspectives such as social bonding and anomie, are as applicable to the elderly as to any other age group. There is no need to construct new theories that apply only to the elderly or only to youth. The fact that research on the theories has been largely confined to youthful subjects is largely a matter of methodological choices, investigator preferences, and the traditionally greater concern for deviance among the young. There is nothing in the logic of the theory that confines it to young people; it is a general theory applicable to any age group. The opportunity to test applications of the theory to a different population came at the University of Florida, even before the Iowa smoking study was complete. With Anthony La Greca as co–principal investigator and Gordon Streib as a senior consultant, I undertook a project to test social learning as an explanation of alcohol behavior among the elderly funded by the National Institute on Alcohol Abuse and Alcoholism (NIAAA). John Cochran, Christine Sellers, Edward Folts, and Jeffery Dwyer joined the project as research assistants. (For descriptions of the research and report of findings, see Akers and La Greca, 1988; Akers et al., 1988; La Greca et al., 1988; Akers et al., 1989; and Akers and La Greca, 1991.)

In the Boys Town and Iowa studies we found some variation in how well the model accounted for (and which social learning variables are

most important in) onset, use, abuse, and cessation of different substances among adolescents. Therefore, one can anticipate some variation
when the model is tested on drinking among an elderly sample. Nevertheless, the general social learning model should do well with the elderly,
as it did with the younger groups.

Drinking Behavior among the Elderly

Drinking by adults is not considered deviant in the general American
culture, but excessive drinking and alcohol abuse are, and to account for
them entails accounting for both conforming and deviant drinking behavior. Moreover, problems related to drinking are often seen as special
ones likely to be encountered by older adults. Studies of institutionalized
or under-treatment populations have led some to conclude that alcohol
abuse by the elderly is a large and serious social problem that is under-
recognized and under-reported (Petersen and Whittington, 1977; National Institute on Alcohol Abuse and Alcoholism, 1982; Glantz, 1982;
Smart and Liban, 1982; Maddox et al., 1984). On the other hand, surveys
of local, regional, and national samples report a different picture. They
have not uncovered high rates of drinking or alcohol abuse among older
people. Instead, they have consistently found drinking behavior to be
negatively associated with age; the elderly are less likely than younger
persons to be drinkers, heavy drinkers, and problem drinkers (Fitzgerald
and Mulford, 1981; Meyers et al., 1981–82; Smart and Liban, 1982; Borgatta et al., 1982; Holzer et al., 1984; Akers and La Greca, 1991). My
concern here is not with comparing levels of drinking behavior or alcoholism among older adults with those among adolescents and younger
adults, or with determining whether the elderly present a special risk
group for alcohol problems. Rather, it is with testing a social learning
explanation of why some elderly persons do not drink, others do drink,
and some drink to excess.

Social Learning Theory and Alcohol Behavior
among the Elderly

Since the theory has been well explicated in earlier chapters, I will present here only a brief restatement as applied specifically to elderly drink-

ing behavior. Social learning theory proposes that the full range of drinking patterns, from abstinence to light, moderate, heavy, or abusive drinking, can be accounted for by variations in the variables of the learning process. The behavior results from experienced or anticipated greater rewarding consequences, on balance, over aversive social and physical contingencies for drinking (differential reinforcement). Further, one's definitions of drinking are conducive to consumption of alcohol when, on balance, one's positive and neutralizing definitions offset negative definitions of drinking (definitions). The greater the extent to which one associates with drinkers and persons who hold favorable attitudes toward drinking (differential association) and provide drinking models to imitate (imitation) than with abstainers and persons who hold negative attitudes toward drinking, the more likely he or she is to drink and to drink more frequently. Therefore, drinking alcohol can be expected to the extent that one has been differentially associated with other drinkers, that drinking has been differentially reinforced over abstinence, and that one defines drinking as at least as justified (if not more desirable) than abstinence.

I knew before embarking on the research that the empirical measures of these theoretical constructs would have to differ somewhat from those we used with the adolescent samples in the Boys Town and Iowa studies to make them more appropriate to an elderly sample. For instance, in our studies of teenagers, imitation of parental and peer models was measured by asking which admired persons the respondents had observed drinking or by asking about exposure to parental and peer models. Obviously, while important for adolescents, current parental drinking models would be nonexistent or irrelevant for elderly adults. We did ask for recollection of parental drinking behavior when the respondents were growing up. To the extent that these recollections can be taken as accurate it is likely that those who later became heavy drinkers had been raised in heavy-drinking families, while lifelong abstainers are most likely to have been raised as children and adolescents in abstinent families. But for all elderly persons this would have occurred a long time ago, and obviously this is not the same thing as measuring the current or recent modeling of drinking behavior of the parents and other substance-using models for teenagers. Recall the discussion in Chapter 8 of the subtleties of measuring peer association and peer imitation among adolescents, and the notion that measures of association as indicated by awareness of friends' behavior could be seen as, indirectly and weakly, also indexing peer modeling. With the elderly, this measure is even more suspect as an indicator of imitation. Therefore, we did not incorporate any measure of imitation in the Florida study of elderly drinking behavior.

We did utilize empirical measures of the three other major social learning concepts, differential association, definitions, and differential reinforcement. There are similarities and differences in how these measures are appropriately conceptualized and utilized in testing social learning among an older population and among an adolescent population. For instance, association with drinking and nondrinking peers and friends should be important for the old as well as for the young; for both, there is a concentration of interaction with others in the same general age group. But the age range of associates is greater for the elderly, and disproportionate interaction with other elderly people is more likely for those living in retirement communities than in age-integrated communities. I noted in Chapter 8 that for adolescents there is no good measure of differential family association comparable to measures of differential peer association. This is not a problem for adult groups, however, because the researcher can ask exactly the same associational question about the behavior and attitudes of spouses and other family members as is asked for friends.

Further, although the drinking norms shared in these groups to which one is exposed and the definitions of drinking adopted by the individual should be important for the elderly just as they are for the adolescent population, the meaningful reference groups and groups reinforcing drinking are somewhat different. For both, the family is important, but for the young it is parents and siblings, perhaps even an extended family with grandparents and other relatives while for the old it is likely to be a spouse (for those not divorced or widowed), adult children, and perhaps siblings. Whereas the peer groups for the young are heavily school related, the relevant friendship groups for the elderly come from a wider range of leisure, social, work, religious, and political groups. For both, media exposure like watching television is frequent, but the nature and content of the programming watched is different.

Differential reinforcement of drinking and abstinence should also be important among the young and the old. But the pattern and sources of the reinforcement differs. In addition to positive social reinforcement for drinking, negative reinforcement may play a greater role in the drinking of some of the elderly than in adolescent drinking. That is, drinking alcohol may be a dysfunctional way for some elderly people to ease the stress or anxiety of unpleasant life events or crises associated with growing old—retirement, death of loved ones, lowered standard of living, health deterioration, social isolation, and so on (Borgatta et al., 1982). We found in the Florida study that stressful life events by themselves account for very little elderly drinking behavior (La Greca et al., 1988). Only a few of those older persons faced with critical life events will respond by turning to alcohol or developing heavy drinking. Nevertheless, in those few cases where excessive drinking is related to stress, social learning theory posits that it develops through negative reinforcement of drinking as escape behavior.

The general hypothesis, then, is that the social learning model will account for drinking behavior among the elderly, just as it has accounted for drinking among adolescents. The social learning variables (singly, in sets, or all together) should be related not only to abstinence or drinking but to the pattern of drinking, continuation of prior drinking patterns, onset of drinking late in life, or other changes in drinking as one enters the elderly years.

Methodology of the Florida Study of Elderly Drinking

SAMPLE AND DATA COLLECTION

We conducted in-home interviews of 1,410 older adults (age 60 and above) in four communities: two retirement communities ($N = 216$ and 516) and two age-integrated communities ($N = 352$ and 326). One of the retirement communities is in New Jersey, and its residents lived near their families and pre-retirement friends. The second retirement community is in Florida, and its residents typically were retired far from pre-retirement home and friends in other counties and often in other states. Both age-integrated communities are in Florida. One is Pinellas County, the locale of St. Petersburg and Clearwater, and there is a high concentration of older adults (25% of the population in 65 years and older, and 35% of the population is 60 and over). The other age-integrated community is in Alachua County, where Gainesville is located and where the proportion of elderly is low (10% are 60 and older, and 7% are 65 and older).

A random sample was generated for Pinellas and Alachua counties through random-digit telephone sampling. Interview completion rates were 67% (N = 326) and 82.1% (N = 352), respectively. We could not generate samples from the two retirement communities by this technique, and entering them for purposes of sampling and interviewing involved the usual restrictions associated with research in such communities (see Streib et al., 1984). Whereas we were able to re-contact and follow up on securing interviews with respondents in the two age-integrated communities, no re-contacts of any type were allowed in the retirement communities. Therefore, only 40% of those initially contacted in the Florida retirement community were interviewed; 25% of those initially contacted in the New Jersey community were interviewed. The age, gender, and race distribution of our two random samples closely approximates that of the census data on Pinellas and Alachua counties, but there were no comparable demographic statistics available for the sampling frame from the retirement communities. The total sample was 52% female, 95% white, and 65% married, with 13 years' median education; the mean age was 70.8. (For additional descriptions of the sample and procedure, see Akers et al., 1987; La Greca et al., 1988; and Akers and La Greca, 1991.)

The difference in response rates and sample sizes from the different communities raises some questions about combining all into a whole sample. Therefore, some of the analyses conducted on the whole sample were repeated using only the random samples from the two age-integrated communities in Florida. There was no difference in conclusions based on findings from the samples from these communities and conclusions based on findings from the whole sample, and there were very few differences in the details of the findings. Moreover, we conducted analyses in which type of community was entered as a variable, with no effect on findings.

MEASURES OF ALCOHOL BEHAVIOR

We used several measures to cover the continuum of alcohol behavior (ranging from abstinence to heavy drinking), as well as measures assessing problem drinking and continuity or change in drinking behavior after age 60. For purposes of this chapter, I define only those drinking variables used in the multivariate analyses. Each variable is given a short label to facilitate reporting the findings and reading the tables.

YFREQALC (frequency of alcohol consumption in the past year) is a measure of drinking during the past twelve months. The responses are: no drinking, once or twice, less than once a month, once a month, two to three times a month, once or twice a week, three to four times a week, nearly every day, daily. MFREQALC is a measure of frequency of drinking in the past month. YFQINDX (frequency/quantity of alcohol consumption in the past year) is a cross-tabulation of the YFREQALC with a measure of the number of cans or bottles of beer, or glasses of wine, or other drinks containing approximately one ounce of liquor consumed on a typical drinking day in the past year. The cells were collapsed and ordinally ranked into five levels: abstinence, light drinking (from 1 to 6 drinks consumed less than once a month, up to 1 to 2 drinks taken once or twice a week), moderate drinking (from 7 to 12 drinks less than once a month, up to 1 to 2 drinks daily), heavy drinking (from 6 to 11 drinks once or twice a week, up to 3 to 6 drinks daily), and excessive drinking (12 or more drinks once or twice a week, up to 7 or more drinks daily). ELDONSET (elderly onset, increase, decrease, or maintenance of drinking) is measured by respondents' retrospective report of their drinking patterns in the decade before age 60 compared with responses for the years after turning 60.

All of these measures relate to the whole continuum of alcohol use, from abstinence to excessive drinking. While any sustained level of drinking by minors is deviant, only excessive or abusive drinking behavior would be socially defined as such for an adult. Alcoholism or problem drinking is socially deviant for all age groups, and we wanted to test the power of the social learning model to differentiate the group of problem drinkers from the rest of the drinkers. Therefore, we constructed a measure of alcohol-related problems in the past year, YPROBALC, to determine whether respondents who drank in the preceding twelve months experienced any difficulties related to alcohol during that time. The list represents the range of problems (physical, psychological, and social) that have long been identified by the National Institute on Alcohol Abuse and Alcoholism (1982) and by the National Institute of Mental Health (Robins et al., 1981) as signs of problem drinking or alcoholism. Differential reinforcement is also measured by positive and negative consequences; therefore we wanted to avoid confounding measures of problem drinking as the dependent variable with measures of differential reinforcement as an independent variable. We did so by making sure that there is no measurement overlap of the two variables. As discussed below, none of the problems listed as diagnostic of alcoholism is included in the measures of differential reinforcement.

We included seven measures of sociodemographic variables in the analysis—age, race, sex, marital status, education, income, and occupational prestige (current if still working, or previous if retired). Education is measured in years of schooling completed, income is measured by monthly household income from all sources, and occupational prestige is measured by the Nam US Census status scores (Nam and Powers, 1983).

Comparing findings on drinking by the elderly with those on substance use by adolescents is facilitated by the fact that measures of the social learning variables in the Florida study are recognizably adapted from those used in the Boys Town and Iowa studies. But since we had no direct measures of modeling or imitation (for the reasons discussed above), beyond those assumed to be operative in differential association with friends and family, there are three main subsets of variables for the social learning model of drinking by older people—definitions (attitudes and beliefs), differential association (interaction and norms), and differential reinforcement (social, mixed, and physical). Again, short labels are used to make identifying variables and reading tables easier.

Definitions

1. BALDEF (balance of positive/negative definitions). This is a single-item Likert measure of the degree to which the respondent's own attitudes, on balance, are approving or disapproving of alcohol.

2. NEUTDEF (neutralizing definitions). This variable is a scale of three Likert items that measures the extent to which the respondent neutralizes negative definitions of alcohol by believing that even heavy drinking is all right as long as it is controlled, if it makes a person happy, and the person watches his or her diet (Cronbach's alpha = .53).

3. NEGDEFA (negative definitions of alcohol behavior). This is a scale of two items indicating negative ("never approve of the use of alcohol") or proscriptive attitudes toward alcohol and getting drunk ("wrong to get drunk") (Cronbach's alpha = .59).

4. PRESDEF (prescriptive definitions). This is a single Likert item on one's own degree of approval of alcohol use under certain circumstances, such as on holidays or special occasions.

5. GENDEF (general definitions). This is a two-item measure of the extent to which the respondent adheres to conventional beliefs (in this case, importance of religious beliefs and belief in the duty to obey the law) that should be unfavorable to frequent or high-quantity drinking and favorable to abstinence or light drinking (Cronbach's alpha = .35).

Differential Association

This concept is measured by two types of variables reflecting its normative and interactional dimensions. One is a series of three items (6, 7, and 8) indicating the respondent's perception of the normative attitudes or definitions of spouse, family, and friends regarding alcohol; the other is a series of items (9, 10, 11, 12, 13) on which the respondent reports the drinking or abstinent behavior of others with whom he or she interacts.

Responses for variables 6, 7, and 8 are "approve," "sometimes approve," "no definite attitude," "sometimes disapprove," and "disapprove."

6. SPNORMS (spouse's drinking norms). This is a one-item measure of the respondent's perception of a spouse's normative definitions of drinking.

7. FAMNORMS (other family's drinking norms). This is a two-item scale of perceived positive or negative definitions of drinking held by adult children and other family members (Cronbach's alpha = .75).

8. FRNORMS (friends' drinking norms). This is measured by a three-item scale of the perceived drinking norms of best friends, friends with whom the respondent most frequently associates, and friends of longest standing (Cronbach's alpha = .95).

   Variables 9 (SPASSN), 10 (CHIASSN), 11 (OFASSN), and 12 (BFASSN) are, respectively, one-item measures of the reported drinking behavior of the respondent's spouse, adult children, other family members, and best friend. Response categories for these were the same as the categories for the measures of alcohol behavior.

13. DIFPASSN (differential peer association). This is the same measure of proportion of friends who are drinkers as was used in the Boys Town and Iowa studies. It is a three-item scale of the proportion of drinkers (none, less than half, more than half, all) among the respondents' best friends, longest time friends, and most frequently associated with friends (Cronbach's alpha = .96).

Differential Reinforcement

14. SREINBAL (balance of reinforcement for drinking or abstinence in social relationships). This is a one-item measure of social reinforcement, indicating whether alcohol use affects one's social relationships and enjoyment in a mainly positive, negative, or balanced way. Nondrinkers were asked about anticipated outcomes if they were to begin drinking alcohol.

Variables 15 through 17 are, respectively, measures of actual (if respondent is a drinker) or anticipated (if one is not a drinker) positive or negative reactions to one's own drinking by a spouse (SPREAC), other family members (FAMREAC), and close friends (FREAC). SPREAC and FREAC are single-item measures; FAMREAC is a two-item scale of adult children's and other family members' reactions to one's drinking (Cronbach's alpha = .92). The question for each of these was "What is the usual reaction of [person] when you drink?" Responses for this reaction were "approve, and encourage my drinking," "approve, but do nothing to encourage," "no reaction," "disapprove, but do nothing about it," and "disapprove, and discourage my drinking."

18. PREINBAL (balance of perceived positive and negative *physical* effects of alcohol). This is a single-item measure of the respondent's perception of whether the direct physical effects felt from alcohol were mainly positive, negative, or balanced between the two. Again, nondrinkers were asked about anticipated effects.

I have stated before that self-report survey data do not provide a direct measure of the physiological effects of drugs, but in the Iowa study we had some success in differentiating between the purely social and physical consequences of smoking. In the Florida study we had even more success in eliciting responses during interviews that allow some separation of reinforcing/aversive effects of the alcohol itself from other social-psychological reinforcing/aversive consequences associated with drinking. We asked respondents about "direct *physical* effects" on reflexes, taste, or health, "not relationships with other people or your emotions." Then we asked about other "outcomes" of drinking "aside from direct physical effects," such as "how it affects your relationships and whether or not you have a good time."

19. BALRC (overall balance of perceived rewards–costs of drinking). This variable is the balance of the perceived rewards of drinking minus the costs of drinking. The perceived rewards are measured from a checklist of eight "good things" resulting from drinking, such as "it helps me to relax," "helps me enjoy leisure activities," "gives me a satisfying/rewarding feeling," or "gives me energy" (Cronbach's alpha = .73). The costs of drinking are measured from a checklist of "bad things" stemming from drinking,

such as "makes me feel guilty," "makes me feel sick or hung-over," or "tastes bad" (Cronbach's alpha = .90).

Findings on Sociodemographic Correlates of Elderly Drinking

Sixty-two percent of our sample reported at least some drinking in the past year. About the same percentage reported drinking in the past month. More than one-fifth reporting drinking every day or nearly every day in the past year and in the past month. About 10% of the drinkers drank heavily or excessively. Of the drinkers, 5.5% (44) reported problems with drinking during the past year. Any survey among the general, noninstitutionalized elderly population will find relatively few problem drinkers. Nevertheless, those identified in our research as falling into this category are indeed those with alcohol-related difficulties, including the same alcohol-crime link that has been found for younger age groups. (For more information on this point, see Akers and La Greca, 1988.) These percentages of drinking and problem drinking are comparable to those found in national and regional surveys on drinking in this age group (Borgatta et al., 1982; Department of Health and Human Services, 1981; Meyers et al., 1981–82; Holzer et al., 1984). The proportion of respondents reporting drinking in the past year was higher in the two retirement communities (68% and 76%) than in the two age-integrated communities (41% and 57%).

The drinking variables YFREQALC and YFQINDX are related to all of the sociodemographic variables—sex, race, education, income, occupation, marital status, and age. The bivariate correlations are statistically significant, with the magnitude of the relationships ranging from weak (r = .08) to moderate (r = .32). A regression model with only these sociodemographic variables accounts for 30% of the variance in YFREQALC (tables not shown).

Findings on Social Learning and Elderly Drinking

Table 9.1 presents the bivariate correlation (r) and the beta weights (standardized regression coefficients) for YFREQALC, YFQINDX, and ELDONSET by each social learning variable. As the data in this table show, all of the drinking variables are moderately to strongly related to each of the social learning variables; for all but GENDEF, the correlation coefficients are .25 or higher, and many are above .5.

The bivariate analysis shows that drinking behavior is consistently related to the social learning variables. The level of drinking during the past year in this age group is related to each of the social learning variables, with zero-order correlations ranging from .19 to .65. The data demonstrate that when the social learning variables are entered into regression equations, the multiple correlations (.71 to .77) are high and substantial amounts of variances are explained. Thus, one can conclude with some confidence that the social learning model applies very well to the drinking and abstaining behavior of the elderly, just as it has been shown to do with adolescents.

Indeed, the social learning variables do a somewhat better job of accounting for drinking behavior among the elderly than among teenagers. The social learning model accounted for 55% of the variance in alcohol use in the Boys Town Study of adolescent substance use (Akers et al., 1979). The model here accounts for the largest proportion of variance (59%) in the frequency of drinking (YFREQALC), as well as for high proportions (52% and 51%) of variance in the quantity-frequency consumption levels (YFQINDX) and the onset or cessation of drinking in old age (ELDONSET).

Table 9.1 also lists the standardized partial regression coefficients, and from this one can see that some measures of each of the major social learning concepts of definitions, differential association, and differential reinforcement retain strong net effects. These observations were made clearer when we ran separate regression equations for the three subsets of social learning variables; those runs showed plainly that any one of the subsets, by itself, has a strong relationship to drinking among the elderly, accounting for 38% (definitions), 45% (differential association), and 50% (differential reinforcement) of the variance in YFREQALC. Also, the subsets account for 27% to 50% of the variance in YFQINDX and ELDONSET. (Tables are not shown.) In each of the models the differential reinforcement subset is the most potent. Note the strength of the effects of reinforcement variables on drinking, and the the effects of associational and definitions variables in this elderly population. This finding

Table 9.1   Social Learning Models of Elderly Drinking Behavior

| | Alcohol Variables | | | | | |
| | YFREQALC | | YFQINDX | | ELDONSET | |
Social Learning Variables	$r=$	$B=$	$r=$	$B=$	$r=$	$B=$
Definitions						
1. BALDEF	.59**	.25**	.55**	.22**	.59**	.12**
2. NEUTDEF	.34**	.05**	.34**	.07**	.30**	.03
3. NEGDEFA	.47**	.02	.44**	.02	.39**	−.04
4. PRESDEF	.44**	.05	.41**	.03	.43**	−.04
5. GENDEF	.19**	.05	.19**	.06*	.15*	.03
Differential Association						
6. SPNORMS	.40**	.08**	.35**	.09**	.30**	−.04
7. FAMNORMS	.35**	.04	.33	.04	.25**	−.04
8. FRNORMS	.48**	.05	.44**	.06*	.39**	−.06*
9. SPASSN	.45**	.17**	.41**	.15**	.33**	.07*
10. CHIASSN	.33**	.01	.31**	.01	.28**	.01
11. OFASSN	.32**	.01	.30**	.01	.27**	−.02
12. BFASSN	.57**	.18**	.54**	.17**	.46**	.04
13. DIFPASSN	.53**	.03	.50**	.03	.50**	.08*
Differential Reinforcement						
14. SREINBAL	.51**	.07*	.50**	.02	.55**	.04
15. SPREAC	.43**	.06*	.39**	.04	.36**	−.02
16. FAMREAC	.46**	.03	.43**	.04	.46**	.02
17. FREAC	.54**	.07*	.51**	.08**	.62**	.15**
18. PREINBAL	.61**	.24**	.58**	.21**	.62**	.25**
19. BALRC	.65**	.18**	.62**	.17**	.65**	.23**
$R^2 =$		.59		.52		.51

$**p < .01; *p < .05$

SOURCE: Adapted from Akers and La Greca (1991).

demonstrates, as do those in Chapters 6 and 7, that critiques of social learning theory claiming that the reinforcement concept adds nothing to the explanatory power of the model are incorrect.

Indeed, in this study of old-age drinking differential reinforcement is the strongest subset, whereas for adolescents both the definitions and differential association variables were stronger. BALRC (the balance of social and physical costs and rewards of drinking) and PREINBAL (the balance of positive and negative physical effects of alcohol) are stronger than the strictly social reinforcement measures of family and friends' reactions to drinking. In none of the studies is there a true measure of the physical effects of alcohol, but in this study of drinking by the elderly we came close to separating out the reinforcing/aversive effects of the alcohol itself from other such consequences associated with drinking in our measure of PREINBAL (see above), finding that it had strong net effects on drinking behavior among the elderly.

These results suggest that adolescents' use of alcohol and other drugs is more "social" and tied to peer contexts and reactions than is drinking among the elderly, for whom the direct effects of the alcohol are more important. This needs to be said with the caveat that controlled experimental studies have shown that consequences of drinking that respondents attribute to the physiologically reinforcing effects of alcohol itself are strongly influenced by learned "expectancy effects" (Lang and Michalec, 1990). Recall that in the Maintenance Model of adolescent smoking reported in Chapter 8, perceived positive and negative physical effects of smoking measured at T2 had direct effects on teenage smoking at T3, but these variables were themselves directly affected by differential peer association and anticipated social reinforcement from friends at T1.

TESTING FOR PROBLEMS OF MULTICOLLINEARITY AND WEAK SCALES

The major concepts of social learning theory are theoretically interrelated because they refer to different aspects of a single underlying general process. Intercorrelations among the independent variables would be expected, then, not only among those within each major subset but among variables in different variable subsets. This raises the issue of multicollinearity effects that may bias coefficients in multivariate analysis. Accordingly, we conducted a collinearity diagnosis. Although there was some multicollinearity among the independent variables, it was well within acceptable limits.

As reported above, the scales for differential association and differential reinforcement variables had high alpha coefficients (alpha = .73 to .96), but the two-item and three-item scales for the neutralizing, general, and negative definitions variables did not scale well (alpha = .35 to .59). Therefore, we ran analyses using only single-item measures of these variables to see if the use of the weak scales biased the findings. They do not. (For more information on how these tests were done, see Akers et al., 1989).

Findings on Social Learning and Problem Drinking among the Elderly

Next we tested the social learning model with abusive or problem drinking (YPROBALC) as the dependent variable. The indicators of independent variables in this model differed somewhat from those in our general model of frequency of drinking. In particular, the measures of the norms, behavior, and reactions of friends and family included in the model for frequency, quantity, and the onset of alcohol behavior in old age asked repondents about alcohol consumption in general. But the relevant questions for such variables in an explanation of problem drinking should ask specifically about problem, or heavy, drinking. Therefore, we included in the interview schedule questions on differential association, definitions, and reinforcement that referred to "heavy drinking" only, and these measures were inserted into the model for problem drinking.

DIFASNHD (differential association with heavy drinkers) is the reported proportion of friends who are heavy drinkers (replaces PFRASSN in the regression equation). NEUTDEFH (neutralizing definitions justifying heavy drinking) is a single item of agreement or disagreement with the statement that even heavy drinking is all right if it makes the person happy (replaces NEUTDEF in the model). NEGDEFHD (negative definitions of heavy drinking) is a two-item scale with one item referring to degree of agreement with the statement that it is wrong to get drunk and the statement that heavy drinkers are more likely to die from heart or liver disease (replaces NEGDEFA in the model). SPREACH (spouse's reactions to one's heavy drinking), FAMREACH (other family members' reactions to one's heavy drinking), and FREACH (friends' reactions to one's heavy drinking) replace SPREAC, FAMREAC, and FREAC. All other social learning variables in the model for YPROBALC remain the same as they were for the models of YFREQALC, YFQINDX, and ELDONSET.

When these variables were substituted in the YPROBALC model for the comparable measures in the YFREQALC model, the bivariate relationships were $r = .20$ or lower, and the amount of explained variance in the ordinary least squares regression equation was fairly low ($R^2 = .07$). (Tables are not shown.) These weaker results are not surprising, because there are only 44 persons in this sample (3.1% of the total and 5.5% of the drinkers) who could be categorized as problem drinkers. This skewed distribution and low number produce almost no variance in the dependent variable. Therefore, it is not surprising that none of the sociodemographic or social learning variables included in the models for other types of old-age drinking behavior is strongly related to problem drinking when the relationship is judged by ordinary least squares statistics.

Because of the skewed distribution, the measure of problem drinking can only be dichotomized (no problems/one or more problems), and logistic regression is the appropriate statistical technique to use with a dichotomous dependent variable. The use of such a maximum likelihood technique overcomes the difficulties presented by the violation of error term assumptions and inadequate linear functional form associated with OLS models in which the dependent variable is dichotomous (Hanushek and Jackson, 1977).

Given the low number of problem drinkers, one would expect to find, as we did, that the percentage of problem drinking is low for all values on any of the independent variables. But it is also clear that scoring high on the social learning variables in the direction of problem drinking dramatically increases the risk that one will be among the small group of abusive drinkers in our sample. For instance, the drinkers who differentially associated with other heavy drinkers (more than half of their friends being heavy drinkers) are six times more likely than those without such friends to have had drinking problems in the past year (18.9% vs. 3.3%). Similarly, those with friends who have responded to his or her own excessive drinking in a supportive or encouraging way (social reinforcement) have a rate of problem drinking (25%) that is five times higher than the rate of problem drinking among those with friends who discourage heavy drinking (5%).

All of this suggests that the social learning variables can predict problem drinking, as well as abstinence and moderate drinking behavior; that is what we found, as shown in Table 9.2. Both standardized and unstandardized logistic regression coefficients are presented in the table. The former permits us to estimate the change in "predicted proportional probability" of problem drinking for each one-unit change in the social learning variables.[1] In addition, the predicted probabilities of problem

Table 9.2   Social Learning (Logistic Regression) Model for Problem Drinking among the Elderly

Social Learning Variables	b=	se(b)=	B[a]=
Definitions			
1. BALDEF	.009	.396	−.000
2. NEUTDEFH	−.447	.270	.014
3. NEGDEFHD	−.796	.326	−.025
4. PRESDEF	−.385	.463	−.010
5. GENDEF	.247	.320	.007
Differential Association			
6. SPNORMS	−.413	.293	−.015
7. FAMNORMS	.150	.356	.005
8. FRNORMS	.658	.432	.002
9. SPASSN	−.025	.088	−.002
10. CHIASSN	.004	.098	.000
11. OFASSN	−.103	.082	−.001
12. BFASSN	.135	.095	.001
13. DIFASNHD	.558	.179	.021
Differential Reinforcement			
14. SREINBAL	.704	.372	.021
15. SPREACH	.292	.433	.006
16. FAMREACH	−.010	.395	−.000
17. FREACHD	.531	.259	.018
18. PREINBAL	−.465	.344	−.016
19. BALRC	.132	.091	.002

Table 9.2 (*continued*)

Intercept   −3.377

	Social Learning Most Conducive to Problem Drinking[c]	Social Learning Most Conducive to Nonproblem Drinking[d]
P(Y, *Predicted Probability of Problem Drinking* = 1)[b] =	.683	.001
−2 Log L (intercept only) =	339.86	
−2 Log L (model) =	282.21	
Model X² =	57.66 w/19df	
Y =	.056	
N =	792	

[a]B = standardized instantaneous rate of change coefficient = $b[p (1 - p)]$, where p = Y.
[b]P = predicted probability = $e^L/1 + e^L$, where $L = a + b_k X_{k \ (min,max)}$.
[c]Problem drinking $(L = a + b_k X_k \ (max))$ refers to a solution for L based on a combination of values for the social learning variables that represent the most extreme context theoretically conducive to problem drinking.
[d]Nonproblem drinking $(L = a + b_k X_k \ (min))$ refers to the solution for L based on a combination of values for social learning variables that represent the most extreme context theoretically least conducive to problem drinking.

drinking P(Y = 1) for various social learning environments are reported in the table.[2]

The most significant finding in Table 9.2 is that the additive effects of the social learning variables have a major influence on the predicted probability of problem drinking among the elderly. Those drinking respondents in our sample who interact with others in the most extreme anti–heavy drinking social learning environment have essentially a zero chance of being classified as problem drinkers—P(Y − 1) = .001. On the other hand, the odds are very high that respondents interacting in a social learning context that is the most permissive or supportive of heavy drinking will be problem drinkers—P(Y − 1) = .683.

In interpreting these findings, one must remember that social learning theory recognizes reciprocal effects and the impact of drinking behavior itself on social learning variables once a pattern of drinking has been established. The noticeable impact of heavy-drinking friends arises not only out of associating with and being rewarded for such drinking by them; it also arises in part because the problem drinkers seek out heavy-drinking friends in order to have a more supportive group environment for using alcohol (see Trice, 1966; Akers, 1985; 1992b).

Additional interpretation is needed, also, for the finding of the negative relationship between problem drinking and PREINBAL—which indicates that problem drinkers are less likely to find drinking a positively rewarding experience, and more likely to report negative outcomes—than those who are not problem drinkers. Our very measure of problem drinking means that a person so classified has had some negative experiences with alcohol in the past year. As noted above, we kept this measure of problem drinking separate from our measure of the effects of excessive drinking, but those effects, too, are also very likely to be viewed as unpleasant by the problem drinker. Similarly, the negative relationship to NEGDEFHD shows that the problem drinker is more likely than the average drinker to hold negative attitudes toward heavy drinking, probably a function of the unpleasant experiences associated with using alcohol.

Other things being equal, these negative outcomes and attitudes should be associated with less, rather than more, heavy drinking. But as shown in the table, other things are not equal. The key to why abusive drinkers would continue to consume alcohol in the face of these unpleasant outcomes and attitudes lies in the balancing principle in social learning. Problem drinkers in our study score high in the positive direction on our measure of the overall balance of rewards/costs of drinking. Some of this is negative reinforcement, in which the heavy drinking helps the person to "escape" from other unpleasant or aversive conditions. Some of it is the social reinforcement that comes from associating with other heavy drinkers. We found that problem drinkers differentially associate with heavy drinkers and that the balance of social reinforcement for heavy drinking was positive. Problem drinking is sustained by support from friends with similar drinking habits and by the fact that the problem drinker experiences the inducements and rewards for drinking as considerably outbalancing its costs and aversive consequences. That is, the person persists in abusing alcohol because it is apt to be escape behavior (drinking negatively reinforced by easing anxiety or temporarily becoming oblivious to problems, even those connected to this kind of drinking itself), because the positive social reinforcement she or he gets from friends with similar drinking habits (FREACHD) counterbalances the negative consequences, and because the problem drinker finds the drinking, on balance, to have more rewardings than aversive consequences (BALRC). This offers a reasonable answer to the age-old question of why all of the difficulties connected with abusing alcohol do not always naturally curtail drinking.

The findings on problem drinking must be viewed as preliminary and only suggestive because of the small number of cases. A fuller analysis would have to be based on a larger sample of problem drinkers and contain greater variability in the number of problems encountered so that the dependent variable may be measured at least ordinally. This could entail the deliberate oversampling of problem drinkers from treatment or institutional populations.

Summary and Conclusions

The social learning explanation of drinking patterns among the elderly was confirmed by the findings from the Florida study reported in this chapter. Thus, the theory is supported in a sample of older people as well as it was in adolescent samples. The social learning model is best supported as an explanation of the frequency of drinking, but it also is supported for other measures of drinking behavior among older adults, such as frequency/quantity and onset after the age of 60. The social learning model, modified to incorporate more appropriate measures, also accounted for problem drinking.

Notes

1. This predicted proportional probability for an independent variable, X_k, controlling for all other variables, is $B_k 1$, where $B_k = b_k p[(1\text{-}p)]$, b_k is the logistic regression coefficient, and $[p(1\text{-}p)]$ is the variance of the dependent variable at the point of comparison (p). These predicted probabilities vary depending on the point of comparison chosen. We choose to place it at the mean of the dependent variable, YPROBALC. Choosing a different value for p would yield different standardized parameter estimates, but the relative size of the coefficients would remain the same.

2. To compute these probabilities, we first solved for L, the logit coefficient. This statistic is a function of the model intercept plus the sum of the products of each of the logistic regression coefficients (b_k) and some value of X_k (i.e., $L = a + \text{Sum } b_k X_k$).

The values for the social learning variables were set at the most extreme pro–heavy drinking and anti–heavy drinking contexts. Once L is computed, the predicted probability of problem drinking can be easily derived by dividing the loginverse of L by 1 + loginverse of L (i.e., $e_1/1 + e_1$).

10

Rape and Sexual Aggression

The dependent variables in the Boys Town, Iowa, and Florida studies clearly involve deviancy, but they have been primarily drug, alcohol, and tobacco use and abuse among the young and the old. Although I include the full range of criminal and deviant behavior in the theory, my previous research did not test the empirical application of social learning propositions to serious property or personal offenses. Much of the research literature on correlates and predictors of crime and delinquency reviewed in Chapters 5 and 6 also focuses primarily on adolescent populations in which the deviant behavior to be explained is either substance use or less serious types of delinquency and deviancy.

As I have noted, the disproportionate focus on adolescent deviance and deviants is partly a matter of methodological convenience, but the use of adolescent samples does have theoretical and methodological justification. All types of deviant patterns, even though they have childhood antecedents, are most likely to be recognizably initiated during adolescence, and most serious crimes peak in incidence and prevalence during the teenage years (see Chapter 12). As Tittle and Ward (1993) have shown, there are empirical grounds for generalizing about causes of crime from one age group to another. Moreover, for any general theoretical perspective (such as social learning) that purports to account for all forms of deviant behavior, from minor norm violations to the most serious crimes, selecting any dependent variable from among that range is suitable for testing the general propositions of the theory.

Restricting samples by age, sex, and race, or restricting dependent variables in theory testing to nonviolent or less-serious offenses, does raise a question, however, in empirically validating the scope claims of a theory. It could be that the theory applies to substance use or minor forms of deviance but does not explain more serious forms of aggression, violence, or property offenses. The scope claims of social learning theory are supported by the research literature on crime and delinquency that reports positive findings on the relationship between such variables as peer associations, attitudes, and modeling and a range of minor to serious offenses among samples (see Chapter 5). But the research on serious offenses reported in this literature infrequently includes tests of fully specified social learning models.

I have long offered specific explanations of professional, organized, white-collar, and violent crime as applications of the general social learning model (Akers, 1985). Also, for some time I contemplated, and often talked with students about, testing social learning theory with empirical data on serious criminal offenses. But neither my own funded research nor the research of students I had directed in master's and doctoral projects had moved to the point of actually doing so. That changed in 1990 when Scot Boeringer, at the time a master's student of mine, undertook a thesis project testing the applicability of social learning to rape behavior. His thesis was intended to lay the groundwork for a larger study of rape, using samples of men in several universities and colleges and samples of convicted rapists. But we were not able to secure funding for such a project, and an alternative plan for an unfunded dissertation project was developed. That project also sampled undergraduate men in one university, but it doubled the size of the male sample, included a sample of women, and enlarged the theoretical issues. In the doctoral study, not only was social learning theory more fully tested but it was empirically compared to other explanatory models of rape based on two other theories—social control and relative deprivation. This chapter presents the social learning theory of rape and reports some findings from these two studies.[1]

Social Learning Explanation of Rape and Sexual Aggression

By definition, rape is both a sexual and a violent act in which nonconsensual sexual intercourse is attempted or consummated through the use or threat of physical force. The more violent the threat or actual aggression in sex, the more deviant it is. Aggression or coercion short of physical force may also be involved in sexual intercourse. Some of these acts, if they render a person unable to consent, may be legally defined as rape; even when they do not constitute rape, they still involve intimidating and aggressive dimensions of behavior. The background and motivation for such acts bear some commonalities with those for rape. All lie along a continuum away from conforming, consensual, noncoercive sexual intercourse. From a social learning perspective, the readiness to use, or a low level of inhibition against, force or violence as a technique for gaining sexual access (and other forms of sexual aggression) is acquired, enacted, and changed through variations in association, definitions, reinforcement, imitation, and discriminative stimuli. I have previously articulated social learning explanations of sexual behavior and violent behavior (Akers, 1985:182–91; 263–69). Specific propositions from these earlier analyses apply to coercive and violent sexual deviance, but I will not reiterate the particulars here. I will, rather, apply the general social learning theory presented in Chapter 3 to individual differences in the tendency for males to commit acts of nonphysical and physical aggression against women to obtain sexual intercourse.[2]

If the groups with which one is and has been in *differential association* are more accepting of and disproportionately engage in sexually coercive behavior, then the person is, himself, more likely to be ready to do the same in given circumstances. *Differential reinforcement* refers to the mix of positive reward or pleasurable consequences and the unpleasant consequences associated with sexually aggressive behavior. These include greater or less physical and psychological sexual stimulation and gratification, social reward or punishment, and greater or less pleasure or displeasure derived from directing coercion or violence against women. If the anticipated outcomes of rape, such as the formal and informal reactions of others, are more positive or rewarding than negative or punishing, the man is more inclined toward using force in sex and, given the right set of circumstances discriminative for it, more likely actually to commit the rape. If the actual outcome of committing such an act is to get what he wanted sexually, to dominate the woman, to suffer no adverse consequences from it, or to gain approval (or to experience no disapproval) from peers or other significant associates, he is likely to repeat it in similar circumstances. In short, if on balance the man has experienced or anticipates greater positive than negative outcomes from using force to obtain sex, there is a greater likelihood that he will initiate or repeat such behavior in a situation discriminative for it.

Definitions are general and specific attitudes and beliefs held by the individual that define rape and other sexual aggression favorably or unfavorably. They may see sexual coercion in positive, "macho" terms as how a man should behave when confronted with resistance to his sexual advances. The vocabulary of motives for rape is more likely, however, to include excuses and justifications that neutralize the deviant nature of sexual coercion, deny the harmfulness of sexual aggression, or define the victim as "asking for it" (Scully and Marolla, 1984). The social source of definitions favorable to sexual aggression may be immediate and more distant reference groups, or the more general attitudes voiced by men toward sex and women that justify various forms of sexual aggression, including rape. Attitudes unfavorable to rape are learned in conventional childhood socialization and through later social controls. The attitudes favorable to rape and the anticipation of social acceptance of it are likely to be picked up in verbal and behavioral interaction within male peer groups currently and over time, but they may also involve childhood socialization and intrafamilial exposure to sexual attitudes and behavior.

Modeling, or imitation effects, in sexual aggression refers to repeating acts one has observed others performing. Vicarious reinforcement, the observation of others being rewarded for the act, is more apt to produce imitation than simply observing the act. Men who have been exposed to conforming models in which aggression is absent or punished are disinclined to practice sexual aggression. Those who are relatively unexposed to such models, but exposed to models of deviant sexual aggression, are not as inhibited. It may be that the man has been in family, peer, or other situations where he has directly observed rape or other types of sexual aggression committed by men with whom he identifies and who escape punishment. But the more deviant the sexual aggression, the less likely this personal observation is to have occurred. Behavioral models do not have to be physically present for observational learning to take place.

Such models of sexual aggression can be favorably depicted in books, films, videos, magazines, and other media. Indeed, this once-removed observation of sexual violence in various forms of pornographic media probably occurs much more frequently than in-person observation. These media depictions can feed fantasies associated with sexual gratification, through masturbation while consuming pornography, in a way that "provides ideal training to develop a strong sexual attraction or preference for the activities depicted in the erotic material" (Marshall and Barbaree, 1984). Moreover, female victimization is frequently portrayed in pornography in a way that is vicariously reinforcing to the male viewer. It is, for instance, extremely improbable that in a real-life rape one would ever observe a woman displaying signs of great enjoyment and sexual fulfillment. Yet that is the recurring theme and the routinely expected outcome in violent pornography—the rapist shows how great forced sex is for him, and it is doubly rewarding because the woman herself, after initial resistance, experiences sexual ecstasy. The more the pornographic models depict rewarded and successful physical coercion in sex, the stronger should be the relationship to sexual aggression. But even "softer," nonviolent pornographic media like the wide-circulation men's magazines depict women's place in society as primarily being sources of male sexual gratification. Consumption of pornography in general has been found to be related to sexual aggression (Baron and Straus, 1987).

Social learning theory, then, would explain committing or refraining from rape and other sexually aggressive behavior as a function of these four main variables. They operate both in the acquisition of higher or lower tendency toward rape (or, stated alternatively, tendency to refrain from it) and in inducing or inhibiting such behavior in particular situations.

Sexual aggression is more likely when one is differentially associated with others who engage in similar behavior, has been or anticipates being differentially reinforced for using sexual coercion under given conditions, defines the behavior as desirable or justified in certain situations, and is exposed to models of forcible sexual behavior. Conversely, one is more likely to refrain from sexual aggression when he is differentially associated with others who are sexually conforming and not involved in such acts, defines the behavior as undesirable, is differentially reinforced for alternative behavior, is relatively isolated from sexually aggressive models, and associates with and is exposed to behavioral models of conforming sexuality. The hypothesis is that empirical measures of rape and sexual aggression will be significantly, substantially, and positively related to indicators of these social learning variables.

Testing the Social Learning Model of Rape and Sexual Aggression

Our studies fit into the growing body of research on "acquaintance" or "date" rape, which focuses not on populations of arrested or convicted rapists or their victims but on victimization surveys or self-reported rape in general populations. Much of this research has been conducted on college campuses. It has included data on forcible rape and on other behavior that may fall short of rape but is nonetheless relevant because it involves sexually oriented aggression by men against women. One-fifth to one-fourth of the college women in the surveys report being physically "forced into intercourse." Much lower proportions (4% to 5%) in the samples of college women report such experience when the word "rape" is used in the question (Koss and Oros, 1982; Lane and Gwartney-Gibbs, 1985; Koss et al., 1987; Garrett-Gooding and Senter, 1987; Rivera and Regoli, 1987). Studies of self-reported sexual coercion and aggression among samples of college men have found that up to 14% report they have committed sexual aggression, but only 3% to 4% report completed or attempted rape when the word "rape" is used in the question (Alder, 1985; Koss et al., 1987; Garrett-Gooding and Senter, 1987).

Previous research on correlates of rape behavior in samples of both officially known populations of rapists and of the general or college male population relate to one or more of the social learning variables. Exposure to models of violent or sexually aggressive behavior can be inferred from research on the relationship between rape and consumption of pornography (Goldstein et al., 1971; Cook and Fosen, 1971), especially pornography that explicitly depicts sexual violence (Malamuth and Check, 1985; Donnerstein and Linz, 1986; Demare et al., 1988; Linz, 1989). Gwartney-Gibbs and her associates (1987) found that abusive and aggressive behavior in courtship situations is related to witnessing abusive or violent behavior by parents. Attitudes and beliefs about women and sexual behavior have been studied as "rape myths" and sex-role stereotyping (Alder, 1985; Murphy et al., 1986; Malamuth, 1989a; 1989b). Some investigations have found one's own sexual aggression to be related to the sexual behavior of peers (Alder, 1985; Kanin, 1985; Gwartney-Gibbs et al., 1987).

The goal of our work in Florida was to move beyond this research to develop and directly test a social learning model of rape and sexual aggression. The first project concentrated solely on the social learning model; the second project compared the empirical validity of social learning with the social bonding/self-control and relative deprivation models. The first study drew on a purposive sample of 282 undergraduate men enrolled in general education courses; the respondents completed self-administered questionnaires in their classrooms. Included in the questions were indicators of the four major social learning concepts of differential association, differential reinforcement, definitions, and modeling. The dependent variables were of two interrelated types. First, there is self-reported readiness to commit, or likelihood of committing, rape in the future. Second, there are self-reports of past or current attempted or committed rape and nonconsensual sex obtained through nonphysical forms of intimidation or coercion. (For more details of methodology, see Boeringer et al., 1991.)

MEASURES OF SEXUALLY AGGRESSIVE BEHAVIOR AND PROCLIVITIES

Two measures of self-perceived likelihood or proclivity toward rape were adapted from Malamuth's (1989a; 1989b) scale of attraction to sexual aggression. The first asked, "If you could be assured that you could in no way be punished for engaging in the following acts, how likely, if at all, would you be to force a female to do something sexual she didn't want to do?" This is a measure of likelihood of using force to gain sexual access. The second question began the same way but ended with "how likely, if at all, would you be to rape a female?" This is labeled "likelihood of committing rape." Responses to both were on a five-point Likert scale, ranging from very unlikely to very likely. Men more frequently report readiness to "use force" against an unwilling woman to coerce her into sexual intercourse than readiness to commit "rape." The two are perceived differently, and the respondents may have some different behavior in mind when answering the questions. But is there a real difference? I come back to this point below.

These were combined into a two-item scale of likelihood of using force and/or committing rape (Cronbach's alpha = .69). Rape and sexually aggressive behavior were measured by two sets of questions adapted from Koss and Oros (1982). Respondents were asked how often to obtain sex they had ever used physical force (four-item scale with an alpha of .86) and had ever used nonphysical coercion (three-item scale with an alpha of .55).

MEASURES OF SOCIAL LEARNING VARIABLES

Differential peer association was measured with a two-question scale that asked respondents to the best of their knowledge how many of their friends had "forced or tried to force sex" on a woman who refused to have sex with them and how many of their friends had gotten a woman "drunk or high in order to have sex with her" (Cronbach's alpha = .55). One measure of differential reinforcement was a three-item scale (Cronbach's alpha = .72) of the respondent's report of his friends' anticipated reactions of approval or disapproval if he were (1) to force a woman to have sex with him after she had "teased" him and then refused to continue with sex, (2) to use alcohol or drugs to get a woman drunk or high in order to have sex with her, and (3) to have sexual intercourse with many women during the academic year. The second measure of differential reinforcement was the overall balance of reinforcement perceived to be contingent on sexual aggression. This general question was intended to capture any physical and psychological pleasant/unpleasant consequences of deviant sexual intercourse involving dominance of women and any social approval/disapproval anticipated from such acts. Therefore, to some extent, it includes portions of the anticipated social reinforcement from peers tapped by the first differential reinforcement measure. A two-item scale (Cronbach's alpha = .76) was created from responses to the question "If you were to rape a woman do you anticipate that the experience would be mainly pleasurable or rewarding to you, mainly negative or unpleasant, or somewhere in between?" and a similar question on "forcing a female to do something sexual she didn't want to do." Definitions favorable and unfavorable were measured on a scale of agreement to disagreement with eleven items (Cronbach's alpha = .81) adapted from Burt's (1980) scales of "rape myths." Behavioral modeling of rape and sexual aggression was measured by questions asking the extent to which the respondent had viewed pornographic depictions of violent sexual acts. We had no measures of direct exposure to live behavioral acts of rape or other types of sexual aggression. Theoretically, such models would have a stronger effect than media portrayals, but social learning theory expects imitation effects even when the models are not actually present. The respondent was asked how often he had viewed women being physically forced into sexual behavior in videos or films and how often he had viewed or read about this behavior in magazines or books. The three items of magazines, books, and videos/films formed a modeling scale with an alpha of .71.

The findings of the multiple regression analysis of the social learning variables and the indicators of sexual aggression are shown in Table 10.1. All of the social learning variables are significantly related to the scale of likelihood of rape/force except for differential association. This is primarily because it is significantly related to responses when the question is about using force to gain sexual access, but not when the word "rape" is in the question. The relationships are not only generally statistically significant but also substantial. The social learning model, with variables measuring the four main concepts of differential association, differential reinforcement, definitions, and modeling, accounts for 53% of the variance in the proclivity to use force and for 41% of the variance in nonphysical coercion.

The social learning model does not do as well in accounting for actual rape behavior (explaining 15% of the variance). Although all of the learning variables are related to use of force in sex at the bivariate level, when they are entered into the regression equation only the measure of reinforcement balance retains significant net effects. This is partly a result of the skewed distribution and truncated variance in reported use of physical force to obtain sex. But it is also true that the social learning model is only moderately successful in explaining actual rape behavior. A very large portion of the individual differences in rape in this university sample of men is left unaccounted for by the empirical indicators of the social learning constructs. Further, it appears that whatever effects one's association, modeling, and definitions have on his use of force in sex comes mainly from their relationship to his perceived balance of reinforcement/punishment for the act.

We were also concerned in this study with the differences between fraternity and nonfraternity students, since fraternities have often been proposed as providing social contexts for learning and committing sexual aggression against women. We found differences only with regard to use of nonphysical coercion. When fraternity membership (dichotomous) is included in the empirical models with social learning variables it no longer shows significant relationships with any of the dependent variables. It is likely that differences in sexually aggressive tendencies are learned before enrollment in college and that there is little additional effect from participation in fraternities. This does not deny that male groupings like these may provide opportunity and social context for male sexual aggression. But to the extent that they do, the contextual impact they have on proclivity to use and actual use of force in sexual behavior is mediated by the operation of the social learning process.

Table 10.1   Social Learning Models of Sexual Aggression

	Measures of Sexual Aggression		
Social Learning Variables	Proclivity to Use Force or Commit Rape $B=$	Use of Nonphysical Coercion $B=$	Use of Physical Force $B=$
Differential peer association	.08	.29***	.02
Differential reinforcement: Peer reactions	.15**	.04	.02
Differential reinforcement: Overall reinforcement balance	.53***	.10**	.18***
Definitions: Attitudes and beliefs	.12*	.00	.00
Modeling: Pornographic media	.11*	.05*	.00
Fraternity membership	.04	.07	−.06
$R^2=$	.53	.41	.15
$N =$	262	262	262

Coefficients are standardized betas from the first study.
$*p < .05; **p < .01; ***p < .001$
Source: Adapted from Boeringer et al. (1991).

Comparison of Theoretical Models of Rape and Sexual Aggression

The second research project on rape and rape proclivity was both a replication and expansion of the first study. Would the initial findings hold up in a separate larger sample? Although the social learning model performed well in the first study, we were not able with the resulting data to address the question of how well it does compared to other models. Absolute validation of social theory is not possible; acceptance of a theory as an adequate explanation is based on the relative strength of its empirical validation compared to other theories applied to the same behavior. Will other models be as strongly or more strongly supported as social learning with regard to proclivity to use force in sexual behavior? Will empirical models based on other theories improve on the smaller levels of explained variance in the social learning model for the use of physical force to obtain sex?

To answer these questions, a model of rape based on social learning theory was compared with models based on two variations on control theory (Hirschi, 1969; Gottfredson and Hirschi, 1990) and a relative deprivation theory (Kanin, 1985). Social learning, control, and relative deprivation do not produce entirely incompatible explanations of rape. However, they are different enough to produce alternative hypotheses and models that can be compared.

SOCIAL BONDING THEORY

This theory proposes that one refrains from crime when social control is strong and commits crime when control is weak (Hirschi, 1969). Control is primarily a function of how strongly one is bonded to others and is committed to conventional society through social attachment, commitment to conformity, involvement in conventional lines of action, and conventional beliefs.

Attachment involves the degree to which the person has close affectional bonds with others. The more closely attached one is to parents, family, and peers, then the more likely he or she is to be constrained from committing deviant acts. The weaker the attachment, the more likely one is to violate conventional social norms. *Commitment* refers to investment of effort, energy, and time in conventional pursuits. Breaking the law jeopardizes reputational, economic, occupational, or emotional investment in conformity, and it is the consideration of this cost or risk of loss that deters deviance. *Involvement* refers to engagement in conventional, nondeviant activities. When the individual's life is filled with such activities, there is less time to engage in deviant acts. *Belief* is acceptance of general moral codes, conventional values, law, and authority. If one does not hold to such beliefs or holds them weakly, then there is greater likelihood of engaging in deviant activity.

Social bonding theory has received empirical support, primarily in research on juvenile delinquency (Hirschi, 1969; Hindelang, 1973; Krohn and Massey, 1980; Wiatrowski et al., 1981; Krohn et al., 1983; William F. Skinner et al., 1985; Marcos and Bahr, 1988; Gardner and Shoemaker, 1989; Cernkovich and Giordano, 1992). But until our study, it had not been tested as an explanation of rape and sexual aggression. As applied to this behavior, the theory would propose that males who are weakly bonded to society are more likely to commit rape and engage in other types of sexual aggression. (For additional specification of social bonding theory, see Chapter 7.)

SELF-CONTROL THEORY

Social bonding has been the dominant control theory in criminology for two decades and has become the most frequently tested theory in the field (Stitt and Giacopassi, 1992). However, Hirschi has moved away from his classic formulation. He has collaborated with Gottfredson (Gottfredson and Hirschi, 1990) to propose a theory of crime based on one type of control only—self-control. Whereas Hirschi's social bonding theory was directed primarily to delinquency, Gottfredson and Hirschi offer self-control theory as a general theory accounting for all crimes and deviance at all ages, under all circumstances. The theory states that individuals with high self-control will be "substantially less likely at all periods of life to engage in criminal acts" (Gottfredson and Hirschi, 1990:89), while those with low self-control are highly likely to commit crime at all times and in all circumstances. The theory, therefore, would expect a negative, significant, and substantial relationship between self-control and rape or other forms of sexual aggression.

There are unresolved problems of tautology in self-control theory (Akers, 1991), and research, thus far, has produced mixed findings. Nagin and Paternoster (1991), using indirect indicators of self-control, report lack of support for the empirical assumptions in the theory. Later, Nagin and Farrington (1992a), using essentially the same approach, report some support for the assumptions regarding stability of criminal potential, but this support holds for onset, not continuation of offending (Nagin and Farrington, 1992b). The support for self-control theory in this research is further compromised because the assumption of stability in behavior is not unique to it. Findings of stable differences in individual propensity to commit crime, therefore, are not necessarily or uniquely favorable to self-control theory. Without further empirical indicators there is no way to know whether the stability comes from stable differences in self-control or from other factors or processes specified in other theories.

Keane and his associates (1993) also report some indirect support for the theory as an explanation of drunk-driving offenses. Grasmick and his colleagues (1993) provide a direct test of the theory with measures designed specifically to tap different dimensions of self-control. They also report mixed support for the theory as an explanation of fraud and force. In commenting on these two studies, Hirschi and Gottfredson maintain that they do not provide an adequate test because "[n]either study invokes an explicitly counter hypothesis or theory on which to base judgments of the validity of our theory. In the absence of explicit competition, control theory cannot lose; nor can it win" (1993:51). Our second project on rape provided for this competition.

SOCIAL BONDING AND SELF-CONTROL

Before Hirschi's version, mechanisms of self-control were central components of social control theories of crime and delinquency, which posited both internal and external controls (see Reiss, 1951a; Nye, 1958). However, Hirschi (1969) did not include self-control as a separate element in his social bonding version of control theory. Instead, he subsumed self-control under the concept of attachment. He argued that the concept of internal, or self, control is too subjective for direct measurement and really is simply a reflection of how strongly one is attached to others. Measuring attachment, therefore, will measure self-control.

Gottfredson and Hirschi (1990) offer no clarification as to how their self-control theory relates to Hirschi's (1969) social bonding theory or to other earlier control theories. They do not explain why they have reversed Hirschi's position and now treat self-control as a general explanation of all crime and delinquency with no reference to attachment. It may be that not only attachment but all elements of social bonding can now be subsumed under, or taken as empirical indicators of, the concept of self-control. It would be just as reasonable, however, to conceptualize self-control as simply another social bond (along with commitment, belief, attachment, and involvement) that prevents crime and promotes conformity. This would integrate social bonding and self-control and move the theory back closer to the external/internal control formulations of earlier social control theories. Either way, self-control would be expected to be related to crime in the same direction as the other elements of social bonding. Therefore, we not only compared social learning models to social bonding and self-control models separately but also to a combined social bonding/self-control model.

RELATIVE DEPRIVATION THEORY

Kanin (1985) has proposed an explanation of acquaintance rape that relies on the concept of relative deprivation of sexual access. The theory proposes that if the individual perceives a discrepancy between his desired and actual level of sexual activity, or if the individual feels peer pressure to be sexually active but believes he has less opportunity or access to sexual partners than others, then he is more apt to use deviant tactics to achieve sexual contact, including physical force.

Although devised specifically to account for rape, Kanin's theory fits especially well into Agnew's (1992) "general strain theory" of deviance. The expanded concept of strain encompasses several sources of stress, not just structurally induced deprivation of means to legitimate goals (Merton, 1957) but also individual inadequacies leading to failure to achieve immediate goals and individually perceived deprivations and pressure. Whatever the source of strain, deviant acts are likely reactions. It is this focus on "negative pressures" toward deviance that Agnew claims clearly distinguishes strain theory from social bonding and social learning theories. Agnew and White (1992) report some empirical support for general strain theory as an explanation of delinquency and drug use.

Kanin found support for his relative deprivation theory in comparing a control group with a small group of men who had admitted raping acquaintances. The rapists were more active sexually than the control group, and they reported a desired level of sexual activity that was substantially greater than that of the control group. The rapists perceived high levels of peer pressure to engage in frequent sexual activity, defined by Kanin as an indication that they felt deprived of sufficient sexual outlets compared to their peers. The hypothesis is that a man is more likely to commit sexual aggression when he feels particularly pressured to engage in a high level of sexual activity, feels that he has a lower level of sexual activity than his peers, and considers his sexual activity to be less than he ideally would have it.

Methodology

SAMPLE AND DATA COLLECTION

The second project was conducted on the same campus as the first, one where the undergraduate male population is approximately 15,000. As before, data were collected through a self-report, self-administered questionnaire. The sample was made up of men enrolled in courses that met general education requirements. The instructors in nine classes granted permission to conduct the survey, and all the men present on the day the questionnaire was administered were asked to take part. A small, undetermined number left the classroom without participating, leaving a total of 515 men to take the survey. Of these, 38 returned questionnaires that were so incomplete or so inappropriately marked that they were unusable, leaving an overall response rate of 92.6% and a sample size of 477.

The female students in the sampled classes were dismissed to provide a research environment intended to limit social-desirability bias in responses. A separate sample of 115 women were administered a self-reported instrument in which they reported on victimization. Although this procedure has limitations, it is commonly used in research on acquaintance rape and sexual aggression (Malamuth, 1989a; Malamuth and Check, 1985; Fischer, 1986; Koss and Gidycz, 1985; Koss et al., 1987; Smeaton and Byrne, 1987). Moreover, research has shown that this procedure produces an environment that counters the tendency toward underreporting deviant sexual behavior better than do procedures that utilize samples of individuals and personal administration of the survey (Shively and Lam, 1991). The percentage distribution of men in the study reporting using nonphysical coercion and physical force to obtain sex are comparable to that found in our first study and in published reports from other surveys of college men (Alder, 1985; Garrett-Gooding and Senter, 1987; Koss et al., 1987). Also, comparing the self-reports of the men in the study with the self-reports of victimization among the women on the same campus indicated no serious under-reporting of male sexual aggression.

MEASURES OF RAPE AND SEXUAL AGGRESSION

Measures of the dependent variables were essentially the same as in the first study.

Rape. We measured this variable by three self-reported items in which respondents were asked to report (on a five-point Likert scale, from never to more than ten times) how often they have (1) attempted to have "sexual acts with a woman when she didn't want to" by using or threatening physical force, (2) completed such sexual acts by threatening to use physical force, and (3) completed sexual acts by actually using some degree of physical force. These three items formed an additive scale of rape (Cronbach's alpha = .90). Ninety-one percent of the respondents scored zero on this scale; 8.6% reported having committed such acts one or more times.

Nonphysical Coercion. Although use or threat of physical force is the most obvious form of sexual aggression, words, gestures, and nonphysical cues short of physical abuse can also be used to intimidate or coerce women into unwanted sex. To measure this nonphysical dimension of sexual aggression we used a two-item scale of how often respondents had obtained sex by (1) threatening to end a relationship if the woman did not consent to sexual intercourse, or (2) told her lies to manipulate her into sexual receptivity. These are rather mild forms of verbal coercion, and the items did not scale well (Cronbach's alpha = .57), but since the scale has been used in previous research (Koss and Oros, 1982; Boeringer et al., 1991) we retained it in the analysis. Over half of the male undergraduates (55.7%) in the study reported using nonphysical coercion at least once. This verbal intimidation is not rape and should not be interpreted as equivalent. But men who engage in such nonphysical aggression are more likely to move toward physical force in sex (in our study the two are correlated, $r = .40$).

Use of Drug/Alcohol Intoxication as an Aggressive Sexual Strategy. Another nonphysical technique employed by college men is to ply a woman with alcohol or drugs with the intent of making her so intoxicated that she will be physically or mentally unable to refuse sexual intercourse—another form of nonconsensual sex. Moreover, in the course of using this stratagem the man is also likely to be drinking or taking drugs. The chance that rape will take place increases when the man has been using alcohol or other drugs, either as a disinhibitor or as an excuse (Scully, 1990).

We measured this behavior with a single item (also taken from Koss and Oros, 1982) asking respondents how often they had used drugs or alcohol for this purpose. About one-fourth of the men (23.7%) reported having "engaged in sexual acts with a woman, or [trying] to engage in sexual acts with a woman who didn't really want to have sex, by giving her alcohol or drugs." Again, men in our study who reported this form of nonphysical sexual aggression are more likely also to report physical aggression in sexual behavior ($r = .44$).

Rape Proclivity. In our cross-sectional design the measures of the dependent variables of nonphysical and physical coercion and measures of the independent variables refer to past and current behavior. This raises questions about the directionality of relationships. As shown in the discussion of delinquency prediction in Chapter 6, how one has behaved before predicts how he will behave in the future. Therefore, current attitudes, associations, social bonds, and perceptions of relative deprivation, while reflecting prior behavior, should in turn be correlated with current and future occurrences of the same behavior. Of course, the concept of differential reinforcement in social learning theory refers specifically to the process in which rewarding of behavior in the past affects the person's anticipation of reinforcement for the behavior and his estimation of the probability of repeating the behavior in the future. When asked how he is likely to behave in the future, the individual is apt to respond based mainly on how he has behaved in the past or is behaving at the time. This self-projected estimation of how one is likely to behave under certain conditions, therefore, introduces an approximation to longitudinal relationships in cross-sectional data.

To produce this approximation, we used a technique developed by Malamuth (1981; 1989a; 1989b; Demare et al., 1988) for measuring what he refers to as rape "proclivity," the self-perceived propensity or readiness to commit rape. The idea is to gauge how willing the man would be to commit acts of rape in a situation with little external restraint, having only his own internal motivations and the behavior of his victim with which to contend. A similar measure of the self-perceived likelihood that one will commit criminal and deviant behavior in the future has been used by Tittle (1995; Tittle et al., 1986). In our study, a situation was described to respondents in which "no one would know and . . . you could in no way be punished for engaging in the following acts." The men were then asked, in this anonymous, no-penalty situation, how likely they would be to engage in (1) "forcing a woman to do something sexual she didn't want to do" and (2) "rape." They responded on a five-point Likert scale ranging from very likely to very unlikely.

Both of these items define rape, but only the second specifically uses the word. Therefore, we refer to the former as Perceived Likelihood of Force in Sex and the latter as Perceived Likelihood of Rape. Just as has been found in previous research, the difference in wording produces variations in the frequency of affirmative responses. Only 7.1% of the respondents perceived that there was some likelihood that they would commit "rape" under the conditions given in the question. Three times as many (22.7%) reported some likelihood that they would use "force" to have sex against the will of the woman. We formed a scale from the two items that we label Rape Proclivity (Cronbach's alpha = .67). This proclivity scale is related to both reported nonphysical coercion and use of force in sexual behavior, but because of the skewed distributions the correlations are modest (r = .27 and .20, respectively).

MEASURES OF SOCIAL LEARNING VARIABLES

Differential Reinforcement. This concept was gauged in two ways, consistent with how I and others have measured it in past research. First, a Friends' Reinforcement Scale was formed from three items that asked about the anticipated positive or negative reactions of a man's friends to his engaging in a high level of sexual activity during the academic year, getting a woman drunk or high in order to have sex with her, and forcing a woman to have sex even when she refused (Cronbach's alpha = .68). Second, a two-item Reinforcement Balance Scale for sexual aggression was formed by asking respondents about the extent to which, overall, they would find it pleasurable or unpleasant to "force a woman to do something sexual she didn't want to do" and to "rape" a woman (Cronbach's alpha = .76).

Definitions. Measures of definitions favorable or unfavorable to sexual aggression applied here are also comparable to measures of the concept in past research. They were derived from Burt's (1980) study of "myths" supportive of rape. Respondents were asked to reject or accept (on a five-point scale) several statements about use of force in sex, violence, sex roles, and attitudes toward women from which a sixteen-item Definitions Scale was constructed (Cronbach's alpha = .90).

Modeling. Exposure to behavioral models was measured by a three-item scale of observation of others' violent sexual behavior as depicted in pornographic media (Cronbach's alpha = .71). Respondents were asked to report the number of times they had encountered magazines, books, and videos/films depicting a woman or women being forced to engage in sexual acts.

Differential Association. This concept was measured by four items. Two were intended to determine the general level of sexual activity within the friendship group. They are Sexually Active Friends (proportion of friends who are sexually active) and Friends' Sexual Partners (average number of sexual partners for each friend in the past year). Two other questions measured the sexually coercive behavior of friends. These are Friends' Use of Drugs for Sex (number of friends who have gotten a woman drunk or high in order to have sex with her) and Friends' Use of Physical Force for Sex (number of friends who have forced or tried to force sex on a woman). These items did not scale well (Cronbach's alpha = .53), and the individual items were entered in the analysis.

SOCIAL BONDING/SELF-CONTROL VARIABLES

Attachment. This variable has been measured by reference to closeness of relationships and identification with peers and family. Attachment to peers and family was measured here by five questions, labeled Number of Close Friends, Importance of Friends' Opinions, Closeness to Parents, Closeness to Family, and Importance of Family's Opinions. These items did not scale well (Cronbach's alpha = .55), and therefore only individual items are used in the analysis.

Commitment. The concept of commitment in social bonding theory has typically been measured in adolescent populations by grade average in schoolwork, educational aspirations, occupational aspirations, and similar indicators of commitment to the conventional system that would be put at risk by involvement in deviance. Commitment is measured in this college male sample with a Commitment Scale of seven items (Cronbach's alpha = .74). Two questions ask about educational goals, and one asks about job aspirations. Two items measure importance of maintaining respectability among peers now and later in life, and two ask about the importance of being thought of as a model student and citizen now and later in life.

Involvement. This variable is usually measured in adolescent samples by the amount of time spent on extracurricular activities and in doing homework. In this study we asked respondents to report Number of Social Activities, Social Time (hours spent per week in social activities), and Academic Time (hours spent each week in classes and studying). These three items did not scale well, however (Cronbach's alpha = .51), and only the individual items were included in the analysis.

Belief. Usually measured by reference to general respect for law and order and the importance of obeying the law, in this study the concept is measured by a three-item Belief Scale (Cronbach's Alpha = .69) of importance of obeying laws and regulations, belief that the laws are good for everyone, and respect for persons in authority.

Self-Control. Although they discuss various dimensions of this variable as a general construct, noting that persons with low self-control seek immediate gratification and tend to be "impulsive, insensitive, physical . . . risk-taking" (Gottfredson and Hirschi, 1990:90), Gottfredson and Hirschi do not provide specific operational measures of their notion of self-control. Grasmick and his colleagues (1993) asked respondents to reply to questions meant to measure directly such concepts as impulsivity, risk taking, and control of temper as different dimensions of self-control and related these to self-reported fraud and force. Keane and his associates (1993) measured low self-control by reported alcohol consumption in the week preceding a drunk-driving charge in a secondary-data analysis of DUI offenses. Hirschi and Gottfredson (1993) express a preference for using indicators of such "analogous" behavior, but believe that measures like control of temper can also be employed as indicators of self-control.

Three items are used here as indicators of the relative absence or presence of self-restraint in different circumstances by responding with, or refraining from, aggression. Respondents were asked on a five-point Likert scale to agree or disagree that it is all right to attack someone physically who "really asks for it" to teach him a lesson (labeled as Physical

Response), that "under some circumstances" a man has to get tough to get what he wants (Get-Tough Response), and "I could become violent" in a situation where someone was "trying to cheat me out of my fair share" (Violent Response). We do not contend that these items measure everything contained in the general concept of self-control, only that they are reasonable indicators of at least one aspect or type of self-control. We conceptualize that aspect as having to do with the lack of self-control over physical or violent responses to situations in which one's will is opposed or thwarted. These are similar to the measures of "temper" used by Grasmick and his colleagues (1993) (e.g., "when I am angry at people I feel more like hurting them than talking"). The items were coded so that a higher score indicates greater self-control; therefore, a negative correlation with our measures of sexual coercion is expected. The three items did not scale well (Cronbach's alpha = .59), and the single items were entered in the empirical models.

Readiness to get one's way by physical action may be taken as an indication of a general inability to control oneself physically in a frustrating situation. It is on this ground that these three items are offered as indicators of lack of self-control. It is obvious that these are relatively weak measures of the self-control concept, however, because they can just as readily be taken as measures of other concepts or processes. For instance, they could be viewed as operational measures of the social learning concept of definitions, in this case definitions favorable to violence or getting one's way by force. They could also be viewed as indicators of "angry aggressions" in Agnew's (1992) revised strain theory. Alternatively, it could be argued that positive responses to these items simply reflect a general behavioral tendency toward interpersonal aggression that can be expressed in both sexual and nonsexual contexts. If so, then their relationship to the measures of physical force in sexual behavior is tautological in that all tap the same violent, or forceful, behavioral syndrome.

MEASURES OF RELATIVE DEPRIVATION VARIABLES

Our measures of the concept of relative deprivation follow those used by Kanin (1985), with the extensions discussed above. We used five items, which did not scale at all (Cronbach's alpha = .11), and they were entered into the analysis as separate variables. These variables are Pressure to Be Sexually Active (perceived amount of pressure felt personally to be sexually active), Relative Opportunity for Sexual Activity (perceived availability of willing females for one's own sexual partners relative to availability for other males), Relative Sexual Deprivation vs Other Males (perceived discrepancy between one's own level of sexual activity and that of the "average guy" on campus), Relative Sexual Deprivation vs Friends (perceived discrepancy between one's own and close friends' level of sexual activity), and Relative Sexual Deprivation vs Own Expectations (perceived discrepancy between one's desired and actual level of sexual activity).

Social Learning Models of Sexual Aggression and Rape Proclivity

At the bivariate level there is no question of the relationship between the social learning and the sexual aggression variables. Seven of the eight social learning variables are significantly and substantially related to each of the four dependent variables, with zero-order correlations ranging from .14 to .67. The eighth variable, number of sexually active friends, is related to nonphysical coercion but is not significantly related to the other dependent variables. The direction of two of these nonsignificant zero-order correlations are opposite theoretical expectation. Thus all but three of the thirty-two correlations are as predicted.

Table 10.2 presents ordinary least squares multiple regression models with social learning variables as the independent variables and with nonphysical coercion, drugs/alcohol, rape behavior, and rape proclivity as the dependent variables. The findings shown in the table offer substantial support for social learning as an explanation of sexual aggression, rape, and rape proclivity. The man in this college sample who anticipates more pleasure than trouble from rape and is more exposed to violent pornography is more likely to engage in sexually coercive behavior and be prepared to do so in the future. The college man with friends who engage in coercive sexual practices, perceives that his friends would positively reward his own sexual aggression, and holds attitudes and beliefs favorable to sexual coercion of women is more likely to employ nonphysical and physical coercion to obtain sex and perceives a greater likelihood that he would use physical force in sex in the hypothetical no-penalty situation.

The regression analyses reported in Table 10.2 show that the variables in the social learning model have strong effects on self-reported sexually aggressive behavior, accounting for more than 20% of the variance in nonphysical coercion, use of drugs or alcohol for sex, and commission of rape. The social learning model does an even better job of accounting for rape proclivity, explaining 54% of the variance in the self-reported probability of committing rape or using physical force in sex.

Within the social learning models, the overall Reinforcement Balance (anticipated pleasurable and unpleasant consequences of rape) and the Modeling Scale (perusal of violent pornography) have the strongest net effects on the dependent variables. Except for the average number of sexual partners of friends in the past year, all of the other social learning

Table 10.2   Social Learning Models of Rape Proclivity and Sexually Aggressive Behavior

Social Learning Variables	Nonphysical Coercion $B=$	Drugs/ Alcohol $B=$	Rape Behavior $B=$	Rape Proclivity $B=$
Differential Reinforcement				
Friends' reinforcement		.14**		.13**
Reinforcement balance	.12**	.17**	.16**	.53**
Definitions Scale	.10*			
Modeling Scale	.15**	.14**	.26**	.15**
Differential Association				
Sexually active friends	.18**		.11**	
Friends' use of drugs for sex	.16**	.20*		
Friends' use of force for sex	.09*	.17**	.08*	
$R^2=$	.22	.22	.21	.54
$N =$	441	440	436	443

Only statistically significant standardized beta coefficients are shown from the second study.

* $= p < .05$; ** $= p < .01$.

SOURCE: Adapted from Boeringer and Akers (1993).

variables in the models also have significant net effects on two or more of the four measures of sexual aggression. As expected, the other individual items measuring differential peer association are related to sexual behavior. The men with greater proportions of sexually active friends are most likely to be engaged in nonphysical coercion, those with greater numbers of friends who use drug or alcohol strategies to obtain sex are more likely to do so themselves, and those with more friends who have used force in sex are more likely themselves to have committed rape and report a greater proclivity to commit rape.

Social Bonding and Self-Control Models of Sexual Aggression and Rape Proclivity

Of the thirty-six possible correlations, the only significant bivariate relationship among any of the measures of the traditional social bonding variables is the correlation ($r = .13$) between one measure of involvement (Number of Social Activities) and the use of nonphysical coercion. That correlation is positive, opposite the direction expected by social bonding theory. But eight of the twelve zero-order correlations between the sexual aggression variables and the measures of self-control are statistically significant and in the theoretically expected negative direction (ranging from $r = -.12$ to $r = -.29$). All of these significant relationships are accounted for by the two measures of Physical Response and Violent Response; the Get-Tough Response is not significantly correlated with any of the dependent variables.

Given the lack of zero-order correlations between social bonding variables and the dependent variables, it is not surprising that regression models with the nine social bonding variables account for no more than 1% of the variance in the dependent variables (tables not shown). There is no support in these findings for the prediction that sexual coercion and rape proclivity will be substantially and negatively related to the elements of the social bond.

There is some support for the hypothesized effect of the self-control models. The three single-item measures of self-control over readiness to use physical aggression to get one's way account for 2% to 7% of the variance in the dependent variables (Table 10.3). The Get-Tough Response is unrelated, but both of the other two items retain significant net effects

Table 10.3   Self-Control Models of Rape Proclivity and Sexually Aggressive Behavior

Self-control *Variables*	Nonphysical Coercion $B=$	Drugs/ Alcohol $B=$	Rape Behavior $B=$	Rape Proclivity $B=$
Physical response	−.18**	−.10*	−.16**	−.22**
Get-tough response	—	—	—	—
Violent response	−.13**	−.12*	−.09	−.11*
$R^2=$	.06	.02	.04	.07
$N =$	463	463	463	492

Only statistically significant standardized beta coefficients are shown.
* $= p < .05;$ ** $= p < .01$.
Source: Adapted from Boeringer and Akers (1993).

on nonphysical and physical behavior and on proclivity to use force in sexual behavior.

When the nine social bonding and the three self-control variables are combined into the same bonding/self-control regression models (Table 10.4), the models still account for relatively little of the variance in non-physical and physical sexual coercion or rape proclivity (3% to 8%). For three of the models in Table 10.4, the only significant net effects come from the Physical Response variable. The social bonding variables of attachment, commitment, involvement, and belief do not conform to theoretical expectation. Their effects are nonsignificant and often run in the opposite direction from expectation. If self-control is viewed as an additional element of the social bond, the empirical validity of social bonding as an explanation of sexual aggression and rape proclivity is considerably enhanced by including it as another bonding element.

Relative Deprivation Models of Sexual Aggression and
Rape Proclivity

Relative deprivation theory predicts that the more a man perceives himself to be relatively deprived of sexual opportunity the greater is the likelihood of his committing rape or other forms of sexual aggression and the greater is the proclivity to commit such acts in the future. Although Kanin applied this theory primarily to acquaintance rape involving college men, there is little confirmation of it in our sample of such respondents. Of the twenty-five zero-order correlation coefficients for our measures of sexual aggression and relative deprivation, only five are sta-

Table 10.4   Social Bonding/Self-Control Models of Rape Proclivity and Sexually Aggressive Behavior

Social Bonding Variables	Nonphysical Coercion $B=$	Drugs/ Alcohol $B=$	Rape Behavior $B=$	Rape Proclivity $B=$
Attachment				
Number of close friends	−.06	−.07	−.04	−.05
Importance of friends' opinions	−.04	.02	−.08	.00
Closeness to family	.04	.05	−.08	−.02
Importance of family's opinions	.00	.00	.04	.04
Commitment Scale	.03	−.02	−.02	.00
Involvement				
Number of social activities	.09	.04	.06	.00
Social time	.05	.10	.03	.07
Academic time	.04	.02	.00	−.01
Belief Scale	−.09	−.06	.00	−.08
Self-control variables				
Physical response	−.18**	−.12**	−.19**	−.22**
Get-tough response	−.04	.04	.06	.03
Violent response	−.12*	−.09	−.05	−.07
$R^2=$	.08	.03	.05	.07
$N=$	452	451	448	458

$*p < .05; **p < .01.$
SOURCE: Adapted from Boeringer and Akers (1993).

tistically significant and in the direction (positive) expected by the theory. The effort to construct a scale of relative sexual deprivation from the five items measuring the concept was not successful (Cronbach's alpha = .11). When the items are entered into a regression equation as five single-item variables, however, they account for about the same amounts of variance (ranging from 3% to 9%) as do the combined social bonding/self-control models, although they account for considerably lower amounts than the social learning models.

Only one of the indicators, Perceived Pressure to Be Sexually Active, has significant net effects in the expected direction on all of the measures of sexually aggressive behavior and measures of rape proclivity (table not shown). The relative deprivation of sexual activity compared to the average man on campus is also significantly related to nonphysical sexual coercion and to all three of the indicators of rape proclivity. The gap between one's own expectations and sexual activity also has a significant effect on rape behavior, but the direction of the relationship is opposite theoretical expectation. That is, the college man who feels relatively more deprived of sexual activity is less likely—not more likely, as the theory predicts—to commit rape.

Conclusion

Empirical models of nonphysical and physical sexual coercion and proclivity for physically forced sex derived from social learning theory are clearly superior to those derived from social control and relative deprivation theories. There are, however, control and deprivation variables that do have statistically significant effects on the dependent variables. Are there elements of these two theories that would retain independent effects as strong or stronger than those of social learning variables and add significantly to the level of explained variance accounted for by the social learning models alone?

To answer this question, regression models containing all of the independent variables from all three models were run for each of the dependent variables. The answer is No. The combined models do not increase explanatory efficacy at all over the social learning models considered alone; the amount of improvement in the adjusted R^2 over that obtained in the social learning models is close to zero (tables not shown). Indeed, in some instances, the combined models lowered explained variance below what was found in the social learning models alone.

The significant net effects (as measured by the standardized beta coefficients) in the combined models come almost exclusively from social learning variables. The Modeling Scale has significant effects in all four models. The Friends' Reinforcement Scale, Reinforcement Balance Scale, Definitions Scale, and one or more of the Differential Association measures have significant beta weights in three of the combined models.

Of the nine social bonding/self-control variables, only the Commitment Scale measure of bonding (in two models) and the Physical Response measure of self-control (in one model) have significant effects. The Sexual Deprivation vs Own Expectations, the Relative Opportunity, and the Sexual Deprivation vs Other Males variables from the relative deprivation model have significant net effects in one model each. Thus, some elements of social bonding/self-control and of relative deprivation variables have separate independent effects on tendency toward rape behavior and proclivity. But neither adds anything to the overall explanation provided by the social learning models.

The full social learning model, with adequate measures of all four of the major concepts, has usually been tested with samples of adolescents and with delinquency or substance use and abuse as the dependent variables. The findings on such a serious offense as rape and on sexual aggression reported in this chapter provide additional empirical validation of the theory with a young adult sample and a concentration on serious deviant behavior. Neither social learning theory nor any other theory is wholly valid or completely incorrect as an explanation of crime and deviance. Judgments of theories, therefore, must be based not only on direct tests of their propositions but also on comparisons of the relative validity of two or more theories. Although this can be done by comparing across studies that test single theories, it is done more effectively by comparing theories within the same study. That is the approach I have taken in previous chapters and in this chapter, where social learning theory is empirically compared to control theory (social bonding and self-control) and to relative deprivation theory.

The principal conclusion to be drawn from this comparative assessment of the theories is that social learning theory offers an explanation of rape and sexual aggression that is empirically supported to a much greater degree than are the social bonding/self-control and the relative deprivation/strain explanations. The same conclusion was reached in previous empirical comparisons of social learning theory, control theory, and strain theory (see Akers and Cochran, 1985; White et al., 1986; McGee, 1992; Benda, 1994). Models derived from social learning theory accounted for about one-fifth of the variance in sexually aggressive behavior and from two-fifths to more than one-half of the variance in rape proclivity. Social learning models accounted for three to ten times more of the variances than were accounted for by the social bonding/self-control and relative deprivation models. When all of the variables from all of the theories were placed in combined models, the overall explained variance did not increase over that of the social learning models by themselves.

Earlier tests of social learning theory with measures of all the main social learning concepts have concentrated on juvenile delinquency and alcohol/drug use. Similarly, the dependent variables in studies of social bonding have usually been measures of nonviolent, less serious deviance or of delinquency. This is the first study of rape behavior testing full models with measures of all of the principal concepts from social bonding and social learning theories, and it is the first to test any aspect of self-control theory as an explanation of rape. It is also the first to attempt a replication of Kanin's study of relative deprivation as a theory of rape and to relate it to general strain theory.

The models are ordinary least square regression models that are based on assumptions of recursive paths from a set of independent variables to a dependent variable. The cross-sectional design, therefore, raises a question of causal ordering in the models. I have argued that temporality and feedback effects are built into the reinforcement concept in social learning theory and that there are theoretically expected reciprocal relationships between patterns of association and the commission of deviant acts. Hirschi and Gottfredson (1993) argue that causal order does not present a problem for self-control theory that cannot be solved simply through conceptual analysis and collateral data in cross-sectional designs. They contend that temporally ordered data in longitudinal designs also have problems that restrict their ability to solve the causal-order question. Further, they argue that the relative magnitude of relationships found in cross-sectional designs will remain about the same in longitudinal studies.

Nonetheless, a study that collects data on its dependent and independent variables at the same time has difficulty in demonstrating directionality of relationships because the temporal ordering is not clearly ascertainable. The measure of rape proclivity introduces a quasi-temporal ordering, in that likelihood of future behavior is reported rather than current or past behavior and the independent variables are related to that measure just as they are to past and current behavioral measures.

Temporal ordering and other methodological issues are equalized when the goal is to compare theories within the same data set. Whatever the temporal-ordering limitations and causal value of the data, they apply in the same way to all of the theories compared. Each theory is susceptible to whatever losses or gains in explanatory power come from the methodology. The benefit of assessing the relative empirical validity of theoretical explanations within the same study is that variations in samples, procedures, and measures of dependent variables that may occur across studies are controlled. Therefore, while methodological limitations may raise questions about the empirical assessment of the absolute explanatory power of a theory, they do not compromise the comparative assessment of theories.

It is possible, of course, for one theory to be compared unequally with others within the same study because of differences in the empirical measures chosen as indicators of the theoretical constructs. In this study, the measures of self-control are the least satisfactory. We had the least conceptual and prior research guidance in operationalizing this concept. We believe that the measures we utilized are reasonable empirical approximations to at least one aspect of self-control, and one can reasonably compare the impact of these with measures of elements of social bonding or of concepts from other theories (for instance, effect of self-control as compared to effect of friends' reinforcement). Since the measures of self-control are limited to this one aspect and the operationalizations of that aspect are questionable, however, the data here cannot be taken as an adequate test of self-control as a general theory.

There should be little question about the adequacy of the measures of the other constructs from social learning, social bonding, and relative deprivation theories. They have strong face validity, closely reflecting the meanings and definitions of concepts given in the original statements of the theories, and they closely parallel the reliable and valid empirical indicators that have been used in previous research testing the theories, including research done by the authors of the theories.

Future research should compare these and additional models of serious criminal behavior in other samples with additional measures and longitudinal data. Such investigations should not concentrate only on comparing such models. The amounts of variance accounted for by the social learning models are impressive, especially the explained variance of more than 50% in rape proclivity. Social learning appears to be the theory of choice in comparison with the other two models. But with all but one of the social learning models we are still left with most of the variance unexplained. Social learning has been shown to be a good explanation, but it leaves much to be explained in male sexual aggression. A fuller accounting of this behavior may come either from other dimensions of the social learning process or from other variables.

All of the measures in this study are in the immediate past, in the present, or projected to the future. For later research to provide a more complete explanation of rape, data would need to be collected on family and peer contexts at periods in the lives of the respondents before they entered college. The self-reported behavior in this study is directly parallel to behavior for which men have been convicted and punished. The study has no reports of arrests or convictions, however; no respondents from arrested or incarcerated populations were sampled. Future research should test social learning, control, and deprivation theories in samples that include convicted rapists. Moreover, future theory and research on rape should examine the kinds of social psychological variables in this study in a broader social structural context. What cultural and structural conditions of our society and communities relate to the high levels of rape in the United States? How do those structural conditions relate to the learning and other social psychological processes whereby some men become disposed to force sexual relations? These are the kinds of questions that the Social Structure–Social Learning (SSSL) model I present in Chapter 12 is designed to address.

Notes

1. This chapter draws heavily on two papers co-authored with Scot Boeringer that were based on his thesis and dissertation research. I gratefully acknowledge my debt to him (and to my colleague Constance Shehan, with whom we collaborated on one of the papers) for the content of this chapter. See Boeringer and others (1991) and Boeringer and Akers (1993).

2. Sexual aggression can be directed against males, but in the great majority of such cases it comes from other males. The social learning principles apply regardless of who the victim of sexual aggression is, but the empirical focus here is on aggression of men against women.

11

Other Studies on Social Learning

Cheating among University Students

Academic dishonesty is another area of deviant behavior investigated from a social learning perspective at the University of Florida. The research on this noncriminal deviance among college students offered yet another opportunity to test the scope and general applicability of the theory. It was first investigated by Lonn Lanza-Kaduce (Lanza-Kaduce and Klug, 1986), who was later joined by Richard Hollinger in a larger, longitudinal study. Cheating on college campuses has been recognized as a significant problem (Michaels and Miethe, 1989), and a major objective of the Florida studies (the second one was carried out with the cooperation and support of the university's office of student services) was to measure the prevalence of academic dishonesty among undergraduates there. But the research also focused on explaining why some individuals do and some do not engage in various kinds of dishonesty in coursework.

> Empirical applications [of social learning] to drug use, smoking, and sexual assault address behaviors that are first confronted, for the most part, in adolescence. The process of initiation and the emergence of patterns in these behaviors may be more readily accessible to researchers, but they may be different from behaviors that are shaped much earlier in life.
>
> Cheating begins in the games children play. In fact, parents routinely teach lessons about honesty by reacting to cheating episodes. Unlike substance use or coercive sexual behaviors, cheating is a "normal" part of childhood. To the extent that . . . deviant and nondeviant behavior are learned in the same way, insight may be gained by focusing on behaviors with which we have all had longstanding experience and for which the definitional process has been subject to interactive learning rather than [only being] received as a cultural pro-

scription. The etiology of cheating behavior is such that we should not be surprised that surveys . . . find a high prevalence of cheating. (Lanza-Kaduce and Hollinger, 1994:2)

As an element of this explanatory goal, partial social learning models were tested and found to offer a good explanation of the frequency, stability, and change of cheating behavior in a college sample. The data also allowed for exploring some of the relationships among social learning variables and reciprocal effects of deviant experiences on those variables. Other than offering some informal advice when asked, I had no hand in either study. Therefore, in describing the research and findings I have relied on data analysis and papers by my colleagues Lonn Lanza-Kaduce and Richard Hollinger and by my students Mary Klug and Kim Lersch; I thank them for access to the findings.

CHEATING STUDY I: CROSS SECTIONAL STUDY OF SOCIAL LEARNING AND MORAL DEVELOPMENT

In the first study on cheating, Lanza-Kaduce and Klug (1986) measured differential association, differential social reinforcement (peer reactions to cheating and negative institutional sanctions), and definitions. No measures of imitation were included. This study also measured levels of moral reasoning taken from Kohlberg's theory of moral development (Kohlberg, 1964; Rest, 1974) and examined the possible convergences of moral development with social learning concepts. The hypotheses of the study revolved around proposing social learning processes as the basic mechanisms in cheating, but with differing magnitudes of effect depending on the level of moral reasoning achieved by the individual at the time of the study.

The sample was made up of 196 undergraduates in a large introductory sociology section who completed a self-report questionnaire administered during class time toward the end of the semester. Cheating was measured by self-reports of the number of times they had cheated on a test in any class during that semester.

The measure of differential association was the proportion of "best" friends whom the respondent believed had cheated on a test. The respondent's own definition favorable or unfavorable to cheating was a single item of the degree of personal approval or disapproval of test cheating. Two variables measured differential reinforcement. One was the perception of how negatively the person's best friends would most likely react if they learned that she or he had cheated on a test. The other asked the respondents what punitive sanctions would be forthcoming from the university if they were caught cheating, ranging from nothing to suspension from school. A short-form measure of the DIT (Defining Issues Test) was used to calculate the respondent's cognitive moral development. The higher the DIT score, the higher the level of postconventional, "principled" moral reasoning.

All of the social learning variables were significantly related to cheating in the expected direction (with zero-order correlations ranging from .20 to .39). The level of moral reasoning as measured by the DIT scores was related to cheating in the expected direction, with respondents scoring higher on the DIT reporting fewer instances of cheating, but the relationship was weak $(r = -.07)$. There was, as expected, some interaction between the DIT score and differential association, and therefore separate regression analyses were done within levels of moral development. As the data in Table 11.1 show, the social learning variables account for considerable amounts of the variance in cheating regardless of the respondents' scores on the DIT, although there is some difference in the strength of the learning variables by level of moral development. The biggest difference, however, lies in how well the social learning model does in explaining cheating by the group of students whose inconsistent responses on the questionnaire items did not allow them to be categorized clearly into low, medium, or high levels of moral reasoning.

CHEATING STUDY 2: LONGITUDINAL STUDY OF SOCIAL LEARNING
AND COLLEGE CHEATING

The social learning model tested in the second Florida study on cheating incorporated measures of three major concepts (differential association, definitions, and differential reinforcement) similar to the ones used in the first study. It also included, in one phase of data analysis, an indirect measure of imitation. Social learning theory refers to these variables in explaining violations of academic norms in the same way that it accounts for any norm violation. Through differential association (first with family, and later with friends and fellow students), the individual is exposed to normative definitions favorable and unfavorable to cheating on exams, term papers, and assignments as being wrong or right, behavioral models of honesty or dishonesty, and social reinforcement for cheating or honesty. To the extent that a student comes to take cheating as acceptable, either in general or under certain circumstances (neutralizing, justifying definitions), he or she is more likely to engage in it when the opportunity arises. Supposedly, the primary reward attached to cheating lies in gaining a better grade or avoiding a poor one, but this could be offset by discovery of the dishonesty and probable application of negative sanctions (lowered grade, failing the course, embarrassment, reprimand, suspension, or, ultimately, expulsion). The balance of reinforcement also involves anticipated permissive, encouraging, or punitive reactions of parents and peers. The social learning variables are expected to be significantly related to frequency of cheating behavior both contemporaneously and longitudinally. Further, the theory is expected to predict maintenance and change in cheating behavior.

Sample and Procedure. The research was a self-report survey group-administered during class time to undergraduate students at the University of Florida, with the Time 1 (T1) measures taken at the beginning of

---

Table 11.1 Social Learning Variables and Test Cheating by Level of Moral Development

Social Learning Variables		Level of Moral Development		
	Low	Medium	High	Inconsistent
Differential association	.30	.22	−.25	.39
Definitions	.20	.10	.22	.29
Differential reinforcement				
Peer reactions	.02	−.10	.29	.11
Institutional sanctions	−.04	−.06	−.03	−.09
R^2 =	.24	.19	.20	.46
N =	.35	56	30	54

Coefficients shown are the unstandardized regression coefficients for the effects of the social learning variables on cheating on tests within each level of moral development. SOURCE: Adapted from Lanza-Kaduce and Klug (1986).

the fall semester ($N = 1,141$) and the Time 2 (T2) measures taken at the end of the semester ($N = 1,766$) in 27 sections of introductory-level undergraduate courses spread across a range of disciplines. Nested within the larger sample was a panel of 503 respondents who completed the survey instrument at both T1 and T2. The researchers were able to identify the panel from anonymous questionnaires by including a series of questions (e.g., month of mother's birth) that could be used to match T1 with T2 questionnaires without name or other information that could be traced to externally identified individuals. The findings presented below are based on this panel of 205 males and 298 females; mean age was 19.4 years, and 83.1% were white.

Measurement of Cheating Behavior. The survey asked for self-reports of the frequency of four types of cheating: knowingly allowed someone to copy your answers to an exam; copied answers from someone else taking the exam; copied published material and turned it in as your own; and turned in another student's work as your own. Although the questions were exactly the same, the time periods and response categories for the four questions on the T1 instrument (a seven-point scale, ranging from never cheated to cheated every day during the year prior to the current semester) differed from those on the T2 instrument (a ten-point scale, ranging from never to nine or more times during the semester). A reliable scale of overall cheating at T1 was formed by summing responses to the four cheating items (CHEAT1; Cronbach's alpha = .75); the same was done for the dependent variable at T2 (CHEAT2; Cronbach's alpha = .80).

In addition to these basic approaches, the researchers devised measures of stability and change in cheating behavior between the two times of data collection. RESISTERS were those students who did not cheat in the past and continued in that pattern during the semester of the study, while PERSISTERS showed the opposite pattern of stable behavior by cheating previously and again by the end of the semester. Two types of changed behavior were identified as DECREASERS (stopped or reduced cheating behavior from T1 to T2) and INCREASERS (increased cheating over the course of the semester). The advantages of this approach in theory testing were specified by Lanza-Kaduce and Hollinger (1994:13):

> This measurement approach incorporates the prior levels of cheating into the dependent variable and simplifies data analysis. It allows us to separate the effects of prior cheating from the social learning variables without resorting to

a technique where prior cheating is introduced as a control. Introducing prior cheating as a control has the limiting consequence of reducing the equation to an analysis of change. If the effects of prior cheating are removed (because they have a feedback effect on learning) so the effects of the social learning variables can be studied, the only variance left to explain is that for persons who changed their cheating patterns. Inasmuch as social learning theory is purported to explain both change (i.e., initiation, increase, cessation) and maintenance of deviance [see Krohn et al., 1985; Akers, 1994], introducing prior deviance as a control results in an analysis that addresses only the change part of the process.

Measures of Social Learning Variables. Definitions favorable and unfavorable to cheating were measured by a summative scale of endorsement of five statements justifying or excusing cheating—for example, cheating is all right if the professor gives unreasonably difficult assignments or tests (NEUTDEF; Cronbach's alpha = .89). They were also measured with a scale summing how strongly one approved or disapproved of each of the four items of cheating (POS/NEGDEF; Cronbach's alpha = .82). These indicators of definitions appeared on the instrument at T1, but neither was included at T2. Differential peer association was measured at T2 by the proportion of the respondent's best friends (from almost none to almost all) who were reported as having committed each of the cheating acts at least occasionally. A scale was constructed by summing the responses to this question for each of the four types of cheating (BFRASSN; Cronbach's alpha = .81).

Questions on the anticipated reactions of friends and father (or head of household) and perceived chances of discovery and penalties for cheating became the operational indicators of differential reinforcement. The first indicator was a four-item scale of the most common reaction of the respondent's best friends if they were to learn of his or her cheating, ranging from "turn you in," to "sympathize or excuse your behavior," to "encourage you" (FRREACT; Cronbach's alpha = .86). The second differential reinforcement measure was the anticipated reaction of the respondent's father (or head of household) if he were to learn of cheating behaviors, ranging from making the student withdraw from school or withholding financial support, to "excuse you and your behavior," to praise or encouragement. Again, a four-item scale was formed from responses to this question on each of the cheating behavior items (FAREACT; Cronbach's alpha = .87).

Both of these social reaction measures represent a range of possible sanctions from very negative to positive, but they appeared on the questionnaire at T1 only. The other scales are perceived informal deterrence measures of probability of the cheating being discovered by the instructor or of the cheater being "turned in" by another student (ranging from almost none to "about 100%"). These items were included at both points of data collection; the respective scales are labeled CHANCE1 and CHANCE2 (Cronbach's alphas = .76 and .83) and CHANCES1 and CHANCES2 (Cronbach's alphas = .90 and .90). The perceived punishment that would be meted out for discovered academic transgressions (SANCTION) was measured only in the first survey by a single item with ten response categories of increasingly serious sanctions, from "nothing" to "kicked out of the university permanently."

Only these three sets of definitions, differential association, and differential reinforcement variables were put in the first series of analysis, which utilized OLS regression models. However, in a second series, based on Discriminant Function Analysis, an indirect indicator of imitation (MODEL) was placed in the social learning function. On the second survey instrument, respondents were asked how often they had the occasion to turn in or refrain from turning in other students whom they "definitely knew cheated" during the semester of the study (in any class, not just the one in which the survey was being conducted.) The number of times the respondent had knowledge of other students' cheating and did or did not turn them in for the academic violation was taken an indicator of the number of times the respondent had been exposed to behavioral "models of cheating" during the semester.

CROSS-SECTIONAL AND LONGITUDINAL FINDINGS ON SOCIAL LEARNING
AND CHEATING BEHAVIOR

Unfortunately for purposes of theory testing, as noted above, measures of differential peer association (proportion of the respondent's best friends who had engaged in each of the types of cheating behavior) were not taken at T1, and measures of definitions (neutralizing definitions and one's own positive/negative attitude toward cheating) were not taken at T2. Similarly, measures of differential reinforcement were taken only in the first survey, and measures of modeling were made only in the second survey. Only perceptions of probability of discovery were measured at both T1 and T2. Therefore, only partial social learning models were tested cross-sectionally or longitudinally. The findings on those partial models provide persuasive support for social learning theory, but there is good reason to believe that much more of the cheating behavior could have been accounted for if indicators of all the major social learning variables had been included in the research at both times of data collection.

Table 11.2 presents the standardized beta coefficients from the OLS multiple regression analysis, with CHEAT1 and CHEAT2 as dependent variables and the social learning variables as the independent variables. The T1 social learning variables explained a considerable amount of variance in T1 cheating (27.8%). Of the social learning variables measured at T1, definitions favorable and unfavorable to academic dishonesty (NEUTDEF and POS/NEGDEF) had the strongest net effects. That the level of explained variance could have been very much higher if a measure of

---

Table 11.2 Cross-Sectional and Longitudinal Analysis of Cheating at T1 and T2

		Cheating Variables	
Social Learning Variables		T1	T2
T1 SL Variables		CHEAT1	CHEAT2
		B =	B =
NEUTDEF		.29***	.17**
POS/NEGDEF		.27***	.15*
CHANCE1		.02	.03
CHANCES1		−.02	.14**
SANCTION		−.01	−.03
FAREACT		−	−.09*
FRREACT		.03	−.04
$R^2=$		.28	.09
T2 SL Variables			
CHANCE2		−	.03
CHANCES2		−	.13**
BFRASSN		−	.49***
$R^2=$			.24

$*p < .05; **p < .01; *** < .001.$
SOURCE: Adapted from Lersch (1993).

differential peer association had been included at T1 is clearly shown by the findings in the lower part of the table. The T2 model accounts for 23.4% of the variance in CHEAT2, with most of that being accounted for by BFRASSN alone (and with CHANCES2 related in the opposite direction from expectation). An analysis (not shown) of the separate effects of each of the social learning variables on the dependent variable confirmed that, while significant effects were observed for each set of the social learning variables, the strongest effects came from the differential peer association variable, which accounted on its own for 23% of the variance in T2 cheating.

In the longitudinal analysis, as can be seen from findings presented in the top right of Table 11.2, the definitions and reinforcement variables at T1 predicted cheating activity at T2. The overall model and four of the relationships in it are statistically significant (although again CHANCES1 is not in the expected direction), but the explained variance was less than in the cross-sectional analysis (9.3%). This modest amount of explained variance by the social learning model arose primarily because there was no measure of differential peer association at T1; it is not due to leaving T1 cheating behavior out of the model. Surprisingly, the relationship between reported cheating at the beginning of the semester was not strongly related to reported cheating during the semester ($r = .24$). Further, when T1 cheating is added to the model, it has no significant net predictive effects on T2 cheating and adds only .001 to the overall amount of explained variance (table not shown). This disconnection between self-reported cheating at the two points of data collection could have come about because the first survey asked for cheating in the past year (which for many of the respondents was the final year of high school) and the second asked for cheating only during the current semester (which could have been affected by the respondent having already participated in the T1 survey at the beginning of the semester).

The findings generally support the social learning explanation of academic dishonesty, providing empirical evidence on yet another type of deviance that can be explained by social learning processes. I believe the findings would have offered even greater support for the theory if all of the major social learning variables had been measured in both the first and second surveys. The way in which the independent variables were measured at the two points in time produced a very conservative test of the predictive power of the model in the OLS regression analysis. But at least one caveat must be entered regarding the extent to which the findings favor the theory. The direction of the relationship of one's cheating to the perceived likelihood that the person would be "turned in" by another student runs counter to theoretical expectations. That is, the higher the perceived probability that another would report one's cheating, the higher the frequency of one's self-reported cheating. Expectations of discovery imply expectations of negative sanctions; the theory would predict that anticipated punishment should reduce, not enhance, the frequency of cheating. Thus, this finding is not supportive of the theory.

However, the direction of the relationship may have been distorted by the skewed distribution on the CHANCES scales. The vast majority of the respondents felt that the odds that other students would inform on them were extremely low. It may be that the few respondents who reported believing that there was a higher probability of being reported by other students and who reported a higher frequency of cheating took some perverse pleasure in committing what they perceived to be high-risk behavior (although in reality there is low risk of sanctions based on "snitching" by another student). It could simply be an anomaly of weak and indirect measures of negative sanctions. The measures of differential reinforcement in the study leaned heavily on measures of deterrence and of certainty and severity of negative sanctions that turned out to be weakly and inconsistently related to cheating behavior, while rewards attached to cheating were under-measured. Future research could rectify this by adding better measures of differential reinforcement, the balance of positive and negative outcomes of cheating. The measures in this study come closer to gauging simple deterrence perceptions than to measuring the concept of differential reinforcement.

LONGITUDINAL FINDINGS ON SOCIAL LEARNING PREDICTIONS OF STABILITY AND CHANGE IN CHEATING BEHAVIOR

As noted above, there was not a strong relationship between cheating at T1 and T2. But even if that relationship were strong (as is usually the case when the same behavior is measured at two different times), Lanza-Kaduce and Hollinger (1994) identify reasons why insertion of T1 deviance into predictive models may undermine efforts to test social learning theory (and perhaps other theories as well):

Because the same learning principles apply to nondeviant as well as deviant behavior, the theory is purported to be able to explain deviance and conformity. Because the theory is processual, it is purported to be able to account for both stability and change. . . . Where behaviors are more stable, as when either non-involvement or a pattern of deviance persists, the nonrecursive elements in the theory are less salient. . . . The reciprocal effects are most crucial during periods of change. As people experiment with a behavior, they get feedback that is novel and which may result in the emergence of a new pattern of deviance. Or when people begin to diminish their involvement, the reinforcement/punishment contingencies may change for both the behavior and the definitions. . . .

[L]ongitudinal work . . . which seeks to control for the effects of prior deviance on the learning variables by introducing a measure of prior deviance into a regression analysis addresses only the change process. The Time 1 deviance measure accounts for the Time 2 deviance for those whose deviance pattern is stable. As such, only part of the overall learning is studied and we should expect more modest magnitudes for relationships in survey research because change is much harder to capture than are the patterns of maintenance. . . . Whenever prior levels of deviance are introduced into the equation, the analysis becomes one of change [only]. (Lanza-Kaduce and Hollinger, 1994:6–7)

Lanza-Kaduce and Hollinger argue, then, that differentiating between those whose cheating behavior or honesty remains relatively unchanged and those whose cheating behavior undergoes some change adequately takes into account these behaviors at T1 and allows for testing social learning predictions.

Our prediction is that learning variables will more aptly discriminate between resisters and persisters (i.e., account for maintenance) than they will differentiate increasers from decreasers (i.e., account for change). However, we expect that a second lesser function will emerge that helps distinguish those with changing cheating patterns. (Lanza-Kaduce and Hollinger, 1994:9)

They were also concerned with examining the effects of definitions and reinforcement of cheating behavior on subsequent patterns of differential association. They contrast Warr's hypothesis of "sticky" deviant friendships, which endure even though the person may stop or reduce involvement in the deviant behavior, with their hypothesis that friendship patterns will be stable for those whose deviant behavior remains about the same, but will change for those whose behavior undergoes alteration. While Warr would predict that friendship patterns will not change for those whose cheating has increased or decreased, Lanza-Kaduce and Hollinger predict that friendship patterns will be stable for those whose cheating (or not cheating) is stable and will change for those whose cheating behavior changes.

The primary finding was that the social learning variables could discriminate successfully among the patterns of cheating and that, even without the more powerful differential peer association variable, the models can predict at least modest amounts of variance in stability and change in cheating behavior. The two theoretically expected functions were identified by the multiple discriminant analysis as statistically significant (table not shown). The first function accounted for about 20% and the second for about 7% of the variance among the resisters, persisters, increasers, and decreasers. The group centroids for the first function also showed a pattern consistent with theoretical expectations, with the resisters (noncheaters) scoring on the social learning functions as expected on one extreme and the cheating increasers scoring at the other extreme, while the decreasers and persisters ranked in between. The findings on the second function, too, were consistent with expectations, differentiating between the two groups who had either increased or decreased their cheating behavior, but not discriminating between the two stable groups. Overall, 56% of the cases could be correctly classified by the social learning variables, a 38% reduction in error from random assignment.

The next step was to analyze the predictive efficacy of the social learning variables on stability of behavior (resisters and persisters) separately from their effects on changes in cheating (decreasers and increasers). The canonical correlations and the group centroids from this separate two-group discriminant analysis (table not shown) confirmed the theoretical expectation that both stability and change in cheating behavior are predictable from the social learning variables, with better prediction of the former (canonical corr. = .54**; 77% correct classification; 47% proportional reduction in chance error) than of the latter (canonical corr. = .34**; 82% correct classification; 41% reduction in chance error).

The strongest learning variable in discriminating persisters from resisters was one's own positive/negative definitions, but since definitions changed very little over the span of one semester they were not related to increasing or decreasing cheating. The imitation variable (MODEL), however, had strong effects on both stability and change. This was a little surprising, since in our previous studies imitation was often weaker than other social learning variables.

> Its [MODEL's] strength was frankly greater than the theory would have led us
> to expect. Perhaps this is due to its operationalization. Almost none of the

> students saw cheating that they reported during the semester. Consequently, almost all the modeled cheating went unreported. To the extent that some kinds of cheating may be pursued with friends (e.g., turning in someone else's work as one's own, copying answers from someone else taking an exam), this measure may be tapping different associations with deviant friends as well as models. (Lanza-Kaduce and Hollinger, 1994:25)

The reinforcement measure of reaction of friends (FRREACT) had weak effects on change and maintenance of cheating behavior, most likely because the campus culture supports norms of noninterference and not "ratting" on others in matters of academic dishonesty. This produced little variation in this independent variable and thereby its weak effects on the dependent variables.

The findings from regressing T2 BFRASSN on T1 measures of definitions, friends' reactions, and perceived risk of being turned in by another student for cheating did not confirm Warr's hypothesis of "sticky" deviant friends (tables not shown). The learning processes that predicted changes in cheating also help predict subsequent friendship patterns.

> The results were consistent with the position that friends are an important source of reinforcement, models, and definitions. . . . Those who reduced their cheating had friends who didn't cheat and who would react negatively to cheating. (Lanza-Kaduce and Hollinger, 1994:29)

Social Learning Theory and Social Reactions to Deviance

Social learning theory posits that the same general process is at work in both conforming and deviant behavior. The focus of the theory and tests of it has been on how that process produces deviant and criminal behavior rather than conformity. Nevertheless, its simultaneous explanation of conformity is usually explicit (and always implicit), since the absence or low levels of the deviant acts under study are taken as indicating conforming behavior. The learning that produces conforming behavior produces less deviance, and the learning that produces deviant alternatives predicts less-conforming behavior. Therefore, it is a theory of conforming/deviant behavior. The basic behavioral learning principles and the sociological principles of reference group and symbolic interaction in my version of social learning theory are applicable to any behavior, deviant or conforming, even when the presence of one does not necessarily imply the absence of the other. Bandura and other social learning theorists, as well as Skinner and other operant theorists, have applied their models to a range of behavior. But beyond accepting the idea that prediction of deviant behavior necessarily involves prediction of a conforming alternative (even when that alternative is no more than refraining from the deviance), I have made no effort to apply or test social learning theory with behavior in which all alternatives are conforming (e.g., spouse/mate selection, sex-role behavior, occupational behavior, etc.) and in which the issue of deviance and crime is not relevant.

On occasion, however, I have moved somewhat in that direction by using the social learning principles to examine legitimate behavior in the form of social reactions to deviance, rather than the absence, presence, or frequency of the deviance itself. The theory predicts that the formal and informal reactions of social audiences and society to deviance is a function of the same variables as the deviant behavior to which those reactions are made—differential association with others who do or do not respond to deviance in certain ways, exposure to norm enforcement and reaction models, definitions of right and wrong, and anticipated rewards and punishment for taking or not taking certain actions in response to deviant or criminal behavior.

SOCIAL LEARNING AS AN ALTERNATIVE TO THE LABELING

AND PSYCHIATRIC PERSPECTIVES ON TREATMENT/CONTROL

OF MENTAL ILLNESS

I first applied the theory in this way, in collaboration with Marvin Krohn, to societal reactions to mental illness (Krohn and Akers, 1977). At that time the two major perspectives on this issue were the psychiatric and the labeling. We reviewed all of the major studies on psychiatric variables (diagnosis and severity of impairment) and extra-psychiatric variables (family, class, legal, and other personal and social characteristics and resources) in decisions on voluntary admissions and involuntary commitments to mental hospitals and treatment programs. We concluded that the preponderance of evidence demonstrated greater impact of extra-psychiatric variables on such decisions, especially with regard to involuntary admissions and discharges from public hospitals, than psychiatric variables. The psychiatric view that only the nature and severity of diagnosis and prognosis enter into such decisions was not supported. At the same time, the nonpsychiatric variables most predictive of decisions (supportive family, marital status, willingness by the patient or family to challenge psychiatric decisions) are not particularly supportive of the labeling view that such decisions are primarily based on differential social status and power. Even those predictive variables that do indicate relative social position and power (class, race, education) are not particularly or solely derivable from labeling theory.

Therefore, we presented social learning theory as an alternative perspective that made better sense, than either the psychiatric or labeling perspective, of the findings that diagnostic, admission, and discharge judgments about mental patients are not context-free decisions and that social variables affect them.

> Both the deviant behavior and the response to it are shaped by stimuli in the social environment, the most important of which are the rewarding or punishing consequences of the behavior. . . .
> [P]sychiatrists and other mental health workers are social actors playing roles in social and organizational contexts which affect their behavior. Their social and educational background (including the training received in the theory and treatment of mental illness), the kind of organizational environment in which they work, the demands and requirements of their job, and the behavior and characteristics of their patients all exert an influence on decisions they make. To this general sociological orientation the learning model adds an explanation of the behavior of psychiatric workers as a function of past learning and responses to present and anticipated stimuli. The hypothesis is that these variables account for diagnosing, treating, and releasing of patients to the extent that they provide discriminative or cue stimuli eliciting given responses and set up reinforcement-punishment contingencies attached to the behavior of psychiatrists and others who make the decisions. In general, decisions will be made which produce greater actual or anticipated rewards and less costs than alternative lines of action. . . .
> [D]iagnosis is, in fact, an inference from verbal and nonverbal behavior. . . . Indeed, some of the same social characteristics associated with the distribution of mental illness in the population provide the cues for applying the label and also serve as indicators of the ability of the patient to control or affect the rewards and costs attached to different psychiatric decisions. (Krohn and Akers, 1977:356–57)

The negative consequences for the psychiatric workers caused by release of patients who have been committed under court order tend to be greater, and the positive consequences tend to be smaller, than for continued commitment. Therefore, there is a tendency for hospital staff to keep such patients under control or treatment longer than they would keep voluntary patients, even for the same diagnosis. Often the diagnosis of the admitting staff does not enter into the decisions to admit civilly or criminally committed patients, and staff assessment of treatment and cure are irrelevant in court-ordered releases. With involuntary patients in public hospitals, the psychiatrists and other workers are more apt to be rewarded for making admission and release decisions in the direction of "control," while professional and economic rewards are greater for "treatment" with voluntary patients.

> The rewards are greater for admitting than refusing treatment to higher-status people who want treatment; they are less for admitting lower-status patients to treatment. Hence, there is a positive relationship between social status and admission to voluntary treatment. Similarly, it is costlier to force higher-status patients into treatment than to make lower-status persons involuntary patients; hence, the negative relationship between admission to treatment and social status among involuntary patients. Once admitted involuntarily to treatment, the lower-status person is less able to make trouble for the staff if not released; therefore, they tend to be kept in longer. Keeping those in who challenge the decision [forcefully or with legal action] is more costly than retaining those who do not challenge; thus, the protestors are more likely to be released. It is more rewarding to go along with what the patient's family wants for both voluntary and involuntary patients even if the seriousness of the case indicates a contrary decision. (Krohn and Akers, 1977:358)

Social Learning Theory and EAP Referrals

The psychiatric and extra-psychiatric variables in mental health decisions are analogous to the legal and extralegal variables that are frequently the objects of research on the law and the criminal-justice system. Thus, it would seem that the social learning perspective could be extended to account for decisions in the law and the criminal-justice system (although they seem to be based more on the nature of offense behavior and legal variables than on extralegal variables). To develop the theory along these lines adequately would require major effort and careful conceptualization. I have not done this, but I have done some additional work, in collaboration with Michael Capece, on the notion that the social learning approach is applicable to the process by which social control decisions are made. His dissertation research, on which I was the major advisor, on reactions of supervisors to impairment of employees on the job, either by alcohol or drug use or by virtue of emotional/mental health problems, offered a good opportunity to apply social learning to behavior in reaction to deviance. The deviance in this case is not specifically substance use or abuse or mental illness but rather how such behavior results in occupational deviance. The specific behavior under study was not deviant; rather, we wanted to explain supervisors' referring or not referring their workers to an employee assistance program (EAP) to help the workers overcome their problems and restore job performance (Capece and Akers, 1995).

In applying social learning theory to supervisors' behavior, we built directly on the Krohn and Akers theorizing about the social learning contingencies surrounding control/treatment decisions by mental health workers. We also built on the use of learning concepts by the late Harrison Trice (Trice and Roman, 1978; Trice and Beyer, 1984). Trice was the pioneer in the development of EAPs and the use of the "constructive confrontation" technique for dealing with job impairment. We also relied on research on EAP referrals by Googins and Kurtz (1981). Of course, we did not view supervisors in work organizations as mental health professionals making diagnoses and treatment decisions about mental or behavioral problems. However, we did see their referral decisions based on perceived substance abuse or emotional problems as functionally equivalent to referrals by health care workers to treatment programs. In EAPs, the work supervisors make no direct decisions about diagnosis, admissions, type of treatment, length of treatment, or discharge from treatment. Nonetheless, supervisors do make decisions regarding referrals for job difficulties or deficiencies that they perceive may result from mental or emotional problems or from drug/alcohol use. In this sense, then, EAP referrals involve a learning process and variables similar to those postulated by Krohn and Akers for control/treatment decisions by psychiatric workers.

Krohn and Akers applied the social learning perspective to help make sense of extant research findings; they did not have any new data against which to gauge the value of the perspective. It was a step forward, then, to have the concepts and measures worked out ahead of time and then collect original data on them. I hesitate to say that this provided a direct or adequate test of the general theory, and we made no claims to making such a a direct test. But social learning theory was used to identify measurable independent variables in the EAP referral process, and to that extent the findings can be taken as being favorable or unfavorable to the theory. We hypothesized that supervisors are likely to refer problem employees to the EAP to the extent that they have experienced or anticipate differential reinforcement (more rewards or positive outcomes than negative outcomes for referring), differentially associate with and model their supervisory decisions on the behavior of colleagues who are supportive of and themselves make use of EAPs, and hold definitions or attitudes favorable to taking such action.

METHODS AND MEASURES IN THE FLORIDA EAP STUDY

We took a sample of supervisors in two large hospitals (one public and one private) in a Florida city, both of which had well-developed EAPs. About half of the sample were nursing supervisors, with the remainder being divided among supervisors in human resources, maintenance, technical services, rehabilitation, and administration. The main data collection instrument was an interview questionnaire administered during regular departmental meetings. The response rate for those present on the day of the data collection in each hospital was 100%, but we missed those who were absent on that day and those who worked other shifts. The sample size was 90 (22% of all supervisors at both hospitals).

The dependent variables were a dichotomous measure of *Referrals/ No Referrals* and the *Number of Referrals* made by the supervisor. The measures of the social learning variables were grouped under the general headings of reinforcement for referrals, definitions favorable or unfavorable to referrals, and differential association. We assumed that modeling effects were operative through interaction with other supervisors, but we had no direct measures of imitation.

Reinforcement for Referrals. We conceptualized reinforcement as the degree to which organizational rewards encouraged or discouraged referring trouble cases to the EAP. The first set of these was the socially rewarding reactions (from strongly supportive to strongly discouraging) for referral anticipated from fellow supervisors and other workers. This was measured separately for referrals for an alcohol problem (REINFA), for drug problems (REINFD), and referral for mental health or emotional problems (REINFE). The next set involved anticipated rewarding support when supervisors referred themselves to the counseling services of the EAP, again for each of the three areas of job impairment (EAPREINA, EAPREIND, and EAPREINE). A similar set of questions was asked about self-referrals to counseling services other than those provided by the hospital's EAP. The hypothesis is that those supervisors who thought they would receive positive reactions from others for utilizing EAP and related services for themselves as well as for the workers under their supervision would be more favorably disposed to making employee referrals.

These measures allow for a balance of positive and negative sanctions in general for referrals, but we also wanted to measure this balance with regard to specific negative sanctions (e.g., the referred employee or one's own superior would be upset or negative about the referral) compared to positive reactions (e.g., gratitude expressed by the referred employee) for EAP referrals, from which we devised a scale of POS/NEG. This idea of support or nonsupport as a type of differential reinforcement for referrals was extended to the general organizational environment regarding EAPs. We asked a series of questions about the number of memos on EAP, informal discussions about EAP, and how much in-service training had been provided by the hospital regarding its EAP; responses to these questions were summed to form a scale of INSTSUP. The final reinforcement measures were directed toward rewards for *not* making referrals (NOREFA, NOREFD, and NOREFE).

Attitudes toward EAP Referrals. Those supervisors who hold generally favorable attitudes toward EAP and the value of referring impaired workers to it should be more likely to make such referrals, and we devised a number of attitudinal items as measures of definitions favorable and unfavorable toward referrals. First, on the assumption that the EAP rested largely on the disease model of substance abuse, we reasoned that supervisors who endorsed this view would be more favorably disposed toward referring employees for help. Therefore, we asked the supervisors about the extent to which they agreed or disagreed with the statement that alcoholism and drug abuse are diseases to form a two-item scale of DISEASE. Next, supervisors were asked if they felt that people addicted to alcohol or drugs could stop on their own if they really wanted to (STOPUSE). Agreement with this statement was assumed to be unfavorable to referrals, on the assumption that such endorsement indicates rejection of the disease concept and a feeling that EAP referrals are not necessary. Similarly, responses to a third question on the degree of responsibility that alcoholics or drug addicts should take for their problems (RESP) were meant to measure attitudes favorable or unfavorable to EAP referrals.

Definitions were also measured by asking how valuable the supervisor believed an EAP would be for persons with alcohol, drug, and emotional problems (HELPFUL) and by asking about the supervisor's overall job satisfaction (JOBSAT).

Differential Association. The key measure of association (DIFFASSN) asked about how many of the supervisor's colleagues had made referrals to the EAP. For some reason the number of nonresponses on this question was high (9), but I have left it in the analysis. The other measure (IMPEAP) was a subjective impression of how much importance the hospital attached to the EAP as an indication of the general organizational climate of opinion about the program.

All of the scales measuring differential reinforcement, definitions, and differential association were highly reliable (Cronbach's alphas ranged from .70 to .97).

Discriminant function analysis was done with Group 1 (Referrals) and Group 2 (No Referrals). Table 11.3 presents the outcome of the discriminant function analysis, listing the standardized canonical correlation coefficients (excluding statistically nonsignificant coefficients) for the social learning variables and the percentage of cases correctly classified by the social learning function. The findings are quite supportive of the social learning function. A high proportion of both referrals (Group 1) and nonreferrals (Group 2) is correctly classified, and, overall, more than three-fourths of the cases were correctly classified by the social learning function. To further place this in perspective, only 21% of the cases could have been correctly predicted by change alone. A substantial proportion (42%) of the variance is explained. The strongest variables in the table are the reinforcement variables, but the definitions variables are also well correlated with referral behavior, and differential association is also (although not as strongly) related to whether the supervisor refers employees to the EAP.

The discriminant function analysis is appropriate for the either/or behavior of making or not making referrals. To account for the frequency with which referrals are made, we entered the social learning variables from the discriminant function analysis into a multiple regression model with the number of referrals as the dependent variable. Table 11.4 pres-

Table 11.3 Discriminant Function Analysis of Social Learning Model of EAP Referrals

Number and Percentage of Correctly Classified Cases

Actual Group Membership	Predicted Group Membership	
	Group 1	Group 2
Group 1—Referral	43	6
	(87.8%)	(12.2%)
Group 2—No Referral	11	20
	(35.5%)	(64.5%)
Total Correct Classification	63	
	(78.7%)	

Standardized Canonical Correlation Coefficients

Differential Reinforcement

REINFA	.68
REINFD	−.69
REINFE	−.33
EAPREINA	−.47
EAPREIND	.69
EAPREINE	−.58
INSTSUP	.59
POS/NEG	.50

Definitions

DISEASE	.25
STOPUSE	−.57
HELPFUL	.53
JOBSAT	−.36

Differential Association

DIFFASSN	.23

Overall Canonical Correlation = .65 N = 80
SOURCE: Adapted from Capece and Akers (1995) and Capece (1991).

ents the results of that analysis (retaining only those beta coefficients significant at the .15 level of lower). The data in this table show that the model can account for more than one-fourth of the variance in the frequency of EAP referrals.

The direction of the relationships is as expected, except for the HELP-FUL definition. The more beneficial the supervisor perceives the EAP to be for the referred employee, the fewer the referrals that were made; perceiving the program as less helpful produced more referrals. Why would this be? On its face, endorsing such programs as helpful is a favorable definition that should produce higher, not lower, frequencies of referrals. But it may be that the supervisors making the most referrals had the highest expectations of the program and were disappointed in the actual improvement made by referred employees. It may be that the more frequently referring supervisors began with a high opinion of the EAP and began to change their attitude somewhat when the results of the referrals became known to them. The expectation is that over time, if this attitude endures, it would reduce the number of referrals, but we did not have the longitudinal data to test this. All that can be said now is that what appears to be an unfavorable definition of the program is associated with using it more often, which is contrary to the theory.

Table 11.4 Effects of Social Learning Variables on Number of EAP Referrals

Social Learning Variables	(Standardized Partial Regression Coefficients)
	$B =$
HELPFUL	$-.28^*$
STOPUSE	$-.19$
INSTSUP	$.31^*$
REINFE	$.30^*$
DIFFASSN	$.25^*$
$R^2 =$	.28

$^*p < .05$
SOURCE: Adapted from Capece and Akers (1995) and Capece (1991).

On the whole, however, the findings are quite consistent with the theory. Paying attention to the social reinforcement for referrals, administrators' attitudes about the EAP, the supervisors' attitudes toward the program, and the pattern of association among supervisors was shown to be useful in understanding referral behavior by the supervisors. The social learning model offers a framework in which to examine workplace supervisors' decisions to respond to certain problems of deviance on the job by referring workers for help. And, as I have argued above, the social learning model could be extended to account for other kinds of social control decisions, including those made in the criminal-justice system.

I have also applied the social learning perspective to reactions to deviance of a very different kind—of fear and precautionary behavior involving crime and victimization. These are not reactions of those in a position to make control and sanctioning decisions about deviants. They are, rather, the responses of frightened citizens.

Social Learning Theory and the Fear of Crime

Earlier, I mentioned our Florida research on type of community and fear of crime among the elderly (Akers et al., 1987). It became clear while doing that research that there is little systematic theory utilized in the study of victimization and the fear of crime and that what theory had been developed had not been very well supported empirically. Research and measures of fear of crime since then have improved considerably (Ferraro and LaGrange, 1992; LaGrange et al., 1992; Ferraro, 1995), but theoretical explanation of fear of crime remains underdeveloped. It seemed to me that the reference group aspects of the concept of differential association in social learning theory might explain variation in fear of crime. I saw a clear parallel with our earlier analysis of Boys Town data on norm qualities and attitudes toward alcohol and drugs by adolescents, where we found that one's own attitudes toward substance use were strongly related to the normative attitudes toward drinking and drug use by family, peers, and coreligionists (see Chapter 7). In social learning theory, one's own definitions or attitudes toward some behavior are learned through differential association with the norms and attitudes of others and through differential reinforcement. If fear of crime could be conceptualized as one type of "definition" or attitude, then theoretically it should be learned in the same way that definitions favorable or unfavorable to committing crime are learned. This fearful attitude would function as a discriminative stimulus or definition favorable to taking some precautionary actions to guard against being a crime victim. In the vast majority of cases, these actions entail legitimate, conforming behavior taken as protection against victimization. In some extreme cases, fear of crime may become a definition favorable to committing crime when it justifies a pre-emptive strike against others. My interest, however, was not in these extreme cases but in exploring the extent to which social learning theory might provide an explanation for variations in attitudes toward, and reactive behavior against, crime.

An opportunity to do this came in 1985 through collaboration with Frank Williams, then at the Criminal Justice Center of Sam Houston State University in Huntsville, Texas. He was preparing to conduct a special poll on Texans' fear of crime and was interested in any ideas I had regarding measurement and theory. He was especially concerned with the possible applicability of a social learning approach and how one would measure such variables in a fear-of-crime survey. Collaborating with Lonn Lanza-Kaduce to work out a social learning model and different measures of fear of crime, we were later joined by our student Frank Biafora, who wrote a master's thesis based on the data from the project. Once again, I am grateful to my colleagues for their contributions. The description of the study and its findings here are based on two unpublished papers on which we collaborated; Lanza-Kaduce was senior author of one, Biafora was senior author of the other.

Because of my prior research on fear of crime among older individuals, I wanted to concentrate on the elderly subsample ($N = 535$) of Williams's 1986 poll ($N = 1,100$). The usual finding in past research has been that old people entertain higher levels of fear of crime, even though they experience relatively low rates of actual victimization (Yin, 1980; Stafford and Galle, 1984). Whether elderly people are more fearful of crime than younger groups, and whether their fear of crime is proportionate to their level of victimization, has not yet been resolved (Ferraro and LaGrange, 1992; LaGrange et al., 1992; Ferraro, 1995). Nonetheless, one's current fear of crime has not been found to relate strongly to prior victimization among either younger or older persons (Lewis and Salem, 1986; Skogan and Maxfield, 1981; Akers et al., 1987). Therefore, there must be additional sources for the person's fear of crime.

Ferraro and LaGrange (1987) and Warr (1990) point to crime-related symbols and messages as probable sources, and there is reason to direct attention to the social sources of the development and maintenance of attitudes, definitions of the situation, or perceptions of the crime problem. Because most elderly people have had little personal experience with serious crime, vicarious sources of experience like personal conversations and exposure to media portrayals (especially local homicide coverage) could play a major role in shaping their impressions (Skogan and Maxfield, 1981; Liska and Baccaglini, 1990; Kennedy and Silverman, 1985).

It is these social sources of fear of crime among the elderly to which social learning theory directs attention. It makes sociological sense to propose, as the theory does, that one's attitudes and perceptions are shaped by those with whom one is in direct interaction, by reference groups with whom one is in indirect interaction, and by exposure to communications media. There should be a link between an individual's perceptions of and attitudes toward crime and those of that person's primary groups of family, friends, neighbors, and workmates, as well as those of more secondary reference groups.

We did not employ the full social learning model, but concentrated on the relationships between "differential association" and fear of crime as a type of "definition" of the situation. Because definitions can be imitated or modeled, the media may be a source of fear-of-crime definitions. However, the more intimate sources (e.g., family/friends) will be more influential sources of definitions than the less intimate ones. Thus, fear of crime is acquired in the same process as other "definitions."

Beyond accounting for fear of crime as a learned definition, we wanted to discover the extent to which such definitions are discriminative for particular behavior, such as taking actions to guard against criminal victimization. If definitions about substance use can be discriminative for abstinence or cessation of drug use, then definitions about crime may be discriminative for taking precautions against crime. In either case the conceptual category is the same—a belief, attitude, or definition of the situation related to some behavior.

Specifically, the hypothesis is that fear of crime will be greater among those older individuals who are differentially exposed to "fearful" crime definitions in their primary and secondary groups and from the media, even when prior victimization is taken into account. The theory also leads to the hypothesis that the more intimate the source of fear-of-crime definitions, the more influence it will have on fear of crime among the elderly. Primary group members should be more influential than secondary groups or the media. Finally, the hypothesis is that attitudes toward the problem of crime will be related to actions taken to guard against crime.

The data were collected in a mailed questionnaire survey of Texas residents randomly drawn from a list of those having valid drivers licenses in the state (age 18 and over), a population representing more than 90 percent of Texas adults. Of the 2,017 questionnaires mailed, 1,141 were returned in usable form, for a response rate of 56.6 percent. The elderly population was oversampled, so that 46.9% (535) of the total sample were persons aged 60 and older; of these respondents, men accounted for 49.4% and women for 50.6%. White respondents made up 89.5% of the sample, black respondents were 4.6%, and respondents with Spanish surnames comprised 4.2%.

Measures of Fear of Crime. Fear-of-crime research has been criticized for its inattentiveness to measurement issues (see Ferraro and LaGrange, 1987; Akers et al., 1987; Ferraro and LaGrange, 1992). Ferraro and LaGrange (1987) classify fear-of-crime measures into indicators of general concern about crime (values), judgments of risk of becoming a crime victim, and emotional worry about crime. While these perceptions are only weakly intercorrelated, a substantial number of studies have used them interchangeably. In our research, we developed separate measures of fear of crime reflecting these three dimensions.

The first measure involves a general concern about crime in society. We asked, "On a scale of 0 to 10, how concerned are you about crime in general?" with 0 representing the lowest concern and 10 the highest (mean = 7.8). This measure directly followed a statement on the survey that asked the respondents to "answer the following questions with only crime in mind." The second measure is judgments of risk of victimization—assessments or evaluations that people make of the probability of becoming crime victims themselves. These risk perceptions do not closely reflect the objective realities of being a victim; they are more related to an individual's proximity to crime than to his or her level of concern about crime (Ferraro and LaGrange, 1987; LaGrange and Ferraro, 1989). We measured the perceived risk of crime among the elderly by asking, "On a scale of 0 to 10, what do you think your chances are of being a victim of any type of crime during the next year?" The scale ranged from 0 ("I will NOT be a victim of crime") to 10 ("I will CERTAINLY be a victim of crime") (mean = 3.8). If general concern about crime and risk perception reflect, respectively, the evaluative and cognitive dimensions of fear of crime, emotional reactions to crime are thought to capture fear as a sense of dread or anxiousness about the issue. We measured this by asking, "Overall, how worried are you about becoming a victim of any of these fifteen crimes [about which the respondent had been asked] during the next year?" Again, the endpoints range from 0 ("Not worried at all") to 10 ("Very worried") (mean = 4.4). The intercorrelations between the three fear-of-crime measures, as expected, are not strong enough (from a low of $r = .21$ to a high of $r = .42$) to support the argument that various measures of fear of crime can be used interchangeably or that they capture the same underlying fear-of-crime construct.

Therefore, we always treated these dimensions separately. Of the three measures, risk judgments are the more or less objective appraisal of one's chances of becoming a crime victim. This appraisal would result mainly from observable circumstances of the individual, and we would not expect it to be related very much to any of the social sources of fear-of-crime definitions. The related emotional response of worrying about the possibility of becoming a victim, on the other hand, should be based on differential association with others sharing similar concerns. General concern about crime is more clearly an attitudinal (or value) orientation, more closely akin to the usual meaning of the concept of definitions in social learning theory, and it should be most highly related to the differential association measures.

Measures of Independent and Control Variables. Respondents were asked, "To the best of your knowledge, how worried are each of the groups about crime in general?" Six groups were listed: spouse, family members, best friends, neighbors, work associates, and organizational members (church, clubs, etc.). Response categories for each ranged from 0 ("Not worried at all") to 10 ("Very worried"). We also asked, "How often do you see reports of violent crime on TV?" and posed the same question about reports in the newspaper; responses ranged from rarely or never to every day. Three scales of differential association were constructed from responses to these questions; we labeled them *Primary* (spouses, family members, best friends), *Secondary* (co-workers, fellow members of organizations, and neighbors), and *Media* (newspaper and television reports). The item-to-scale correlations for each of these scales are high (ranging from .69 to .88). Primary and Secondary scales are highly correlated ($r = .69$), but neither is related strongly to the measures of media exposure ($r = .11$ and $r = .17$). The analysis also employed three dummy variables as controls: *Sex* (females = 0 and males = 1); *Age* ("younger elderly," 60 to 70 years old = 0, and "older elderly," older than 70 = 1); and *Prior victimization* (0 = no prior victimization, and 1 = one or more prior victimizations).

Each of the three fear-of-crime measures—concern, judgment of risk, and worry about being victimized—was regressed separately on the control variables and the differential association scales. Also, interaction terms were computed between each of the differential association scales and sex, and between each of the scales and age group, which were forced into the regression analyses after the other variables had been entered. Standardized regression coefficients (betas) are reported for comparison of statistics across variables within each separate analysis; unstandardized coefficients (betas) are reported for comparison of statistics across analyses. No significant interactions were found in the analyses of worry and judgment of risk, while a weak but statistically significant interaction was found between sex and *Primary* associations in the analysis of general concern about crime. Therefore, regression equations for this measure of fear of crime were run separately for men and women.

The results of the multiple regression analysis for judgments of risk and emotional worry about crime and of crime as a general concern or value orientation are presented in Table 11.5.

Sex, Age, and Prior Victimization. Earlier research has found a strong relationship between sex of respondent and fear of crime, but we found a significant difference only for general concern about crime. There was a slight tendency for the younger elderly in our sample to perceive a greater likelihood of victimization than did the older group of respondents. Our oldest respondents did not judge themselves to be more vulnerable to the

Table 11.5 Differential Association and Fear of Crime

	Judgment of Risk ($N = 535$)		Worry ($N = 535$)	
	$B =$	$b =$	$B =$	$b =$
Control Variables				
Sex	.05	.27	−.03	−.09
Age	−.09*	−.47*	−.03	−.16
Victimization	.13*	.78*	.08*	.54*
Increment in $R^2 =$		.03		.02
Differential Association Variables				
Primary Group	.05	.02	.24***	.11***
Secondary Groups	.05	.02	.09	.05
Media Sources	.10**	.13**	.14***	.19***
Increment in $R^2 =$		.02		.12
Total $R^2 =$		.05		.14

	General Concern about Crime			
	Male ($N = 261$)		Female ($N = 268$)	
	$B =$	$b =$	$B =$	$b =$
Control Variables				
Age	.10*	.55*	.14**	.70**
Victimization	.05	.28	.04	.25
Increment in $R^2 =$		.01		.03
Differential Association Variables				
Primary Groups	.64***	.25***	.50***	.20***
Secondary Groups	.12*	.05*	.03	−.02
Media Sources	.02	.03	.08	.09
Increment in $R^2 =$		.53		.24
Total $R^2 =$		.54		.27

*$p < .05$; **$p < .01$; ***$p < .001$.

risk of crime victimization, but age is positively related to fear of crime as measured by a concern about crime in general. Prior victimization is weakly related to old people's judgment of risk and their emotional worry, but not to their general concern about crime (see Table 11.5). Clearly, their fear is not just a function of past crime victimization. The regression analyses, which include only prior victimization, sex, and age, account for only tiny fractions (1% to 3%) of the variance for any of the measures of fear of crime.

Differential Association. The relationships of these variables to fear of crime are also reported in Table 11.5. The degree to which one's primary group members worry about crime, as expected, appears not to affect an individual's judgment of personal risk of victimization; the media variable, however, unexpectedly has a significant, though small, impact $(B = .10)$. None of the variables in this study has much impact on judgments by the elderly about their risk of becoming crime victims. The variables do have a moderate relationship with fear of crime as worry, with almost all of the explained variance being attributable to the differential association variables. As predicted from the theory, exposure to fear of crime through association in primary groups has a stronger effect on one's own fear of crime than exposure to fear of crime in secondary groups and the media. Although primary group definitions are most salient, the media effect is significant; considered along with the significant effect on judgment of risk, it appears that crime coverage in the media can encourage some kinds of fear of crime (for other evidence see Lab, 1988).

The hypothesis that fear of crime is learned from association with others sharing that fear receives its strongest support when fear of crime is measured as a concern for crime in general. One's own fear of crime will reflect the perceived level of fear of crime among those with whom one is in association; 53% of the variance is explained among men, and 24% is explained among women. The magnitude of these relationships is best appreciated by noting that the very best models (containing many variables) in previous research have been able to explain only between 7% and 12% of the variance in fear of crime (Taylor and Hale, 1986). It is quite obvious from the table that for both elderly men and elderly women, the perceptions of the concern about crime held by the members of their primary groups are important for their own definitions. Those who think family and friends are worried about crime tend to report more personal concern with crime, while those who think these primary group members are less worried are personally less concerned with crime.

These results provide strong, but not unequivocal, support for the hypothesis that fear of crime is greater among older persons who are exposed to high fear-of-crime definitions through association and that primary groups will be more influential in this regard than secondary groups or media. However, the media also had some net effect on the emotional fear of crime was the only statistically significant variable (albeit with small effects) for judgment of risk of victimization. The theoretical model overall does not help much in understanding the social sources of fear of crime as measured by emotional worry about crime or by judgments of the risks of being victimized as crime (Table 11.5).

Given that concern about crime comes the closest of the three measures to the concept of definitions in social learning theory, these differences among the three measures of crime was expected. Theoretically, the differential association process refers to normative definitions as being acquired through interaction with and exposure to the normative definitions of others. Thus, the fear-of-crime measure, which taps concern with crime as a normative issue, should be most similar to the concept of definitions in the theory. Emotional reactions and personal worry are less clearly normative, and assessments of risk can be made without regard to beliefs or normative attitudes. Some people may judge their risk of victimization to be high but not be worried about it or concerned about crime generally. Emotional fear of crime is more affective than value oriented; judgment of risk has a rational and "objective" component that occurs over and above the value consideration.

Aside from these conceptual and theoretical considerations, the wording of the questions designed to measure each dimension of fear of crime may have further weakened the effect of the differential association scales on the measures of worry about crime and judgments of risk. Recall that the differential association items were measured by asking respondents to report their perceptions of "how worried" about crime "in general" the various primary and secondary groups were. The measure of fear of crime as an emotional response on the part of the respondent also included the word "worry," and the measure of fear as a concern about crime included the phrase "in general." The measure of fear as a judgment of the risk of victimization, on the other hand, did not include either of these. Hence, its weak relationship to the differential association measures may be, in part, a measurement artifact. Recall also that the media items did not ask directly about crime attitudes or values expressed in the media, but only about frequency of exposure to television and newspaper reports of violent crimes. In spite of this weak measurement, media exposure has some relationship to the fear-of-crime measures. With a different wording, the media variable may have had a stronger relationship to fear of crime. To the extent that media coverage heightens awareness about crime, it may serve a positive function. If, however, it raises fear levels that do not reflect objective victimization risks, crime coverage is dysfunctional, especially if it also increases the emotional fear experienced by the elderly.

FINDINGS ON PRECAUTIONS AGAINST CRIME

The next step in our application of social learning theory to fear of crime was to gauge the relationships among measures of social learning variables (the various measures of fear of crime) and measures of precautionary behavior (steps taken to guard against crime). I have pointed out the relationship between fear of crime and exposure to fearful attitudes toward crime through differential association. The model for crime precautions takes this a step further and proposes that fear of crime will in turn operate as "definitions favorable" to, or discriminative for, a variety of personal fearful actions, including the adoption of crime precautions.

To test this model, we added measures of social reinforcement for fear of crime to differential association variables as the independent, or exogenous, variables. Also, instead of treating prior personal victimization as a control variable, as was done above, we entered it in the model along with vicarious victimization as indexing social learning processes. Fear-of-crime measures are entered as the mediating variables, and measures of crime precautions appear as the endogenous, or dependent, variables. The hypothesis is that those persons who are exposed to fear-of-crime attitudes, whose own fear of crime is reinforced by family and friends, and who have been exposed directly or vicariously to victimization are more likely to develop fearful definitions of crime, and that these more fearful attitudes will be discriminative for precautionary behavior.

Direct victimization (the person having been a crime victim) may be viewed, at least in part, as a form of punishment or negative outcome for failing to take sufficient precautions against crime in the past; it is therefore relevant as a partial measure of differential reinforcement. But simply knowing that persons have been crime victims does not really tell us much about whether they perceive the victimization as the consequence of their own inaction or as unrelated to anything they could have done. Therefore, the punishment effect would be only weakly indexed by a measure of past victimization, and it would not index at all whatever negative reinforcement (by avoiding future victimization) was attached to taking precautions. This may be one of the reasons past research, including our Florida studies, has found only a weak relationship between fear of crime and prior victimization.

We expect the relationships of prior victimization to precautionary behavior also to be weak. Vicarious, or indirect, victimization (the person knows of others' victimization) can be viewed as modeling, or observational, learning—vicarious punishment when others have failed to take sufficient precautions. The modeling effects can be derived either from observing family, friends, neighbors, and others who have been crime victims or from observing media portrayals of crime victimization. Again, because this measure captures only part of the modeling process, the expectation is that the relationships will be modest.

Exposure to attitudes of fear toward crime also may come through the media or interpersonal interaction. Again, the intimate sources of definitions should be more strongly related to the attitudes than are the more secondary sources. The effect that this exposure has on precautionary behavior should be mediated by the extent to which one has adopted attitudes of fear.

The fear-of-crime measures were, as described above, concern about crime in general, perceived risk of victimization, and personal worry about crime. To measure crime precautions we created two indexes. The first, *Personal Precautions,* was constructed from a set of ten questions on actions taken to protect oneself from personal or theft while away from home; these included taking someone with you when going out after dark, taking protection (e.g., a whistle, Mace, a gun, or a knife), keeping the car doors locked, and carrying very little cash. The second index, *Home Precautions,* was constructed from seventeen items asking about steps taken to protect person and property in the residence; these included keeping a gun in the house, installing a burglar alarm system, keeping windows and doors locked, forming a crime watch group in the neighborhood, having someone check on the home during one's absence, installing window bars, and putting extra security locks on the doors. There are three subsets of social learning variables: *Exposure to victimization*, both direct and vicarious, through knowledge of victimization of friends, family, and neighbors, and through media portrayals; *Differential association*, or exposure to others' (media, family, and friends) fear-of-crime definitions (worry about crime and perceived risk of victimization); and *Social reinforcement of fear of crime* (approval or disapproval of one's own concern about crime by family, best friends, and neighbors).

This is still only a partial social learning model, however, because we did not have measures of direct reinforcement of precautionary behavior itself, measures of association with others who engage in various kinds of precautionary behavior against crime, or measures of discriminative stimuli or definitions favorable to crime precautions directly. Nevertheless, the measures we did have are derivable from the theory, and they provided a reasonable, if incomplete, testing of it as an explanation not only of fear of crime but also of actions taken to protect the persons or their property from crime.

Since women have significantly higher levels of fear of crime than do men, regardless of what measure of fear of crime is used and regardless of the actual experience of victimization (Akers et al., 1987), we ran separate analyses for elderly men ($N = 264$) and women ($N = 264$). All of the zero-order correlations (table not shown) were in the expected direction, ranging from weak (.08) to strong (.57), and were stronger for the men's than the women's sample. As expected, there was a weak correlation of direct victimization with fear of crime; the same is true for the correlation with crime precautions. Indeed, the correlations were even lower than the relationship of fear of crime and crime precautions with vicarious victimization. One's own fear of crime was more strongly related to behavioral precautions than were the victimization, exposure, and reinforcement variables.

The model was tested using path analysis (model and paths not shown). The findings were consistent with theoretical expectations, although, for both the male and female samples, the magnitude of the relationships was modest. Worry about crime had a direct effect on taking precautionary action against becoming a victim of personal crime for both elderly women ($b = .27$) and men ($b = .30$). Worry about crime was also somewhat predictive of women's efforts against home crime ($b = .23$), and general concern about crime among men was related to taking steps for personal safety ($b = .15$). Exposure to victimization increased fear of crime and taking precautions against crime; the effects on precautions were, as expected, primarily indirect through fear of crime. There were weak direct effects of vicarious victimization and exposure to crime, more through family and friends than the media. Similarly, we found the expected indirect effect of exposure to others' fear of crime on precautions mediated by one's own fear of crime. Exposure to the attitudes of family and friends was weakly to moderately related to one's own fear of crime, which then had an effect on crime precautions. Finally, the hypothesis was supported that social reinforcement for fearful attitudes toward crime is related to the attitudes held by the individual and the crime precautions he or she takes against both personal and home crime.

The findings for precautions against crimes involving home, person, or both conform, at least for some of the measures of the independent variables, to what was expected from social learning theory. Fear of crime (as worry or general concern about crime) does function, at least to some extent, as definitions favorable to the elderly person's engaging in crime-precaution behavior. These definitions, in turn, are related to indirect exposure to victimization and social exposure to and reinforcement of fear of crime.

The essential findings of the study were that the differential association measures, while weakly related to the judgment of risk and moderately related to the emotional concern or worry connected with risk of victimization, were very highly related to general fear of crime. Also, consistent with social learning theory, the greatest net effect on fear of crime came from the primary group associations. This was true for both men (54% of the variance explained) and women (26% of the variance explained). Also, the social learning variables were able to account, in part, for the extent to which people take precautions against crime. There is recognition in the literature that studies of fear of crime, whether among the elderly or other age groups, have needed, and are moving toward, greater theoretical sophistication (Taylor and Hale, 1986;

Akers et al., 1987). The findings in our study show that social learning has promise as an explanation of fear of crime and citizens' actions taken in response to crime. Future research would be strengthened by including social learning variables. Not only can more powerful explanations be expected, but the explanations can be tied into a more general theoretical tradition that is not restricted specifically to the issue of fear of crime.

12

Social Structure and Social Learning in Crime and Deviance

In this concluding chapter I will present a Social Structure–Social Learning (SSSL) theory of crime. Its basic assumption is that social learning is the primary process linking social structure to individual behavior. Its main proposition is that variations in the social structure, culture, and locations of individuals and groups in the social system explain variations in crime rates, principally through their influence on differences among individuals on the social learning variables—mainly, differential association, differential reinforcement, imitation, and definitions favorable and unfavorable and other discriminative stimuli for crime. The social structural variables are indicators of the primary distal macro-level and meso-level causes of crime, while the social learning variables reflect the primary proximate causes of criminal behavior by individuals that mediate the relationship between social structure and crime rates. Some structural variables are not related to crime and do not explain the crime rate because they do not have a crime-relevant effect on the social learning variables.

Deviance-producing environments have an impact on individual conduct through the operation of learning mechanisms. The general culture and structure of society and the particular communities, groups, and other contexts of social interaction provide learning environments in which the norms define what is approved and disapproved, behavioral models are present, and the reactions of other people (for example, in applying social sanctions) and the existence of other stimuli attach different reinforcing or punishing consequences to individuals' behavior. Social structure can be conceptualized as an arrangement of sets and schedules of reinforcement contingencies and other social behavioral variables. The family, peers, schools, churches, and other groups provide the more immediate contexts that promote or discourage the criminal or conforming behavior of the individual. Differences in the societal or group rates of criminal behavior are a function of the extent to which cultural traditions, norms, social organization, and social control systems provide socialization, learning environments, reinforcement schedules, opportunities, and immediate situations conducive to conformity or deviance.

I have made assertions like these over a great many years, and I have sketched out ways in which social learning is congruent with and could be integrated with social structural theories of crime rates (Burgess and Akers, 1966b; Akers, 1968; Akers, 1973; 1977; 1985; Akers et al., 1979; Akers, 1992b; 1994). Both these earlier statements and the current sssl model harken back to the theme introduced by Sutherland fifty years ago.

> It is not necessary, at this level of explanation, to explain why a person has the associations which he has; this certainly involves a complex of many things. . . . The person's associations are determined in the general context of social organization. . . . Many other factors enter into this social organization, including many of the small personal group relationships.
>
> The preceding explanation of criminal behavior [differential association theory] was stated from the point of view of the person who engages in criminal behavior. It is possible, also, to state theories of criminal behavior from the point of view of the community, nation, or other group. The problem, when thus stated, is generally concerned with crime rates and involves a comparison of the crime rates of various groups or the crime rates of a particular group at different times. One of the best explanations of crime rates from this point of view is that a high crime rate is due to social disorganization. The term "social disorganization" is not entirely satisfactory and it seems preferable to substitute for it the term "differential social organization." The postulate on which this theory is based, regardless of the name, is that crime is rooted in the social organization and is an expression of that social organization. A group may be organized for criminal behavior or organized against criminal behavior. Most communities are organized both for criminal and anti-criminal behavior and in that sense the crime rate is an expression of the differential group organization. Differential group organization as an explanation of a crime rate must be consistent with the explanation of the criminal behavior of the person, since the crime rate is a summary statement of the number of persons in the group who commit crimes and the frequency with which they commit crimes. (Sutherland, 1947:8–9)

This is a concise statement of the relationship between differential association as a causal process in criminal behavior at the individual level and social disorganization (or differential social organization) as an explanation of crime at the structural level (see Chapter 3). However, Sutherland did not develop this link systematically. Rather, he came back to it occasionally with brief references to the connection between differential association and social organization in his chapters on social disorganization and culture conflict. He also came back to it indirectly by pointing to the operation of differential association in various "factors" in crime, such as family, age, sex, class, and race. Sutherland also referred to associations and value codes in his chapter dealing with behavior systems in crime, which can be taken as well as a discussion of differential social organization and association (Sutherland, 1947).

Cressey developed the connection between differential social organization (epidemiology) and differential association (individual conduct) more clearly, noting that, "for example, a high crime rate in urban areas can be considered the end product of social conditions that lead to a situation in which relatively large proportions of persons are presented with an excess of criminal behavior patterns" (Sutherland and Cressey, 1960:55). In his revisions of *Principles of Criminology*, Cressey stressed that a general theory must be evaluated on the basis of its "capacity to 'make sense' of the facts" about the "variations of crime and delinquency rates with age, sex, race, poverty, educational status, urbanization, and other variables, as well as the incidence among criminals and delinquents of various biological, psychological, and social traits, characteristics, and processes" (Sutherland and Cressey, 1960:v; 1970:v). This is sometimes mistakenly taken to mean that differential association is a theory of group-level crime rates and does not really apply to individual behavior. Neither Sutherland nor Cressey proposed that differential association was a theory of crime rates rather than a theory of individual criminal behavior. Rather, they proposed that when combined consistently with an explanation such as differential social organization, differential association as an explanation of individual criminality was more capable of "making sense" of these group variations in crime than any other theory.

> Certain of these ratios, and variations in ratios, seem to be crucial for the explanation of criminal behavior. These may be called definitive facts; that is, facts which define or limit the explanations which can be regarded as valid. . . . Some of the ratios and variations in ratios may be explained by one or another of the general theories of criminal behavior, but the differential association theory seems to explain *all* of these ratios and variations more adequately than the other theories. Although this theory has many defects, it seems to fit gen-

eral facts better than does any other general theory. (Sutherland and Cressey, 1960:149; emphasis in original)

This is a clear-cut reiteration and elaboration by Cressey of Sutherland's view that differential association can make sense of the widely known correlates of crime and that it does so in a way that is consistent with a structural explanation of crime rates—for example, differential social organization or social disorganization. But Cressey's position does not offer a systematic statement of the theory of differential social organization or of an integrated theory of social organization and association.

In the Burgess and Akers (1966b) article, we stressed that our task was to revise Sutherland's processual theory of differential association *only*; we left undone connecting that process with the social structure. But we made it equally clear that this was something that should be undertaken later:

> Sutherland, himself . . . was convinced that the two-edged theory—(1) genetic, differential association and (2) structural, differential social organization—accounted for the known data on the full range of crimes.
>
> Sutherland, of course, was as interested in explaining the "epidemiology" of crime as in explaining how the individual comes to engage in behavior in violation of the law and insisted that the two explanations must be consistent.
>
> That Sutherland intended an explanation of the two-fold problem of rates of crime and individual criminal behavior is, of course, the basic point of Cressey's paper "Epidemiology and Individual Conduct."
>
> Our main concern here, of course, is with the nine statements of the theory as genetic [non-biological] explanation of the process by which the individual comes to engage in illegal behavior. We do not lose sight of the fact, however, that this must be integrated with explanations of the variation and location of crime. (Burgess and Akers, 1966:128–30)

I followed up on these statements in a later article outlining the structural and processual questions and theories in the sociology of crime and deviance with remarks showing the general thrust of how social learning and structural theories can be integrated.

> The structural theories contend that more people in certain groups, located in certain positions in, or encountering particular pressures created by the social structure, will engage in deviancy than those in other groups and locations.
>
> The differential association–reinforcement theory formulated by Burgess and Akers avoids some of the problems of Sutherland's original formulation and describes the general process (consistently and integrally with a broader theory of behavior) of deviant behavior. It is capable of identifying the common elements in the separate processual theories and provides the groundwork for integrating structural and processual explanations. By conceptualizing groups

and social structure as learning environments which structure the patterns of associations and reinforcement, a long step is taken in the direction of bringing the two together. Differential association–reinforcement spells out the *mechanisms* by which environmental stimuli produce and maintain behavior and the structural theories explicate the type of *environments* most likely to sustain norm and law-violating behavior. (Akers, 1968:457–58; emphasis in original)

These ideas about social structure as arranging different sets of learning environments or patterns of associations and reinforcement were incorporated in the first and subsequent editions of *Deviant Behavior* and in the first research article from the Boys Town project.

> [W]hile other theories delineate the structural variables (class, race, anomic conditions, breakdown in social control, etc.) that yield differential rates of deviance, social learning stresses the behavioral mechanisms by which these variables produce the behavior comprising the rates. As such, social learning is complementary to other sociological theories and could be used to integrate extant formulations to achieve more comprehensive explanations of deviance. (Akers et al., 1979:637)

As shown below, I also conducted research on the links between the social learning variables and social structure in the form of "community context" (Krohn et al., 1984; Akers and La Greca, 1991). And in subsequent publications I have returned to the issue of an integrated structural-process model of crime and deviance (1992b; 1994). The purposes here are to present the sssl model in a full and clear form, offer some empirical evidence on the model, and point to the need for future research testing the relationships specified in the model.

Social Structure, Social Correlates, and Individual Behavior: Issues in Cross-Level Integration of Explanations of Crime

Purely social structural theories of crime of the form shown in Figure 12.1 can stand on their own without the necessity of positing the mediating or intervening variables or of specifying the mechanisms by which the social structure produces higher or lower rates of crime, delinquency, or deviance. It is perfectly legitimate to hold that the question of "by what mechanism" or "by what mediating process" is outside the explanatory intent of the theory. This would not deny the importance of asking the question, but simply would define it as a question the theory was not designed to answer. Thus, differences in anomie, social disorganization, or other conditions of the social structure may be posited as structural sources of differences in crime rates across societies, among subparts of the same society, or through time for the same society or group. Such an explanation would be sufficient to identify the macro-level causes of differences in crime rates, without the necessity of also explaining what micro-level mechanisms are involved in producing criminal acts. However, the question of how anomie produces crime rates is a good one, and a formulation that explicitly inserts elements into the theory that show how this occurs is a more complete explanation.

Similarly, purely social psychological (or purely biological or psychological) explanations, either of differences between individuals or variations in the behavior of the same individuals by time, place, and situation (shown in simplified form in Figure 12.1), can legitimately be formulated without also offering an answer to the question of what social structural conditions differentially distribute the processual variables in society. But it is a fuller explanation if the process can be tied to social structural sources of the variations.

Theories emphasizing social structure propose that the proportions of crimes among groups, classes, communities, or societies differ because of variations in their social or cultural makeup. Most structural theories, however, also include assumptions, and sometimes more explicit state-

---

Figure 12.1   Simplified Models of Social Structure, Process, and Crime

Social Structure and Crime Rates

Social Structure ——————————→ Crime Rate

Social Process and Criminal Behavior

Social Psychological Process ——————————→ Criminal Behavior

Social Structure and Social Process
in Criminal Behavior and Crime Rates

Social Structure ——→ Social Psychological ——→ Criminal Behavior ——→ Crime Rate
Process

ments, regarding the process by which these structural conditions produce high or low crime rates. For instance, although variations in individual perceptions of the social structure are not an explicit part of Merton's
anomie theory, most researchers, myself included, have operationalized
the theory as if such perceptions were at least implicit in it (see the discussion of anomie and strain in Chapter 7). In order for objective differential opportunities to have an effect on deviant adaptations, the reasoning
goes, individuals must perceive a discrepancy between their educational/
occupational aspirations (goals) and realistic expectations of achieving
those aspirations legitimately (perceived access to socially approved
means). Therefore, the greater the perceived discrepancy, the greater the
chance of deviant involvement. Indeed, this micro-level perceptual counterpart of the macro-level condition of anomie has become such a routine
part of later interpretations and research on Merton's anomie theory that
some have protested that the structural version of anomie theory has
never really been tested (Bernard, 1987; Messner, 1988). Similarly, micro-
level theories assert that an individual commits criminal acts because he
or she has experienced a particular life history, possesses a particular set
of individual characteristics, or has encountered a particular situation.
Such theories imply something about the deviance-producing structures
that an individual must encounter in order to increase the probability of
his or her committing a crime.

Thus, theories of criminal behavior are neither purely structural nor
processual. Nevertheless, structural variables are clearly separable from
social psychological variables, regardless of how they are folded into a
particular theory. In spite of its frequent operationalization at the social
psychological level, for instance, anomie theory is still clearly and rightly
classified as a structural theory. And the structural conditions of anomie
are clearly separable from the social psychological process by which
those conditions affect perceptions and individual behavior.

None of the structural approaches makes assumptions or produces
hypotheses that would run counter to the basic, empirically sound,
premise of the social learning approach that both conforming and deviant
behavior are learned in the same way; the substance and direction of the
learning is different, but the general process is the same for both. All
would agree that the individual's behavior is shaped by the situations
experienced in life. In fact, as I have noted, the primary burden of these

theories, whatever social psychological processes they imply, is to show what kinds of social structures lead to high levels of delinquent, deviant, or criminal behavior. It is the burden of social learning theory to specify the process by which social structure produces variations in individual behavior. Thus, social learning is complementary to, not in competition with, any of the empirically validated structural theories.

I have long held that social behaviorism is the perspective on individual behavior that is most compatible with sociological theories and most able to explicate the process by which structural correlates of crime do or do not have an effect on criminal behavior. I have previously outlined in some detail the ways in which same-level conceptual integration of social learning with other social psychological theories of crime and deviance, most notably social bonding theory, can be done (Akers, 1989; 1994). That integration involves primarily conceptual absorption rather than propositional integration, and I will not take up this topic here. Also, I will not review the efforts of others to integrate theories either at the same level or cross-level (see the various papers in Messner et al., 1989, and the various theoretical integrations reviewed in Akers, 1997). The purpose, rather, is to integrate across levels by linking the variables, causes, and explanations at the structural/macro level (that account for different absolute and relative levels of crime) to probable effects on individual behavior through social learning variables.

When social learning is used to specify the process by which some conceptually defined structural conditions, such as social disorganization, central to a particular theory, affects crime, then we have a clear-cut instance of cross-level theoretical integration. It is less clear that it is theoretical integration when social learning variables are used, without reference to any given structural theory, to "make sense" of or "mediate" the empirical effects of the social correlates on criminal behavior. However, since virtually all of the social correlates have been used at one time or another as indicators of some theoretical construct, tying any of them together with social learning variables in an sssl explanatory model is tantamount to integrating theories across levels of explanation. Therefore, both uses of sssl are considered here to be cross-level theoretical integration. However, the sssl model may be interpreted as not truly a "propositional integration" of social learning (see Elliott et al., 1985; Messner et al., 1989). Rather, it may be seen as more in the nature of a "theoretical elaboration" (Thornberry, 1989). That is, it begins with the existing social learning theory and adds structural variables from different sources to produce the sssl model. It makes no difference, for my purpose of linking social structure to crime rates through the social learning process, which of these interpretations is accepted.

Such cross-level integration is possible because in the final analysis both kinds of theory, structural/macro and processual/micro, propose answers to the same overall question of why people do or do not commit criminal and deviant acts. The dependent variable in macro-level theories is based ultimately on the same behavior that is the dependent variable in micro-level theories. Social structure and the crime rates are embodied in the actions and reactions of real people. Crime rates are summary statements of relative amounts of individual behavior in different groups or social categories. When individual behavior is counted and summed (the number of criminal acts committed by individuals, including multiple offenses by the same individuals and/or the number of individuals committing at least one act in a given time period) for a given social system or sociodemographic category, the result is a measure of the absolute level of offenses committed by and against members of that system. When divided by the proper population base, this number produces the crime rate, or rate of criminal offending for a society, group, or sociodemographic category. The absolute number of offenders and the absolute number of offenses, when summed and divided by the base population, produce the prevalence rates. When the first offenses in a given time period are summed and divided by the proper population base, we have the incidence rate. All general crude rates, category-specific rates, place-specific rates, and ratios are predicated on the commission of crimes by some individuals against others in the group or category for which the rates are calculated.

Social Structure and Social Learning in Crime and Deviance

MAIN COMPONENTS OF THE SSSL MODEL

The sssl model is diagrammed in Figure 12.2. The social learning variables in the model have been extensively defined, measured, and discussed in previous chapters, and the dependent variables of criminal be-

Figure 12.2   The SSSL Model: Social Structure and Social Learning in Crime

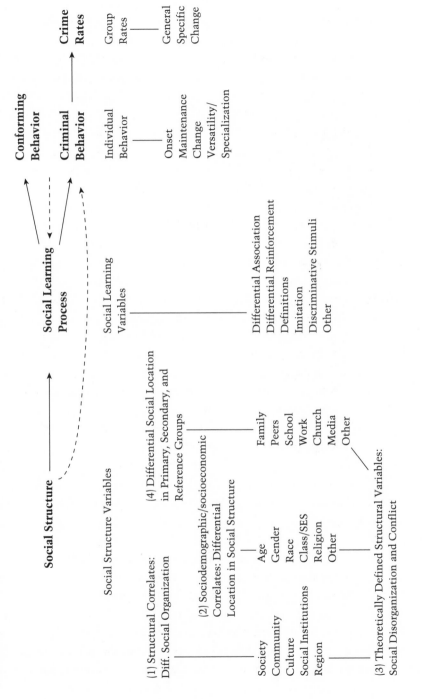

havior and crime rates are self-explanatory. The other sets of variables need further definition and comment. There are four dimensions, contexts, or elements of social structure that are expected to be related to social process and individual behavior and hence to crime rates in the sssl model. The first two of these have to do with the social correlates or "structural covariates" of crime, that is, the often-studied and well-known distributions of crime by age, sex, gender, community, inequality, population density and composition, and so on (Land et al., 1990). These can be and have been identified on purely empirical grounds without regard to their theoretical relevance in explaining crime. In fact, they are routinely entered into tests of theoretical models as nontheoretical control variables. The third has to do with the conceptually defined features or conditions of social structure that sociological theories of social disorganization, anomie, and conflict hypothesize to be the cause(s) of crime. The fourth has to do with the small group level of social structure.

Social Structural Correlates: Differential Social Organization. First, there are the known ecological, community, or geographical differences across systems (urban versus rural communities, cross-national comparisons, regional variations in rates, differences by ecological areas of the city, differences in population size or density, etc.). The empirical variations in rates of crime and delinquency can be established, with or without specification of the causative structural or cultural characteristics of these systems. From this point of view, it makes little difference what the specific theoretical explanations of the variations are, although a particular set of authors or researchers may conceptualize them as operational measures of theoretical constructs. But the measure could be tapping some unspecified combination of the features of the social organization, culture, or social backgrounds of the people who form the community or society. I see these differences across social systems or areas as indicating in part what Sutherland meant by groups "organized for and against crime." That is, there are some known or unknown characteristics of the social structure and/or culture of the society, community, or group that lean it toward relatively high or relatively low crime rates. Following Sutherland, I identify these variations in structural conditions by the general label of differential social organization, and I reiterate his view that "crime is rooted in the social organization." However, I do not agree with Sutherland that this term is essentially synonymous with, and should substitute for, the "less satisfactory" concept of social disorganization.

Sociodemographic/Socioeconomic Correlates: Differential Location in the Social Structure. Second, there are the known or probable variations in crime rates by sociodemographic characteristics, groupings, aggregates, collectivities, or categories, such as race/ethnicity, class, gender, age, marital status, religion, occupation, and other dimensions of social differentiation that exist in societies, regions, and communities. These may be viewed as the direct causes of crime (e.g., there is something inherent in being male that makes men more prone to crime than women), but more frequently the relationship between them and crime is viewed as the thing to be explained. For instance, one may attempt to account for the high ratio of male to female crime by explaining that crime-proneness reflects gender-role expectations in society. At one level these are descriptive characteristics of individuals and may be measured as sources of variation in individual behavior. At the structural level, however, I conceptualize them as direct indicators of the differential location of groups or categories of individuals in the social structure. They are commonly conceptualized as defining sociocultural categories or collectivities. Many structural variables incorporated into empirical models of crime are simply the aggregation or proportional composition of social systems of individuals with these characteristics (e.g., racial and class composition of the population of a city or proportion of males aged 15 to 24).

Theoretically Defined Structural Causes: Social Disorganization and Conflict. Third, there are the conceptually defined structural variables that have been captured in particular theoretical formulations that propose them as structural causes of crime. I am referring here to the well-known structural theories of crime and deviance that propose elevated rates in those societies, or segments of societies, that are hypothesized to have higher levels of some abstractly defined condition like anomie, conflict, social disorganization, patriarchy, or class oppression. The explanatory variables in these theories typically do not simply reiterate the correlates of crime. Rather, the structural theories offer explanations for one or more of the known or assumed correlations between general or offense-specific crime rates and race, class, gender, region, city, neighborhood, and population size, density, and composition. Often, the sociodemographic or socioeconomic variables are taken as empirical indicators of the explanatory concepts in these theories.

In the sssl model, the most relevant of these explanatory concepts are drawn primarily from anomie, social disorganization, and conflict theories. Although they have evolved from different theoretical and research traditions in sociology, social disorganization and anomie theories propose essentially the same explanation for crime. Both view social order, stability, and integration as conducive to conformity, and disorder and malintegration as conducive to crime and deviance. A social system (a society, community, or subsystem within a society, such as a family) is socially organized and integrated if there is an internal consensus on its norms and values, a strong cohesion exists among its members, social interaction proceeds in an orderly way, and there is a low level of disruptive conflict. Conversely, the system is disorganized or anomic if there is a disruption in its social cohesion or integration, weakened formal or informal social control, or malalignment or disjuncture between its social and cultural elements. The greater the homogeneity and common loyalties to shared values and norms or functional interdependence, the lower the crime rate. The less solidarity, cohesion, or integration there is within a group, community, or society, the higher will be the rate of crime and deviance. The more disorganized or weakened the institutions of conventional formal and informal control and socialization (family, education, religion, government), the higher the crime rate. Social, political, and economic disparities and inequalities that produce group and culture conflict relate to crime both as indicators of general social disorganization and as indicators that some of the groups in the conflict, while they may be internally organized, have interests or normative expectations that violate the social and legal norms of the larger society.[1]

Differential Social Location in Primary, Secondary, and Reference Groups. Fourth, there are the more immediate primary, secondary, and reference groups comprising the small-group and personal networks that impinge directly on the individual. These are the agents of informal and semiformal social control and socialization and are referred to specifically in social learning theory's concept of differential association. These are the groups to which the individual relates and which provide or filter the social environments, situations, and opportunities that promote or discourage his or her criminal or conforming behavior. Real and symbolic (through utilization of communications media) as well as direct and indirect participation, interaction, and identification with these groups provide the immediate social context in which differential social organization, differential social location, and social disorganization and conflict impinge on the individual and the operation of the social learning variables. Families, peers, schools, and other groups may be incomplete, disorganized, or ineffective agents of social control. They reflect the differential social organization and conflicts of the larger society or community and are the social locations for the operation of statuses and roles indicated by age, sex, race, and class. They provide the small-group, meso- or micro-level social contexts. From the perspective of the individual they are closely linked to the concept of differential association and entangled with the other social learning variables.

Please note that I am writing here about all of the social learning variables and primary groups, including the family. I am not postulating that peer group association is the only thing that counts. Sampson and Laub (1993:122) mistakenly believe that differential association theory hypothesizes that "family, school, and other effects are *fully mediated by learning in delinquent groups*" (emphasis added). They incorrectly cite Matsueda (1982) on this point. Social learning theory would not hypothesize that only delinquent peer groups mediate the effects of family and school or that such delinquent groups "fully" mediate other effects of these other groups. Rather, these are all primary and secondary groups that define the immediate social contexts within which the behavioral mechanisms operate.

FURTHER SPECIFICATION AND CAVEATS

The sssl model portrayed in Figure 12.2 shows that the effects of social structure on crime rates are expected to be mediated by the social learning process. The macro- and meso-level variables determine the probabilities that an individual has been, is, or will be exposed to different levels of the social learning variables. The different levels of these variables determine the probability that the individual will begin, persist, or desist from behavior, and at what frequency and degree of specialization or versatility. This behavior is translated into crime rates.

The lists of macro- and meso-level variables under differential organization and differential social location are not exhaustive, and it has not been unequivocally demonstrated that crime rates are related to all of them. The sociodemographic and socioeconomic variables listed under these headings are not equally related to crime rates, and certain relationships (e.g., that between class and crime) remain controversial. But all have been shown to be related to some extent to crime and delinquency. Of these, the strongest and most consistent differences in criminal and deviant behavior are by age and sex. The same caveat must be entered about empirical support for social disorganization and group/culture conflict. Social disorganization and anomie theory have some empirical support, but neither social disorganization nor group conflict as theoretical constructs are often measured directly, and as I noted above and in Chapter 7, anomie has been measured almost exclusively as individually perceived strain (Akers, 1997). The model predicts, however, that those structural correlates under differential organization, differential location, or social disorganization/anomie that are strongly related to crime rates will be related to the social learning variables, and those that are not highly or consistently correlated with the crime rates will not be highly or consistently correlated with the social learning variables.

The theory takes the structural conditions or variables that have been or can be shown to be correlated with crime rates as independent variables. There is no attempt to use principles of behavior or social exchange to account for social structure as the dependent variable, as Kunkel (1970), Emerson (1972b), Blau (1987), and others have done. The theory does not attempt to explain why a society has the culture, age structure, class system, race system, family system, economic system, gender/sex role system, or religious system that it has. The theory does not explain (by reference to history, social change, or other macro-level variables) why there is social disorganization, conflict, or inequality in society. For instance, suppose it can be shown that American society has a higher level of anomie (greater disjuncture between cultural goals and socially approved means, and more restricted access to legitimate opportunities for some segments of society) or is more socially disorganized, with a greater amount of intrasocietal heterogeneity and conflict among different segments of society, than is true of Japanese society. Further, assume it has been shown that crimes are more frequent in the United States and among the lower classes in both societies. Social structure–social learning theory would answer the question of how such a difference in anomie and disorganization produces the difference in individual behavior and hence the difference in crime rates. It does not attempt to explain why American society came to have higher levels of anomie (and Japanese society lower) or why the lower class has more restricted access to legitimate means. And in fact neither anomie nor social disorganization theory, in themselves, attempt such explanations. Similarly, why society is structured by gender in the way it is lies outside the purview of the theory; it simply hypothesizes that the gender structure of society produces crime-related differences in male and female socialization, associations, rewards, definitions, and models.

That is, the different patterns to which individuals are exposed in society are not the objects of explanation here and, typically, not the object of explanation in the structural theories of crime. Rather, the object of a theory such as disorganization/anomie is to explain why American society has higher rates of crime than other societies and why disadvantaged groups within American society have higher rates of crime than other groups. There is a high rate of crime in the United States because of a general societal discrepancy between culturally prescribed goals and socially approved means or because of some other disintegrating or disorganizing condition. There is a high rate of crime in the lower class or in depressed urban areas because of the anomic social condition created by unequal access to approved avenues of material success on the part of disadvantaged persons equally aspiring to the cultural goal of success or created by conditions of social disorganization. Anomie theory does not attempt to explain why such discrepancies exist between ends and means in a society, only to predict that when the discrepancies exist there will be (1) an overall high rate of crime in that society and (2) a particularly high rate of crime in its disadvantaged groups. Although social disorganization is often attributed to industrialization, urbanization, disruptive population movement, and other social changes, social disorganization theory is not geared toward uncovering the sources of disorganization. Social disorganization is not treated as the dependent variable. Rather, the theory proposes social disorganization as the independent variable; when it exists crime rates will be high. Similarly, the object of correlating race to crime is not to explain why race disparities and inequities exist in American society in the first place, but to determine if those group disparities make a difference in crime rates.

The sssl model explains the relationship between the structural variable(s), such as disorganization or race, and crime by proposing that the relationship is mediated by the social learning variables. For instance, higher levels of anomie produce higher probabilities that illegitimate means for acquiring material goods will be differentially reinforced over legitimate means for those most affected by the anomic conditions. Social disorganization reduces the availability and effectiveness of a consistent conventional moral climate and the application of formal and informal social rewards for conforming and punishment for deviance.

> Explicitly or implicitly, the sociological perspectives . . . make assumptions about the conditions affecting the differential reinforcement of criminal and conforming behavior. For example, "social disorganization" perspectives attribute variation in crime to variation in the vitality of certain institutions that have traditionally rewarded conformity and punished deviance (such as the family, the neighborhood, the church, and the school). If these social institutions are "disorganized" because of such factors as population change, urbanization, and industrialization, the probability that crime will be punished and conformity rewarded may be quite low. (Jensen and Rojek, 1992:204–5)

Groups in conflict may internally provide strong social support through modeling, definitions favorable, and social rewards for committing offenses against one another or against the sociolegal norms of the larger society.

We can account for the gender gap in crime by noting that male socialization (social learning) in the family and in peer groups is less likely than socialization of females to produce conformity to social and legal norms. Girls and women are subjected to more conforming-inducing social control (role expectations, informal social rewards, less freedom from conforming adult supervision, and so on). Adolescent male patterns of association differ significantly from female patterns, ranging from a vastly greater tendency to become involved in delinquent gangs to the much greater tendency to associate with peers who hold deviant attitudes and engage in deviant behavior. The social costs of violative behavior are greater and the rewards are smaller for females than males. The frequency of exposure to deviant models is higher for males than females. Similarly, age has an impact on crime because age is one of the factors that affects associations, reinforcement, models, and definitions favorable and unfavorable to crime. Age-specific rates differ because individuals are differentially exposed to the learning variables at different ages.

Rates are higher in the adolescent and young adult years because that is when the reinforcement balance, differential association, and attitudes are more apt to lean in a deviant direction. Crime rates decline with age because these variables, for most offenses, change in the conforming direction as individuals grow older. Crime rates are higher in urban than in rural areas because the greater diversity of urban environments "makes it easier to associate with deviant others, learn definitions favorable for deviance, and have deviant behavior reinforced by those in one's social environment. . . . This is more likely (but does not have) to occur in cities" (Krohn et al., 1984:357).

These propositions do not predict that the group-level probabilities uniformly affect all persons in the group or category. An individual in a low-crime group or category who is nonetheless more exposed to criminal associations, models, definitions, and reinforcement than someone in a high-crime group or category will have a higher probability of committing criminal or deviant acts. The theory explains the high male-female ratio in crime (and for most, but not all, specific types of deviance) by reference to gender ratios in the social learning variables. The way in which males are more exposed than females to learning variables mediates the effects of being male or female on criminal behavior. The probability that males will be exposed to deviance-producing patterns of associations, reinforcement, definitions, and models is higher than it is for females. However, if an individual female scores higher on these variables in the deviance-prone direction for a particular type of behavior than an individual male, she will have a higher probability than he will of committing the deviant act.

Figure 12.2 shows (with the broken-line reverse arrow) the reciprocal effects between the social learning variables and criminal and deviant behavior to reflect the discussion of the sequential and feedback aspects of the social learning process in Chapter 3. It is recognized that one's socioeconomic status, marital status, employment, and other indicators of social location can be affected by his or her criminal status; crime can exacerbate social disorganization and group conflict. However, for most of the social structural and sociodemographic variables indicating differential social organization and differential location in the social structure, the assumption is that they have a recursive relationship to criminal behavior and the crime rate. For instance, one's criminal behavior cannot cause race, gender, age, place of birth, or population density. Therefore, nonrecursive relationships between crime and the social structural variables are not shown.

The model in Figure 12.2 is depicted in the way it is to show that it can be tested with empirical data in a multivariate statistical model. What kind of empirical findings, what magnitude of coefficients from such a statistical analysis, will be taken as confirming or disconfirming the theory? It depends on how strongly or unequivocally the expected relationships are stated.

The strongest expectation is that the variations and stabilities in the behavioral and cognitive variables in the social learning process account for *all* variations and stabilities in criminal behavior and thereby mediate *all* of the significant relationships between the structural variables and crime. The more realistic statement is that variations and stabilities in the behavioral and cognitive variables specified in the social learning process account for a *substantial portion* of individual variations and stabilities in crime and deviance and mediate a *substantial portion* of the relationship between *most* of the structural variables in the model and crime. A weak statement of the theory is that the social learning process accounts for *some* portion of the variation and stability in criminal behavior and mediates *some* portion of the relationship between the correlates and crime.

Although I report empirical models below that come very close to fitting it, the strong statement is probably destined for failure most of the time. Direct and full empirical support for this version of the theory (or the strong version of any general theory, for that matter) is unlikely for two reasons. First, completely adequate empirical support for or refutation of this or any theory assumes totally unbiased sampling, full measurement of all relevant variables with no measurement error, full specification of the empirical model, and control of all extraneous or confounding conditions, factors, or variables. Obviously, no empirical research can meet these assumptions, and any given set of data will be insufficient to the task. Second, neither this nor any other theory can be entirely true, even assuming no methodological errors in testing. There are almost certain to be sources of variation and stability in crime that are not captured by the theory or by the variables it specifies that are included in the model. Some of these unmeasured sources of variation may be compatible with the theory, while others would not. Furthermore, as I and others have argued (Akers, 1997), a fully causative, deterministic model is inappropriate for human behavior. It will never be achieved and ought to be abandoned in principle. The principle of partial, or "soft," determinism (Matza, 1964) is quite appropriate and adequate for valid explanations of criminal and deviant behavior, and most sociologists and criminologists no longer employ thoroughgoing, "strong" determinism (Gibbons, 1994).

Thus, the strong version should be treated as no more than an ideal model to guide the construction of empirical models. The issue, then, is how close to this ideal, fully specified statement of the theory the empirical models come. The more closely the results of the analysis show relationships as predicted by the model, the more one can conclude that the theory has been supported. The weaker the empirical relationships predicted by the model, the less support there is for it.

For these reasons, I consider the moderate statement to be the operative one. If substantial portions of the variations (by normally accepted standards in social science) are accounted for by the variables in the theory, then it is confirmed. Weaker relationships can still be taken as support for the theoretical model in its weak form. In order to reject this weak statement, empirical findings would have to show that the theoretical variables are unrelated or related in the wrong direction to crime and delinquency. This would provide a minimum standard for judging the theory, however, and could be taken as insufficient to support the theory as stated. Adequate and acceptable tests of the theory, then, do not need to demonstrate absolute confirmation or falsification, but only the preponderance of credible evidence on the theory considered on its own or relative to alternative explanations over a series of tests with adequate methodology. Are the direction and relative magnitude of relationships in support of or counter to the theory? Are they stronger or weaker than relationships predicted by other theories?[2]

Empirical Evidence on SSSL

The model could be supported by reviewing the research findings on the major structural theories of crime and demonstrating that these findings are consistent with SSSL. (See the reviews of this research literature in

Akers, 1994; Gibbons, 1994; Curran and Renzetti, 1994; and Vold and Bernard, 1986, or in virtually any text for criminology, delinquency, and deviance courses.) Similarly, a post hoc application could show that the social correlates of crime or the known "facts" about crime are consistent with the theory. These include the well-known systematic variations in crime rates by age, race/ethnicity, gender, class/socioeconomic status, community, urbanism, and region that are reported in any criminology textbook and in many summary articles and book chapters (see Land et al., 1990; Braithwaite, 1989; Gottfredson and Hirschi, 1990; Tittle, 1995). This does not mean that all studies have found exactly the same relationships or that the relationships between, say, class and crime or age and crime are beyond dispute. But the nature of these disagreements is known and taken into account in reviews of the facts of crime that any valid theory must fit.

A theory that is useful and successful in accounting for these variations is accorded greater confidence and credibility. But the empirical test of a theory is not that it "fits the known facts"; without direct empirical measures of the explanatory variables, more than one (I am tempted to say virtually any) post hoc interpretation can make plausible sense of the same set of facts. For instance, Gottfredson and Hirschi (1990) claim low self-control fits all of the facts of crime. Braithwaite (1989) claims that his model of integrative and nonintegrative shaming fits all the major known social variations in crime. Tittle (1995) claims that his theory of control balance is consistent with the evidence on gender, age, race, marital status, urban residence, and socioeconomic status. And in each case these claims are reasonably and plausibly supported by post hoc consideration of known crime correlates. I briefly make a plausible case above with regard to crime and social disorganization/anomie, gender, age, and community. The real test of the model, however, must come from direct and full examination of the propositions and derived hypotheses of the theory with data collected specifically for that purpose.

At this time there has been no such direct test of the full sssl model. However, some recent research (Heimer, 1997) has moved in the direction of testing models of the mediating effects of certain social learning variables (delinquent friends and definitions favorable to violence) on the relationship of delinquency to social structural variables (e. g., socioeconomic status, age, race, and urban resident). In addition, there is research (my own and others') testing the effects of sociodemographic variables (indicative in the model of differential location in the social structure) and one or more social learning variables on crime and delinquency. The findings from this research are relevant to examining the probable empirical validity of the sssl model. Among these investigations, I will concentrate on some specific studies of crime and age/life course. Moreover, some of my own research has more directly tested the sssl model, with regard to the effects not only of sociodemographic variables but also the social learning mediation of community context as an indicator of being differentially organized for higher or lower rates of drug and alcohol use among adolescent and elderly populations. I do not pretend that these studies constitute definitive tests of the model, but they provide support for it and suggest ways of testing the model more thoroughly with other structural variables and other dependent variables. Finally, the empirical review must be even more tentative with regard to evidence on the relationship of social disorganization and conflict to social learning and rates of crime or deviance.

AGE, CRIME, AND SOCIAL LEARNING VARIABLES

Hirschi and Gottfredson (1983; Gottfredson and Hirschi, 1990) have argued that there is an inverted-J curve relationship between crime and age that is invariant across time, cross-culturally, across groups within the same society, and across all types of criminal behavior. This assertion has been vigorously countered by a number of researchers, and, if taken literally, it is not true (Greenberg, 1985; 1988; Steffensmeier et al., 1989; Tittle, 1995; Reed and Yeager, 1996; Shavit and Ruttner, 1988; Gartner and Noch, 1990; Britt, 1992; Jang and Krohn, 1995.). The ages at which the crime curve peaks and declines vary to some extent cross-culturally, and some types of offense, such as white-collar and corporate crimes, peak out later than others. Age-specific rates of drug addiction and alcoholism do not decline in the late teenage years and peak out much later than rates of violence and theft. However, the general shape of this curve for most criminal offenses, in which age-specific crime rates for offenses peak in the late teenage years and early twenties and decline thereafter, is generally accepted. What is not generally accepted is Hirschi and Gottfredson's related contention that no known criminological theory or set of known causal variables can account for this phenomenon, even in part

(Greenberg, 1988; Warr, 1993b; Sampson and Laub, 1993; Tittle, 1995). They also make the claim, supported by Tittle (1995), that the causes of crime are the same regardless of age.

I will not try to settle the issue of what the exact shape of the age-crime curve is and whether or not this shape is invariant by time, place, group, or offense. I will simply take it as empirically established that the age-specific rates for most offenses increase from childhood to late adolescence or early adulthood and decline thereafter. I agree with Gott-fredson and Hirschi (1990) that the causes of crime are the same regard-less of age of the offender. I agree also with Tittle's argument (1995; Tittle and Ward, 1993) that this does not mean that the values of the causative variables or the magnitude of their relationship to the dependent vari-ables are the same at each age.

I go one step further and hypothesize that these causes are the vari-ables specified in social learning theory. Thus, variations in the social learning variables at each age, created by age-related changes in social circumstances, are hypothesized to account for variations in criminal and deviant behavior at each age. The theory would predict that persis-tence or desistance, increase or decrease in deviant behavior as persons grow older accompanies deviant or conforming changes (persistence, in-crease, or decrease) in the social learning variables in the life course, op-erating in the sequential and reciprocal manner presented in Chapter 3.

Obviously, then, I do not agree with Gottfredson and Hirschi that the age-crime relationship cannot be explained by any known theory or set of intervening variables. It is not clear to me, however, whether they mean that it is the general inverted-J shape of the crime-age relationship or that it is the invariance of the shape that is beyond explanation. If they mean that the shape of the curve is the explanatory problem, then I see a contradiction in their firm argument that the age-crime relationship cannot be explained by any known theory or set of causes and their equally firm argument that the causes of crime are the same regardless of age. It seems apparent that if the same variables that explain adolescent delinquency also explain adult crime, then variations in those causes by age should sufficiently account for variations in crime that occur from the teenage to the adult years. Of course, Gottfredson and Hirschi may mean that low self-control (once it has been formed after childhood so-cialization) is the cause of deviance, coming into play to produce the first commission of crime in adolescence, with its value or magnitude remaining constant and unchanging with age. In order for the inverted-J curve to be explained by this process, not only the average difference in self-control across individuals but also the level of self-control exercised by the same individual must remain relatively constant throughout life. A constant, of course, cannot explain changes. I think Gottfredson and Hirschi are correct that there is little change in adulthood (at least for most people) in the individual's internalized self-control. On the other hand, their efforts to show that research has been unable to substantiate that other variables, which do change with age, cannot explain the increase in crime throughout adolescence and its rapid decline after the young adult years is sketchy and unconvincing (see Warr, 1993b).

David Greenberg (1985; 1988) has argued that the social control variables from Hirschi's bonding theory could explain the relationship between age and crime because, if it be true that control stems "from the formal and informal institutional memberships and affiliations of social life, it is difficult to believe that control variables could be independent of age" (Greenberg, 1988:18). Greenberg makes the case that if adolescents are more involved in crime than are adults this comes from how their lives differ. He offers a plausible and reasonable explanation that refers to such differences in four main areas—labor force, school, family status, and legal status. In so doing, however, he leans heavily on notions of differential reward and punishment for adolescent deviance and other concepts that are drawn more from social learning than from control theory.

Marvin D. Krohn and his associates (1989) tested the direct and indirect effects of bonding variables from Hirschi's control theory in the context of examining the relationship between age and adolescent cigarette smoking. But they conceptualized the effects of family and peer attachment, school commitment and involvement, and beliefs as primarily indirect through differential association with smoking and nonsmoking friends. Therefore, the findings are relevant to the question of whether social learning variables mediate age effects on adolescent deviance. The data came from the Iowa smoking study (see Chapter 8), but I had nothing to do with the conceptualization, analysis, or report. Krohn and his colleagues (1989) report total and direct effects for each of these variables for each grade level from 7 through 12 for each of the five years of the study. Smoking behavior increased from the seventh to twelfth grades, but they found age or cohort effects interacting with only the social bonding variables. The peer association variable, on the other hand, operated on smoking behavior in essentially the same way regardless of age and explains the changes in smoking behavior from early to later adolescence. This variable mediated not only the age and cohort factors but also the effects of the social bonding variables. Krohn and his associates (1989:124–25) conclude that differential peer association is the "most powerful prediction of smoking for all panels, cross-section and age groups" and that "there was no discernible age effect for association with friends who smoke."

Randy LaGrange and Helene White (1985) examined the issue of "age generalizability" in a sample of males aged 12, 15, and 18. The model tested is primarily one of social bonding, with measures of parental attachment, school attachment, and educational commitment. However, they did include a good measure of differential peer association, and their findings are relevant to the question of the effects of this social learning variable at different stages of the adolescent years. They found the magnitude of the relationship between delinquent behavior and the bonding and learning variables (as well as a measure of socioeconomic status, or ses) varied somewhat depending upon the age category. All of the variables in the model had significant effects in the combined sample of all ages. However, the bonding variables had their strongest net effects at the mid-adolescent age of 15 (in fact, they had no significant net effects at ages 12 and 18), and ses had a significant net effect only among the 18-year-olds. Differential peer association had significant effects in all models, but its strongest impact was seen among 18-year-old males; it was weaker in the mid-adolescent group.

LaGrange and White do not conclude from their findings that the causes of delinquency vary by age, but they do conclude that lumping all ages from 12 to 18 into overall adolescent samples, as is common in research, may mask some age-dependent relationships. I think this is a reasonable conclusion, but there are some caveats that the authors did not mention. These point in the other direction of age generalizability and provide some evidence in favor of social learning (or a combination of social learning and bonding variables) as furnishing the mediating variables between age and delinquency. The social learning variable of differential peer association had the largest relative effect in the overall model and in two of the three age-specific models (ages 12 and 18), and it was the only variable to have significant net effects in all models. Since all of the variables in the combined model had significant path coefficients, it is reasonable to assume that the bonding and SES variables continued to have effects at all ages, but were mediated by the peer association variable. The overall level of explained variance in delinquent behavior was of the same order of magnitude at all ages (from 27% to 36%). The same set of variables operates (with different configurations) at each age. Changes in delinquent behavior from early to later adolescence accompany changes in parental, school, and peer variables.

Robert J. Sampson and John H. Laub (Sampson and Laub, 1993; Laub and Sampson, 1993) propose an "age-integrated" theory of informal social control as an explanation of crime and the life cycle, that is, the persistence and change in delinquency and crime from childhood, to adolescence, and into adulthood. Their major hypothesis is that increases in the strength of social bonds for most people reduce crime rates in adulthood. But for those individuals for whom the social bonds are not strengthened with age or who experience abrupt changes weakening existing bonds, the likelihood of criminal behavior is increased. Structural contexts are mediated by informal family and school controls. Early childhood behavior and differences in self-control are important, but Sampson and Laub found that later adult events also have an impact on criminal behavior. Informal social bonds to family and occupation that develop and change in adulthood explain changes in criminality over the life span.

Sampson and Laub (1993) revisit the Gluecks' famous data set that matched 500 official delinquents by delinquency rate of neighborhood, age, ethnicity, and IQ with 500 nondelinquents who were all white males from Boston public schools, selected to maximize differences. The Gluecks' data were collected by intensive in-person interviews and from social welfare agencies, with delinquency measured by self-reports, parent reports, and teacher reports and by arrest data. The two groups were followed up at age 25 and again at age 32. Of the delinquents, 55% had arrests as adults; of the nondelinquents, 20% had arrests as adults. Compared to the persisters, the 45% of the delinquents who had desisted enough from law violation to avoid arrest as adults had experienced greater marriage success, employment stability, and other life changes that worked against continuing in crime. The 20% of nondelinquents who became criminal as adults were more likely than those who had continued their conforming ways to have experienced family disruption, marriage failure, employment instability, and other changes. Sampson and Laub found that there is both stability and change in the trajectory or pathway of criminal and conforming behavior over the life span. These long-term patterns are a function of the sequence, timing, and duration of transitions, life events, and significant turning points associated with aging. Continuities in individual behavior are associated with lack of change, and change in behavior is associated with change in social experiences.

Therefore, Sampson and Laub (1993) take a position that is contrary to the assertions by Gottfredson and Hirschi (1990) that life events have little or no effect on adult crime. They point out that, while behavior at an earlier age is predictive of behavior at a later age, it does so fairly imprecisely with a high proportion of false positives. While there may be stable average differences in deviance propensity across individuals, there are fairly large within-individual changes in offending behavior over time. Most anti-social children do not become anti-social adults. The majority of adult criminals have no history of delinquency. Looking at behavior retrospectively, beginning with adult offenders and tracing back to adolescence or beginning in adolescence and tracing back to childhood, overstates stability. Looked at prospectively, behavior appears to be much less stable. Adult criminality is often preceded by childhood misconduct, but most childhood misconduct does not lead to adult criminality. Sampson and Laub found significant changes in criminal propensity later in life, and these were correlated with changes in the person's family, employment, and social circumstances. While some individuals involved in adolescent deviance persist in crime in adulthood, most delinquency is "adolescence-limited" rather than "life-course persistent" (Moffitt, 1993). Just as most anti-social children do not become anti-social adults; most adolescent delinquents do not become adult criminals. Moreover, merely finding behavioral stability does not by itself show that the stability is based on some context-free, within-person personality or biological factor. The finding of behavioral stability is as consistent with stability of social contexts as it is with self-control or some other persistent within-individual condition that does not change with age. Sampson and Laub (1993) conclude that it is the stability of causative factors in the social environment as one ages that produces stability of behavior, and that it is changes in those same factors that produce changes in behavior from youth to adulthood and through the life course.

Other researchers have examined the persistence or change in individual tendencies toward delinquency and the extent to which these can be attributed to stable/changing individual characteristics or to stable/changing life circumstances (Nagin and Paternoster, 1991; Nagin and Farrington, 1992a; Nagin and Farrington, 1992b; Benson and Moore, 1992; Creechan, 1994). Persistence of deviant behavior is seen in this research as an indirect indicator of low self-control. According to Gottfredson and Hirschi (1990) persons with low self-control will have a persistently greater tendency to commit deviance across all social circumstances and at all stages of life after childhood. As I have indicated, however, the empirical evidence from this research shows change and inconsistencies along with stability of behavior patterns.

I interpret the findings by Sampson and Laub and other researchers (e.g., Conger and Simons, 1995) on crime through the life course as consistent with the sssl model. Age is an indicator of location in the social structure, and it is accompanied by both stable and changing life experiences. These in turn have stable or changing effects on the social learning variables and hence on conforming and deviant behavior. Although I am sure that Sampson and Laub would not agree with this interpretation, a careful look at their own model reveals a considerable amount of overlap and consistency with social learning theory.

Sampson and Laub (1993) have become the leading proponents of a "developmental" or "life-course" perspective in criminology (see also Loeber and LeBlanc, 1990; Moffitt, 1993; Conger and Simons, 1995; Bartusch et al., 1997; Paternoster and Brame, 1997). But the perspective does not represent a new theory of crime with a new set of explanatory variables; rather, it seems to be a systematic way of raising questions about how important variables drawn from extant criminological theories do or do not operate at different life stages. However, it is unclear from which theories the supporters of the developmental perspective draw these variables. Moffitt (1993) and Loeber and LeBlanc (1990) draw from concepts in developmental psychology. But the models tested include childhood socialization and peer associations as significant variables (Bartusch et al., 1997). Sampson and Laub use the language of "social bonds" and "informal social control," downplay the relevance of association with delinquent peers, and otherwise take a social bonding approach to life-course changes. But, in fact, they do not stick with control or bonding theory. They propose that the effects of "family context" (e.g., family size, disruption, social class, parental criminality) on delinquency during the adolescent years are mediated by internal family dynamics of discipline, supervision, and rejection. Their discussion of how and why family context is so important in the development of delinquent behavior leans very heavily upon Gerald R. Patterson's (1982) "coercion theory," which is explicitly an application of social learning concepts of parental modeling, reinforcement, and punishment of children's conforming and deviant behavior. Patterson found that parents who are least likely to have delinquent children (1) notice what the child is doing, (2) monitor the child's behavior, (3) provide good models for the child's social skills, (4) clearly state rules and standards of behavior, (5) administer consistent and sane punishment for rule violations, (6) provide consistent reinforcement for conforming, and (7) negotiate disagreements and conflicts with the child. "[L]ess skilled parents inadvertently reinforce their children's anti-social behavior and fail to provide effective punishment for transgressions" (Sampson and Laub, 1993:67).

Sampson and Laub point out the similarity of Patterson's theory to the social control theories of Hirschi and others (but not to Gottfredson and Hirschi's self-control theory). Their reference to parental discipline and supervision echoes parts of Hirschi's original formulation of social bonding theory. But beyond that there is very little in their model that relates directly to control theory. There is nothing in their data that directly measures the specific concepts of attachment, commitment, beliefs, and involvement found in social bonding theory or the personal and social controls as defined in other control theories. At the same time, they describe a family process that draws extensively on social learning concepts of modeling pro-social skills and the absence of criminality in the family (imitation, observational learning), clear statements of rules (normative definitions unfavorable to deviance), supervision and monitoring of behavior, and following up with reward for conformity and punishment for nonconformity (differential reinforcement). In spite of the fact that Patterson directs the Oregon Social Learning Center and the obviously close affinity of his explanatory concepts to those in Akers's social learning theory, Sampson and Laub label the process "informal social control." But whatever the label, it would seem that each aspect of this informal social control process is specified in social learning theory.

Sampson and Laub interpret their findings that abrupt "turning points" (e.g., getting married or finding stable employment) and gradual changes in a person's life explain why individuals discontinue law violations to be inconsistent with Gottfredson and Hirschi's (1990) low-self-control theory. They also interpret their findings as being inconsistent with Gottfredson and Hirschi's assertion that *no* variables known to criminological theory can account for the age-crime relationship. This interpretation may be correct. Nevertheless, their view that these findings are consistent with, or interpretable in terms of, social bonding theory misses the point that the findings are as readily interpretable in terms of social learning theory. Indeed, as I have just shown, their interpretative discussions, although they do not identify them as such, clearly invoke social learning mechanisms as the primary ones in the effects of age on stability and change in deviance. Their findings are consistent with the sssl explanation of the age-crime relationship. It would seem self-evident that variables such as parents' criminality and disciplinary practices are measures of the social learning concepts of social reinforcement and imitation/modeling in the family. Further, getting married, finding stable employment, and other significant turning points can be expected to affect differential association, reinforcement balance, exposure to conforming and deviant models, and pro- or anti-deviant definitions. Therefore, in spite of their disavowal of peer associations as a mediating variable and their endorsement of social bonding theory, Sampson and Laub's empirical findings are very largely compatible with the predictions about the age-crime relationship in the sssl model I have presented here. Thus, I see this model as falling in the "theoretical middle ground," identified by Paternoster and Brame (1997), between the "pure static/general" theory of Gottfredson and Hirschi (1990) that stresses the invariance of behavior at different ages and the pure "developmental" theory of Moffitt (1993; Bartusch et al., 1997) that stresses variation in causes of behavior at different ages.

Another example of empirical research that is purported to be an "empirical test of social control theory" but which, in fact, provides empirical evidence supportive of the sssl model is reported by Josine Junger-Tas (1992). Junger-Tas calls the empirical model tested in her study a "social control" or "social integration" model (family, school, and leisure integration). Nevertheless, the meaning and measures of social integration show that a more accurate view would be that it is a combined social bonding/social learning model; the findings show, moreover, that the strongest variables in the model come from social learning theory. Junger-Tas conducted the two-year longitudinal research project among adolescents in the Netherlands. The strongest predictor of delinquency in the study was peer associations, but she inexplicably excludes this variable from the final model. Endorsement of normative statements (an obvious but unrecognized measure of favorable and unfavorable definitions) was included in the final model. Junger-Tas reports that delinquents are less attached to friends than nondelinquents (consistent with social bonding theory), but this relationship is not strong, and the real difference lies in whether the attachment is to conforming or delinquent friends (consistent with social learning theory). Among the adolescents with no delinquent friends, 41% reported delinquent offenses. On the other hand, 69% of those with one delinquent friend engaged in delinquent behavior, 86% of those with two to three delinquent friends were themselves delinquent, and an adolescent with four or more deviant friends was almost certain (93%) to have committed delinquent offenses. Only 2.3% of adolescents with no delinquent friends reported frequent offenses, while 50% of those with four or more delinquent friends reported frequently committing offenses.

These results support social learning theory, and Junger-Tas's findings on stability and change in behavior over time are also consistent with how the sssl model would explain age differences in offending. She found that the persistence of delinquency from the first year to the next depended on the level of the adolescent's social integration, not a persistent difference in some personality trait, any other inherent individual characteristic, or some context-free stability factor in behavior.

Another comment concerns the relation between earlier and later delinquency. One would expect such a relationship, and indeed path analysis produces a correlation. . . . However, controlling for integration levels, the relation disappears. This suggests that the best predictor of delinquency is not earlier delinquency, but current levels of social integration. The reason we think otherwise is because in most lives social integration tends to be a constant factor, at least over a number of years. Our research indicates that, when social conditions change, social behavior will also change. (Junger-Tas, 1992:21)

Erich Labouvie (1996) reports findings from the Rutgers Health and Human Development study, which has tracked substance use and abuse in two birth cohorts from adolescence (ages 15 and 18) into young adulthood (tested at ages 21/24 and again at 28/31), that also parallel the findings from Sampson and Laub's analysis. Stable and new marriage, having children, and maintaining or changing patterns of differential association with friends similarly situated with regard both to family status and to substance use were related to stability as well as change in drinking, smoking, and drug use at these different ages. The changes, reflecting the processes of selection and socialization, tended toward reduction in illicit drug use and in smoking and drinking by age 28/31. The expected deviance reduction after young adulthood is accounted for by changes in family and friends that accompanied the aging process.

Charles R. Tittle and David A. Ward (1993; Tittle, 1995) found significant interactions between age and other variables in specific offense categories. However, they conclude that these were not substantial enough to restrict generalizing from youth to adult samples. They support the general thrust of the Gottfredson and Hirschi hypothesis that the causes of crime at any age are essentially the same at all ages. Other researchers have also found this to be true, but most of their studies have been of adolescent samples and look at age variations within the teenage years. Tittle and Ward sampled the entire age span from adolescence to old age. If causes are the same, we may continue to generalize from adolescent samples to adult samples; if not, age-specific theories will have to be devised. Tittle and Ward conclude that the causes are essentially the same (only the values of the causative variables differ) for each age category. Predicting offense behavior at any age using the significant independent variables from any other age produced no more errors than expected by chance. Interestingly, they found the least error in generalizing from significant variables among the elderly (60+) to other age categories.

They base this conclusion on an analysis of data from a 1972 survey of persons aged 15 to 94 in Iowa, Oregon, and New Jersey (Tittle, 1980), which allowed testing whether causes of crime and delinquency interact with age. The independent variables in their model are seven sociodemographic variables (gender, SES, size of place of residence, geographic mobility, race, intactness of home, childhood place of residence) and five theoretical variables (differential association, social integration, anomie, social control, and deterrence). The dependent variables are having committed six criminal acts (petty theft, grand theft, marijuana smoking, gambling, assault, and income tax cheating) and the self-projected likelihood of committing these acts in the future.

Of the many variables in the model, my interests lie specifically in two areas. Differential association was measured by asking respondents, for each of five types of criminal behavior, the proportion of people they personally knew who committed that offense at least once a year; "informal social control" (anticipated negative responses of individuals important to a person if they found out he or she had committed the offense) is a partial measure of the punishment dimension of differential reinforcement. The logistic regression coefficients for the relationships of differential association and each of the five crimes, as measured by self-reported offenses in the past and by self-projection of offenses in the future, are strong and essentially the same at all age categories; there is no significant difference in the relationship across ages. There are some significant differences among coefficients for informal social control with regard to previous behavior, but none with regard to projected behavior. The findings with regard to differential associations and informal punishment are what would be predicted by the sssl model. These and other variables are effective predictors of violative behavior at all ages; controlling for age makes no differences. Tittle and Ward do not run models of age effects on crime with differential association and reinforcement in the equation, nor do they run models of age effects on offenses controlling for other independent variables.

Tittle and Ward (1993:41) caution that their findings do not relate to the Gottfredson and Hirschi hypotheses that an inverted-J pattern best describes the age-crime relationship (although their age-specific rates do take a similar shape for most of the offenses), that the shape of this curve is invariant, and that the relationship between age and "crime is inexplicable with currently known variables." Rather, they focus only on the Gottfredson and Hirschi proposal that causes of crime found to be operative in the adolescent years are the same ones operative in adulthood at any age. They find support for this hypothesis.

Nevertheless, as noted above, Gottfredson and Hirschi's dual hypotheses that nothing yet known can explain the age-crime relationship and that the same causes of crime are operative at each age seem contradictory to me. If the causes are the same for each age and crime changes by age, is it not reasonable to conclude or hypothesize that the inverted-J pattern is a function of changes in the values, distribution, or variation in the causes of crime by age? For instance, suppose it can be demonstrated that differential reinforcement accounts for variations in criminal behavior among persons who are 18 years of age and also for persons who are 45. Does it not seem reasonable to propose that the higher rate of crime for the former and the lower rate for the latter are the result of greater reinforcement on balance for deviance among 18-year-olds compared to 45-year-olds? The explanatory variable is the same, but just as there must be significant individual variations in reinforcement for offense behavior within the same age category (otherwise the variable would not be related to within-age differences in individual offending) there should be across-age differences in the average level of reinforcement for offense behavior. Given the empirical finding that crime is related to these causative factors at any given age, then variations in the causes of crime by age should sufficiently account for variations in crime by age. Therefore, is it logically consistent to propose that no set of variables can explain the relationship of crime to age and simultaneously to hypothesize that the same variables that explain delinquency also explain adult crime?

In explicating his control balance theory, Tittle (1995) argues that if the causes of crime are the same regardless of age, then those same causes can explain age differences in crime. First, he maintains that the inverted-J curve pattern holds more for "predatory and defiant crime" (for instance, ordinary personal and property crimes by adults and adolescents) than it does for "exploitative, decadent and plunderous crime" (for instance, white-collar and corporate crimes). The former are concentrated in the late teens and early twenties, while the latter are concentrated among the middle-aged. Then, he argues that these differences are explained by control deficits for the former crimes and by control surpluses for the latter crimes. Thus, the causes of crime are the same regardless of age:

> However, this does not imply that the actual values of the variables are the same for all ages. Indeed, it is age variation in the magnitude of the variables that accounts for the age-deviance relationship. (Tittle, 1995:248)

Mark Warr (1993b) also offers evidence that differential association is one of those variables that account for the age-deviance relationship. Gottfredson and Hirschi argue that the "age distribution of crime cannot be explained by any known variables, and they point specifically to the failure of sociological theories to explain this phenomenon" (Warr, 1993b:17). Warr believes that Gottfredson and Hirschi are too quick to dismiss sociological explanations and variables. For instance, they reject the explanation of the age distribution of crime by changes in crime-related peer associations by age, but they cite only one study, and that study used the wrong age categories to allow a proper test of the explanation. The theory does not require that differential association with delinquent and nondelinquent peers during the adolescent years produce a lifetime effect. It requires only that associations do vary by age and that their effects remain while controlling for age. Any explanation must account for the rapid increase in offense behavior from the pre-adolescent through the adolescent years, followed by a rapid decrease for most offenses in the late teens or early adult years. There must be strong age-graded changes taking place in the independent variables to account for this strong change in the dependent variable. Drawing data from the National Youth Survey (NYS; ages 11–21), Warr tested the hypothesis that among these are significant changes in differential association; he did so by relating age and crime to various measures of differential peer association, exposure to delinquent peers (number of delinquent friends), time spent with peers, importance of friends, and commitment or loyalty to friends.

To account for the rapid and large changes in criminal behavior from the pre-teen to the young adult years, there must be correspondingly quick and substantial changes in the relationship between age and differential peer associations. This is exactly what Warr found. The rate of age-specific exposure to delinquent peers increases rapidly through the adolescent years; it then decreases in the late teenage years for some offenses or levels off in the young adult years for other behavior. At age 11, for instance, only 5% of the NYS respondents reported having one or more friends who had smoked marijuana. Among those aged 16, this had increased to 60%. By age 18 it was around 75% and stayed at about that level through age 21. A similar pattern, with somewhat higher percentages at each age, was observed for alcohol. These results are very close to the curves found for the age distribution of self-reported marijuana and alcohol use in national household and high school surveys. The age distributions for exposure to peers for other offenses like vandalism, burglary, and theft showed exposure to peers engaged in those acts increasing rapidly, peaking at about age 16 to 17, and then decreasing. Again, these distributions fit the distribution of reported crimes and arrests for these offenses by age. The age distribution of the other elements of peer relations (time, importance, loyalty) also track the age distribution of delinquency and crime. Peer associations do change dramatically with age, and these changes closely parallel the age-pattern of changes in crime.

When these peer influence variables are controlled, the age effects on offense behavior become nonsignificant. Warr ran regression models testing only age effects for different self-reported offenses and found that most offenses differed significantly by age. But when only one variable, exposure to delinquent friends, is added to the baseline equations, the significant age effects for all offenses were considerably reduced and, in the cases of marijuana use, serious theft, and burglary, disappeared altogether. Adding time spent with peers, loyalty to peers, and importance of peer relations reduced the age effects even more, but it did not really add much beyond the effects of the variable of number of delinquent peers alone. This seems to me to be a fairly clear demonstration of how just one variable from social learning theory (differential peer association) can explain why the age-specific rate of delinquency increases rapidly through the adolescent years and then decreases just as rapidly toward the late teens and into young adulthood. In other words, the inverted-J curve of the age-deviance relationship is explained. Warr (1993b:35) concludes:

> Hirschi and Gottfredson contend that the age distribution of crime cannot be explained by any variables known to criminology. The analysis presented herein shows that when measures of peer influence are held constant, the association between age and crime is substantially weakened, and for some of-

fenses, disappears entirely. Instead of an impenetrable conundrum, the age-crime relation appears to be at least partially explicable by . . . differential association.

Criminal and deviant behavior has a large, consistent, and well-established relationship to age. It also has a large, consistent, and well-established relationship to differential peer association. Warr shows that deviance-relevant peer relationships also have a large and consistent relationship to age. It could be that all of these arise simply from the common association with age, and, since age causes both differences in associations and in offending behavior, the relationship between the two is spurious and without causal significance.

> That conclusion, however, is contradicted by the analysis. Recall that when age and peer behavior are introduced into the same equation, it is age—not peer behavior—that is rendered insignificant. Consequently, it is difficult to avoid the conclusion that it is *age* that is spuriously associated with delinquency. (Warr, 1993b:37)

I would not conclude that the age-delinquency relationship is spurious, only that differential peer associations is an important variable mediating the effects of age on delinquency. Thus, Warr's evidence and the evidence of the other research I have reviewed here conforms to the prediction from the sssl model that age effects on delinquency behavior are indirect, operating through the social learning process. That the impact of age is mediated by other social learning variables (definitions and differential reinforcement) in addition to peer association is shown by analysis of data from my own Boys Town research, to which I now turn.

AGE, COMMUNITY CONTEXT, AND SOCIAL LEARNING IN ADOLESCENT DEVIANCE

The Boys Town Study (see Chapter 7) provided two kinds of data and findings that are relevant to the sssl model. First, they allow examining the relationship between adolescent drug use and the sociodemographic variables of age, sex, race, and socioeconomic status. Second, the Boys Town data allowed an analysis of the interplay between the effects of "community context" as a macro-level variable and the effects of social learning variables on teenage substance use that is directly relevant to the empirical validity of the sssl model (Krohn et al., 1984).

Recall that the Boys Town Study demonstrated strong effects of the social learning variables on adolescent drinking, smoking, and use of other drugs. When sociodemographic variables were controlled, they had little effect on the general level of variance in these dependent variables explained by the social learning variables. Sex, socioeconomic status, and race (there were very few black youngsters in the community) were not related to drug and alcohol behavior, and hence controlling for them would not be expected to make a difference. However, age and grade in school were significantly related to the dependent variables of alcohol and marijuana use and abuse. For both adolescent boys and girls there are decided differences in the age-specific and grade-specific rates of substance use and abuse.

Age and grade in school are not the same, but they are so highly correlated ($r = .9$) that they measure essentially the same thing. Therefore, we used grade-level as the independent variable to test the hypothesis that age effects on substance use are mediated by social learning variables. Grade in school sets an age-related social context for behavior, and as such should also set an age-related context in which the social learning mechanisms differentially move some toward conforming and some toward deviant behavior. Substance use was measured by frequency of marijuana use. Consumption increases noticeably from the seventh grade to the eleventh grade, and then declines slightly in the twelfth grade. The curve describing changes in marijuana use from the seventh to the twelfth grade is matched almost exactly by the pattern of changes by grade in the social learning variables of definitions, differential peer association, and reinforcement balance. Both marijuana use and the social learning variables are significantly related to grade in school, at about the same level (for marijuana, $r = .24$; for the three social learning variables, $r = $ to .21 to .26).

Marijuana use is strongly correlated with each of the social learning variables ($r = .58$ to .78). When separate social learning models are run for each grade, the correlation of marijuana use with each of these social learning variables remains high for each grade, and the level of explained variance in marijuana smoking remains at remarkably similar levels in each of the models (tables not shown). Moreover, as shown in the LISREL model in Figure 12.3, the direct effect of Age (measured by grade in school) on marijuana use becomes statistically nonsignificant and is reduced to nearly zero when entered in the same model with the Social

Learning construct (measured by differential reinforcement, differential association, and definition). Grade in school retains a significant direct effect on the social learning variables, and the social learning construct retains a very strong effect on marijuana use, conforming very closely to the relationships predicted by the sssl model. Age produces changes in the social learning variables that in turn make for changes in marijuana use (recognizing, of course, that the cross-sectional model does not show the reciprocal effects of marijuana use in previous grades on the social learning variables in higher grades). The different rates of marijuana use from the seventh to the twelfth grade are a function of the differential probabilities that individuals at different locations in the adolescent age

Figure 12.3   Age and Social Learning in Adolescent Marijuana Use

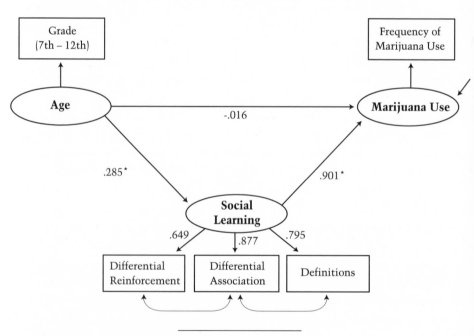

Chi-square (2) = 13.73 (p = .001)
Good-of-fit index = .998
Adjusted good-of-fit index = .985
N = 2,826

structure are exposed to associations, reinforcement, and definitions favorable to substance use and abuse.

We also uncovered significant systematic variations in the rates of adolescent drug and drinking behavior among the different types of communities (rural farm, rural nonfarm, suburban, and urban) included in the Boys Town Study. Theoretically, the social learning process should be operating in each community so that the community-level differences in normative and social structure, traditions, and social control system produce the differences in adolescent behavior because they produce differences in associating with delinquent peers, of having models who use alcohol and other drugs available, in developing definitions favorable to delinquency, of having substance use reinforced, and so on.

> Social learning theory would predict that the same variables explain delinquency equally well across contexts and that any differences in rates of delinquency will merely reflect different levels of reinforcement, association with deviant others, and definitions favorable to deviance found in the respective communities
>
> Communities will have more deviance wherever the diversity makes it easier to associate with deviant others, learn definitions favorable for deviance, and have deviant behavior reinforced by those in one's social environment. . . . Differences in rates of delinquency across communities should only reflect different levels of the learning variables present; there should be no interactions between community contexts and the learning process. (Krohn et al., 1984:357)
>
> Different mean levels of association, definitions, and reinforcement among respondents in the contexts should have accounted for the observed community differentials in use. (Krohn et al., 1984:362)

That is what we found. There were significant differences among the communities in the mean levels of adolescent marijuana and alcohol use (although they did not correspond exactly to a rural-urban distinction, since the highest level was found in the rural-nonfarm community rather than in the urban community) and parallel significant differences among the communities in the mean levels of definitions favorable to use, reinforcement balance, and peer associations. These social learning variables mediated virtually all of the community variations in rate of adolescent substance use. There were some significant interactions of social learning by community context. The model was not perfect, and there remained some impact of community context that could not be completely accounted for by intervening social learning processes. However, community context by itself added no explained variance, and the interaction terms added only 1% to the total 68% of the variance explained by the model for marijuana use. The community context and interaction terms added zero explained variance in the model for alcohol use.

We also examined the models to locate any confounding or interaction effects of class and race, since the communities differed significantly on these two structural dimensions. Including them had no significant effect on the explained variance in any of the models, and there was no significant interaction effect. The strong support given to the sssl model by these findings on the mediation of community context effects on these forms of adolescent deviance by social learning variables is apparent and needs no further comment. (See Elliott et al., 1989, who also found that social learning variables intervened in the effects of urban-rural residence on delinquency.)

COMMUNITY CONTEXT AND SOCIAL LEARNING IN DRINKING AMONG
THE ELDERLY

The Florida study of elderly drinking behavior (see Chapter 9) also provided data relevant to the sssl model. In that study we found noticeable differences among the four communities in rates of alcohol consumption. The proportions of drinkers were 41.5% in Alachua County, 57.1% in Pinellas County, 67.1% in the New Jersey retirement community, and 76.4% in the Florida retirement community. Moreover, 30% of the respondents in the Florida retirement community reported drinking daily, which is more than twice the level of daily drinking in Alachua County and in the retirement community in New Jersey. Clearly, there was systematic variation in level of alcohol consumption by community, proportions of abstainers, amount of daily drinking, and levels of heavy or excessive drinking. Were there systematic structural differences among the communities that could account for these differences in rates?

The level of drinking in a community also reflects differences in the social background, drinking experiences, traditions, and sociodemographic characteristics of its residents. Homogeneity of drinking behavior, as well as homogeneity of sociodemographic characteristics to which drinking behavior is correlated, may be among those social factors that influence the selective process by which people come to live in different communities. In the Florida study, drinking varied by race, sex, marital status, education, income, and occupation. A regression model containing only these sociodemographic variables accounted for about 30% of the variance in frequency of drinking. This finding suggests that sociodemographic composition is another aspect of community context that should be related to the rate of alcohol consumption in that community.

Even though the respondents were all older people, the communities differed systematically in how densely concentrated the residents were in elderly-only communities. The most age-dense was the New Jersey retirement community, which was itself totally surrounded by other elderly-only retirement communities. The Florida retirement community is also age segregated, separated but not far from an age-integrated community; it is age-dense, but not quite so much as the New Jersey community. Although the New Jersey community did not have the highest level of drinking, it had the second highest proportion of drinkers, well above both Alachua and Pinellas counties. The two age-dense communities both had higher levels and frequencies of alcohol consumption than the two age-integrated communities. Of the two age-integrated communities, Pinellas County (with 35% of the population 60 and over) has a greater proportion of older people than Alachua County (with only 10% of the population 60 and over). And it was the latter that had the fewest drinkers among the elderly respondents. Alachua County is smaller and less urbanized, and it is less affected by in-migration than the St. Petersburg area of Pinellas, which is part of the large Tampa/St. Petersburg metropolitan area. Alachua County still maintains many of the traditional religious and other southern community traditions, and this rural-urban difference probably also affects the finding that Alachua County had the fewest drinkers among the elderly respondents. Thus, while not perfectly related, the age density of the community appears to be one factor in drinking among its older residents. We used these differences in concentrations of the elderly as a measure of community context by ranking and assigning an ordinal age-density score to each community. We devised a second measure of community context by aggregating the education and income of their residents (the two sociodemographic variables most strongly related to drinking, $r = .28$ and $.32$, respectively).

We ran regression equations for the social learning models (the full models, as well as each of the subset models) with sociodemographic variables included. This made essentially no difference in the relative effects of the subsets of social learning variables, and made no differences in the total explained variances in the models (tables not shown). In addition, we ran a multiple regression equation for frequency of drinking in the past year that included the sociodemographic variables and each community as a dummy variable. The dummy variables for two of the communities did show statistically significant partial effects. However, the magnitude of the effect was small (B = .05 in each case), and the addition of the community variables and all of the sociodemographic variables added only 1 percent to the variance explained by social learning variables alone. We ran the same equation substituting for the dummy community variables a variable created by coding the four communities on the ordinal scale of age density. The new variable had zero effect. Finally, we ran the analysis only on the two age-heterogeneous communities where probability samples were drawn (N = 677, a high response rate). The amount of variance explained by the model in these two communities was only slightly less (adj R^2 = .56) than for the whole sample, and there were only minor changes in the beta coefficients.

Next, we tested a LISREL model with age density, educational level of the community, and income distribution in the community as indicators of a Community Context as a social structural construct and the social learning constructs of Differential Association, Definitions, and Differential Reinforcement with frequency of individual drinking behavior (including abstinence as the zero value of the drinking variable). In the LISREL model these social learning constructs themselves were treated as different dimensions of a single second-order construct labeled Social Learning. The measurement model had a good fit to the data (X^2 = 3.78, df = 3, P = .44, and adjusted goodness-of-fit index = .99). A structural model was run with the definitions, association, and reinforcement indicators from this social learning model as exogenous, the second-order Social Learning construct as the first endogenous variable, and frequency of yearly and monthly drinking as indicators of the second endogenous construct, Drinking (dependent variable). Again, there was a good fit to the data (a significant X^2 at 45.16 with df = 12, but with a Wheaton index of 3.9).

Then, a good-fitting structural model (Figure 12.4) was run including

Figure 12.4 Community Context and Social Learning in Elderly Drinking

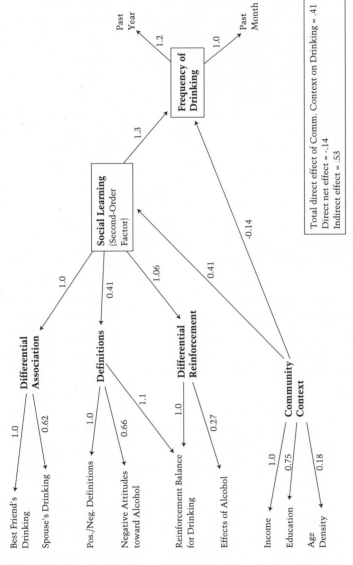

$X^2 = 104$; $df = 33$; $p < .001$; Wheaton Index = 3.15; Adj. Goodness-of-Fit Index = .97; $N = 1410$.
Squared Multiple Correlation for Drinking = .76.
SOURCE: Adapted from Akers and La Greca (1991).

EOT neakercp12

the social learning constructs and a Community Context construct with Age Density, Education, and Income as the indicators. Community Context had a direct effect on Drinking (Beta = .41). This indicates that there is something about each of the communities that directly affects how much drinking takes place in it. This social structural effect may come from the age density and sociodemographic composition of the community that we measured in the model or from other unmeasured community characteristics correlated with them. If the sssl model is correct, however, community context should relate to the social learning process operative at the individual level, which in turn should mediate the impact of community context on drinking behavior.

That is, the community in which one lives makes a difference in his or her drinking because the social and normative context of that community differentially affects the chances that one will differentially associate with other drinkers, develop attitudes favorable to drinking, and receive or perceive differentially rewarding outcomes for drinking. The social learning variables, in turn, are the mechanisms by which community context gets translated down to the individual level of behavior.

The findings supported this expectation. When the social learning constructs were inserted into the model, the direct effect of community context became nonsignificant (Figure 12.4). Community Context retained an indirect relationship to Drinking through the Social Learning construct that is, in fact, somewhat stronger than the original direct affect. The LISREL Beta coefficients showed a strong direct effect of Community Context on the Social Learning second-order construct (B = .58). The social learning construct had an even stronger direct effect on frequency of Drinking among the elderly (B = .95). Thus, as would be expected by the sssl model, the impact of Community Context on drinking patterns among the elderly are primarily felt indirectly through the social learning process. The Social Learning factor explains 74% of the variance in Drinking on its own. The Community Context construct accounts for 24% of the explained variance on its own, but adds only 2% to the total explained variance when placed in the structural model with the social learning constructs. The conclusion to be drawn is that the sssl model is supported. As theoretically expected, the structural variable of community context is mediated through the micro-level process of social learning. Community context has a direct effect on the social learning process, with whom one associates, the normative orientations to which one is exposed and which one internalizes, and how reinforcing one finds alcohol use to be (and perhaps other variables not included in the model), which, in turn, affects one's drinking behavior.

SOCIAL DISORGANIZATION, SOCIAL LEARNING VARIABLES, AND CRIME

There is essentially no research at this time relating any of the theoretical variables of social disorganization, anomie, and conflict to social learning variables and crime. Since the pioneering studies of Shaw and McKay (1942), a great deal of research has been done on the ecology of urban crime and delinquency and social disorganization.[3] Although this research continues to find that arrests, convictions, incarcerations, and other measures of official rates of crime and delinquency are high among people living in neighborhoods and communities that are characterized as socially disorganized, the degree to which the high crime rate in the inner city is the result of social disorganization remains uncertain. Often the research does not measure social disorganization carefully. The very fact that crime and deviance are high within a community, neighborhood, or social area is itself sometimes used, tautologically, as an empirical indicator that the area is socially disorganized (see Bursik's 1988 review of this issue). What physical, economic, population, or family conditions, then, are the best operational measures of social disorganization?

In recent years, social disorganization has received renewed theoretical attention through the work of Robert Bursik, Robert Sampson, and others, who have addressed some of the questions about it (Sampson, 1995). Bursik (1988) points out that Shaw and McKay did not view urban economic and social conditions as the direct causes of crime and delinquency. Rather, they were proposing that these indicators of social disorganization undermine or hinder informal social controls within the community and neighborhood, making it more difficult to sustain patterns of conformity and reduce deviant behavior, which sets the stage for high rates of crime. Therefore, the absence or breakdown of social control is a key component behind the concept of social disorganization, which Bursik contends, ties it to modern social control theory. My argument is that insofar as informal social control entails family socialization, peer interaction, exposure to conforming models, and application of social sanctions to conforming or deviant behavior, then social disorganization's link to social control also links it to social learning. Sampson and Groves (1989) also point out that the indicators of urban decay, economic deprivation, and racial inequality are often used as measures of social disorganization theory without further measuring actual breakdown in social control, lack of social integration and cohesion, or other components of social disorganization itself. Therefore, Sampson and Groves concluded that "while past researchers have examined Shaw and McKay's prediction concerning community change and extra-local influence on delinquency, *no one* has directly tested their theory of social disorganization" (1989:775; emphasis added).

Sampson and Groves (1989) proffered an empirical model of social disorganization that remedied this problem. Their model contains the usual measures of "external" factors affecting social disorganization, such as social class, residential mobility, and family disruption, but then goes beyond these variables to include what they describe as measures of three key components of the concept of social disorganization: community supervision of teenage gangs, informal friendship networks, and participation in formal organizations. Their data from British communities supported this model. They found that most of the external factors were related to social disorganization, as predicted. The links in the model were completed by showing that the measures of social disorganization were good predictors of rates of crime victimization. Though not very adequately, the model also explained the rates of criminal offenses. Delinquent gangs, low level of friendship networks, and low participation in secondary groups are relevant to social learning, but none of the analyses by Sampson and Groves related these indicators of community social disorganization to individual participation in these groups and individual criminal behavior.

More recent research has not followed the Sampson and Groves model of measuring social disorganization directly. Social disorganization continues to be measured indirectly by social conditions in different areas of a city. In a household survey of victimization, E. Britt Patterson (1991) found violent crime in a community to be related to measures of "absolute poverty" (proportion of homes with very low incomes), as well as to measures of residential instability, low social integration, population density, proportion of nonwhite residents, and age composition, but not to measures of relative poverty (income inequality). He concludes that these findings support the hypothesis that poverty, family disorganization, and population density undermine a community's social integration and mechanisms of social control, but he has no measures of social disorganization or breakdown in social control. Warner and Pierce (1993) report strong relationships between rates of telephone calls to police (by victims of assaults, robbery, and burglary) and neighborhood poverty, racial heterogeneity, residential instability, family disruption, and high density of housing units as measures of social disorganization. Again, there are no direct measures of social disorganization as conceptualized by Sampson and Groves, nor are there measures of family or peer associations, definitions, reinforcement, or models.

Adequate tests of the SSSL model will have to go beyond these typical studies of social disorganization to the "multilevel" kind of research done by Simcha-Fagan and Schwartz (1986) and Gottfredson and her colleagues (1991). Simcha-Fagan and Schwartz related community-level measures of family disorganization, economic deprivation, formal and informal control systems, and the existence of a criminal subculture to both self-reported and official delinquency. They found that neither attachment to school nor association with delinquent peers mediated the effects of community disorganization on rates of delinquency.

Gottfredson and her associates (1991) tested social disorganization theory by correlating block-level census data on disrupted families, poverty, unemployment, income, and education with individual-level self-reports of delinquent behavior of interpersonal aggression, theft and vandalism, and drug use. The independent variables accounted for individuals' delinquency, but the relationships were not strong and varied by type of delinquency and gender. Most of the interview items measured social bonding concepts, but two measures relevant to social learning were included. The first was "negative peer influence," measured by two items. The second, "belief in conventional rules," was intended to be a measure of the social bonding concept of belief, but the six items contained some that were neutralizing definitions favorable to delinquency. Both of these variables were significantly related to self-reported delinquency for both boys and girls and mediated the effects of social disorganization on delinquent behavior.

Conclusion

For the most part, these findings from my own and others' research show results that are predicted by the SSSL model. However, there has as yet been so little research on the relationship between social learning and social structure, especially with regard to theoretical variables like social disorganization, expected by the theory that it cannot be said to have been adequately tested. I end, therefore, with a call for more research both on social learning mechanisms and processes in criminal and deviant behavior and on the SSSL model of social structure and social learning in crime.

First, research should continue testing the social learning theory as a processual explanation of criminal and deviant behavior. I have shown how I and others have tested it, and those same approaches can be used. But I also encourage the use and development of other approaches to testing the theory. Research is particularly needed on the imitation variables in a way that produces stronger measures separating them more clearly from the measures of other learning variables. I believe that when this is done, imitation will be found to have a stronger effect than has so far been observed. My work, and that of some others, has tested more or less full models of the theory with a range of measures of association, reinforcement, definitions, and imitation. But too many studies still include only peer association, and too many times even that is not adequately measured. Of course, differential peer association is very important and should not be neglected. However, future research needs to move away from so much reliance on measures of peer association and incorporate more measures of other social learning variables, particularly with regard to the family and other important groups beyond peers. Much more research needs to be done on the sequential and reciprocal effects of social learning variables and deviant behavior. I believe that much progress can continue to be made using cross-sectional data. But longitudinal studies should also be carried out, especially with a view to testing the claims I made in Chapter 6 that predictive models will be more successful if they begin with a clearer focus on identifying and measuring social learning variables than has thus far been done. Much more research is needed testing general social learning models on serious crime in adult samples, white-collar crime, violence, and organized crime. At the same time, there are many areas of noncriminal deviance, such as suicide, sexual deviance, cheating, and problem drinking, where social learning theory has been under-tested or not tested at all. I hope that the brief attention given in Chapter 11 to how accounting for social control and reaction to crime can benefit from social learning theory can be the basis for also expanding social learning research in this area.

Second, I suggest that the SSSL model presented in this chapter be tested for its validity. Such research would, of course, be complementary to the kind of research I have just suggested on social learning processes in deviance without regard to the structural context in which those processes operate. Studies testing SSSL should use both official and unofficial measures of criminal behavior and rates of crime. Future research can build on the studies and the tests I have reviewed in this chapter, but must go beyond them. Multilevel data collection and analyses are needed to test the model adequately, from aggregate, system-level data to individual-level data. The empirical models need to include measures of all of the major sets of variables—social disorganization, group and culture conflict, differential social organization, differential location in the social structure, differential location in primary and other groups, and the social learning variables. As noted above, it is important that the social learning measures include more than differential peer association. The macro-level structural variables should be measured not only at the social area or community level but also at the societal level in cross-cultural studies. Adumbrations of the SSSL model have been in existence for some time, and it is specified here as carefully as I am able to do. Nevertheless, it should be viewed as a work in progress, not as a finished product. I welcome others' critiques, tests, and modifications.

Notes

1. Although derived mainly from social disorganization/anomie and conflict theories (for a specific effort to integrate conflict and social learning theories, see Vold and Bernard, 1986), the structural conditions that would be indicative of social disorganization and conflict overlap with the explanatory variables of a number of structural theories of crime. The element of weak or inadequate social control in social disorganization of the family, community, or society is found in both control theory (informal control) and deterrence theory (formal control). Notions of crime related to conflict and social, economic, or political inequality are found in Marxist, feminist, and radical

theories. The relevance of a cohesive and integrated system for low levels of crime is found in some modified versions of labeling theory, such as Braithwaite's (1989) idea of the reintegrative shaming found in communitarian societies. To the extent that the notion of differential location in the social structure and the concept of social and cultural conflict invokes the existence of subgroups or subcultures within the larger society, there is overlap with subcultural theories. For instance, the subculture-of-violence thesis attempts to explain the high correlation of violent crime with young male, urban, lower-class status (Wolfgang and Ferracuti, 1982) and the high rates of violence in the southern region of the United States (Gastil, 1971).

2. As noted above, I am not interested here in making comparisons with other theories. But one obvious implication of this statement of sssl is that I would be prepared to defend the claim that there is no alternative, nonoverlapping, incompatible explanation of the link between social structure and crime rates that is empirically superior. There are other micro-level theories that can provide plausible links between social structure and crime rates; for instance, Gottfredson and Hirschi (1990:117) claim that their self-control theory explains all crime at all times and under all circumstances, so that it accounts for all the known correlations of crime with sociodemographic and other variables. This implies that low self-control is *the* mediating variable. Gottfredson and Hirschi view self-control theory as incompatible with all "positivistic" theories (under which they classify social learning theory). It remains to be seen if measures of low social control mediate social structural effects on crime rates, but the concepts of social control and self-control are, in fact, not contradictory to social learning theory. "Self-control presumably is a product of socialization and the current circumstances of life" (Gottfredson and Hirschi, 1990:179). Since socialization is itself a social learning process, this statement by Gottfredson and Hirschi recognizes that self-control is itself a product of social learning (Akers, 1991). Any variation and stability in self-control is a function of variations and stabilities in the socialization process, past learning history, and current and anticipated learning contingencies.

3. See Lander (1954), Shaw and McKay (1969), Voss and Petersen (1971), Simcha-Fagan and Schwartz (1986), William Julius Wilson (1987), Sampson and Groves (1989), E. Britt Patterson (1991), Warner and Pierce (1993), and Sampson (1995).

Bibliography

Adler, Patricia, and Peter Adler

1978 "Tinydopers: a case study of deviant socialization," Symbolic Interaction 1:90–105.

Agnew, Robert

1985 "Social control theory and delinquency: a longitudinal test," Criminology 23:47–62.

1991a "The interactive effects of peer variables on delinquency," Criminology 29:47–72.

1991b "A longitudinal test of social control theory and delinquency," Journal of Research in Crime and Delinquency 28:126–156.

1992 "Foundation for a general strain theory of crime and delinquency," Criminology 30:47–88.

1993 "Why do they do? An examination of the intervening mechanisms between 'social control' variables and delinquency," Journal of Research in Crime and Delinquency 30:245–266.

1994 "The techniques of neutralization and violence," Criminology 32:555–580.

Agnew, Robert, and Helene Raskin White

1992 "An empirical test of general strain theory," Criminology 30:475–500.

Akers, Ronald L.

1964 "Socio-economic status and delinquent behavior: a re-test," Journal of Research in Crime and Delinquency 1:38–46.

1965 "Toward a comparative definition of law," Journal of Criminal Law, Criminology, and Police Science 56:301–306.

1968 "Problems in the sociology of deviance: social definitions and behavior," Social Forces 46:455–465.

1973 Deviant Behavior: A Social Learning Approach. Belmont, CA: Wadsworth.

1977 Deviant Behavior: A Social Learning Approach. Second Edition. Belmont, CA: Wadsworth.

1985 Deviant Behavior: A Social Learning Approach. Third Edition. Belmont, CA: Wadsworth. Reprinted 1992. Fairfax, VA: Techbooks.

373

1988 "Social learning and adolescent deviance: theory, research, and prediction of delinquent behavior," Paper presented to the International Conference of The Republic of China and The United States of America on Social and Psychological Factors in Juvenile Delinquency, Taipei, ROC.

1989 "A social behaviorist's perspective on integration of theories of crime and deviance," pp. 23–36 in Steven Messner, Marvin D. Krohn, and Allen Liska, eds., Theoretical Integration in the Study of Deviance and Crime: Problems and Prospects. Albany: SUNY Press.

1990 "Rational choice, deterrence, and social learning theory: the path not taken," Journal of Criminal Law and Criminology 81:653–676.

1991 "Self-control as a general theory of crime," Journal of Quantitative Criminology 7:201–211.

1992a "Linking sociology and its specialties: the case of criminology," Social Forces 71:1–16.

1992b Drugs, Alcohol, and Society: Social Structure, Process, and Policy. Belmont, CA: Wadsworth.

1994 Criminological Theories: Introduction and Evaluation. Los Angeles: Roxbury.

1996 "Is differential association/social learning cultural deviance theory?" Criminology 34:229–248.

1997 Criminological Theories: Introduction and Evaluation. Second Edition. Los Angeles: Roxbury.

Akers, Ronald L., Robert L. Burgess, and Weldon Johnson

1968 "Opiate use, addiction, and relapse," Social Problems 15:459–469.

Akers, Ronald L., and John K. Cochran

1985 "Adolescent marijuana use: a test of three theories of deviant behavior," Deviant Behavior 6:323–346.

Akers, Ronald L., Marvin D. Krohn, Lonn Lanza-Kaduce, and Marcia Radosevich

1979 "Social learning and deviant behavior: a specific test of a general theory," American Sociological Review 44:635–655.

1980 "Social characteristics and self-reported delinquency: differences in extreme types," pp. 48–62 in Gary F. Jensen, ed., Sociology of Delinquency: Current Issues. Beverly Hills, CA: Sage.

Akers, Ronald L., and Anthony J. La Greca

1988 "Alcohol, contact with the legal system, and illegal behavior among the elderly," pp. 51–61 in Belinda McCarthy and Robert Langworthy, eds., Older Offenders. New York: Praeger.

1991 "Alcohol use among the elderly: social learning, community context, and life events," pp. 242–262 in David J. Pittman and Helene Raskin White, eds., Society, Culture, and Drinking Patterns Re-examined. New Brunswick, NJ: Rutgers Center of Alcohol Studies.

Akers, Ronald L., Anthony J. La Greca, John Cochran, and Christine Sellers

1989 "Social learning theory and alcohol behavior among the elderly," Sociological Quarterly 30:625–638.

Akers, Ronald L., Anthony J. La Greca, Christine Sellers, and John Cochran

1987 "Fear of crime and victimization among the elderly in different types of communities," Criminology 25:487–505.

Akers, Ronald L., Anthony J. La Greca, and Christine Sellers

1988 "Theoretical perspectives on deviant behavior among the elderly," pp. 35–50 in Belinda McCarthy and Robert Langworthy, eds., Older Offenders. New York: Praeger.

Akers, Ronald L., and Gang Lee

1996 "A longitudinal test of social learning theory: adolescent smoking," Journal of Drug Issues 26:317–343.

Akers, Ronald L., James Massey, Ronald L. Lauer, and William Clarke

1983 "Are self-reports of adolescent deviance valid? bio-chemical measures, randomized response, and the bogus pipeline in smoking behavior," Social Forces 62:234–251.

Akers, Ronald L., and Ross Matsueda

1989 "Donald Cressey: an intellectual portrait of a criminologist," Sociological Inquiry 29:423–438.

Alder, Christine

1985 "An exploration of self-reported sexually aggressive behavior," Crime and Delinquency 31:306–331.

Anderson, Linda S., Theodore G. Chiricos, and Gordon P. Waldo

1977 "Formal and informal sanctions: a comparison of deterrent effects," Social Problems 25:103–112.

Andrews, D. A.

1980 "Some experimental investigations of the principles of differential association through deliberate manipulations of the structure of service systems," American Sociological Review 45:448–462.

Andrews, Kenneth H., and Denise B. Kandel

1979 "Attitude and behavior: a specification of the contingent consistency hypothesis," American Sociological Review 44:298–310.

Austin, Roy L.

1977 "Commitment, neutralization, and delinquency," pp. 121–137 in Theodore N. Ferdinand, ed., Juvenile Delinquency: Little Brother Grows Up. Beverly Hills, CA: Sage.

Baldwin, John D., and Baldwin, Janice I.

1981 Behavior Principles in Everyday Life. Englewood Cliffs, NJ: Prentice Hall.

Ball, Richard A.

1968 "An empirical exploration of neutralization theory," pp. 255–265 in Mark Lefton, James K. Skipper, and Charles H. McCaghy, eds., Approaches to Deviance. New York: Appleton-Century-Crofts.

Bandura, Albert

1969 Principles of Behavior Modification. New York: Holt, Rinehart, and Winston.

1973 Agression: A Social Learning Analysis. Englewood Cliffs, NJ: Prentice Hall.

1976 Analysis of Delinquency and Aggression. New York: L. Erlbaum Associates, distributed by Halsted Press.

1977a Social Learning Theory. Englewood Cliffs, NJ: Prentice Hall.

1977b "Self-efficacy: toward a unifying theory of behavioral change," Psychological Review 84:191–215.

1983 "Psychological mechanisms of aggression," pp. 1–40 in R. G. Green and Edward Donnerstein, eds., Aggression: Theoretical and Empirical Reviews. New York: Academic Press.

1986a Social Foundations of Thought and Action: A Social Cognitive Theory. Englewood Cliffs, NJ: Prentice Hall.

1986b "Human agency in social cognitive theory," American Psychologist 44: 1175–1184.

1989 "Regulation of cognitive processes through perceived self-efficacy," Developmental Psychology 25:729–735.

1990 "Selective activation and disengagement of moral control," Journal of Social Issues 46:27–46.

in press "Mechanism of moral disengagement in the exercise of moral agency," Journal of Personality and Social Psychology.

Bandura, Albert, and Richard H. Walters

1963 Social Learning and Personality Development. New York: Holt, Rinehart, and Winston.

Barlow, Hugh D.

1987 Introduction to Criminology. Fourth Edition. Boston: Little, Brown.

Barlow, Hugh D., and Theodore N. Ferdinand

1992 Understanding Delinquency. New York: HarperCollins.

Baron, James N., and Reiss, Peter C.

1985 "Same time, next year: aggregate analyses of the mass media and violent behavior," American Sociological Review 50:347–363.

Baron, Larry, and Murray A. Straus

1987 "Four theories of rape: a macrosociological analysis," Social Problems 34:467–488.

Bartusch, Dawn, R. Jeglum, Donald R. Lynam, Terrie E. Moffitt, and Phil A. Silva

1997 "Is age important? testing a general versus a developmental theory of antisocial behavior," Criminology 35:13–48.

Becker, Howard S.

1963 Outsiders: Studies in the Sociology of Deviance. New York: Free Press.

1964 The Other Side. New York: Free Press.

Benda, Brent B.

1994 "Testing competing theoretical concepts: adolescent alcohol consumption," Deviant Behavior 15:375–396.

Benson, Michael L., and Elizabeth Moore

1992 "Are white-collar and common offenders the same? an empirical and theoretical critique of a recently proposed general theory of crime," Journal of Research in Crime and Delinquency 29:251–272.

Bernard, Thomas J.

1987 "Testing structural strain theories," Journal of Research in Crime and Delinquency 24:262–290.

Bernard, Thomas J., and Jeffrey B. Snipes

1995 "Theoretical integration in criminology," pp. 1–48 in Michael Tonry, ed., Crime and Justice. Chicago: University of Chicago Press.

Beschner, George M., and Bovelle, Elliott I.

1985 "Life with heroin: voices of experience," pp. 75–107 in Bill Hanson, George Beschner, James Walter, and Elliott Bovelle, eds., Life with Heroin: Voices from the Inner City. Lexington, MA: Lexington Books.

Blackman, Derek

1974 Operant Conditioning: An Experimental Analysis of Behaviour. London: Methuen and Co.

Blau, Peter

1987 "Microprocess and macrostructure," pp. 83–100 in Karen Cook, ed., Social Exchange Theory. Beverly Hills, CA: Sage.

Blumstein, Alfred, Jacqueline Cohen, Jeffrey A. Roth, and Christy Visher, eds.

1986 Criminal Careers and "Career Criminals." Vol. 1. Washington, DC: National Academy Press.

Blumstein, Alfred, David P. Farrington, and S. Moitra

1985 "Delinquency careers: innocents, desisters, and persisters," pp. 137–168 in Michael Tonry and Norval Morris, eds., Crime and Justice. Vol. 6. Chicago: University of Chicago Press.

Boeringer, Scot

1992 Sexual Coercion among College Males: Assessing Three Theoretical Models of Coercive Sexual Behavior. Ph.D. Dissertation. University of Florida.

Boeringer, Scot, and Ronald L. Akers

1993 "Rape and rape proclivity: a comparison of social learning, social control, and relative deprivation models," unpublished paper, Department of Sociology, University of Florida.

Boeringer, Scot, Constance L. Shehan, and Ronald L. Akers

1991 "Social contexts and social learning in sexual coercion and aggression: assessing the contribution of fraternity membership," Family Relations 40:558–564.

Borgatta, Edgar F., R. Montgomery, and M. L. Borgatta

1982 Alcohol use and abuse, life crisis events, and the elderly. Research on Aging 4:378–408.

Braithwaite, John

1989 Crime, Shame, and Reintegration. Cambridge: Cambridge University Press.

Britt, Chester L.

1992 "Constancy and change in the U.S. age distribution of crime: a test of the 'invariance hypothesis,' " Journal of Quantitative Criminology 8:175–187.

Bruinsma, Gerben J. N.

1992 "Differential association theory reconsidered: an extension and its empirical test," Journal of Quantitative Criminology 8:29–49.

Burgess, Robert L., and Ronald L. Akers

1966a "Are operant principles tautological?" Psychological Record 16:305–312.
1966b "A differential association–reinforcement theory of criminal behavior," Social Problems 14:128–147.

Burgess, Robert L., and Don Bushell, eds.

1969 Behavioral Sociology. New York: Columbia University Press.

Burkett, Steven, and Eric L. Jensen

1975 "Conventional ties, peer influence, and the fear of apprehension: a study of adolescent marijuana use," Sociological Quarterly 16:522–533.

Burkett, Steven R., and Bruce O. Warren

1987 "Religiosity, peer associations, and adolescent marijuana use: a panel study of underlying causal structures," Criminology 25:109–131.

Bursik, Robert J.

1988 "Social disorganization and theories of crime and delinquency: problems and prospects," Criminology 26:519–551.

Burt, Martha R.

1980 "Cultural myths and supports for rape," Journal of Personality and Social Psychology 38:217–230.

Burton, Velmer S., Francis Cullen, David Evans, and R. Gregory Dunaway

1994 "Reconsidering strain theory: operationalization, rival theories, and adult criminality," Journal of Quantitative Criminology 10:213–239.

Bynum, Jack E., and William E. Thompson

1992 Juvenile Delinquency: A Sociological Approach. Boston: Allyn and Bacon.

Capece, Michael

1991 Supervisor Referrals to Employee Assistance Programs. Ph.D. Dissertation. Gainesville: University of Florida.

Capece, Michael, and Ronald L. Akers

1995 "Supervisor referrals to an employee assistance program: a social learning perspective," Journal of Drug Issues 25:341–361.

Carmines, E. G., and J. P. McIver

1981 "Analyzing models with unobserved variables: analysis of covariance structures," pp. 65–115 in G. W. Bohrnstedt and E. F. Borgatta, eds., Social Measurement: Current Issues. Beverly Hills, CA: Sage.

Carmody, T.

1992 "Preventing relapse in the treatment of nicotine addiction: current issues and future directions," Journal of Psychoactive Drugs 24:131–158.

Catalano, Richard F., and J. David Hawkins

in press "The social development model: a theory of anti-social behavior," in J. David Hawkins, ed., Some Current Theories of Delinquency and Crime. New York: Springer-Verlag.

Catalano, Richard F., Rick Kosterman, J. David Hawkins, Michael D. Newcomb, and Robert D. Abbott

1996 "Modeling the etiology of adolescent substance use: a test of the social development model," Journal of Drug Issues 26:429–455.

Catania, A. Charles.

1979 Learning. Englewood Cliffs, NJ: Prentice Hall.

Cernkovich, Stephen A., and Peggy C. Giordano

1992 "School bonding, race, and delinquency," Criminology 30:261–291.

Chadwick-Jones, J. K.

1976 Social Exchange Theory: Its Structure and Influence in Social Psychology. London: Academic Press.

Chance, Paul

1979 Learning and Behavior. Belmont, CA: Wadsworth.

Clark, John P., and Eugene P. Wenninger

1962 "Socio-economic class and area as correlates of illegal behavior among juveniles," American Sociological Review 27:826–834.

Clinard, Marshall B.

1952 The Black Market. New York: Holt, Rinehart, and Winston.

Cloward, Richard, and Lloyd Ohlin

1959 "Illegitimate means, anomie, and deviant behavior," American Sociological Review 24:164–177.
1960 Delinquency and Opportunity. Glencoe, IL: Free Press.

Cochran, John K., and Ronald L. Akers

1989 "Beyond hellfire: an exploration of the variable effects of religiosity on adolescent marijuana and alcohol use," Journal of Research on Crime and Delinquency 26:198–225.

Cohen, Albert K.

1955 Delinquent Boys. Glencoe, IL: Free Press.

Cohen, Albert K., Alfred R. Lindesmith, and Karl F. Schuessler, eds.

1956 The Sutherland Papers. Bloomington: Indiana University Press.

Cohn, Ellen, and David P. Farrington

1994a "Who are the most influential criminologists in the English-speaking world," British Journal of Criminology 34:204–225.

1994b "Who are the most-cited authors and what are the most-cited works in crime and justice," unpublished paper.

1996a "Crime and justice and the criminal justice and criminology literature," pp. 193–228 in Michael Tonry, ed., Crime and Justice. Vol. 20. Chicago: University of Chicago Press.

1996b "Changes in the most-cited scholars in major American criminology and criminal justice journals," unpublished paper, Florida International University.

Comstock, G. A., and E. A. Rubinstein, eds.

1972 Television and Social Behavior. Vols. 1 and 3. Washington, DC: US Government Printing Office.

Conger, Rand

1976 "Social control and social learning models of delinquency: a synthesis," Criminology 14:17–40.

Conger, Rand D., and Ronald L. Simons

1995 "Life-course contingencies in the development of adolescent antisocial behavior: a matching law approach," pp. 55–99 in Terence P. Thornberry, ed., Developmental Theories of Crime and Delinquency. New Brunswick, NJ: Transaction Books.

Cook, R. F., and R. H. Fosen

1971 Pornography and the Sex Offender: Patterns of Exposure and Immediate Arousal Effects of Pornographic Stimuli. Commission on Obscenity and Pornography, Technical Reports. Washington, DC: US Government Printing Office.

Cornish, Derek B., and Ronald V. Clarke, eds.

1986 The Reasoning Criminal: Rational Choice Perspectives on Offending. New York: Springer-Verlag.

Corcoran, Kevin J.

1991 "Efficacy, 'skills,' reinforcement, and choice behavior," American Psychologist 49:155–157.

Craig, Maude, and Selma J. Glick

1963 "Ten years experience with the Glueck Social Prediction Table," Crime and Delinquency 9:249–261.

Craighead, W. Edward, Alan E. Kazdin, and Michael J. Mahoney, eds.

1976 Behavior Modification: Principles, Issues, and Applications. Boston: Houghton Mifflin.

Creechan, James H.

1994 "A test of the general theory of crime: delinquency and school dropouts," pp. 233–256 in James H. Creechan and Robert A. Silverman, eds., Canadian Juvenile Delinquency. Canada: Prentice Hall.

Cressey, Donald R.

1952 "Application and verification of the differential association theory," Journal of Criminal Law, Criminology, and Police Science, 43:43–52.

1953 Other People's Money. Glencoe, IL: Free Press.

1954 "The differential association theory and compulsive crimes," Journal of Criminal Law, Criminology, and Police Science 45:29–40.

1960 "Epidemiology and individual conduct: a case from criminology," Pacific Sociological Review 3:47–58.

Curran, Daniel J., and Claire M. Renzetti

1994 Theories of Crime. Boston: Allyn and Bacon.

Dabney, Dean

1995 "Neutralization and deviance in the workplace: theft of supplies and medicines by hospital nurses," Deviant Behavior 16:313–331.

Davey, Graham

1988 "Trends in human operant theory," pp. 1–14 in Graham Davey and Chris Cullen, eds., Human Operant Conditioning and Behavior Modification. New York: John Wiley and Sons.

Davey, Graham, and Chris Cullen, eds.

1988 Human Operant Conditioning and Behavior Modification. New York: John Wiley and Sons.

Decker, Scott, Richard Wright, and Robert Logie

1993 "Perceptual deterrence among active residential burglars: a research note," Criminology 31:135–147.

DeFleur, Melvin L., and Richard Quinney

1966 "A reformulation of Sutherland's differential association theory and a strategy for empirical verification," Journal of Research in Crime and Delinquency 3:1–22.

Demare, Dano, John Briere, and Hilary Lips

1988 "Violent pornography and self-reported likelihood of sexual aggression," Journal of Research in Personality 22:140–153.

Dembo, Richard, Gary Grandon, Lawrence La Voie, James Schmeidler, and William Burgos

1986 "Parents and drugs revisited: some further evidence in support of social learning theory," Criminology 24:85–104.

Dentler, Robert, and Lawrence Monroe

1961 "Social correlates of early adolescent theft," American Sociological Review 26:733–743.

Department of Health and Human Services

1981 Alcohol and Health. Washington, DC: US Government Printing Office.

Dinitz, Simon, Frank R. Scarpitti, and Walter C. Reckless

1962 "Delinquency vulnerability: a cross-group and longitudinal analysis," American Sociological Review 27:515–517.

Dishion, Thomas J., Gerald R. Patterson, and Kathryn A. Kavanagh

1992 "An experimental test of the coercion model: linking theory, measurement, and intervention," pp. 253–282 in Joan McCord and Richard E. Tremblay, eds., Preventing AntiSocial Behavior: Interventions from Birth through Adolescence. New York: Guilford Press.

Donnerstein, Edward, and Daniel Linz

1986 "Mass media sexual violence and the male viewer," American Behavioral Scientist 29:601–618.

1995 "The media," pp. 237–266 in James Q. Wilson and Joan Petersilia, eds., Crime. San Francisco: ICS Press.

Dull, R. Thomas

1983 "Friends' use and adult drug and drinking behavior: a further test of differential association theory," Journal of Criminal Law and Criminology 74:1608–1619.

Dunford, Frank W., and Delbert S. Elliott

1984 "Identifying career offenders using self-reported data," Journal of Research in Crime and Delinquency 21:57–86.

Dutile, Ferdinand, Cleon Foust, and D. Robert Webster

1981 Early Childhood Intervention and Juvenile Delinquency. Lexington, MA: D. C. Heath and Company.

Elliott, Delbert S.

1994 "Serious violent offenders: onset, developmental course, and termination," Criminology 32:1–22.

Elliott, Delbert, Franklyn Dunford, and David Huizinga

1987 "The identification and prediction of career offenders utilizing self-reported and official data," pp. 90–121 in J. Burchard and S. Burchard, eds., Prevention of Delinquent Behavior. Newbury Park, CA: Sage.

Elliott, Delbert S., David Huizinga, and Suzanne S. Ageton

1985 Explaining Delinquency and Drug Use. Beverly Hills, CA: Sage.

1989 Multiple Problem Youth: Delinquency, Substance Use and Mental Health Problems. New York: Springer-Verlag.

Elliott, Delbert S., and Scott Menard

1991 "Delinquent friends and delinquent behavior: temporal and developmental patterns," The Institute of Behavioral Science, University of Colorado.

in press "Delinquent friends and delinquent behavior: temporal and developmental patterns," in David Hawkins, ed., Current Theories of Crime and Deviance. New York: Springer-Verlag.

Emerson, Richard N.

1962 "Power-dependence relations," American Sociological Review 27:31–43.

1972a "Exchange theory, part I: a psychological basis for social exchange," pp. 38–57 in Joseph Berger, Morris Zelditch, Jr., and Bo Anderson, eds., Sociological Theories in Progress. Vol. 2. Boston: Houghton Mifflin.

1972b "Exchange theory, part II: exchange relations and networks," pp. 58–87 in Joseph Berger, Morris Zelditch, Jr., and Bo Anderson, eds., Sociological Theories in Progress. Vol. 2. Boston: Houghton Mifflin.

1981 "Social exchange theory," pp. 30–65 in Morris Rosenberg and Ralph Turner, eds., Social Psychology. New York: Basic Books.

Empey, LaMar T., and Mark Stafford

1991 American Delinquency: Its Meaning and Construction. Belmont, CA: Wadsworth.

Ensminger, M. E., S. G. Kellam, and B. R. Rubin

1983 "School and family origins of delinquency: comparisons by sex," pp. 73–98 in K. T. Van Dusen and S. A. Mednick, eds., Antecedents of Aggression and Antisocial Behavior. Boston: Kluwer-Nijhoff.

Epling, W. Frank, and W. David Pierce

1988 "Applied behavior analysis: new directions from the laboratory," pp. 43–58 in Graham Davey and Chris Cullen, eds., Human Operant Conditioning and Behavior Modification. New York: John Wiley and Sons.

Esbensen, Finn-Aage, and Delbert S. Elliott

1994 "Continuity and discontinuity in illicit drug use: patterns and antecedents," Journal of Drug Issues 24:75–97.

Esbensen, Finn-Aage, and David Huizinga

1993 "Gangs, drugs, and delinquency in a survey of urban youth," Criminology 31:565–590.

Fagan, Jeffrey, and Sandra Wexler

1987 "Family origins of violent delinquents," Criminology 24:439–471.

Farnworth, Margaret, and Michael J. Leiber

1989 "Strain theory revisited: economic goals, educational means, and delinquency," American Sociological Review 54:263–274.

Farrington, David

1983 "Offending from 10 to 25 years of age," pp. 17–38 in K. T. Van Dusen and S. A. Mednick, eds., Prospective Studies of Crime and Delinquency. Boston: Kluwer-Nijhoff.

1985 "Predicting self-reported and official delinquency," pp. 150–173 in D. Farrington and R. Tarling, eds., Prediction in Criminology. New York: State University of New York Press.

Farrington, David P., and D. J. West

1981 "The Cambridge Study in delinquent development," in Sarnoff A. Mednick and A. E. Baert, eds., Prospective Longitudinal Research. Oxford: Oxford University Press.

Feldman, Michael P.

1977 Criminal Behavior: A Psychological Analysis. London: Wiley.

Ferraro, Kenneth F.

1995 Fear of Crime: Interpreting Victimization Risk. Albany: State University of New York Press.

Ferraro, Kenneth F., and Randy L. LaGrange

1987 "The measurement of fear of crime," Sociological Inquiry 57:70–101.

1992 "Are older people most afraid of crime? reconsidering age differences in fear of victimization," Journal of Gerontology 47:S233–S244.

Fischer, Gloria J.

1986 "College student attitudes toward forcible date rape: I: cognitive predictors," Archives of Sexual Behavior 15:457–466.

Fishbein, D. H., and S. E. Pease

1996 The Dynamics of Drug Abuse. Boston: Allyn and Bacon.

Fitzgerald, J. L., and Harold A. Mulford

1981 "The prevalence and extent of drinking in Iowa, 1979," Journal of Studies on Alcohol 42:38–47.

Gardner, L., and Donald J. Shoemaker

1989 "Social bonding and delinquency: a comparative analysis," Sociological Quarterly 30:481–500.

Garrett-Gooding, Joy, and Richard Senter, Jr.

1987 "Attitudes and acts of sexual aggression on a university campus," Sociological Inquiry 57:348–371.

Gartner, Rosemary, and Robert Nash Parker

1990 "Cross-national evidence on homicide and the age structure of the population," Social Forces 69:351–371.

Gastil, Raymond D.

1971 "Homicide and a regional culture of violence," American Sociological Review 36:412–427.

Gaylord, Mark S., and John F. Galliher

1988 The Criminology of Edwin Sutherland. New Brunswick, NJ: Transaction.

Gibbons, Don C.

1994 Talking about Crime and Criminals: Problems and Issues in Theory Development in Criminology. Englewood Cliffs, NJ: Prentice Hall.

Gibbons, Don, and Marvin D. Krohn

1986 Delinquent Behavior. Fourth Edition. Englewood Cliffs, NJ: Prentice Hall.

Gilmore, Samuel

1992 "Culture," pp. 404–411 in Edgar F. Borgatta and Marie L. Borgatta, eds., Encyclopedia of Sociology. New York: Macmillan.

Glantz, M.

1982 "Predictions of elderly drug abuse," pp. 7–16 in D. M. Petersen and F. J. Whittington, eds., Drugs, Alcohol, and Aging. Dubuque, IA: Kendall/Hunt.

Glaser, Daniel

1956 "Criminality theories and behavioral images," American Journal of Sociology 61:433–444.

1960 "Differential association and criminological prediction," Social Problems 8:6–14.

1978 Crime in Our Changing Society. New York: Holt.

Glueck, Sheldon, and Eleanor Glueck

1950 Unraveling Juvenile Delinquency. Cambridge, MA: Harvard University Press.

1959 Predicting Delinquency and Crime. Cambridge, MA: Harvard University Press.

1968 Delinquents and Non-Delinquents in Perspective. Cambridge, MA: Harvard University Press.

1970 Toward a Typology of Juvenile Delinquency. New York: Grune and Stratton.

1974 Of Delinquency and Crime: A Panorama of Years of Search and Research. Springfield, IL: Charles C. Thomas.

Goldstein, M. J., H. S. Kant, L. L. Judd, C. J. Rice, and R. Green

1971 Exposure to Pornography and Sexual Behavior in Deviant and Nondeviant Groups. Commission on Obscenity and Pornography, Technical Reports. Washington, DC: US Government Printing Office.

Gomme, Ian M.

1985 "Predictors of status and criminal offences among male and female adolescents in an Ontario community," Canadian Journal of Criminology 2:219–236.

Goode, Erich

1993 Drugs in American Society. Fourth Edition. New York: McGraw-Hill.

Googins, B., and N. Kurtz

1981 "Factors inhibiting supervisory referrals to occupational alcoholism intervention programs," Journal of Studies on Alcohol 41:1196–1208.

Gottfredson, Denise C., Richard J. McNeil, III, and Gary Gottfredson

1991 "Social area influences on delinquency: a multilevel analysis," Journal of Research in Crime and Delinquency 28:197–226.

Gottfredson, Michael, and Travis Hirschi

1987 "The methodological adequacy of longitudinal research on crime," Criminology 25:581–614.

1990 A General Theory of Crime. Stanford, CA: Stanford University Press.

Grasmick, Harold G., and Donald E. Green

1980 "Legal punishment, social disapproval, and internalization as inhibitors of illegal behavior," Journal of Criminal Law and Criminology 71:325–335.

Grasmick, Harold G., Charles R. Tittle, Robert J. Bursik, Jr., and Bruce J. Arneklev

1993 "Testing the core empirical implications of Gottfredson and Hirschi's general theory of crime," Journal of Research in Crime and Delinquency 30:5–29.

Greenberg, David F.

1985 "Age, crime, and social explanation," American Journal of Sociology 91: 1–21.

1988 "The controversial age-crime relationship," Paper presented to the International Conference of The Republic of China and The United States of America on Social and Psychological Factors in Juvenile Delinquency, Taipei, ROC.

1994 "The historical variability of the age-crime relationship," Journal of Quantitative Criminology 10:361–373.

Grusec, Joan E.

1992 "Social learning theory and developmental psychology: the legacies of Robert Sears and Albert Bandura," Developmental Psychology 28:776–786.

Gwartney-Gibbs, P. A., J. Stockard, and S. Bohmer

1987 "Learning courtship aggression: the influence of parents, peers, and personal experience," Family Relations 36:276–282.

Hamblin, Robert L.

1979 "Behavioral choice and social reinforcement: step function versus matching," Social Forces 57:1141–1156.

Hamblin, Robert L., and John H. Kunkel, eds.

1977 Behavioral Theory in Sociology: Essays in Honor of George C. Homans. New Brunswick, NJ: Transaction Books.

Hanushek, Eric A., and John E. Jackson

1977 Statistical Methods for Social Scientists. New York: Academic Press.

Hardt, Robert H., and S. Peterson-Hardt

1977 "On determining the quality of the delinquency self-report methods," Journal of Research in Crime and Delinquency 14:247–257.

Hartung, Frank E.

1965 Crime, Law, and Society. Detroit: Wayne State University Press.

Hathaway, Starke, and Paul E. Meehl

1951 An Atlas for the Clinical Use of the MMPI. Minneapolis: University of Minnesota Press.

Hathaway, Starke, and Elio Monachesi

1953 Analyzing and Predicting Juvenile Delinquency with the MMPI. Minneapolis: University of Minnesota Press.

1957 "The personalities of predelinquent boys," Journal of Criminal Law, Criminology, and Police Science 48:149–163.

1963 Adolescent Personality and Behavior. Minneapolis: University of Minnesota Press.

Hawkins, J. David, Richard F. Catalano, and J. Y. Miller

1992 "Risk and protective factors for alcohol and other drug problems in adolescence and early adulthood: implications for substance abuse prevention," Psychological Bulletin 112:64–105.

Hawkins, J. David, Richard F. Catalano, Diane M. Morrison, Julie O'Donnell, Robert D. Abbott, and L. Edward Day

1992 "The Seattle Social Development Project: Protective factors and problem behaviors," pp. 139–161 in Joan McCord and Richard E. Tremblay, eds., Preventing AntiSocial Behavior: Interventions from Birth through Adolescence. New York: Guilford Press.

Hawkins, J. David, and Joseph G. Weis

1985 "The social development model: an integrated approach to delinquency prevention," Journal of Primary Prevention 6:73–97.

Hawkins, J. David, and T. Lam

1987 "Teacher practices, social development and delinquency," pp. 241–274 in J. D. Burchard and S. N. Burchard, eds., Primary Prevention of Psychopathology. Vol. 10. The Prevention of Delinquent Behavior. Newbury Park, CA: Sage.

Heimer, Karen

1997 "Socioeconomic status, subcultural definitions, and violent delinquency," Social Forces 75:799–833.

Heimer, Karen, and Ross Matsueda

1994 "Role-taking, role-commitment, and delinquency: a theory of differential social control," American Sociological Review 59:365–390.

Herrnstein, Richard J.

1961 "Relative and absolute strength of response as a function of frequency of reinforcement," Journal of the Experimental Analysis of Behavior 4:267–272.

1970 "On the law of effect," Journal of the Experimental Analysis of Behavior 13:243–266.

Hertzog, C., and J. R. Nesselroade

1987 "Beyond autoregressive models: some implications of the trait-state distinction for the structural modeling of developmental change," Child Development 58:93–109.

Hewitt, John P., and Randall Stokes

1975 "Disclaimers," American Sociological Review 40:1–11.

Hindelang, Michael J.

1973 "Causes of delinquency: a partial replication and extension," Social Problems 20:471–487.

Hindelang, Michael J., Travis Hirschi, and Joseph Weiss

1981 Measuring Delinquency. Beverly Hills, CA: Sage.

Hirschi, Travis

1969 Causes of Delinquency. Berkeley: University of California Press.
1996 "Theory without ideas: reply to Akers," Criminology 34:249–256.

Hirschi, Travis, and Michael Gottfredson

1979 "Introduction: the Sutherland tradition in criminology," pp. 7–19 in Travis Hirschi and Michael Gottfredson, eds., Understanding Crime: Current Theory and Research. Beverly Hills, CA: Sage.
1983 "Age and the explanation of crime," American Journal of Sociology 89:552–584.
1993 "Commentary: testing the general theory of crime," Journal Research in Crime and Delinquency 30:47–54.

Hirschi, Travis, and Hanan C. Selvin

1967 Delinquency Research: An Appraisal of Analytic Methods. New York: Free Press.

Hollinger, Richard C.

1991 "Neutralizing in the workplace: an empirical analysis of property theft and production deviance," Deviant Behavior 12:169–202.

Holman, John E., and James F. Quinn

1992 Criminology: Applying Theory. St. Paul, MN: West.

Holzer, C., L. Robins, J. Meyers, M. Weissman, G. Tischler, P. Leaf, J. Anthony, and P. Bednarski

1984 "Antecedents and correlates of alcohol abuse and dependence in the elderly," pp. 217–244 in George Maddox, Lee Robins, and Nathan Rosenberg, eds., Nature and Extent of Alcohol Abuse among the Elderly. Washington, DC: US Government Printing Office.

Homans, George C.

1974 Social Behavior: Its Elementary Forms. Revised Edition. New York: Harcourt Brace Jovanovich.

Horn, Margo

1986 " 'Gee, Officer Krupke, what are we to do?': the politics of professing and the prevention of delinquency, 1909–1940," pp. 57–81 in Steven Spitzer and Andrew Scull, eds., Research in Law, Deviance, and Social Control: A Research Annual. Vol. 8. Greenwich, CT: JAI Press.

Huizinga, David, Finn-Aage Esbensen, and Anne Wylie Weither

1991 "Are there multiple paths to delinquency?" Journal of Criminal Law and Criminology 82:83–118.

Inciardi, James A., Ruth Horowitz, and Anne E. Pottiger

1993 Street Kids, Street Drugs, Street Crime: An Examination of Drug Use and Serious Delinquency in Miami. Belmont, CA: Wadsworth.

Jackson, Elton F., Charles R. Tittle, and Mary Jean Burke

1986 "Offense-specific models of the differential association process," Social Problems 33:335–356.

Jacoby, Joseph E., ed.

1994 Classics of Criminology. Second Edition. Prospect Heights, IL: Waveland Press.

Jang, Sung-Joon, and Marvin D. Krohn

1995 "Developmental patterns of sex differences in delinquency among African American adolescents: a test of the sex-invariance hypothesis," Journal of Quantitative Criminology 11:195–222.

Janson, Carl-Gunnar

1983 "Delinquency among metropolitan boys," pp. 147–180 in K. T. Van Dusen and S. A. Mednick, eds., Prospective Studies of Crime and Delinquency. Boston: Kluwer-Nijhoff.

Jeffery, C. Ray

1965 "Criminal behavior and learning theory," Journal of Criminal Law, Criminology, and Police Science 56:294–300.

Jensen, Gary F.

1972 "Parents, peers, and delinquent action: a test of the differential association perspective," American Journal of Sociology 78:63–72.

Jensen, Gary F., Maynard L. Erickson, and Jack P. Gibbs

1978 "Perceived risk of punishment and self-reported delinquency," Social Forces 57:57–78.

Jensen, Gary F., and Dean G. Rojek

1992 Delinquency and Youth Crime. Second Edition. Prospect Heights, IL: Waveland Press.

Jessor, Richard, and Shirley L. Jessor

1977 Problem Behavior and Psychosocial Development. New York: Academic Press.

Jessor, Richard, Shirley L. Jessor, and John Finney

1973 "A social psychology of marijuana use: longitudinal studies of high school and college youth," Journal of Personality and Social Psychology 26:1–15.

Johnson, Richard E.

1979 Juvenile Delinquency and Its Origins: An Integrated Theoretical Approach. New York: Cambridge University Press.

Johnson, Richard E., Anastasios C. Marcos, and Stephen J. Bahr

1987 "The role of peers in the complex etiology of adolescent drug use," Criminology 25:323–340.

Jöreskog, K. G.

1971 "Statistical analysis of sets of congeneric tests," Psychometrika 36:109–133.

Jöreskog, K. G., and D. Sörbom

1989 LISREL VII: A Guide to the Program and Application. Second Edition. Chicago: SPSS.

Junger-Tas, Josine

1992 "An empirical test of social control theory," Journal of Quantitative Criminology 8:9–28.

Jussim, Lee, and D. Wayne Osgood

1989 "Influence and similarity among friends: an integrative model applied to incarcerated adolescents," Social Psychology Quarterly 52:98–112.

Kandel, Denise B.

1974 "Interpersonal influences on adolescent illegal drug use," pp. 207–240 in Eric Josephson and Eleanor E. Carrol, eds., Drug Use: Epidemiological and Sociological Approaches. New York: Wiley.

1978 "Homophily, selection, and socialization in adolescent friendships," American Journal of Sociology 84:427–436.

1996 "The parental and peer contexts of adolescent deviance: an algebra of interpersonal influences," Journal of Drug Issues 26:289–316.

Kandel, Denise B., and Israel Adler

1982 "Socialization into marijuana use among French adolescents: a cross-cultural comparison with the United States," Journal of Health and Social Behavior 23:295–309.

Kandel, Denise B., and Kenneth Andrews

1987 "Processes of adolescent socialization by parents and peers," International Journal of the Addictions 22:319–342.

Kandel, Denise, and Mark Davies

1991 "Friendship networks, intimacy, and illicit drug use in young adulthood: a comparison of two competing theories," Criminology 29:441–469.

Kandel, Elizabeth, and Sarnoff Mednick

1991 "Perinatal complications predict violent offending," Criminology 29: 519–529.

Kanin, Eugene J.

1985 "Date rapists: differential sexual socialization and relative deprivation," Archives of Sexual Behavior 14:219–231.

Kaplan, Howard B.

1975 Self-Attitudes and Deviant Behavior. Pacific Palisades, CA: Goodyear Press.
1996 "Empirical validation of the applicability of an integrative theory of deviant behavior to the study of drug use," Journal of Drug Issues 26:345–377.

Kaplan, Howard B., Richard J. Johnson, and C. A. Bailey

1987 "Deviant peers and deviant behavior: further elaboration of a model," Social Psychology Quarterly 50:277–284.

Kaplan, Howard B., and Cynthia Robbins

1983 "Testing a general theory of deviant behavior in longitudinal perspective," pp. 117–146 in K. T. Van Dusen and S. A. Mednick, eds., Prospective Studies of Crime and Delinquency. Boston: Kluwer-Nijhoff.

Keane, Carl, Paul S. Maxim, and James J. Teevan

1993 "Drinking and driving, self-control, and gender: testing a general theory of crime," Journal of Research in Crime and Delinquency 30:30–45.

Kempf, Kimberly

1987 "Specialization and the criminal career," Criminology 25:399–420.
1993 "The empirical status of Hirschi's control theory," pp. 143–185 in Freda Adler and William S. Laufer, eds., New Directions in Criminological Theory. New Brunswick, NJ: Transaction.

Kennedy, Leslie W., and Robert A. Silverman

1985 "Significant others and fear of crime among the elderly," International Journal of Aging and Human Development 20:241–255.

Klein, Stephen B., and Robert R. Mowrer, eds.

1989 Contemporary Learning Theories: Instrumental Conditioning Theory and the Impact of Biological Constraints on Learning. Hillsdale, NJ: Erlbaum Associates.

Kohlberg, Lawrence

1964 "Development of children's orientations toward a moral order: I. Sequence in the development of moral thought," Vita Humana 6:11–33.
1969 "Stage and sequence: the cognitive-developmental approach to socialization," pp. 347–481 in D. A. Goslin, ed., Handbook of Socialization Theory and Research. Chicago: Rand-McNally.
1981 The Philosophy of Moral Development: Moral Stages and the Idea of Justice. San Francisco: Harper and Row.

Kornhauser, Ruth Rosner

1978 Social Sources of Delinquency: An Appraisal of Analytic Models. Chicago: University of Chicago Press.

Koss, Mary P., and Christine A. Gidycz

1985 "Sexual experiences survey: reliability and validity," Journal of Consulting and Clinical Psychology 53:422–423.

Koss, Mary P., Christine A. Gidycz, and Nadine Wisniewski

1987 "The scope of rape: incidence and prevalence of sexual aggression and victimization in a national sample of higher education students," Journal of Consulting and Clinical Psychology 55:162–170.

Koss, Mary P., and Cheryl J. Oros

1982 "Sexual experiences survey: a research instrument investigating sexual aggression and victimization," Journal of Consulting and Clinical Psychology 50:455–457.

Kroeber, Alfred, and Talcott Parsons

1958 "The concepts of culture and of social system," American Sociological Review 23:582–83.

Krohn, Marvin D.

1974 "An investigation of the effect of parental and peer associations on marijuana use: an empirical test of differential association theory," pp. 75–89 in Marc Riedel and Terence P. Thornberry, eds., Crime and Delinquency: Dimensions of Deviance. New York: Praeger.

Krohn, Marvin D., and Ronald L. Akers

1977 "An alternative view of the labeling versus psychiatric perspectives on social reaction to mental illness," Social Forces 56:341–61.

Krohn, Marvin D., Ronald L. Akers, Marcia J. Radosevich, and Lonn Lanza-Kaduce

1982 "Norm qualities and adolescent drinking and drug behavior," Journal of Drug Issues 12:343–359.

Krohn, Marvin D., Lonn Lanza-Kaduce, and Ronald L. Akers

1984 "Community context and theories of deviant behavior: an examination of social learning and social bonding theories," Sociological Quarterly 25: 353–371.

Krohn, Marvin D., Alan J. Lizotte, Terence P. Thornberry, Carolyn Smith, and David McDowall

1996 "Reciprocal causal relationships among drug use, peers, and beliefs: a five-wave panel model," Journal of Drug Issues 26:405–428.

Krohn, Marvin D., and James L. Massey

1980 "Social control and delinquent behavior: an examination of the elements of the social bond," Sociological Quarterly 21:529–543.

Krohn, Marvin D., James L. Massey, William F. Skinner, and Ronald M. Lauer

1983 "Social bonding theory and adolescent cigarette smoking: a longitudinal analysis," Journal of Health and Social Behavior 24:337–349.

Krohn, Marvin D., William F. Skinner, James L. Massey, and Ronald L. Akers

1985 "Social learning theory and adolescent cigarette smoking: a longitudinal study," Social Problems 32:455–473.

Krohn, Marvin D., William F. Skinner, Mary Zielinski, and Michelle Naughton

1989 "Elaborating the relationship between age and adolescent cigarette smoking," Deviant Behavior 10:105–129.

Kunkel, John H.

1970 Society and Economic Growth: A Behavioral Perspective of Social Change. New York: Oxford University Press.

Lab, Steven

1988 Crime Prevention: Approaches, Practices, and Evaluation. Cincinnati: Anderson.

Labouvie, Erich

1996 "Maturing out of substance use: selection and self-correction," Journal of Drug Issues 26:457–476.

LaGrange, Randy L., and Kenneth F. Ferraro

1989 "Assessing age and gender differences in perceived risk and fear of crime," Criminology 27:697–719.

LaGrange, Randy L., Kenneth F. Ferraro, and Michael Supancic

1992 "Perceived risk and fear of crime: role of social and physical incivilities," Journal of Research in Crime and Delinquency 29:311–334.

LaGrange, Randy L., and Helene Raskin White

1985 "Age differences in delinquency: a test of theory," Criminology 23:19–46.

La Greca, Anthony J., Ronald L. Akers, and Jeffrey Dwyer

1988 "Life events and alcohol behavior among older adults," Gerontologist 4:552–558.

Land, Kenneth C., Patricia L. McCall, and Lawrence E. Cohen

1990 "Structural covariates of homicide rates: are there any invariances across time and social space?" American Journal of Sociology 95:922–963.

Lander, Bernard

1954 Towards an Understanding of Juvenile Delinquency. New York: Columbia University Press.

Lane, Katherine E., and Patricia A. Gwartney-Gibbs

1985 "Violence in the context of dating and sex," Journal of Family Issues 6:45–59.

Lang, Alan R., and Elizabeth M. Michalec

1990 "Expectancy effects in reinforcement from alcohol," pp. 192–232 in Miles Cox, ed., Why People Drink. New York: Gardner.

Lanza-Kaduce, Lonn

1988 "Perceptual deterrence and drinking and driving among college students," Criminology 26:321–342.

Lanza-Kaduce, Lonn, Ronald L. Akers, Marvin D. Krohn, and Marcia Radosevich

1982 "Conceptual and analytical models in testing social learning theory: reply to Stafford and Ekland-Olsen and Strictland," American Sociological Review 47:169–173.

1984 "Cessation of alcohol and drug use among adolescents: a social learning model," Deviant Behavior 5:79–96.

Lanza-Kaduce, Lonn, and Richard Hollinger

1994 "Change and stability in cheating: exploring social learning theory," Paper presented to the annual meeting of the American Society of Criminology, Miami, November 1994.

Lanza-Kaduce, Lonn, and Mary Klug

1986 "Learning to cheat: the interaction of moral-development and social learning theories," Deviant Behavior 7:243–259.

Larsen, Donald D., and Abu-Laban, Baha

1968 "Norm qualities and deviant drinking behavior," Social Problems 15:441–449.

Lasley, James R.

1988 "Toward a control theory of white-collar offending," Journal of Quantitative Criminology 4:347–359.

Laub, John H., and Robert J. Sampson

1993 "Turning points in the life course: why change matters to the study of crime," Criminology 31:301–326.

Lauer, Ronald M., Ronald L. Akers, James Massey, and William Clarke

1982 "The evaluation of cigarette smoking among adolescents: the Muscatine study," Preventive Medicine 11:417–428.

Lauritsen, Janet L.

1993 "Sibling resemblance in juvenile delinquency: findings from the national youth survey," Criminology 31:387–410.

Lee, Ching-Mei

1989 The Study of Social Learning and Social Bonding Variables as Predictors of Cigarette Smoking Behavior among Ninth-Grade Male Students in Taipei, Taiwan, The Republic of China. Ph. D. Dissertation. Department of School and Community Health, University of Oregon, Eugene.

Lefkowitz, M. M., L. D. Eron, L. O. Walder, and L. R. Huesmann

1972 "Television violence and childhood aggression: a follow-up study," pp. 35–135 in G. A. Comstock and E. A. Rubinstein, eds., Television and Social Behavior. Vol. 3. Washington, DC: US Government Printing Office.

Lemert, Edwin M.

1953 "An isolation and closure theory of naive check forgery," Journal of Criminal Law, Criminology, and Police Science 44:296–307.

1958 "The behavior of the systematic check forger," Social Problems 6:141–149.

Lersch, Kim M.

1993 "The effects of social learning concepts on academic dishonesty," unpublished paper, Department of Sociology, University of Florida, Gainesville.

Lewis, Dan A., and Greta Salem

1986 Fear of Crime: Incivility and the Production of a Social Problem. New Brunswick, NJ: Transaction.

Liebert, Robert M.

1972 "Television and social learning: some relationships between viewing violence and behaving aggressively," pp. 1–41 in George A. Comstock and Eli A. Rubinstein, eds., Television and Social Behavior Vol. 2. Washington, DC: US Government Printing Office.

Lilly, J. Robert, Francis T. Cullen, and Richard A. Ball

1989 Criminological Theory: Context and Consequences. Newbury Park, CA: Sage.

Linz, Daniel

1989 "Exposure to sexually explicit materials and attitudes towards rape: a comparison of study results," Journal of Sex Research 26:50–84.

Liska, Allen E.

1969 "Uses and misuses of tautologies in social psychology," Sociometry 33:444–457.

1971 "Aspirations, expectations, and delinquency: stress and additive models," Sociological Quarterly 12:99–107.

1987 Perspectives on Deviance. Englewood Cliffs, NJ: Prentice Hall.

Liska, Allen E., and William Baccaglini

1990 "Feeling safe by comparison: crime in the newspaper," Social Problems 37:360–374.

Loeber, Rolf, and Thomas J. Dishion

1983 "Early predictors of male delinquency: a review," Psychological Bulletin 94:68–99.

1987 "Antisocial and delinquent youths: methods for their early identification," pp. 75–89 in J. D. Burchard and Sara Burchard, eds., Prevention of Delinquent Behavior. Newbury Park, CA: Sage.

Loeber, Rolf, and M. LeBlanc

1990 "Toward a developmental criminology," pp. 375–473 in Michael Tonry and Norvel Morris, eds., Crime and Justice: A Review of Research. Vol. 12. Chicago: University of Chicago Press.

Loeber, Rolf, and Magda Stouthamer-Loeber

1986 "Family factors as correlates and predictors of juvenile conduct problems and delinquency," pp. 29–149 in Michael Tonry and Norval Morris, eds., Crime and Justice. Vol. 7. Chicago: University of Chicago Press.

1987 "Prediction," pp. 325–382 in Herbert C. Quay, ed., Handbook of Juvenile Delinquency. New York: Wiley.

Loeber, Rolf, Magda Stouthamer-Loeber, Welmoet Van Kammen, and David P. Farrington

1991 "Initiation, escalation, and desistance in juvenile offending and their correlates," Journal of Criminal Law and Criminology 82:36–82.

Lundman, Richard J.

1993 Prevention and Control of Juvenile Delinquency. Second Edition. New York: Oxford University Press.

Lyman, Stanford M., and Marvin B. Scott

1970 A Sociology of the Absurd. New York: Appleton-Century-Crofts.

Maddox, George L., Lee D. Robins, and Nathan Rosenberg, eds.

1984 Nature and Extent of Alcohol Problems among the Elderly. Washington, DC: US Government Printing Office.

Magnusson, D., H. Stattin, and A. Duner

1983 "Aggression and criminality in a longitudinal perspective," pp. 277–302 in K. T. Van Dusen and S. A. Mednick, eds., Antecedents of Aggression and Antisocial Behavior. Boston: Kluwer-Nijhoff.

Mahoney, Michael J.

1974 Cognition and Behavior Modification. Cambridge, MA: Ballinger.

Malamuth, Neil M.

1981 "Rape proclivity among males," Journal of Social Issues 29:138–157.

1989a "The attraction to sexual aggression scale: part one," Journal of Sex Research 26:26–49.

1989b "The attraction to sexual aggression scale: part two," Journal of Sex Research 26:324–354.

Malamuth, Neil M., and James V. P. Check

1985 "The effects of aggressive pornography on beliefs in rape myths: individual differences," Journal of Research in Personality 19:299–320.

Marcos, Anastasios C., and Stephen J. Bahr

1988 "Control theory and adolescent drug use," Youth and Society 19:395–425.

Marcos, Anastasios C., Stephen J. Bahr, and Richard E. Johnson

1986 "Test of a bonding/association theory of adolescent drug use," Social Forces 65:135–161.

Marshall, W. L., and H. E. Barbaree

1984 "A behavioral view of rape," International Journal of Law and Psychiatry 7:51–77.

Massey, James L., and Marvin D. Krohn

1986 "A longitudinal examination of an integrated social process model of deviant behavior," Social Forces 65:106–134.

Matsueda, Ross L.

1982 "Testing control theory and differential association," American Sociological Review 47:489–504.

1988 "The current state of differential association theory," Crime and Delinquency 34:277–306.

Matsueda, Ross L., and Karen Heimer

1987 "Race, family structure, and delinquency: a test of differential association and social control theories," American Sociological Review 52:826–840.

Matthews, Victor M.

1968 "Differential identification: an empirical note," Social Problems 14:376–83.

Matza, David

1964 Delinquency and Drift. New York: Wiley.

Matza, David, and Gresham M. Sykes

1961 "Juvenile delinquency and subterranean values," American Sociological Review 26:712–719.

McCord, Joan

in press The Cambridge-Somerville Study: Thirty Years Later. New York: Springer-Verlag.

1991a "Family relationships, juvenile delinquency, and adult criminality," Criminology 29:397–418.

1991b "The cycle of crime and socialization practices," Journal of Criminal Law and Criminology 82:211–228.

McCord, Joan, and John H. Laub, eds.

1995 Contemporary Masters in Criminology. New York: Plenum Press.

McCord, William, and Joan McCord

1959 Origins of Crime. New York: Columbia University.

McCord, Joan, and Richard E. Tremblay, eds.

1992 Preventing AntiSocial Behavior: Interventions from Birth through Adolescence. New York: Guilford Press.

McDowell, J. J.

1982 "The importance of Herrnstein's mathematical statement of the law of effect for behavior therapy," American Psychologist 37:771–779.

McGee, Zina T.

1992 "Social class differences in parental and peer influence on adolescent drug use," Deviant Behavior 13:349–372.

Mednick, Sarnoff, and K. O. Christiansen, eds.

1977 Biosocial Basis of Criminal Behavior. New York: Gardner Press.

Mednick, Sarnoff, William F. Gabrielli, Jr., and Barry Hutchings

1983 "Genetic influence in criminal behavior: evidence from an adoption cohort," pp. 39–56 in K. T. Van Dusen and S. A. Mednick, eds., Prospective Studies of Crime and Delinquency. Boston: Kluwer-Nijhoff.

Meier, Robert, Steven Burkett, and Carol Hickman

1984 "Sanctions, peers, and deviance: preliminary models of a social control process," Sociological Quarterly 25:67–82.

Meier, Robert F., and Weldon T. Johnson

1977 "Deterrence as social control: legal and extralegal production of conformity," American Sociological Review 42:292–304.

Menard, Scott, and Delbert S. Elliott

1990 "Longitudinal and cross-sectional data collection and analysis in the study of crime and delinquency," Justice Quarterly 7:11–55.

1994 "Delinquent bonding, moral beliefs, and illegal behavior: a three-wave panel model," Justice Quarterly 11:173–188.

Merton, Robert K.

1938 "Social structure and anomie," American Sociological Review 3:672–682.

1957 Social Theory and Social Structure. Glencoe, IL: Free Press.

Messner, Steven F.

1988 "Merton's 'Social structure and anomie': the road not taken," Deviant Behavior 9:33–53.

Messner, Steven, Marvin D. Krohn, and Allen Liska, eds.

1989 Theoretical Integration in the Study of Deviance and Crime: Problems and Prospects. Albany: SUNY Press

Messner, Steven F., and Richard Rosenfeld

1994 Crime and the American Dream. Belmont, CA: Wadsworth.

Meyers, A. R., E. Goldman, R. Hingson, N. Scotch, and T. Mangione

1981–82 "Evidence of cohort and generational differences in drinking behavior of older adults," International Journal of Aging and Human Development 14:31–44.

Michaels, J. W., and T. D. Miethe
1989 "Applying theories of deviance to academic cheating," Social Science Quarterly 70:870–885.

Millenson, J. R., and Julian C. Leslie
1979 Principles of Behavior Analysis. New York: Macmillan.

Miller, Walter B.
1958 "Lower class culture as a generating milieu of gang delinquency," Journal of Social Issues 14:5–19.

Minor, W. William
1980 "The neutralization of criminal offense," Criminology 18:103–120.
1981 "Techniques of neutralization: a reconceptualization and empirical examination," Journal of Research in Crime and Delinquency 18:295–318.
1984 "Neutralization as a hardening process: considerations in the modeling of change," Social Forces 62:995–1019.

Mizruchi, Ephraim H., and Robert Perruci
1962 "Norm qualities and differential effects of deviant behavior," American Sociological Review 27:391–399.

Moffitt, Terrie E.
1993 "Adolescence-limited and life-course-persistent antisocial behavior: a developmental taxonomy," Psychological Review 100:674–701.

Molm, Linda D.
1981 "The legitimacy of behavioral theory as a sociological perspective," American Sociologist 16:153–165.

Monahan, John D.
1981 "Childhood predictors of adult criminal behavior," pp. 11–21 in F. N. Dutile, C. H. Foust, and D. R. Webster, eds., Early Childhood Intervention and Juvenile Delinquency. Lexington, MA: Lexington Books.

Morris, Edward K., and Curtis J. Braukmann, eds.
1987 Behavioral Approaches to Crime and Delinquency: A Handbook of Application, Research, and Concepts. New York: Plenum Press.

Murphy, William D., Emily M. Coleman, and Mary R. Haynes
1986 "Factors related to coercive sexual behavior in a nonclinical sample of males," Violence and Victims 1:255–278.

Murray, John P., Eli A. Rubinstein, and George A. Comstock, eds.
1972 Television and Social Behavior. Vol. 3. Washington, DC: US Government Printing Office.

Nagin, Daniel, and David P. Farrington
1992a "The stability of criminal potential from childhood to adulthood," Criminology 30:235–260.
1992b "The onset and persistence of offending," Criminology 30:501–523.

Nagin, Daniel S., David P. Farrington, and Terrie E. Moffitt

1995 "Life-course trajectories of different types of offenders," Criminology 33:111–140.

Nagin, Daniel S., and Raymond Paternoster

1991 "On the relationship of past to future participation in delinquency," Criminology 29:163–189.

Nam, Charles B., and M. G. Powers

1983 The Socioeconomic Approach to Status Measurement. Houston: Cap and Gown.

National Institute on Alcohol Abuse and Alcoholism

1982 "Alcohol problems in the elderly compounded by many factors," Information and Feature Service 103 (Dec.):1.

Nolan, Margretta

1994 Adolescents and Alcohol: A Social Learning Approach. Senior Thesis. Department of Psychology, University College, Dublin, Ireland.

Nye, F. Ivan

1958 Family Relationships and Delinquent Behavior. New York: Wiley.

O'Donnell, Julie, J. David Hawkins, and Robert D. Abbott

1993 "Predicting avoidance of later problem behavior among aggressive boys," Social Development Research Group, University of Washington, Seattle.

Orcutt, James D.

1983 Analyzing Deviance. Homewood, IL: Dorsey.
1987 "Differential association and marijuana use: a closer look at Sutherland (with a little help from Becker)," Criminology 25:341–358.

Pallone, Nathaniel J., and James J. Hennessy

1992 Criminal Behavior: A Process Psychology Analysis. New Brunswick, NJ: Transaction.

Paternoster, Raymond, and Robert Brame

1997 "Multiple routes to delinquency? a test of developmental and general theories of crime," Criminology 35:49–84.

Paternoster, Raymond, Linda E. Saltzman, Gordon P. Waldo, and Theodore G. Chiricos

1983 "Perceived risk and social control: do sanctions really deter?" Law and Society Review 17:457–480.

Patterson, E. Britt

1991 "Poverty, income inequality, and community crime rates," Criminology 29:755–776.

Patterson, Gerald R.

1975 Families: Applications of Social Learning to Family Life. Champaign, IL: Research Press.

1982 A Social Learning Approach, vol. 3: Coercive Family Process. Eugene, OR: Castalia.

1995 "Coercion as a basis for early age of onset for arrest," pp. 81–105 in Joan McCord, ed., Coercion and Punishment in Long-Term Perspectives. Cambridge: Cambridge University Press.

1996 "Some characteristics of a development theory for early-onset delinquency," pp. 81–124 in Mark F. Lenzenweger and Jeffrey J. Haugaard, eds., Frontiers of Developmental Psychopathology. New York: Oxford University Press.

Patterson, G. R., D. Capaldi, and L. Bank

1991 "The development and treatment of childhood aggression," pp. 139–168 in D. Pepler and R. K. Rubin, eds., The Development and Treatment of Childhood Aggression. Hillsdale, IL: Erlbaum.

Patterson, Gerald R., and Patricia Chamberlain

1994 "A functional analysis of resistance during parent training therapy," Clinical Psychology: Science and Practice 1:53–70.

Patterson, G. R., B. D. Debaryshe, and E. Ramsey

1989 "A developmental perspective on antisocial behavior," American Psychologist 44:329–335.

Patterson, Gerald R., and Thomas J. Dishion

1985 "Contributions of families and peers to delinquency," Criminology 23:63–79.

Patterson, G. R., and J. B. Reid

1973 "Intervention for families of aggressive boys: a replication study," Behaviour Research and Therapy 11:383–394.

Patterson, Gerald R., John B. Reid, and Thomas J. Dishion

1992 Antisocial Boys. Eugene, OR: Castalia.

Patterson, G. R., J. B. Reid, R. Q. Jones, and R. E. Conger

1975 A Social Learning Approach to Family Intervention. Vol. 1. Eugene, OR: Castalia.

Pearl, David, Lorraine Bouthilet, and Joyce Lazar, eds.

1982 Television and Behavior: Ten Years of Scientific Progress and Implications for the Eighties. Rockville, MD: National Institute of Mental Health.

Petersen, David M., and F. J. Whittington

1977 "Drug use among the elderly: a review," Journal of Psychedelic Drugs 9:25–37.

Phillips, David P.

1982 "The behavioral impact of violence in the mass media: a review of the evidence from laboratory and non-laboratory investigations," Sociology and Social Research 66:387–398.

1983 "The impact of mass media violence on US homicides," American Sociological Review 48:560–568.

Phillips, David P., and Hensley, John E.

1984 "When violence is rewarded or punished: the impact of mass media stories on homicide," Journal of Communication 34:101–116.

Pittman, David J.

1967 "International overview: social and cultural factors in drinking patterns," pp. 3–20 in David J. Pittman, ed., Alcoholism. New York: Harper and Row.

Pittman, David J., and Helene Raskin White, eds.

1991 Society, Culture, and Drinking Patterns Re-examined. New Brunswick, NJ: Rutgers Center of Alcohol Studies.

Pomerleau, O. F., and C. S. Pomerleau

1988 "A biobehavioral view of substance abuse and addiction," pp. 117–139 in Stanton Peele, ed., Visions of Addiction. Lexington, MA: Heath.

Poole, Eric D., and Robert M. Regoli

1979 "Parental support, delinquent friends, and delinquency: a test of interaction effects," Journal of Criminal Law and Criminology 70:188–193.

Powers, Edwin, and Helen Witmer

1951 An Experiment in the Prevention of Delinquency. New York: Columbia University Press.

Premack, David

1965 "Reinforcement theory," in David Levine, ed., Nebraska Symposium on Motivation. Vol 13. Lincoln: University of Nebraska Press.

Radosevich, Marcia, Lonn Lanza-Kaduce, Ronald L. Akers, and Marvin D. Krohn

1979 "The sociology of adolescent drug and drinking behavior: a review of the state of the field: part I," Deviant Behavior 1:15–35.

Ray, O., and C. Ksir

1993 Drugs, Society, and Human Behavior. St. Louis: Mosby.

Reckless, Walter C.

1961 "A new theory of delinquency and crime," Federal Probation 25:42–46.

Reckless, Walter C., Simon Dinitz, and Ellen Murray

1956 "Self concept as an insulator against delinquency," American Sociological Review 21:744–746.

1957 "The 'good' boy in a high delinquency area," Journal of Criminal Law, Criminology, and Police Science 48:18–26.

Reed, Gary E., and Peter Cleary Yeager

1996 "Organizational offending and neoclassical criminology: challenging the reach of a general theory of crime," Criminology 34:357–382.

Reid, Sue Titus

1988 Crime and Criminology. Fifth Edition. New York: Holt, Rinehart.

Reiss, Albert J., Jr.

1951a "Delinquency as the failure of personal and social control," American Sociological Review 16:196–207.

1951b "Unraveling juvenile delinquency, II: an appraisal of the research methods," American Journal of Sociology 57:115–120.

Reiss, Albert J., Jr., and Albert Lewis Rhodes

1961 "The distribution of juvenile delinquency in the social class structure," American Sociological Review 26:720–732.

Rest, James R.

1974 "The cognitive-developmental approach to morality: the state of the art," Counseling and Values 18:64–78.

1979 Development in Judging Moral Issues. Minneapolis: University of Minnesota Press.

Ritzer, George

1992 Sociological Theory. Third Edition. New York: McGraw-Hill.

Rivera, George F., and Robert M. Regoli

1987 "Sexual victimization experiences of sorority women," Sociology and Social Research 72:39–42.

Robins, Lee N.

1966 Deviant Children Grow Up: A Sociological and Psychiatric Study of Sociopathic Personality. Baltimore: Williams and Williams.

Robins, Lee N., W. M. Bates, and Patricia O'Neal

1962 "Adult drinking patterns of former problem children," pp. 395–412 in David J. Pittman and Charles R. Snyder, eds., Society, Culture, and Drinking Patterns. New York: John Wiley & Sons.

Robins, L. N., J. E. Helzer, J. Croughan, and K. S. Ratcliff

1981 "National Institute of Mental Health Diagnostic Interview Schedule: its history, characteristics, and validity," Archives of General Psychiatry 38:381–389.

Robins, Lee N., and Shirley Hill

1966 "Assessing the contribution of family structure, class, and peer groups to juvenile delinquency," Journal of Criminal Law, Criminology, and Police Science 57:325–334.

Rotter, Julian

1954 Social Learning and Clinical Psychology. Englewood Cliffs, NJ: Prentice Hall.

Rowe, David C.

1985 "Sibling interaction and self-reported delinquent behavior: a study of 265 twin pairs," Criminology 23:223–240.

Rowe, David C., and Bill L. Gulley

1992 "Sibling effects on substance use and delinquency," Criminology 30: 217–234.

Rubin, Sol

1951 "Unraveling juvenile delinquency, I: illusions in a research project using matched pairs," American Journal of Sociology 57:107–114.

Rushton, J. Philippe

1980 Altruism, Socialization, and Society. Englewood Cliffs, NJ: Prentice Hall.

1982 "Television and prosocial behavior," pp. 248–255 in David Pearl, Lorraine Bouthilet, and Joyce Lazar, eds., Television and Behavior: Ten Years of Scientific Progress and Implications for the Eighties. Rockville, MD: National Institute of Mental Health.

Sampson, Robert J.

1995 "The community," pp. 193–216 in James Q. Wilson and Joan Petersilia, eds., Crime. San Francisco: ICS Press.

Sampson, Robert J., and W. Byron Groves

1989 "Community structure and crime: testing social-disorganization theory," American Journal of Sociology 94:774–802.

Sampson, Robert J., and John H. Laub

1993 Crime in the Making: Pathways and Turning Points through Life. Cambridge, MA: Harvard University Press.

Scarpitti, Frank, Ellen Murray, Simon Dinitz, and Walter Reckless

1960 "The good boy in a high-delinquency area: four years later," American Sociological Review 23:555–558.

Schuessler, Karl, ed. and intro.

1973 Edwin H. Sutherland: On Analyzing Crime. Chicago: University of Chicago Press.

Scott, John Finley

1971 Internalization of Norms: A Sociological Theory of Moral Commitment. Englewood Cliffs, NJ: Prentice Hall.

Scully, Diana

1990 Understanding Sexual Violence: A Study of Convicted Rapists. New York: Unwin Hyman.

Scully, Diana, and Joseph Moralla

1984 "Convicted rapists' vocabulary of motives: excuses and justifications," Social Problems 31:530–544.

Sellers, Christine S., and Thomas L. Winfree

1990 "Differential associations and definitions: a panel study of youthful drinking behavior," International Journal of the Addictions 25:755–771.

Sellin, Thorsten

1938 Culture Conflict and Crime. New York: Social Science Research Council.

Shannon, Lyle W.

1978 "A longitudinal study of delinquency and crime," pp. 121–146 in Charles Wellford, ed., Quantitative Studies of Criminology. Beverly Hills, CA: Sage.

1980 "Assessing the relationship of adult criminal careers to juvenile careers," pp. 232–246 in C. Abt, ed., Problems in American Social Policy Research. Cambridge, MA: Abt Books.

1982 Assessing the Relationship of Adult Criminal Careers to Juvenile Careers. Washington, DC: US Government Printing Office.

Shaplin, Judson T., and David V. Tiedman

1951 "Comment on the juvenile delinquency prediction tables in the Gluecks' Unraveling Juvenile Delinquency," American Sociological Review 16:544–548.

Shavit, Yossi, and Arye Rattner

1988 "Age, crime, and the early life course," American Journal of Sociology 93:1457–1470.

Shaw, Clifford R., and Henry D. McKay

1942 Juvenile Delinquency and Urban Areas. Chicago: University of Chicago Press.

1969 Juvenile Delinquency and Urban Areas. Revised Edition. Chicago: University of Chicago Press.

Shaw, Clifford R., and others

1929 Delinquency Areas. Chicago: University of Chicago Press.

Shively, Michael, and Julie A. Lam

1991 "Sampling methods and admissions of sexual aggression among college men," Deviant Behavior 12:345–360.

Shoemaker, Donald J.

1990 Theories of Delinquency: An Examination of Explanations of Delinquent Behavior. Second Edition. New York: Oxford University Press.

Shoham, S. Giora, and John Hoffman

1991 A Primer in the Sociology of Crime. New York: Harrow and Heston.

Short, James F.

1957 "Differential association and delinquency," Social Problems 4:233–239.

1958 "Differential association with delinquent friends and delinquent behavior," Pacific Sociological Review 1:20–25.

1960 "Differential association as a hypothesis: problems of empirical testing," Social Problems 8:14–25.

Siegel, Larry J., and Joseph J. Senna

1991 Juvenile Delinquency: Theory, Practice, and Law. Fourth Edition. St. Paul, MN: West.

Simcha-Fagan, Ora

1979 "The prediction of delinquent behavior over time: sex-specific patterns related to official and survey-reported delinquent behavior," in R. G. Simmons, ed., Research in Community and Mental Health. Greenwich, CT: JAI.

Simcha-Fagan, Ora, and Joseph E. Schwartz

1986 "Neighborhood and delinquency: an assessment of contextual effects," Criminology 24:667–704.

Simons, Ronald L., C. Wu, Rand D. Conger, and F. O. Lorenz

1994 "Two routes to delinquency: differences between early and late starters in the impact of parenting and deviant peers," Criminology 32:247–276.

Skinner, B. F.

1953 Science and Human Behavior. New York: Macmillan.
1959 Cumulative Record. New York: Appleton-Century-Crofts.
1971 Beyond Freedom and Dignity. New York: Knopf.
1974 About Behaviorism. New York: Knopf.

Skinner, William F., James L. Massey, Marvin D. Krohn, and Ronald M. Lauer

1985 "Social influences and constraints on the initiation and cessation of adolescent tobacco use," Journal of Behavioral Medicine 8:353–368.

Skogan, Wesley, and Michael G. Maxfield

1981 Coping with Crime: Individual and neighborhood reactions. Beverly Hills, CA: Sage.

Smart, G., and C. B. Liban

1982 "Predictors of problem drinking among elderly, middle-aged and youthful drinkers," pp. 43–53 in David M. Petersen and F. J. Whittington, eds., Drugs, Alcohol, and Aging. Dubuque, IA: Kendall/Hunt.

Smeaton, George, and Donn Byrne

1987 "The effects of R-rated violence and erotica: individual differences, and victim characteristics on rape proclivity," Journal of Research in Personality 21:171–184.

Snyder, James J., and Gerald R. Patterson

1995 "Individual differences in social aggression: a test of a reinforcement model of socialization in the natural environment," Behavior Therapy 26:371–391.

Spear, Sherilyn, and Ronald L. Akers

1988 "Social learning variables and the risk of habitual smoking among adolescents: the Muscatine Study," American Journal of Preventive Medicine 4:336–348.

Spivack, George, and Norma Cianci

1987 "High-risk early behavior pattern and later delinquency," pp. 44–74 in J. Burchard and S. Burchard, eds., Prevention of Delinquent Behavior. Newbury Park, CA: Sage.

Staats, Arthur

1964 Human Learning. New York: Holt, Rinehart, Winston.
1975 Social Behaviorism. Homewood, IL: Dorsey.

Stafford, Mark C., and Sheldon Ekland-Olson

1982 "On social learning and deviant behavior: a reappraisal of the findings," American Sociological Review 47:167–169.

Stafford, Mark C., and Omer R. Galle

1984 "Victimization rates, exposure to risk, and fear of crime," Criminology 22:173–185.

Stafford, Mark C., and Mark Warr

1993 "A reconceptualization of general and specific deterrence," Journal of Research in Crime and Delinquency 30:123–135.

Steffensmeier, Darrell J., E. A. Allen, M. D. Harer, and Cathy Streifel

1989 "Age and the distribution of crime," American Journal of Sociology 94:803–831.

Stitt, B. Grant, and David J. Giacopassi

1992 "Trends in the connectivity of theory and research in criminology," Criminologist 17:1, 3–6.

Streib, Gordon F., W. Edward Folts, and Anthony J. La Greca

1984 "Entry into retirement communities: process and related problems," Research on Aging 6:257–272.

Strictland, Donald E.

1982 Social learning and deviant behavior: a specific test of a general theory: a comment and critique," American Sociological Review 47:162–167.

Stumphauzer, Jerome S.

1986 Helping Delinquents Change: A Treatment Manual of Social Learning Approaches. New York: Haworth Press.

Sutherland, Edwin H.

1924 Criminology. Philadelphia: J. B. Lippincott.

1934 Principles of Criminology. Second Edition. Philadelphia: J. B. Lippincott.

1937 The Professional Thief. Chicago: University of Chicago Press.

1939 Principles of Criminology. Third Edition. Philadelphia: J. B. Lippincott.

1940 "White collar criminality," American Sociological Review 5:1–12.

1947 Principles of Criminology. Fourth Edition. Philadelphia: J. B. Lippincott.

1949 White-collar Crime. New York: Holt, Rinehart, Winston.

1956 The Sutherland Papers. Edited by Albert K. Cohen, Alfred R. Lindesmith, and Karl F. Shcuessler. Bloomington: Indiana University Press.

1961 White-collar Crime. Paperback Edition with Introduction by Donald R. Cressey. New York: Holt, Rinehart, Winston.

1973 On Analyzing Crime. Edited with an Introduction by Karl Schuessler. Chicago: University of Chicago Press.

Sutherland, Edwin H., and Donald R. Cressey

1955 Principles of Criminology. Fifth Edition. Chicago: J. B. Lippincott.

1960 Principles of Criminology. Sixth Edition. Philadelphia: J. B. Lippincott.

1970 Criminology. Eighth Edition. Philadelphia: J. B. Lippincott

1974 Criminology. Ninth Edition. Philadelphia: J. B. Lippincott.

1978 Criminology. Tenth Edition. Philadelphia: J. B. Lippincott.

Sutherland, Edwin H., Donald R. Cressey, and David F. Luckenbill

1992 Principles of Criminology. Eleventh Edition. Dix Hills, NY: General Hall.

Swenson, Leland C.

1980 Theories of Learning: Traditional Perspectives/Contemporary Developments. Belmont, CA: Wadsworth.

Sykes, Gresham, and David Matza

1957 "Techniques of neutralization: a theory of delinquency," American Journal of Sociology 22:664–670.

Tait, C. D., and E. F. Hodges

1972 "Follow-up study of the Glueck Table applied to a school population of problem boys and girls between the ages of five and fourteen," pp. 49–59 in Sheldon Glueck and Eleanor Glueck, eds., Identification of Pre-Delinquents. New York: Intercontinental Medical Book.

Tarter, Donald E.

1979 Turning Behavior Inside Out. Washington, DC: University Press of America.

Taylor, Ian, Paul Walton, and Jock Young

1973 The New Criminology. New York: Harper and Row.

Taylor, Ralph B., and Margaret Hale

1986 "Testing alternative models of fear of crime," Criminology 77:151–189.

Thomas, Charles W., and John R. Hepburn

1983 Crime, Criminal Law, and Criminology. Dubuque, IA: Wm. C. Brown.

Thomas, William I., and Dorothy S. Thomas

1928 The Child in America: Behavior Problems and Programs. New York: Knopf.

Thompson, Travis, and John G. Grabowski

1972 Reinforcement Schedules and Multioperant Analysis. New York: Appleton-Century-Crofts.

Thornberry, Terence P.

1989 "Reflections on the advantages and disadvantages of theoretical integration," pp. 51–60 in Steven F. Messner, Marvin D. Krohn, and Allen E. Liska, eds., Theoretical Integration in the Study of Deviance and Crime. Albany: State University of New York Press.

Thornberry, Terence P., Alan J. Lizotte, Marvin D. Krohn, Margaret Farnworth, and Sung Joon Jang

1991 "Testing interactional theory: an examination of reciprocal causal relationships among family, school, and delinquency," Journal of Criminal Law and Criminology 82:3–33.

1994 "Delinquent peers, beliefs, and delinquent behavior: a longitudinal test of interactional theory," Criminology 32:47–84.

Thornberry, Terence, M. Moore, and R. L. Christian

1985 "The effect of dropping out of high school on subsequent criminal behavior," Criminology 23:3–18.

Tittle, Charles R.

1980 Sanctions and Social Deviance. New York: Praeger.

1995 Control Balance: Toward a General Theory of Deviance. Boulder, CO: Westview Press.

Tittle, Charles R., Mary Jean Burke, and Elton F. Jackson

1986 "Modeling Sutherland's theory of differential association: toward an empirical clarification," Social Forces 65:405–432.

Tittle, Charles R., and David A. Ward

1993 "The interaction of age with the correlates and causes of crime," Journal of Quantitative Criminology 9:3–53.

Toby, Jackson

1957 "Social disorganization and stake in conformity: complementary factors in the predatory behavior of hoodlums," Journal of Criminal Law, Criminology, and Police Science 48:12–17.

1965 "An evaluation of early identification and intensive treatment programs for predelinquents," Social Problems 13:160–175.

Tremblay, R. E., B. Masse, D. Perron, M. LeBlanc, A. E. Schwartzman, and J. E. Ledingham

1992 "Early disruptive behavior, poor school achievement, delinquent behavior and delinquent personality: longitudinal analyses," Journal of Consulting and Clinical Psychology 60:64–72.

Trice, Harrison M.

1966 Alcoholism in America. New York: McGraw-Hill.

Trice, Harrison, and Janice M. Beyer

1984 "Work-related outcomes of the constructive-confrontation strategy in a job-based alcoholism program," Journal of Studies on Alcohol 45:393–404.

Trice, Harrison, and Paul M. Roman

1978 Spirits and Demons at Work: Alcohol and Other Drugs on the Job. Second Edition. Ithaca, NY: Cornell University Press.

Troyer, Ronald J., and Gerald F. Markle

1983 Cigarettes: The Battle over Smoking. New Brunswick, NJ: Rutgers University Press.

Ullman, Leonard P., and Leonard Krasner

1969 A Psychological Approach to Abnormal Behavior. Englewood Cliffs, NJ: Prentice Hall.

Urberg, K. A., C. Cheng, and S. Shyu

1991 "Grade change in peer influence on adolescent cigarette smoking: A comparison of two measures," Addictive Behaviors 16:21–28.

Van Dusen, K. T., and S. A. Mednick, eds.

1983 Prospective Studies of Crime and Delinquency. Boston: Kluwer-Nijhoff.

Van Dusen, Katherine T., Sarnoff A. Mednick, William F. Gabrielli, and Barry Hutchings

1983 "Social class and crime in an adoption cohort," Journal of Criminal Law and Criminology 74:249–269.

Visher, Christy A., Pamela K. Lattimore, and Richard L. Linster

1991 "Predicting the recidivism of serious youthful offenders using survival models," Criminology 29:329–366.

Vold, George B.

1958 Theoretical Criminology. New York: Oxford University Press.

Vold, George B., and Thomas J. Bernard

1986 Theoretical Criminology. Third Edition. New York: Oxford University Press.

Voss, Harwin

1963 "The predictive efficiency of the Glueck Social Prediction Table," Journal of Criminal Law, Criminology, and Police Science 54:421–430.

1964 "Differential association and reported delinquent behavior: a replication," Social Problems 12:78–85.

1969 "Differential association and containment theory: a theoretical convergence," Social Forces 47:381–391.

Voss, Harwin, and David M. Petersen, eds.
1971 Ecology, Crime, and Delinquency. New York: Appleton-Century-Crofts.

Warner, Barbara D., and Glenn L. Pierce
1993 "Reexamining social disorganization theory using calls to the police as a measure of crime," Criminology 31:493–518.

Warr, Mark
1990 "Dangerous situations: social context and fear of victimization," Social Forces 68:891–907.
1993a "Parents, peers, and delinquency," Social Forces 72:247–264.
1993b "Age, peers, and delinquency," Criminology 31:17–40.
1996 "Organization and instigation in delinquent groups," Criminology 34:11–38.

Warr, Mark, and Mark Stafford
1991 "The influence of delinquent peers: what they think or what they do?" Criminology 4:851–866.

Wells, Edward, and Joseph H. Rankin
1988 "Direct parental controls and delinquency," Criminology 26:263–285.

Weis, Joseph G., and J. David Hawkins
1981 Preventing Delinquency. Report of the National Juvenile Justice Assessment Centers. Washington, DC: US Government Printing Office.

Werner, E. E., and R. S. Smith
1982 Vulnerable, but Invincible: Children and Youth. New York: McGraw-Hill.

Werner, Emmy E.
1987 "Vulnerability and resiliency in children at risk for delinquency: a longitudinal study from birth to young adulthood," pp. 16–43 in J. Burchard and S. Burchard, eds., Prevention of Delinquent Behavior. Newbury Park, CA: Sage.

West, Donald J.
1969 Present Conduct and Future Delinquency. London: Heinemann.
1982 Delinquency: Its Roots, Careers, and Prospects. London: Heinemann.

West, Donald J., and David P. Farrington
1973 Who Becomes Delinquent? London: Heinemann.
1977 The Delinquent Way of Life. London: Heinemann.

White, Helene Raskin, Marsha E. Bates, and Valerie Johnson
1991 "Learning to drink: familial, peer, and media influences," pp. 177–197 in David J. Pittman and Helene Raskin White, eds., Society, Culture, and Drinking Patterns Re-examined. New Brunswick, NJ: Rutgers Center of Alcohol Studies.

White, Helene R., Valerie Johnson, and A. Horowitz
1986 "An application of three deviance theories for adolescent substance use," International Journal of the Addictions 21:347–366.

White, Helene Raskin, Robert J. Pandina, and Randy L. LaGrange

1987 "Longitudinal predictors of serious substance use and delinquency," Criminology 25:715–740.

White, Jennifer, Terrie E. Moffitt, Felton Earls, Lee Robins, and Phil A. Silva

1990 "How early can we tell? predictors of childhood conduct disorder and adolescent delinquency," Criminology 28:507–534.

Whitehead, Paul C., and Reginald G. Smart

1972 "Validity and reliability of self-reported drug use," Canadian Journal of Criminology and Corrections 14:1–8.

Wiatrowski, Michael D., David B. Griswold, and Mary K. Roberts

1981 "Social control theory and delinquency," American Sociological Review 46:525–541.

Williams, Frank P., and Marilyn D. McShane

1988 Criminological Theory. Englewood Cliffs, NJ: Prentice Hall.
1993 Criminology Theory: Selected Classic Readings. Cincinnati: Anderson.

Wilson, James Q.

1991 "Thinking about cohorts," Journal of Criminal Law and Criminology 82:119–124.

Wilson, James Q., and Richard J. Herrnstein

1985 Crime and Human Nature. New York: Simon and Schuster.

Wilson, James Q., and Joan Petersilia, eds.

1995 Crime. San Francisco: ICS Press.

Wilson, K., R. Faison, and G. M. Britton

1983 Cultural aspects of male sex aggression. Deviant Behavior, 4:241–255.

Wilson, William Julius

1987 The Truly Disadvantaged: The Inner City, the Underclass, and Public Policy. Chicago: University of Chicago Press.

Winfree, L. Thomas, and Curt T. Griffiths

1983 "Social learning and marijuana use: a trend study of deviant behavior in a rural middle school," Rural Sociology 48:219–239.

Winfree, L. Thomas, Curt T. Griffiths, and Christine S. Sellers

1989 "Social learning theory, drug use, and American Indian youths: a cross-cultural test," Justice Quarterly 6:395–417.

Winfree, L. Thomas, Jr., G. Larry Mays, and Teresa Vigil-Backstrom

1994 "Youth gangs and incarcerated delinquents: exploring the ties between gang membership, delinquency, and social learning theory," Justice Quarterly 11:229–256.

Winfree, L. Thomas, Christine Sellers, and Dennis L. Clason

1993 "Social learning and adolescent deviance abstention: toward understanding reasons for initiating, quitting, and avoiding drugs," Journal of Quantitative Criminology 9:101–125.

Wolfgang, Marvin E.

1983 "Delinquency in two birth cohorts," pp. 7–16 in K. T. Van Dusen and S. A. Mednick, eds., Prospective Studies of Crime and Delinquency. Boston: Kluwer-Nijhoff.

Wolfgang, Marvin E., and Franco Ferracuti

1967 The Subculture of Violence. London: Ravistock Publications.

Wolfgang, Marvin E., Robert M. Figlio, and Thorsten Sellin

1972 Delinquency in a Birth Cohort. Chicago: University of Chicago Press.

Wolfgang, Marvin E., Robert M. Figlio, and Terence P. Thornberry

1978 Evaluating Criminology. New York: Elsevier.

Wolfgang, Marvin E., Terence P. Thornberry, and Robert M. Figlio

1987 From Boy to Man, from Delinquency to Crime. Chicago: University of Chicago Press.

Wood, Peter B., John K. Cochran, Betty Pfefferbaum, and Bruce J. Arneklev

1995 "Sensation-seeking and delinquent substance use: an extension of learning theory," Journal of Drug Issues 25:173–193.

Yin, Peter P.

1980 "Fear of crime among the elderly: some issues and suggestions," Social Problems 27:492–504.

Young, Alice M., and Seymore Herling

1986 "Drugs as reinforcers: studies in laboratory animals," pp. 9–67 in Steven R. Goldberg and Ian P. Stolerman, eds., Behavioral Analysis of Drug Dependence. Orlando, FL: Academic Press.

Zhang, Lening, and Steven F. Messner

1995 "Family deviance and delinquency in China," Criminology 33:359–388.

Index